Learning TypeScript
Second Edition

Develop and maintain captivating web applications with ease

Remo H. Jansen

Packt>

BIRMINGHAM - MUMBAI

Learning TypeScript 2.x
Second Edition

Copyright © 2018 Packt Publishing

All rights reserved. No part of this book may be reproduced, stored in a retrieval system, or transmitted in any form or by any means, without the prior written permission of the publisher, except in the case of brief quotations embedded in critical articles or reviews.

Every effort has been made in the preparation of this book to ensure the accuracy of the information presented. However, the information contained in this book is sold without warranty, either express or implied. Neither the author, nor Packt Publishing or its dealers and distributors, will be held liable for any damages caused or alleged to have been caused directly or indirectly by this book.

Packt Publishing has endeavored to provide trademark information about all of the companies and products mentioned in this book by the appropriate use of capitals. However, Packt Publishing cannot guarantee the accuracy of this information.

Commissioning Editor: Merint Mathew
Acquisition Editor: Denim Pinto
Content Development Editor: Nikhil Borkar
Technical Editor: Madhunikita Sunil Chindarkar
Copy Editor: Safis Editing
Project Coordinator: Ulhas Kambali
Proofreader: Safis Editing
Indexer: Aishwarya Gangawane
Graphics: Tania Dutta
Production Coordinator: Arvindkumar Gupta

First published: September 2015
Second edition: April 2018

Production reference: 1270418

Published by Packt Publishing Ltd.
Livery Place
35 Livery Street
Birmingham
B3 2PB, UK.

ISBN 978-1-78839-147-4

www.packtpub.com

In memory of Kay Mc Andrew

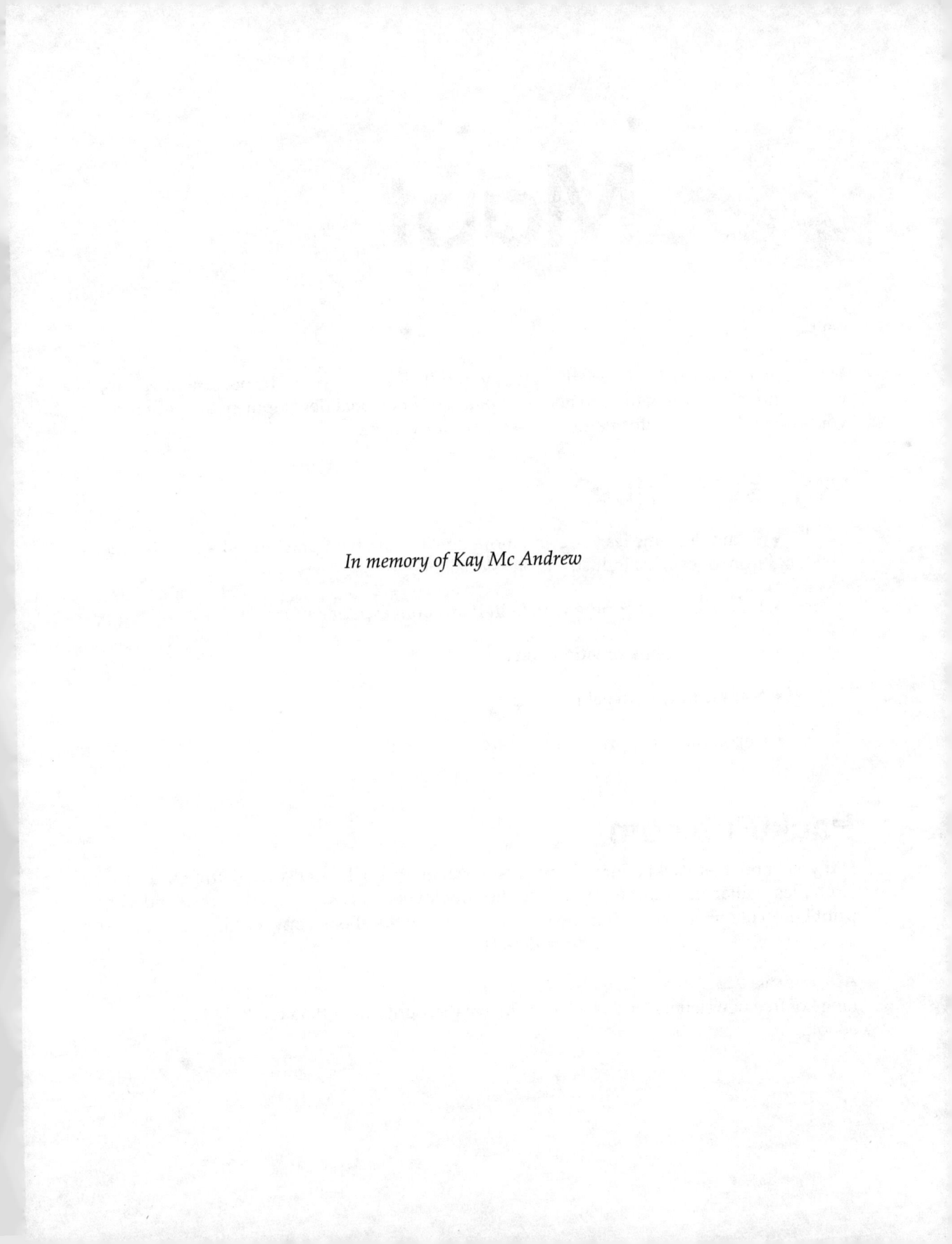

Mapt

`mapt.io`

Mapt is an online digital library that gives you full access to over 5,000 books and videos, as well as industry leading tools to help you plan your personal development and advance your career. For more information, please visit our website.

Why subscribe?

- Spend less time learning and more time coding with practical eBooks and Videos from over 4,000 industry professionals
- Improve your learning with Skill Plans built especially for you
- Get a free eBook or video every month
- Mapt is fully searchable
- Copy and paste, print, and bookmark content

PacktPub.com

Did you know that Packt offers eBook versions of every book published, with PDF and ePub files available? You can upgrade to the eBook version at `www.PacktPub.com` and as a print book customer, you are entitled to a discount on the eBook copy. Get in touch with us at `service@packtpub.com` for more details.

At `www.PacktPub.com`, you can also read a collection of free technical articles, sign up for a range of free newsletters, and receive exclusive discounts and offers on Packt books and eBooks.

Contributors

About the author

Remo H. Jansen is originally from Seville, Spain, but he currently lives in Dublin, Ireland, where he works as a web engineer at Stellwagen Technology and as a part-time lecturer at CCT College Dublin.

Remo is a Microsoft MVP and an active member of the TS community. He organizes the Dublin TypeScript and Dublin OSS meetups, writes a blog, and maintains InversifyJS on GitHub.

> *Thanks to everyone who participated in this book for your support and hardwork. My friends, Lorraine, and my family, for your support and patience. My other family in Ireland, for adopting me as one of your own. In particular, to Kay, who sadly left us while I was working on this book and whose caring memories and advice I will cherish forever.*

About the reviewers

Alejandro Lora Gómez is a software developer residing in Seville, Spain. He is an instructor at Udemy, where he teaches his best-selling courses on Android and Kotlin to over 25K students. Alejandro has a keen interest in web development with Angular and has been working with Angular for several years in multiple contexts (consulting, start-ups, and contracting) and countries (Spain, Ireland, and France), which has added professional value and experience to his career. Nowadays, he works remotely for a multinational corporation based in the USA as an Angular developer.

Carlos Landeras has been a Software Engineer for the past 10 years, being focused on .NET platform and JavaScript development for web solutions. He has been awarded the Microsoft MVP in Visual Studio and development technologies and has a large number of contributions as a speaker in different conferences and user groups. He works at Plain Concepts, a Microsoft Partner Company that provides innovative and engaging custom solutions. Plain Concepts is specialized in web, apps, ALM, Cloud, VR and AR, AI, and DevOps.

Andrew Leith Macrae first cut his programming teeth on an Apple IIe poking bytes into RAM. Over the years he has developed interactive applications with Hypercard, Director, Flash and HTML. He is currently a frontend developer at Arithmos. Andrew is convinced that TypeScript is the future, bringing the structure and discipline of strongly-typed object-oriented language to the web.

David Sherret is the author of ts-simple-ast. He is a software developer in the health-care industry, currently working on surgical planning and navigation software for neurosurgery at Synaptive Medical in Toronto, Canada. In the past, he has worked on several projects, including a project that supported the logistics behind specialty pharmaceuticals and technology for reducing health insurance fraud.

Packt is searching for authors like you

If you're interested in becoming an author for Packt, please visit `authors.packtpub.com` and apply today. We have worked with thousands of developers and tech professionals, just like you, to help them share their insight with the global tech community. You can make a general application, apply for a specific hot topic that we are recruiting an author for, or submit your own idea.

Table of Contents

Preface — 1

Chapter 1: Introducing TypeScript — 7
  The TypeScript architecture — 7
    Design goals — 8
    TypeScript components — 9
  TypeScript language features — 10
    Types — 13
      Type inference and optional static type annotations — 13
    Variables, basic types, and operators — 14
      Variable scope (var, let, and const) — 17
      Arithmetic operators — 18
      Comparison operators — 18
      Logical operators — 19
      Bitwise operators — 20
      Assignment operators — 21
      Spread operator — 21
    Flow control statements — 22
      The single-selection structure (if) — 22
      The double-selection structure (if...else) — 22
      The inline ternary operator (?) — 23
      The multiple-selection structure (switch) — 23
      The expression is tested at the top of the loop (while) — 25
      The expression is tested at the bottom of the loop (do...while) — 25
      Iterate on each object's properties (for...in) — 25
      Iterate values in an iterable (for...of) — 26
      Counter-controlled repetition (for) — 27
    Functions — 27
    Classes — 29
    Interfaces — 30
    Namespaces — 31
  Putting everything together — 32
  Summary — 34

Chapter 2: Working with Types — 35
  The TypeScript type system's characteristics — 35
    The line between TypeScript and JavaScript — 36
    Type inference — 36
    Optional static type annotations — 37
    Structural type system — 39
  Core features of the TypeScript type system — 41

Table of Contents

    Union types   41
    Type aliases   42
    Intersection types   43
    Non-nullable types   44
    The --strict mode   47
    The typeof operator   48
    Type guards   48
    Custom type guards   48
    Control flow analysis   51

Literal types   52
    Discriminated unions   52
    The never type   53
    Enumerations   55
    Object literals   56
    Weak types   56
    The keyof operator   57
    Index signature   57
    Local types   58
    Type casting   59

Advanced features of the TypeScript type system   59
    Generic types   59
    Generic constraints   60
    Mapped types   61
    Lookup types   63
    Mapped type modifiers   63
    Conditional types   65
    The infer keyword   66
    Built-in conditional types   66
    The polymorphic this type   67
    Ambient declarations   69
    Type declarations – .d.ts   70

Summary   71

Chapter 3: Working with Functions   73
  Working with functions in TypeScript   74
    Function declarations and function expressions   74
    Function types   75
    Trailing commas in function arguments   76
    Functions with optional parameters   77
    Functions with default parameters   78
    Functions with REST parameters   80
    Function overloading   82
    Specialized overloading signature   83
    Function scope   84
    Immediately invoked functions   87

Table of Contents

    Tag functions and tagged templates   91
  Asynchronous programming in TypeScript   92
    Callbacks and higher-order functions   92
    Arrow functions   93
    Callback hell   95
    Promises   98
    Covariant checking in callback parameters   102
    Generators   104
    Asynchronous functions – async and await   106
    Asynchronous generators   108
    Asynchronous iteration (for await...of)   109
    Delegating to another generator (yield*)   109
  Summary   110
Chapter 4: Object-Oriented Programming with TypeScript   111
  Classes   111
    Strict property initialization   112
    Inheritance   114
      Depth of the inheritance tree (DIT)   115
    Access modifiers   116
      The public access modifier   116
      The private access modifier   117
      The protected access modifier   119
    Parameter properties   120
    Class expressions   121
    Static members   121
    Optional members   123
    Read-only properties   124
    Method overriding   126
    Generic classes   127
      Generic constraints   130
      Multiple types in generic type constraints   134
      The new operator in generic types   135
    Association, aggregation, and composition   136
      Association   136
      Aggregation   136
      Composition   137
    Mixins (multiple inheritance)   138
      The diamond problem   139
      Implementing mixins   140
    Iterables   144
  Abstract classes   146
  Interfaces   147
  SOLID principles, encapsulation, and polymorphism   149
    SOLID – the single responsibility principle   150
      Encapsulation   152

[iii]

Table of Contents

- SOLID – the open/closed principle — 153
  - Polymorphism — 155
- SOLID – the Liskov substitution principle — 155
- SOLID – the interface segregation principle — 157
- SOLID – the dependency inversion principle — 159
- Summary — 160

Chapter 5: Working with Dependencies — 161
- Third-party dependencies — 161
  - Package management tools — 162
    - The rise and fall of package management tools — 162
    - npm — 162
    - Type definitions — 166
      - Modules with native support for TypeScript — 166
      - Modules with external support for TypeScript — 166
      - Modules with no support for TypeScript — 167
      - The ECMAScript specification type definitions (lib.d.ts) — 169
      - External TypeScript helpers (tslib) — 170
- Internal modules (module and namespace) — 171
  - Nested internal modules — 171
  - Cross-file internal modules — 172
  - Internal module aliases — 173
  - Compiling internal modules — 173
- External modules — 173
  - Module loaders and module definition syntaxes — 174
  - External modules at design time and runtime — 175
  - ES6 modules (runtime and design time) — 176
  - Legacy external modules (design time only) — 178
  - AMD modules (runtime only) — 179
  - CommonJS modules (runtime only) — 180
  - UMD modules (runtime only) — 181
  - SystemJS modules (runtime only) — 182
  - Modules summary — 182
- Managing dependencies in OOP — 183
  - Dependency injection versus dependency inversion — 183
  - Inversion of control containers — 185
    - InversifyJS basics — 186
  - Circular dependencies — 188
- Summary — 188

Chapter 6: Understanding the Runtime — 189
- The execution environment — 190
- Understanding the event loop — 191
  - Frames — 192
  - Stack — 193
  - Queue — 193
  - Heap — 193

[iv]

The event loop	193
The this operator	194
The this operator in the global context	195
The this operator in a function context	195
The call, apply, and bind methods	196
Prototypes	199
Instance properties versus class properties	201
Prototypal inheritance	204
The prototype chain and property shadowing	207
Accessing the prototype of an object	209
The new operator	210
Closures	210
Static variables powered by closures	212
Private members powered by closures	214
Summary	216
Chapter 7: Functional Programming with TypeScript	217
FP concepts	218
Pure functions	219
Side effects	220
Referential transparency	221
Immutability	221
Functions as first-class citizens	221
Lambda expressions	221
Function arity	222
Higher-order functions	223
The benefits of FP	224
Is TypeScript a FP language?	225
FP techniques	225
Composition	225
Partial application	227
Currying	230
Pipes	231
Pointfree style	232
Recursion	235
Category theory	235
Functor	237
Applicative	237
Maybe	238
Either	240
Monad	243
Real-world FP	245
Immutable.js	245
Ramda	247
React and MobX	247

Table of Contents

Summary — 248
Chapter 8: Working with Decorators — 249
Prerequisites — 249
Annotations versus decorators — 250
- The class decorators — 251
- The method decorators — 253
- The property decorators — 257
- The parameter decorators — 259
- Decorators with arguments — 262
- The reflect metadata API — 262
- The decorator factory — 267
Summary — 270
Chapter 9: Automating Your Development Workflow — 271
A modern development workflow — 271
Prerequisites — 272
- Node.js — 272
- Visual Studio Code — 272
- Git and GitHub — 273
- Companion source code — 274
Source control tools — 276
Package management tools — 281
The TypeScript compiler — 281
Linting tools — 282
Working with npm scripts — 284
Gulp — 285
- Controlling the gulp task execution order — 287
  - Passing in a callback to the task definition function — 288
  - Returning a promise — 288
  - Returning a stream — 288
Webpack — 290
Webpack development server — 295
Unit testing and test coverage — 296
Visual Studio Code — 299
- Quick fixes — 299
- Debugging utilities — 300
- Source control utilities — 303
ts-node — 304
Continuous integration (CI) tools — 305
Scaffolding tools — 306
Why does the command line win? — 307
Summary — 308
Chapter 10: Node.js Development with TypeScript — 309

[vi]

Understanding Node.js 309
Understanding non-blocking I/O 309
The main components of Node.js 312
V8 313
Libuv 313
Bindings 313
The Node.js core API (node-core) 313
Node.js environment versus browser environment 314
The Node.js ecosystem 314
The Node.js core API 314
The style of the Node.js core API 316
The npm ecosystem 318
Setting up Node.js 319
Node.js development 320
Working with the filesystem 320
Working with databases 323
Working with REST APIs 327
Hello world (http) 327
Hello world (Express.js) 328
Routing with Express 328
Express middleware 329
Architecting Node.js application – the MVC design pattern 331
Model 332
Repository 332
Controller 332
Database 334
View 335
Index 335
Controllers and routing with inversify-express-utils 335
Model, repository, database, and view 336
Types 336
Controller 336
InversifyJS configuration 339
Index 339
Other applications of Node.js 340
Summary 340
Chapter 11: Frontend Development with React and TypeScript 341
Working with React 342
About the sample application 344
Serving a React application with Node.js 348
Working with react-dom and JSX 350
Working with the react-router 351
Working with React components 353
Components as classes 354
Properties and state 355
Functional stateless components 357
React component life cycle 358

Table of Contents

        Smart components and dumb components — 359
    Working with MobX — 360
        Understanding the MobX architecture — 360
        Working with actions and observables — 360
        Dependency injection in MobX — 368
        MobX alternatives — 370
    Development tools — 370
    Summary — 371

Chapter 12: Frontend Development with Angular and TypeScript — 373
    Working with Angular — 373
    About the sample application — 376
    Serving an Angular application with Node.js — 377
    Bootstrapping an Angular application — 377
    Working with NgModules — 378
    Working with Angular components — 380
        Our first component — 380
        Components and directives — 382
        Data binding — 382
        Working with @Attribute and @Input — 383
        Using structural directives — 385
        Using the <ng-content> directive — 386
        Working with @Output and EventEmitter — 386
        Working with the component's host — 388
        Working with the Angular router — 389
        Angular component life cycle hooks — 391
        Working with services — 391
        Smart components and dumb components — 393
        Dependency injection in Angular — 399
    Summary — 400

Chapter 13: Application Performance — 401
    Prerequisites — 402
        Google Chrome — 402
        Node.js — 402
    Performance and resources — 402
    Common performance metrics — 404
        Availability — 404
        Response time — 404
        Processing speed — 405
        Bandwidth — 405
        Latency — 405
        Scalability — 405
    Performance analysis — 406
        Network performance analysis — 406

Table of Contents

    Network performance and user experience — 412
        Network performance best practices and rules — 413
    GPU performance analysis — 417
        Frames per second (FPS) — 417
    CPU performance analysis — 420
    Memory performance analysis — 422
    The garbage collector — 425
    Performance analysis in Node.js applications — 427
Performance automation — 428
    Performance optimization automation — 428
    Performance monitoring automation — 428
    Performance testing automation — 430
Exception handling — 431
    The Error class — 431
    The try...catch statements and throw statements — 432
Summary — 432
Chapter 14: Application Testing — 433
    Testing terminology — 433
        Assertions — 433
        Specs — 435
        Test cases — 435
        Suites — 435
        Spies — 436
        Dummies — 436
        Stubs — 436
        Mocks — 436
        Test coverage — 437
    Prerequisites — 437
        Mocha — 438
        Chai — 438
        Sinon.JS — 438
        nyc — 438
        Webpack — 439
        Enzyme — 439
        SuperTest — 439
        PM2 — 439
        Nightwatch.js and ChromeDriver — 440
    Testing methodologies — 440
        Test-driven development (TDD) — 440
        Behavior-driven development (BDD) — 441
    Tests plans and test types — 442
        Unit tests — 442
        Integration tests — 443
        Regression tests — 443

Performance and load tests	443
End-to-end (e2e) tests	443
User-acceptance tests (UAT)	443
The example application	444
Unit tests and integration tests with Mocha	446
Back to basics	447
Testing asynchronous code	450
Asserting exceptions	451
Testing a web service with SuperTest	452
Working with tests suites	454
Isolating components with Sinon.JS	456
jsdom	457
Testing React web components with Enzyme	458
TDD versus BDD with Mocha and Chai	462
End-to-end tests with Nightwatch.js	463
Summary	467

Chapter 15: Working with the TypeScript Compiler and the Language Services — 469

The TypeScript compiler's internal architecture	470
Scanner	470
Lexemes and tokens	471
Parser	472
AST	472
Symbols	473
Binder	473
Type checker	474
Emitter	474
Language service	474
Understanding the abstract syntax tree (AST)	475
TypeScript AST Viewer	478
Sample application	479
interfaces.ts	479
katana.ts	479
ninja.ts	480
main.ts	480
broken.ts	480
Traversing the TypeScript AST	481
Working with ts-simple-ast	483
Traversing the AST with ts-simple-ast	484
Diagnostics with ts-simple-ast	485
Accessing class details with ts-simple-ast	487
Accessing module details with ts-simple-ast	489
Accessing the language services API	491
Implementing a yUML compiler	493
VS Code extensions	500

Table of Contents

Summary	500
Other Books You May Enjoy	501
Index	505

Preface

Over the past decade, the JavaScript code base of an average web application has been growing exponentially. However, the current version of JavaScript was designed several years ago and lacks some features necessary to cope with the level of complexity that we may find in a modern JavaScript application. Owing to these missing features, maintainability problems have arisen.

The **ECMAScript 2015** specification is meant to solve some of the maintainability issues of JavaScript, but its implementation is in progress, and many incompatible web browsers are still in use today. For these reasons, wide adoption of the **ECMAScript 2015** specification is expected to be a slow process.

To resolve the maintainability and scalability problems of JavaScript, TypeScript was publicly announced in October 2012, after 2 years of internal development at Microsoft:

> "We designed TypeScript to meet the needs of the JavaScript programming teams that build and maintain large JavaScript programs. TypeScript helps programming teams to define interfaces between software components and to gain insight into the behavior of existing JavaScript libraries. TypeScript also enables teams to reduce naming conflicts by organizing their code into dynamically loadable modules. TypeScript's optional type system enables JavaScript programmers to use highly-productive development tools and practices: static checking, symbol-based navigation, statement completion, and code refactoring."
>
> —TypeScript Language Specification 1.0

Some developers with many years, experience in web development will find it challenging to define a large-scale JavaScript application. When referring to this term, we will avoid considering the number of lines of code in the application. It is much better to consider the number of modules and entities in an application, and the number of dependencies between them as units of measurement of the application's scale. We will define large-scale applications as nontrivial applications that require significant developer effort to be maintained.

Preface

Learning TypeScript 2.x Second Edition, introduces many of the TypeScript features in a simple and easy-to-understand format. This book will teach you everything you need to know to implement a large-scale JavaScript application using TypeScript. Not only does it teach TypeScript's core features, which are essential to implement a web application, but it also explores some powerful development tools, design principles, and good practices, and demonstrates how to apply them to real-life applications.

The second edition has been upgraded and extended, with five additional chapters that cover topics such as functional programming, advanced type system features, an introduction to frontend development with React and Angular, an introduction to Node.js development, and an introduction to the internal APIs of the TypeScript compiler.

The new edition contains a total of 15 chapters. Seven of these chapters are completely new and were not included in the first edition.

Who this book is for

If you are a developer aiming to learn TypeScript to build attractive web applications, this book is for you. No prior knowledge of TypeScript is required. However, a basic understanding of JavaScript would be an added advantage.

What this book covers

Chapter 1, *Introducing TypeScript*, helps you to get familiar with the TypeScript basics. This chapter explores the purpose, main features, and benefits of the TypeScript programming language.

Chapter 2, *Working with Types*, teaches you how to make the most out of the TypeScript type annotations and its type inference system. This chapter will teach you how to use powerful features, such as union types or mapped types.

Chapter 3, *Working with Functions*, covers how to work with functions in depth. This chapter will teach you how to take advantage of the power of functions and asynchronous programming in TypeScript.

Chapter 4, *Object-Oriented Programming with TypeScript*, deals with the core concepts of the object-oriented programming (OOP) paradigm, such as polymorphism, inheritance, and encapsulation. This chapter also explores some OOP best practices, such as the SOLID principles.

Chapter 5, *Working with Dependencies*, explores how to work with application dependencies, third-party dependencies, and type definitions. This chapter explores multiple module systems, such as CommonJS and ES6 modules, and concepts such as dependency injection.

Chapter 6, *Understanding the Runtime*, teaches you how the JavaScript runtime works and helps you gain a good understanding of concepts such as the event loop, closures, and hoisting.

Chapter 7, *Functional Programming with TypeScript*, explores the core building blocks of the functional programming paradigm, including concepts such as function composition, function partial application, and referential transparency.

Chapter 8, *Working with Decorators*, showcases how to apply and declare decorators and how to use decorators to create and read metadata that can be used to power tools such as testing frameworks and inversion of control containers.

Chapter 9, *Automating Your Development Workflow*, focuses on how to automate certain tasks in your development workflow and reduce the number of integration issues, using tools, such as TSLint, webpack, Gulp and npm scripts.

Chapter 10, *Node.js Development with TypeScript*, teaches you how to use REST APIs powered by Node.js and TypeScript.

Chapter 11, *Frontend Development with React and TypeScript*, enables you to learn how to develop single-page web applications powered by React and TypeScript.

Chapter 12, *Frontend Development with Angular and TypeScript*, teaches you how to develop single-page web applications powered by Angular and TypeScript.

Chapter 13, *Application Performance*, makes you understand how the availability of system resources can affect the performance of a TypeScript application, and how to use the Node.js inspector and the Chrome Development tools to analyze the performance of a TypeScript application.

Chapter 14, *Application Testing*, teaches you how to implement automated tests such as unit tests or end-to-end tests powered by tools such as Mocha, Chai, Sinon.JS, Supertest, and Karma.

Chapter 15, *Working with the TypeScript Compiler and the Language Services*, explores how to leverage the TypeScript language services to create your own code analysis tools.

Preface

To get the most out of this book

Nothing external is required for this book. You will be able to make the most out of this book by following just what's mentioned in this book.

Download the example code files

You can download the example code files for this book from your account at `www.packtpub.com`. If you purchased this book elsewhere, you can visit `www.packtpub.com/support` and register to have the files emailed directly to you.

You can download the code files by following these steps:

1. Log in or register at `www.packtpub.com`.
2. Select the **SUPPORT** tab.
3. Click on **Code Downloads & Errata**.
4. Enter the name of the book in the **Search** box and follow the onscreen instructions.

Once the file is downloaded, please make sure that you unzip or extract the folder using the latest version of:

- WinRAR/7-Zip for Windows
- Zipeg/iZip/UnRarX for Mac
- 7-Zip/PeaZip for Linux

The code bundle for the book is also hosted on GitHub at `https://github.com/remojansen/LearningTypeScript`. In case there's an update to the code, it will be updated on the existing GitHub repository. The GitHub repository will include detailed instructions about how to run each of the examples.

We also have other code bundles from our rich catalog of books and videos available at `https://github.com/PacktPublishing/`. Check them out!

Download the color images

We also provide a PDF file that has color images of the screenshots/diagrams used in this book. You can download it here: `https://www.packtpub.com/sites/default/files/downloads/LearningTypeScript2xSecondEdition_ColorImages.pdf`.

Conventions used

There are a number of text conventions used throughout this book.

`CodeInText`: Indicates code words in text, database table names, folder names, filenames, file extensions, pathnames, dummy URLs, user input, and Twitter handles. Here is an example: "If we try to predict the result of invoking the `isIndexPage`, we will need to know the current state."

A block of code is set as follows:

```
function addMany(...numbers: number[]) {
    numbers.reduce((p, c) => p + c, 0);
}
```

Any command-line input or output is written as follows:

```
npm install typescript -g
```

Bold: Indicates a new term, an important word, or words that you see onscreen. For example, words in menus or dialog boxes appear in the text like this. Here is an example: "Select **System info** from the **Administration** panel."

> Warnings or important notes appear like this.

> Tips and tricks appear like this.

Get in touch

Feedback from our readers is always welcome.

General feedback: Email `feedback@packtpub.com` and mention the book title in the subject of your message. If you have questions about any aspect of this book, please email us at `questions@packtpub.com`.

Preface

Errata: Although we have taken every care to ensure the accuracy of our content, mistakes do happen. If you have found a mistake in this book, we would be grateful if you would report this to us. Please visit `www.packtpub.com/submit-errata`, selecting your book, clicking on the Errata Submission Form link, and entering the details.

Piracy: If you come across any illegal copies of our works in any form on the Internet, we would be grateful if you would provide us with the location address or website name. Please contact us at `copyright@packtpub.com` with a link to the material.

If you are interested in becoming an author: If there is a topic that you have expertise in and you are interested in either writing or contributing to a book, please visit `authors.packtpub.com`.

Reviews

Please leave a review. Once you have read and used this book, why not leave a review on the site that you purchased it from? Potential readers can then see and use your unbiased opinion to make purchase decisions, we at Packt can understand what you think about our products, and our authors can see your feedback on their book. Thank you!

For more information about Packt, please visit `packtpub.com`.

Introducing TypeScript

This book aims to provide you with a broad overview of TypeScript's features, its limitations, and its ecosystem. You will learn about the TypeScript language, development tools, design patterns, and recommended practices.

This chapter will give you an overview of the history behind TypeScript and introduce you to some of its basics.

In this chapter, you will learn about the following concepts:

- The TypeScript architecture
- Type annotations
- Variables and primitive data types
- Operators
- Flow control statements
- Functions
- Classes
- Interfaces
- Namespaces

The TypeScript architecture

In this section, we will focus on TypeScript's internal architecture and its original design goals.

Design goals

The following list describes the main design goals and architectural decisions that shaped the way the TypeScript programming language looks today:

- **Statically identify JavaScript constructs that are likely to be errors**: The engineers at Microsoft decided that the best way to identify and prevent potential runtime issues was to create a strongly-typed programming language and perform static type checking at compile time. The engineers also designed a language services layer to provide developers with better tools.
- **High compatibility with existing JavaScript code**: TypeScript is a superset of JavaScript; this means that any valid JavaScript program is also a valid TypeScript program (with a few small exceptions).
- **Provide a structuring mechanism for larger pieces of code**: TypeScript adds class-based object-orientation, interfaces, namespaces, and modules. These features will help us to structure our code in a much better way. We will also reduce potential integration issues within our development team and our code will become easier to maintain and scale by adhering to the best object-oriented principles and recommended practices.
- **Impose no runtime overhead on emitted programs**: It is common to differentiate between design time and execution time when thinking about TypeScript. We use the term *design time* or *compile time* to refer to the TypeScript code that we write while designing an application, while we use the term *execution time* or *runtime* to refer to the JavaScript code executed after compiling some TypeScript code.

TypeScript adds some features to JavaScript, but those features are only available at design time. For example, we can declare interfaces in TypeScript, but since JavaScript doesn't support interfaces, the TypeScript compiler will not declare or try to emulate this feature at runtime (in the output JavaScript code).

The Microsoft engineers provided the TypeScript compiler with some mechanisms, such as **code transformations** (converting TypeScript features into plain JavaScript implementations) and **type erasure** (removing static type notation), to generate clean JavaScript code. Type erasure removes not only the type annotations, but also all the TypeScript-exclusive language features such as interfaces.

Furthermore, the generated code is highly compatible with web browsers as it targets the ECMAScript 3 specification by default, but it also supports ECMAScript 5 and ECMAScript 6. In general, we can use the TypeScript features when compiling to any of the available compilation targets, but sometimes some features will require ECMAScript 5 or a higher version as the compilation target.

- **Align with current and future ECMAScript proposals**: TypeScript is not just compatible with existing JavaScript code; it is also compatible with some future versions of JavaScript. At first glance, we may think that some TypeScript features make it quite different from JavaScript, but the reality is that all the features available in TypeScript (except the type system features) follow the ECMAScript proposals, which means that many of the TypeScript files will eventually be available as native JavaScript features.
- **Be a cross-platform development tool**: Microsoft released TypeScript under the open source Apache license and it can be installed and executed in all major operating systems.

TypeScript components

The TypeScript language has three main internal layers. Each of these layers is, in turn, divided into sublayers or components. In the following diagram, we can see the three layers (three different shades of gray) and each of their internal components (boxes):

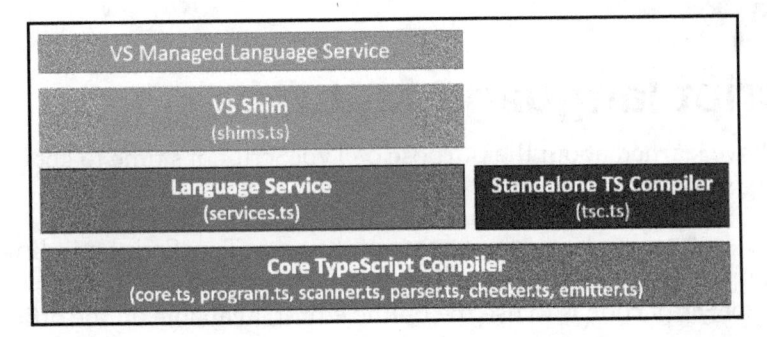

VS Managed Language Service
VS Shim (shims.ts)
Language Service (services.ts)   **Standalone TS Compiler** (tsc.ts)
Core TypeScript Compiler (core.ts, program.ts, scanner.ts, parser.ts, checker.ts, emitter.ts)

> In the preceding diagram, the acronym **VS** refers to Microsoft's Visual Studio, which is the official family of **integrated development environments** (**IDEs**) for all Microsoft products (including TypeScript). We will learn more about this and the other IDEs in `Chapter 9`, *Automating Your Development Workflow*.

Each of these main layers has a different purpose:

- **Language**: Features the TypeScript language elements.
- **Compiler** Performs the parsing, type checking, and transformation of your TypeScript code to JavaScript code.
- **Language services**: Generates information that helps editors and other tools provide better assistance features, such as IntelliSense or automated refactoring.
- **IDE integration (VS Shim)**: The developers of the IDEs and text editors must perform some integration work to take advantage of the TypeScript features. TypeScript was designed to facilitate the development of tools that help to increase the productivity of JavaScript developers. Because of these efforts, integrating TypeScript with an IDE is not a complicated task. A proof of this is that the most popular IDEs these days include good TypeScript support.

> In other books and online resources, you may find references to the term *transpiler* instead of *compiler*. A **transpiler** is a type of compiler that takes the source code of a programming language as its input and outputs the source code into another programming language with a similar level of abstraction.

We will learn more about the TypeScript language services and the TypeScript compiler in `Chapter 15`, *Working with the TypeScript Compiler and the Language Services*.

TypeScript language features

Now that you have learned about the purpose of TypeScript, it's time to get our hands dirty and start writing some code.

Before you can start learning how to use some of the basic TypeScript building blocks, you will need to set up your development environment. The easiest and fastest way to start writing some TypeScript code is to use the online editor, available on the official TypeScript website at `https://www.typescriptlang.org/play/index.html`:

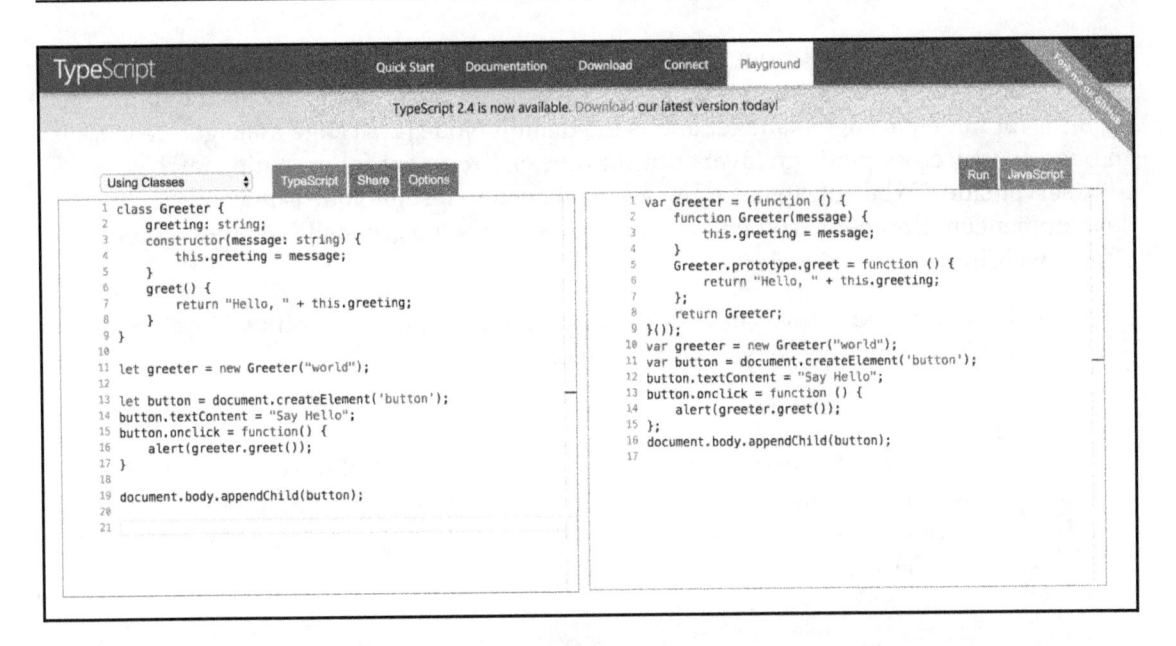

```
1  class Greeter {                                    1  var Greeter = (function () {
2      greeting: string;                              2      function Greeter(message) {
3      constructor(message: string) {                 3          this.greeting = message;
4          this.greeting = message;                   4      }
5      }                                              5      Greeter.prototype.greet = function () {
6      greet() {                                      6          return "Hello, " + this.greeting;
7          return "Hello, " + this.greeting;          7      };
8      }                                              8      return Greeter;
9  }                                                  9  }());
10                                                   10  var greeter = new Greeter("world");
11 let greeter = new Greeter("world");                11  var button = document.createElement('button');
12                                                   12  button.textContent = "Say Hello";
13 let button = document.createElement('button');     13  button.onclick = function () {
14 button.textContent = "Say Hello";                  14      alert(greeter.greet());
15 button.onclick = function() {                      15  };
16     alert(greeter.greet());                        16  document.body.appendChild(button);
17 }                                                  17
18
19 document.body.appendChild(button);
20
21
```

The preceding screenshot shows the appearance of the TypeScript playground. If you visit the playground, you will be able to use the text editor on the left-hand side of the screen to write TypeScript code. The code will then be automatically compiled into JavaScript. The output code will be inserted in the text editor located on the right-hand side of the screen. If your TypeScript code is invalid, the JavaScript code on the right-hand side will not be updated.

Alternatively, if you prefer to be able to work offline, you can download and install the TypeScript compiler. If you work with a Visual Studio version older than Visual Studio 2015, you will need to download the official TypeScript extension from `https://marketplace.visualstudio.com/`. If you are working with a version of Visual Studio released after the 2015 version (or Visual Studio Code), you will not need to install the extension, as these versions includes TypeScript support by default.

> There are TypeScript plugins available for many popular editors such as Sublime (`https://github.com/Microsoft/TypeScript-Sublime-Plugin`) or Atom (`https://atom.io/packages/atom-typescript`).

Introducing TypeScript

You can also use TypeScript from the command-line interface by downloading it as an npm module. Don't worry if you are not familiar with npm. For now, you only need to know that it stands for **node package manager** and is the default Node.js package manager. Node.js is an open source, cross-platform JavaScript runtime environment for executing JavaScript code server-side. To be able to use npm, you will need to install Node.js in your development environment. You will be able to find the Node.js installation files on the official website at https://nodejs.org/.

Once you have installed Node.js in your development environment, you will be able to run the following command in a console or Terminal:

```
npm install -g typescript
```

> Unix-based operating systems may require the use of the sudo command when installing global (-g) npm packages. The sudo command will prompt the user credentials and install the package using administrative privileges:

```
sudo npm install -g typescript
```

Create a new file named test.ts, and add the following code to it:

```
let myNumberVariable: number = 1;
console.log(myNumberVariable);
```

Save the file into a directory of your choice and open a command-line interface. Navigate to the directory in which you saved the file and execute the following command:

```
tsc test.ts
```

If everything goes well, you will find a file named test.js in the same directory in which the test.ts file is located. Now you know how to compile your TypeScript code into JavaScript code.

You can execute the output JavaScript code using Node.js:

```
node test.js
```

Now that we know how to compile and execute TypeScript source code, we can start learning about some of the TypeScript features.

> You will be able to learn more about editors, compiler options, and other TypeScript tools in Chapter 9, *Automating Your Development Workflow*.

[12]

Types

As we have already learned, TypeScript is a typed superset of JavaScript. TypeScript added a static type system and optional static type annotations to JavaScript to transform it into a strongly-typed programming language.

TypeScript's type analysis occurs entirely at compile time and adds no runtime overhead to program execution.

Type inference and optional static type annotations

The TypeScript language service is great at automatically detecting the type of a variable. However, there are certain cases where it is not able to automatically detect a type.

When the type inference system is not able to identify the type of a variable, it uses a type known as the *any* type. The any type is a value that represents all the existing types, and as a result, it is too flexible and unable to detect most errors, which is not a problem because TypeScript allows us to explicitly declare the type of a variable using what is known as **optional static type annotations**.

The optional static type annotations are used as constraints on program entities such as functions, variables, and properties so that compilers and development tools can offer better verification and assistance (such as IntelliSense) during software development.

Strong typing allows programmers to express their intentions in their code, both to themselves and to others in the development team.

For a variable, a type notation comes preceded by a colon after the name of a variable:

```
let counter; // unknown (any) type
let counter = 0; // number (inferred)
let counter: number; // number
let counter: number = 0; // number
```

> We have used the `let` keyword instead of the `var` keyword. The `let` keyword is a newer JavaScript construct that TypeScript makes available. We'll discuss the details later, but some common problems in JavaScript can be solved by using `let`, so, you should use `let` instead of `var` whenever possible.

As you can see, we declare the type of a variable after its name; this style of type notation is based on type theory and helps to reinforce the idea of types being optional.

When no type annotations are available, TypeScript will try to guess the type of the variable by examining the assigned values. For example, in the second line, in the preceding code snippet, we can see that the variable counter has been identified as a numeric variable, because its value is a numeric value. There is a process known as **type inference** that can automatically detect and assign a type to a variable. The any type is used as the type of a variable when the type inference system is not able to detect its type.

Please note that the companion source code might be slightly different from the code presented during the chapters. The companion source code uses namespaces to isolate each demo from all the other demos and sometimes appends numbers to the name of the variables to prevent naming conflicts. For example, the preceding code is included in the companion source code as follows:

```
namespace type_inference_demo {
    let counter1; // unknown (any) type
    let counter2 = 0; // number (inferred)
    let counter3: number; // number
    let counter4: number = 0; // number
}
```

> You will be able to learn more about the TypeScript type system in Chapter 2, *Working with Types*.

Variables, basic types, and operators

The basic types are boolean, number, string, array, tuple, Object, object, null, undefined, {}, void, and enumerations. Let's learn about each of these basic types:

Data type	Description
Boolean	Whereas the string and number data types can have a virtually unlimited number of different values, the boolean data type can only have two. They are the literals: `true` and `false`. A boolean value is a truth value; it specifies whether the condition is true or not: `let isDone:   boolean = false;`
Number	As in JavaScript, all numbers in TypeScript are floating-point values. These floating-point numbers get the type `number`: `let height:   number = 6;`

[14]

String	We use the `string` data type to represent text in TypeScript. You include string literals in your scripts by enclosing them in single or double quotation marks. Double quotation marks can be contained in strings surrounded by single quotation marks and single quotation marks can be contained in strings surrounded by double quotation marks: ```\nlet name: string = "bob";\nname = 'Smith';\n```

Array	We use the `array` data type to represent a collection of values. The `array` type can be written using two different syntax styles. We can use the type of the elements in the array followed by brackets `[]` to annotate a collection of that element type:
	```\nlet list: number[] = [1, 2, 3];\n```
	The second syntax style uses a generic array type named `Array<T>`:
	```\nlet list: Array<number> = [1, 2, 3];\n```

Tuple	Tuple types can be used to represent an array with a fixed number of elements with different types where the type is known. For example, we can represent a value as a pair of a string and a number: ```\nlet x: [string, number];\nx = ["hello", 10]; // OK\nx = ["world", 20]; // OK\nx = [10, "hello"]; // Error\nx = [20, "world"]; // Error\n```
Enum	We use enumerations to add more meaning to a set of values. Enumerations can be numeric or text-based. By default, numeric enumerations assign the value 0 to the first member in the enumeration and increase it by one for each of the members in the enumeration: ```\nenum Color {Red, Green, Blue};\nlet c: Color = Color.Green;\n```

Any	All types in TypeScript are subtypes of a single top type called the **any type**. The `any` keyword references this type. The any type eliminates most of the TypeScript type checks and represents all the possible types:
	```\nlet notSure: any = 4; // OK\nnotSure = "maybe a string instead"; // OK\nnotSure = false; // OK\n```
	The `any` type can be useful while migrating existing JavaScript code to TypeScript, or when we know some details about a type but we don't know all its details. For example, when we know that a type is an array, but we don't know the type of the elements in such an array:
	```\nlet list: any[] = [1, true, "free"];\nlist[1] = 100;\n```

Introducing TypeScript

object (lowercase)	The `object` type represents any non-primitive type. The following types are considered to be primitive types in JavaScript: boolean, number, string, symbol, null, and undefined.
Object (uppercase)	In JavaScript, all objects are derived from the `Object` class. `Object` (uppercase) describes functionality that is common to all JavaScript objects. That includes the `toString()` and the `hasOwnProperty()` methods, for example.

Empty object type {}	This describes an object that has no members of its own. TypeScript issues a compile-time error when you try to access arbitrary properties of such an object:
	`const obj = {};`
	`obj.prop = "value"; // Error`

Null and undefined	In TypeScript, both undefined and null are types. By default, null and undefined are subtypes of all other types. That means you can assign null and undefined to something like a number. However, when using the `--strictNullChecks` flag, null and undefined are only assignable to void and their respective types.

Never	The `never` type is used in the following two places:
	• As the return type of functions that never return
	• As the type of variables under type guards that are never true
	`function impossibleTypeGuard(value: any) {`
	`    if (`
	`        typeof value === "string" &&`
	`        typeof value === "number"`
	`    ) {`
	`        value; // Type never`
	`    }`
	`}`

Void	In some ways the opposite of any is `void`, the absence of having any type at all. You will see this as the return type of functions that do not return a value:
	`function warnUser(): void {`
	`    console.log("This is my warning message");`
	`}`

In TypeScript and JavaScript, undefined is a property in the global scope that is assigned as a value to variables that have been declared but have not yet been initialized. The value `null` is a literal (not a property of the global object) and it can be assigned to a variable as a representation of no value:

```
let testVar; // variable is declared but not initialized
consoe.log(testVar); // shows undefined
console.log(typeof testVar); // shows undefined

let testVar = null; // variable is declared, and null is assigned as its
value
cosole.log(testVar); // shows null
console.log(typeof testVar); // shows object
```

Variable scope (var, let, and const)

When we declare a variable in TypeScript, we can use the `var`, `let`, or `const` keywords:

```
var myNumber: number = 1;
let isValid: boolean = true;
const apiKey: string = "0E5CE8BD-6341-4CC2-904D-C4A94ACD276E";
```

Variables declared with `var` are scoped to the nearest function block (or global, if outside a function block).

Variables declared with `let` are scoped to the nearest enclosing block (or global, if outside any block), which can be smaller than a function block.

The `const` keyword creates a constant that can be global or local to the block in which it is declared. This means that constants are block-scoped.

> You will learn more about scopes in Chapter 6, *Understanding the Runtime*.

Arithmetic operators

TypeScript supports the following arithmetic operators. We must assume that variable A holds 10 and variable B holds 20 to understand the following examples:

Operator	Description	Example
−	Subtracts the second operand from the first.	A - B will give −10
+	Adds two operands.	A + B will give 30
*	Multiplies both the operands.	A * B will give 200
**	Multiplies the first operand by itself a number of times which is indicated by the second operand.	A ** B will give 1e+20
%	This is the modulus operator and remainder after an integer division.	B % A will give 0
/	Divides the numerator by the denominator.	B / A will give 2
--	Decreases an integer value by one.	A-- will give 9
++	Increases an integer value by one.	A++ will give 11

Comparison operators

TypeScript supports the following comparison operators. To understand the examples, you must assume that variable A holds 10 as value and variable B holds 20 as value:

Operator	Description	Example
==	Checks whether the values of two operands are equal or not. This operator uses type coercion. If yes, then the condition becomes true.	(A == B) is false. A == "10" is true.
===	Checks whether the value and type of two operands are equal or not. This operator doesn't use type coercion. If yes, then the condition becomes true.	A === B is false. A === "10" is false.
!=	Checks whether the value of two operands are equal or not. If the values are not equal, then the condition becomes true. This operator uses type coercion.	(A != B) is true. A != "10" is false.

!==	Checks whether the value of two operands are equal or not. If the values are not equal, then the condition becomes true. This operator doesn't use type coercion.	A !== B is true. A !== "10" is true.
>	Checks whether the value of the left operand is greater than the value of the right operand. If yes, then the condition becomes true.	(A > B) is false.
<	Checks whether the value of the left operand is less than the value of the right operand. If yes, then the condition becomes true.	(A < B) is true.
>=	Checks whether the value of the left operand is greater than or equal to the value of the right operand. If yes, then the condition becomes true.	(A >= B) is false.
<=	Checks whether the value of the left operand is less than or equal to the value of the right operand. If yes, then the condition becomes true.	(A <= B) is true.

Logical operators

TypeScript supports the following logical operators. To understand the examples, you must assume that variable A holds 10 and variable B holds 20:

Operator	Description	Example
&&	Known as the logical AND operator. If both the operands are nonzero, then the condition becomes true.	(A && B) is true.
||	Known as the logical OR operator. If any of the two operands are nonzero, then the condition becomes true.	(A || B) is true.
!	Known as the logical NOT operator. It is used to reverse the logical state of its operand. If a condition is true, then the logical NOT operator will make it false.	!(A && B) is false.

Introducing TypeScript

Bitwise operators

TypeScript supports the following bitwise operators. To understand the examples, you must assume that variable A holds 2 as value and variable B holds 3 as value:

Operator	Description	Example
&	Known as the bitwise AND operator, it performs a boolean AND operation on each bit of its integer arguments.	(A & B) is 2
|	Known as the bitwise OR operator, it performs a boolean OR operation on each bit of its integer arguments.	(A | B) is 3.
^	Known as the bitwise XOR operator, it performs a boolean exclusive OR operation on each bit of its integer arguments. Exclusive OR means that either operand one is true or operand two is true, but not both.	(A ^ B) is 1.
~	Known as the bitwise NOT operator, it is a unary operator and operates by reversing all bits in the operand.	(~B) is -4
<<	Known as the bitwise shift-left operator. It moves all bits in its first operand to the left by the number of places specified in the second operand. New bits are filled with zeros. Shifting a value left by one position is equivalent to multiplying by two, shifting two positions is equivalent to multiplying by four, and so on.	(A << 1) is 4
>>	Known as the bitwise shift-right with sign operator. It moves all bits in its first operand to the right by the number of places specified in the second operand.	(A >> 1) is 1
>>>	Known as the bitwise shift-right with zero operators. This operator is just like the >> operator, except that the bits shifted from the left are always zero.	(A >>> 1) is 1

One of the main reasons to use bitwise operators in languages such as C++, Java, or C# is that they're extremely fast. However, bitwise operators are often considered not that efficient in TypeScript and JavaScript. The bitwise operators are less efficient in JavaScript, because it is necessary to cast from floating-point representation (how JavaScript stores all of its numbers) to a 32-bit integer to perform the bit manipulation and back.

[20]

Assignment operators

TypeScript supports the following assignment operators:

Operator	Description	Example
=	Assigns the values from the right-side operands to the left-side operand.	C = A + B will assign the value of A + B into C
+=	Adds the right operand to the left operand and assigns the result to the left operand.	C += A is equivalent to C = C + A
-=	Substracts the right operand from the left operand and assigns the result to the left operand.	C -= A is equivalent to C = C - A
*=	Multiplies the right operand by the left operand and assigns the result to the left operand.	C *= A is equivalent to C = C * A
/=	Divides the left operand by the right operand and assigns the result to the left operand.	C /= A is equivalent to C = C / A
%=	Calculates the modulus using two operands and assigns the result to the left operand.	C %= A is equivalent to C = C % A

Spread operator

The spread operator can be used to initialize arrays and objects from another array or object:

```
let originalArr1 = [ 1, 2, 3];
let originalArr2 = [ 4, 5, 6];
let copyArr = [...originalArr1];
let mergedArr = [...originalArr1, ...originalArr2];
let newObjArr = [...originalArr1, 7, 8];
```

The preceding code snippet showcases the usage of the spread operator with arrays, while the following code snippet showcases its usage with object literals:

```
let originalObj1 = {a: 1, b: 2, c: 3};
let originalObj2 = {d: 4, e: 5, f: 6};
let copyObj = {...originalObj1};
let mergedObj = {...originalObj1, ...originalObj2};
let newObjObj = {... originalObj1, g: 7, h: 8};
```

Introducing TypeScript

The spread operator can also be used to expand to an expression into multiple arguments (in function calls), but we will skip that use case for now.

> We will learn more about the spread operator in `Chapter 3`, *Working with Functions* and `Chapter 4`, *Object-Oriented Programming with TypeScript*.

Flow control statements

This section describes the decision-making statements, the looping statements, and the branching statements supported by the TypeScript programming language.

The single-selection structure (if)

The following code snippet declares a variable of type boolean and name `isValid`. Then, an `if` statement will check whether the value of `isValid` is equal to `true`. If the statement turns out to be `true`, the `Is valid!` message will be displayed on the screen:

```
let isValid: boolean = true;

if (isValid) {
  console.log("is valid!");
}
```

The double-selection structure (if...else)

The following code snippet declares a variable of type boolean and name `isValid`. Then, an `if` statement will check whether the value of `isValid` is equal to `true`. If the statement turns out to be `true`, the message `Is valid!` will be displayed on the screen. On the other hand, if the statement turns out to be `false`, the message `Is NOT valid!` will be displayed on the screen:

```
let isValid: boolean = true;

if (isValid) {
  console.log("Is valid!");
} else {
  console.log("Is NOT valid!");
}
```

The inline ternary operator (?)

The inline ternary operator is just an alternative way of declaring a double-selection structure:

```
let isValid: boolean = true;
let message = isValid ? "Is valid!" : "Is NOT valid!";
console.log(message);
```

The preceding code snippet declares a variable of type boolean and name `isValid`. Then, it checks whether the variable or expression on the left-hand side of the operator `?` is equal to `true`.

If the statement turns out to be `true`, the expression on the left-hand side of the character will be executed and the message `Is valid!` will be assigned to the message variable.

On the other hand, if the statement turns out to be `false`, the expression on the right-hand side of the operator will be executed and the message, `Is NOT valid!` will be assigned to the message variable.

Finally, the value of the message variable is displayed on the screen.

The multiple-selection structure (switch)

The `switch` statement evaluates an expression, matches the expression's value to a case clause, and executes statements associated with that case. Switch statements and enumerations are often used together to improve the readability of the code.

In the following example, we declare a function that takes an enumeration named `AlertLevel`.

> You will learn more about enumerations in Chapter 2, *Working with Types*.

Inside the function, we will generate an array of strings to store email addresses and execute a `switch` structure. Each of the options of the enumeration is a case in the `switch` structure:

```
enum AlertLevel{
  info,
    warning,
```

Introducing TypeScript

```typescript
      error
   }

   function getAlertSubscribers(level: AlertLevel){
      let emails = new Array<string>();
      switch(level){
      case AlertLevel.info:
         emails.push("cst@domain.com");
         break;
      case AlertLevel.warning:
         emails.push("development@domain.com");
         emails.push("sysadmin@domain.com");
         break;
      case AlertLevel.error:
         emails.push("development@domain.com");
         emails.push("sysadmin@domain.com");
         emails.push("management@domain.com");
         break;
      default:
         throw new Error("Invalid argument!");
      }
      return emails;
   }

   getAlertSubscribers(AlertLevel.info); // ["cst@domain.com"]
   getAlertSubscribers(AlertLevel.warning); //
    ["development@domain.com", "sysadmin@domain.com"]
```

The value of the `level` variable is tested against all the cases in the `switch`. If the variable matches one of the cases, the statement associated with that case is executed. Once the `case` statement has been executed, the variable is tested against the next case.

Once the execution of the statement associated with a matching case is finalized, the next case will be evaluated. If the `break` keyword is present, the program will not continue the execution of the following `case` statement.

If no matching case clause is found, the program looks for the optional `default` clause, and if found, it transfers control to that clause and executes the associated statements.

If no `default` clause is found, the program continues execution at the statement following the end of switch. By convention, the `default` clause is the last clause, but it does not have to be so.

The expression is tested at the top of the loop (while)

The `while` expression is used to repeat an operation while a certain requirement is satisfied. For example, the following code snippet declares a numeric variable `i`. If the requirement (the value of `i` is less than 5) is satisfied, an operation takes place (increase the value of `i` by one and display its value in the browser console). Once the operation has completed, the accomplishment of the requirement will be checked again:

```
let i: number = 0;
while (i < 5) {
  i += 1;
  console.log(i);
}
```

In a `while` expression, the operation will take place only if the requirement is satisfied.

The expression is tested at the bottom of the loop (do...while)

The `do...while` expression can be used to repeat an instruction until a certain requirement is not satisfied. For example, the following code snippet declares a numeric variable `i` and repeats an operation (increase the value of `i` by one and display its value in the browser console) for as long as the requirement (the value of `i` is less than `five`) is satisfied:

```
let i: number = 0;
do {
  i += 1;
  console.log(i);
} while (i < 5);
```

Unlike the `while` loop, the `do...while` expression will execute at least once, regardless of the tested expression, as the operation will take place before checking whether a certain requirement is satisfied or not.

Iterate on each object's properties (for...in)

The `for...in` statement by itself is not a *bad practice*; however, it can be misused, for example, to iterate over arrays or array-like objects. The purpose of the `for...in` statement is to enumerate over object properties:

```
let obj: any = { a: 1, b: 2, c: 3 };
```

```
for (let key in obj) {
    if (obj.hasOwnProperty(key)) {
        console.log(key + " = " + obj[key]);
    }
}

// Output:
// "a = 1"
// "b = 2"
// "c = 3"
```

The following code snippet will go up in the prototype chain, also enumerating the inherited properties. The `for...in` statement iterates the entire prototype chain, also enumerating the inherited properties. When you want to enumerate only the object's properties that aren't inherited, you can use the `hasOwnProperty` method.

Iterate values in an iterable (for...of)

In JavaScript, some built-in types are built-in iterables with a default iteration behavior. To be an iterable, an object must implement the `@@iterator` method, meaning that the object (or one of the objects in its prototype chain) must have a property with a `@@iterator` key, which is available via constant `Symbol.iterator`.

The `for...of` statement creates a loop iterating over iterable objects (including array, map, set, string, arguments object, and so on):

```
let iterable = [10, 20, 30];

for (let value of iterable) {
  value += 1;
  console.log(value);
}
```

> You will learn more about iterables in `Chapter 4`, *Object-Oriented Programming with TypeScript*.

Counter-controlled repetition (for)

The `for` statement creates a loop that consists of three optional expressions, enclosed in parentheses and separated by semicolons, followed by a statement or a set of statements executed in the loop:

```
for (let i: number = 0; i < 9; i++) {
   console.log(i);
}
```

The preceding code snippet contains a `for` statement. It starts by declaring the variable `i` and initializing it to `0`. It checks whether `i` is less than `9`, performs the two succeeding statements, and increments `i` by one after each pass through the loop.

Functions

Just as in JavaScript, TypeScript functions can be created either as a named function or as an anonymous function, which allows us to choose the most appropriate approach for an application, whether we are building a list of functions in an API or a one-off function to hand over to another function:

```
// named function
function greet(name?: string): string {
  if(name) {
    return "Hi! " + name;
  } else {
    return "Hi!";
  }
}

// anonymous function
let greet = function(name?: string): string {
  if (name) {
    return "Hi! " + name;
  } else {
    return "Hi!";
  }
}
```

As we can see in the preceding code snippet, in TypeScript, we can add types to each of the parameters and then to the function itself to add a return type. TypeScript can infer the return type by looking at the `return` statements, so we can also optionally leave this off in many cases.

Introducing TypeScript

There is an alternative syntax for functions that use the => operator after the return type and don't use the `function` keyword:

```
let greet = (name: string): string => {
   if(name){
      return "Hi! " + name;
   }
   else
   {
      return "Hi";
   }
};
```

Now that we have learned about this alternative syntax, we can return to the previous example, in which we were assigning an anonymous function to the `greet` variable. We can now add the type annotations to the `greet` variable to match the anonymous function signature:

```
let greet: (name: string) => string = function(name: string):
  string {
      if (name) {
         return "Hi! " + name;
      } else {
         return "Hi!";
      }
};
```

> Keep in mind that the arrow function (=>) syntax changes the way the `this` keyword works when working with classes. We will learn more about this in the upcoming chapters.

Now you know how to add type annotations to force a variable to be a function with a specific signature. The usage of this kind of annotation is really common when we use a callback (functions used as an argument of another function):

```
function add(
     a: number, b: number, callback: (result: number) => void
) {
     callback(a + b);
}
```

In the preceding example, we are declaring a function named `add` that takes two numbers and a `callback` as a function. The type annotations will force the callback to return `void` and take a number as its only argument.

> We will focus on functions in Chapter 3, *Working with Functions*.

Classes

ECMAScript 6, the next version of JavaScript, adds class-based object-orientation to JavaScript and, since TypeScript includes all the features available in ES6, developers are allowed to use class-based object orientation today, and compile them down to JavaScript that works across all major browsers and platforms, without having to wait for the next version of JavaScript.

Let's take a look at a simple TypeScript class definition example:

```
class Character {
  public fullname: string;
  public constructor(firstname: string, lastname: string) {
    this.fullname = `${firstname} ${lastname}`;
  }
  public greet(name?: string) {
    if (name) {
      return `Hi! ${name}! my name is ${this.fullname}`;
    } else {
      return `Hi! my name is ${this.fullname}`;
    }
  }
}

let spark = new Character("Jacob","Keyes");
let msg = spark.greet();
console.log(msg); // "Hi! my name is Jacob Keyes"

let msg1 = spark.greet("Dr. Halsey");
console.log(msg1); // "Hi! Dr. Halsey! my name is Jacob Keyes"
```

In the preceding example, we have declared a new class, `Character`. This class has three members: a property called `fullname`, a `constructor`, and a method `greet`. When we declare a class in TypeScript, all the methods and properties are public by default. We have used the `public` keyword to be more explicit; being explicit about the accessibility of the class members is recommended but it is not a requirement.

Introducing TypeScript

You'll notice that when we refer to one of the members of the class (from within itself), we prepend the `this` operator. The `this` operator denotes that it's a member access. In the last lines, we construct an instance of the `Character` class using a `new` operator. This calls into the constructor we defined earlier, creating a new object with the `Character` shape and running the constructor to initialize it.

TypeScript classes are compiled into JavaScript functions in order to achieve compatibility with ECMAScript 3 and ECMAScript 5.

> We will learn more about classes and other object-oriented programming concepts in `Chapter 4`, *Object-Oriented Programming with TypeScript*.

Interfaces

In TypeScript, we can use interfaces to ensure that a class follows a particular specification:

```
interface LoggerInterface{
    log(arg: any): void;
}

class Logger implements LoggerInterface {
    log (arg: any){
        if (typeof console.log === "function") {
            console.log(arg);
        } else {
            console.log(arg);
        }
    }
}
```

In the preceding example, we have defined an interface `LoggerInterface` and a class `Logger`, which implements it. TypeScript will also allow you to use interfaces to declare the type of an object. This can help us to prevent many potential issues, especially when working with object literals:

```
interface UserInterface {
    name: string;
    password: string;
}

// Error property password is missing
let user: UserInterface = {
```

```
    name: ""
};
```

> We will learn more about interfaces and other object-oriented programming concepts in Chapter 4, *Object-Oriented Programming with TypeScript*.

Namespaces

Namespaces, also known as **internal modules**, are used to encapsulate features and objects that share a certain relationship. Namespaces will help you to organize your code. To declare a namespace in TypeScript, you will use the namespace and export keywords:

> In older versions of TypeScript, the keyword to define an internal module was module instead of namespace.

```
namespace geometry {
    interface VectorInterface {
        /* ... */
    }
    export interface Vector2DInterface {
        /* ... */
    }
    export interface Vector3DInterface {
        /* ... */
    }
    export class Vector2D
        implements VectorInterface, Vector2dInterface {
        /* ... */
    }
    export class Vector3D
        implements VectorInterface, Vector3DInterface {
        /* ... */
    }
}

let vector2DInstance: geometry.Vector2DInterface = new
geometry.Vector2D();
let vector3DInstance: geometry.Vector3DInterface = new
geometry.Vector3d();
```

[31]

Introducing TypeScript

In the preceding code snippet, we have declared a namespace that contains the classes `vector2D` and `vector3D` and the interfaces `VectorInterface`, `Vector2DInterface`, and `Vector3DInterface`. Note that the first interface is missing the keyword `export`. As a result, the interface `VectorInterface` will not be accessible from outside the module's scope.

> Namespaces are a good way to organize your code; however, they are **not the recommended way to organize your code** in a TypeScript application. We will not get into more details about this topic for now, but we will learn more about internal and external modules and we'll discuss when each is appropriate and how to use them in Chapter 4, *Object-Oriented Programming with TypeScript*.

Putting everything together

Now that we have learned how to use the basic TypeScript building blocks individually, let's take a look at a final example in which we will use modules, classes, functions, and type annotations for each of these elements:

```
namespace geometry_demo {
    export interface Vector2DInterface {
        toArray(callback: (x: number[]) => void): void;
        length(): number;
        normalize(): void;
    }

    export class Vector2D implements Vector2DInterface {
        private _x: number;
        private _y: number;
        constructor(x: number, y: number) {
            this._x = x;
            this._y = y;
        }
        public toArray(callback: (x: number[]) => void): void {
            callback([this._x, this._y]);
        }
        public length(): number {
            return Math.sqrt(
                this._x * this._x + this._y * this._y
            );
        }
        public normalize() {
            let len = 1 / this.length();
```

[32]

```
            this._x *= len;
            this._y *= len;
        }
    }
}
```

The preceding example is just a small portion of a basic 3D engine written in JavaScript. In 3D engines, there are a lot of mathematical calculations involving matrices and vectors. As you can see, we have defined a module `Geometry` that will contain some entities; to keep the example simple, we have only added the class `Vector2D`. This class stores two coordinates (x and y) in 2D space and performs some operations on the coordinates. One of the most widely used operations in vectors is normalization, which is one of the methods in our `Vector2D` class.

3D engines are complex software solutions, and as a developer, you are much more likely to use a third-party 3D engine than create your own. For this reason, it is important to understand that TypeScript will not only help you develop large-scale applications but also interact with complex libraries.

In the following code snippet, we will use the module declared earlier to create a `Vector2D` instance:

```
let vector: geometry_demo.Vector2DInterface = new
geometry_demo.Vector2D(2,3);
vector.normalize();
vector.toArray(function(vectorAsArray: number[]){
    console.log(`x: ${vectorAsArray[0]}, y: ${vectorAsArray[1]}`);
});
```

The type-checking and IntelliSense features will help us create a `Vector2D` instance, normalize its value, and convert it into an array to finally show its value on the screen with ease:

```
28  var vector : Geometry.Vector2dInterface = new Geometry.Vector2d(2,3);
29  vector.|
30          ⊘ length (method) Geometry.Vector2dInterface.length(): number
            ⊘ normalize
            ⊘ toArray
```

Summary

In this chapter, you have learned about the purposes of TypeScript. You have also learned about some of the design decisions made by the TypeScript engineers at Microsoft.

Toward the end of this chapter, you learned a lot about the basic building blocks of a TypeScript application, and we started to write some TypeScript code for the first time.

We now know the basics of type annotations, variables, primitive data types, operators, flow control statements, functions, interfaces, classes, and namespaces.

In the next chapter, we will learn more about the TypeScript type system.

2
Working with Types

In the preceding chapter, we learned some basic concepts about the TypeScript type system, including the basics about the type inference system and the optional static type annotations.

In this chapter, you will learn about the main features of the TypeScript type system, including the following concepts:

- The line between TypeScript and JavaScript
- The features of the type system
- Union types, intersection types, and discriminated unions
- Type aliases and local types
- The `typeof` and `keyof` operators
- Control flow analysis and type guards
- Non-nullable types
- Generic types
- Mapped types, lookup types, and conditional types

The TypeScript type system's characteristics

In this section, we are going to learn about the main characteristics of the TypeScript type system, including concepts such as type inference, optional type annotation, and the differences between a nominal type system and a structural type system.

The line between TypeScript and JavaScript

One of the most important things that you are going to need to master to become a good TypeScript programmer is to be able to understand where TypeScript ends and JavaScript begins. It is very important to be able to understand what happens with our TypeScript code at three important phases:

- **Design time**: This takes place when we are writing our TypeScript code and designing our application.
- **Compilation time**: This takes place when we compile our TypeScript into JavaScript code (some compilation errors may take place). Compilation time has subphases, such as parsing the TypeScript code, creating an abstract syntax tree (ATS), and emitting JavaScript code.
- **Execution time** (also known as runtime): This takes place when we execute the output JavaScript code generated by the TypeScript compiler.

The TypeScript types are declared or inferred at design time and used during compilation time, but they are not available at execution time because they are not part of JavaScript.

In this chapter, we are going to learn about many of the TypeScript type system features. If you are familiar with JavaScript, you will notice the differences straight away but, if you are not familiar with JavaScript, I would recommend examining the generated JavaScript output after compiling the code samples included in this chapter. Over time, you will slowly earn the experience required to have a clear vision of the line between TypeScript and JavaScript.

> Please refer to `Chapter 6`, *Understanding the Runtime*, to learn more about the execution time phase (JavaScript).

Type inference

TypeScript tries to find the types of the variables and objects in our application using what is known as **type inference**. When we declare a variable, TypeScript will try to observe the value assigned to the variables in the application to identify its type. Let's examine some examples:

```
let myVariable1 = 3;
```

The type of the variable `myVariable1` is inferred as a number.

```
let myVariable2 = "Hello";
```

The type of the variable `myVariable2` is inferred as a string.

```
let myVariable3 = {
  name: "Remo",
  surname: "Jansen",
  age: 29
};
```

The type of the variable `myVariable3` is inferred as the following type:

```
{ name: string; surname: string; age: number; }
```

The type any is assigned in the cases in which TypeScript is not able to identify the type of a variable. For example, given the following function:

```
function add(a, b) {
    return a + b;
}
```

The type of the function `add` is inferred as the following type:

```
(a: any, b: any) => any;
```

The type `any` is problematic because it prevents the TypeScript compiler from identifying many potential errors. Fortunately, TypeScript features optional type annotations that can be used to solve this problem.

Optional static type annotations

TypeScript allows us to use type annotations to overcome the scenarios in which the type inference system is not powerful enough to automatically detect the type of a variable.

Let's consider the `add` function one more time:

```
function add(a, b) {
    return a + b;
}
```

The type of the function `add` is inferred as the following type:

```
(a: any, b: any) => any;
```

Working with Types

The preceding type is a problem because the usage of the any type effectively prevents the TypeScript compiler from detecting certain errors. For example, we might expect the add function to add two numbers:

```
let result1 = add(2, 3); // 5
```

However, if we pass a string as input, we will encounter an unexpected result:

```
let result2 = add("2", 3); // "23"
```

The preceding error can happen very easily if, for example, the arguments provided to the add function have been extracted from an HTML input and we forget to parse them as a number.

We can fix the add function by adding optional type annotations:

```
function add(a: number, b: number): number {
  return a + b;
}
```

We can add an optional type annotation by adding a colon (:) after the declaration of a variable followed by the type:

```
let myVariable: string = "Hello";
```

> In the case of functions, we can add annotations to the arguments of the function and its returned value.

Now that the type of the arguments of the add function are number, instead of any, the TypeScript compiler will be able to detect potential issues if we provide arguments of the worn type:

```
let result1 = add(2, 3); // OK
let result2 = add("2", 3); // Error
```

> In general, we should try to leverage the type inference system and use optional static type annotations only when the type inference system is not powerful enough to automatically detect the type of a variable.

Structural type system

In the type system of a programming language, a type is an object with a name and a structure. Some types have very simple data structures (such as primitives) while others use complex structures (such as classes).

The type system can use two different strategies to validate that a given value matches the desired type:

- **Nominal type system**: In this type system, values are matched against a type by its name
- **Structural type system**: In this type system, values are matched against a type by its structure

The TypeScript type system is a structural type system because the values are matched against a type by its structure, as the following code snippet demonstrates:

```
interface Person {
  name: string;
  surname: string;
}

function getFullName(person: Person) {
  return `${person.name} ${person.surname}`;
}

class Employer {
  constructor(
    public name: string,
    public surname: string
  ) {}
}

getFullName(new Employer("remo", "jansen")); // OK

const p1 = { name: "remo", surname: "jansen" };
getFullName(p1); // OK

const p2 = { name: "remo", familyName: "jansen" };
getFullName(p2); // Error
```

In the preceding code snippet, we can observe how the first two calls to the getFullName function are successful because the structure (properties and types) of both the Employer instance and the object literal match the structure of the Person interface.

Working with Types

The following code snippet showcases how TypeScript would work if it used a nominal type system:

```
interface Person {
  name: string;
  surname: string;
}

function getFullName(person: Person) {
  return `${person.name} ${person.surname}`;
}

class Employer implements Person { // Named!
  constructor(
    public name: string,
    public surname: string
  ) {}
}

getFullName(new Employer("remo", "jansen")); // OK

const p1: Person = { name: "remo", surname: "jansen" }; // Named!
getFullName(p1); // OK

const p2: Person = { name: "remo", familyName: "jansen" }; // Error
getFullName(p2); // OK
```

The first call to `getFullName` works because the `Employer` class implements the `Person` interface, and the name of the type of the interface can then be matched against the name of the type of the function argument.

> The TypeScript team is currently investigating the possibility of potentially adding support for a nominal type system as well. You can learn more about the progress at `https://github.com/Microsoft/TypeScript/issues/202`.

Core features of the TypeScript type system

In this section, we are going to learn about some of the core features of the TypeScript type system. This includes concepts such as union types, intersection guards, type guards, and type aliases.

Union types

TypeScript allows you to declare union types:

```
let path: string[]|string;
path = "/temp/log.xml";
path = ["/temp/log.xml", "/temp/errors.xml"];
path = 1; // Error
```

In the preceding example, we have declared a variable named path that can contain a single path (string) or a collection of paths (array of strings). In the example, we have also set the value of the variable. We assigned a string and an array of strings without errors; however, when we attempted to assign a numeric value, we got a compilation error, because the union type didn't declare a number as one of the valid types of the variable.

Union types are used to declare a variable that can store a value of two or more types. Only the properties available in all the types present in the intersection type are considered valid:

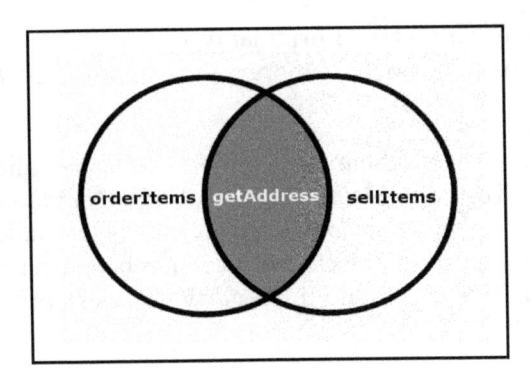

[41]

Working with Types

We can appreciate this behavior in the following example:

```
interface Supplier {
    orderItems(): void;
    getAddress(): void;
}

interface Customer {
    sellItems(): void;
    getAddress(): void;
}

declare let person: Supplier | Customer;
person.getAddress();  // OK
person.orderItems();  // Error
person.sellItems();   // Error
```

Type aliases

TypeScript allows us to declare type aliases by using the `type` keyword:

```
type PrimitiveArray = Array<string|number|boolean>;
type MyNumber = number;
type Callback = () => void
```

Type aliases are exactly the same as their original types; they are simply alternative names. Type aliases can help us to make our code more readable, but it can also lead to some problems.

If you work as part of a large team, the indiscriminate creation of aliases can lead to maintainability problems. The book *Maintainable JavaScript*, Nicholas C. Zakas recommends that you *"avoid modifying the objects you don't own"*. Nicholas was talking about adding, removing, or overriding methods in objects that have not been declared by you (DOM objects, BOM objects, primitive types, and third-party libraries), but we can apply this rule to the use of aliases as well.

Intersection types

When Anders Hejlsberg added intersection types to TypeScript for the first time, he defined them as follows:

> *"Intersection types are the logical complement of union types. A union type A | B represents an entity that has either type A or type B, whereas an intersection type A & B represents an entity that has both type A and type B."*

The following example declares three interfaces named A, B, and C. Then it declares an object named abc, whose type is the intersection type of the interfaces A, B, and C. As a result, the abc object has properties named a, b, and c, but not d:

```
interface A { a: string }
interface B { b: string }
interface C { c: string }
declare let abc: A & B & C;
abc.a = "hello"; // OK
abc.b = "hello"; // OK
abc.c = "hello"; // OK
abc.d = "hello"; // Error
```

Intersection types can also be applied to subproperties:

```
interface X { x: A }
interface Y { x: B }
interface Z { x: C }
declare let xyz: X & Y & Z;
xyz.x.a = "hello"; // OK
xyz.x.b = "hello"; // OK
xyz.x.c = "hello"; // OK
xyz.x.d = "hello"; // Error
```

They can also be applied to functions:

```
type F1 = (x: string) => string;
type F2 = (x: number) => number;
declare let f: F1 & F2;
let s = f("hello"); // OK
let n = f(42); // OK
let t = f(true); // Error
```

Working with Types

The properties available in one or all the types present in the intersection type are considered valid:

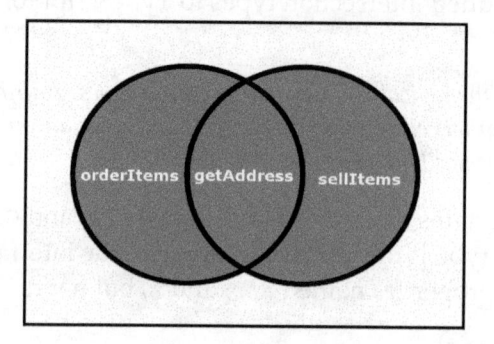

We can appreciate this behavior in the following example:

```
interface Supplier {
    orderItems(): void;
    getAddress(): void;
}

interface Customer {
    sellItems(): void;
    getAddress(): void;
}

declare let person: Supplier & Customer;
person.getAddress();  // OK
person.orderItems();  // OK
person.sellItems();   // OK
```

Non-nullable types

TypeScript 2.0 introduced what are known as non-nullable types. TypeScript used to consider null and undefined to be valid values of every type.

The following diagram represents the values that can be assigned to the type number when non-nullable types are disabled:

[44]

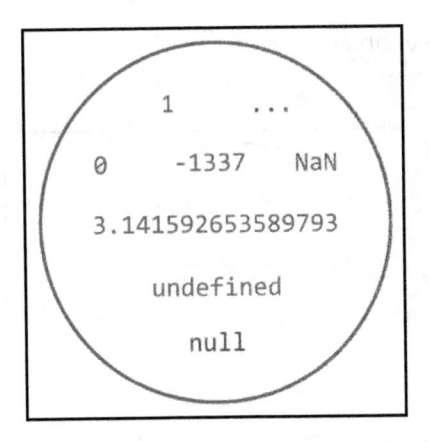

As we can see in the preceding diagram, `undefined` and `null` are allowed as values of the type number, together with the `NaN` value and all the possible numbers.

> NaN, standing for not a number, is a numeric data type value representing an undefined or non-representable value, especially in floating-point calculations. Systematic use of NaNs was introduced by the IEEE 754 floating-point standard in 1985, along with the representation of other non-finite quantities such as infinities.

The following code snippet demonstrates how `undefined` and `null` are allowed as values of the type number when non-nullable types are disabled:

```
let name: string;
name = "Remo"; // OK
name = null; // OK
name = undefined; // OK
```

The same can be said about all other types:

```
let age: number;
age = 28; // OK
age = null; // OK
age = undefined; // OK

let person: { name: string, age: number};
person = { name: "Remo", age: 28 }; // OK
person = { name: null, age: null }; // OK
person = { name: undefined, age: undefined }; // OK
person = null;        // OK
person = undefined;   // OK
```

When non-nullable types are enabled, the values `null` and `undefined` are considered independent types and stop being considered as valid values of the type number:

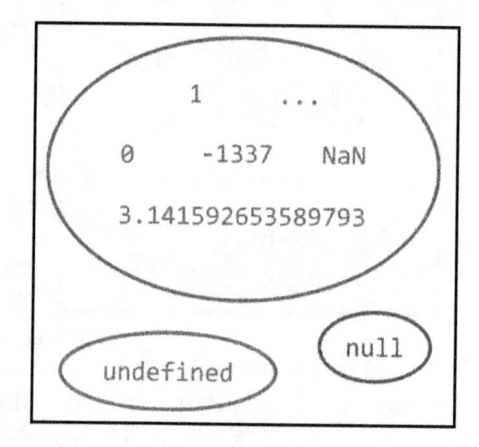

The following code snippet demonstrates how `undefined` and `null` are not allowed as values of the type number when non-nullable types are enabled:

```
let name: string;
name = "Remo"; // OK
name = null; // Error
name = undefined; // Error
```

The same can be said about all other types:

```
let age: number;
age = 28; // OK
age = null; // Error
age = undefined; // Error

let person: { name: string, age: number};
person = { name: "Remo", age: 28 }; // OK
person = { name: null, age: null }; // Error
person = { name: undefined, age: undefined }; // Error
person = null; // Error
person = undefined; // Error
```

We can enable non-nullable types by using the `--strictNullChecks` compilation flag:

```
tsc -strictNullChecks file.ts
```

When non-nullable types are enabled, we can use union types to create nullable versions of a type:

```
type NullableNumber = number | null;
```

The --strict mode

TypeScript allows us to use the `--strict` compilation flag to enable all strict type checking options. Enabling `--strict` enables `--noImplicitAny`, `--noImplicitThis`, `--alwaysStrict`, `--strictPropertyInitialization`, and `--strictNullChecks`:

- The `--strictNullChecks` compilation flag enables non-nullable types.
- The `--noImplicitAny` flag forces us to explicitly declare the type of a variable when the type inference system is not able to automatically infer the correct type.
- The `--alwaysStrict` flag forces the TypeScript parse to use the strict mode.
- The `--noImplicitThis` flag forces us to explicitly declare the type of the this operator in functions when the type inference system is not able to automatically infer the correct type.
- The `--strictPropertyInitialization` flag forces class properties to be initialized.

> We will learn more about the JavaScript use strict and the this operator in `Chapter 6`, *Understanding the Runtime*.

Using the `--strict` compilation flag makes the TypeScript compiler much stricter. Enabling this option in existing large TypeScript projects can lead to the discovery of many errors that may require a significant effort to fix. For this reason, it is recommended to enable the `--strict` compilation flag in greenfield TypeScript projects and enable the individual flags (`--noImplicitAny`, `--noImplicitThis`, `--alwaysStrict`, and `--strictNullChecks`) progressively in existing TypeScript projects.

The `--noImplicitReturns` compilation flag is not one of the flags enabled by the `--strict` flag. The flag throws an error when not all code paths in function return a value. It is also recommended that you enable this flag in greenfield TypeScript projects or when possible on existing projects.

The typeof operator

The `typeof` operator can be used at runtime (JavaScript):

```
let myNumber = 5;
console.log(typeof myNumber === "number");
```

It is important to note that it can also be used at design time (TypeScript) only:

```
let myNumber = 5;
type NumberType = typeof myNumber;
```

Type guards

We can examine the type of an expression at runtime by using the `typeof` or `instanceof` operators. The TypeScript language service looks for these operators and will narrow down the inferred type accordingly when used in an `if` block:

```
let x: any = { /* ... */ };
if(typeof x === 'string') {
    console.log(x.splice(3, 1)); // Error, 'splice' does not exist
      on 'string'
}
// x is still any
x.foo(); // OK
```

In the preceding code snippet, we have declared a variable named x of type `any`. Later, we check the type of x at runtime by using the `typeof` operator. If the type of x results to be a string, we will try to invoke the method `splice`, which is supposed to be a member of the x variable. The TypeScript language service can understand the usage of `typeof` in a conditional statement. TypeScript will automatically assume that x must be a string and let us know that the `splice` method does not exist on the type string. This feature is known as **type guards**.

Custom type guards

We can define custom type guards using by declaring a function with a special return type:

```
interface Supplier {
    orderItems(): void;
    getAddress(): void;
}
```

```
interface Customer {
    sellItems(): void;
    getAddress(): void;
}

function isSupplier(person: Supplier | Customer): person is Supplier {
    return (<Supplier> person).orderItems !== undefined;
}

function handleItems(person: Supplier | Customer) {
    if (isSupplier(person)) {
        person.orderItems(); // OK
    } else {
        person.sellItems(); // OK
    }
}
```

The preceding code snippet declares two types (`Supplier` and `Customer`); it then declares a custom type guard function. The custom type guard returns a Boolean value. The function returns true when the provided value `person` has a property named `orderItems` and false when the property is missing.

The function is trying to identify the type at runtime by examining the properties of the value. This kind of type matching is known as **pattern matching**.

> We will learn more about pattern matching in `Chapter 7`, *Functional Programming with TypeScript*.

Pattern matching is not the only technique that we can use to identify if a value matches a type. We can also use the `instanceof` operator:

```
class Supplier {
    public orderItems(): void {
        // do something...
    }
    public getAddress(): void {
        // do something...
    }
}


class Customer {
    public sellItems(): void {
        // do something...
```

Working with Types

```
        }
        public getAddress(): void {
            // do something...
        }
    }


    function isSupplier(person: Supplier | Customer): person is Supplier {
        return person instanceof Supplier;
    }


    function handleItems(person: Supplier | Customer) {
        if (isSupplier(person)) {
            person.orderItems(); // OK
        } else {
            person.sellItems(); // OK
        }
    }
```

Another technique that we can use to identify if a value matches a type is to use the `typeof` operator:

```
    function doSomething(x: number | string) {
        if (typeof x === 'string') {
            console.log(x.subtr(1)); // Error
            console.log(x.substr(1)); // OK
        }
        x.substr(1); // Error
    }
```

The preceding code snippet throws a compilation error within the `if` block because TypeScript knows that the variable x must be a string within the block. Another error is thrown outside of the `if` block, because TypeScript cannot guarantee that the type of the variable x is string at that point.

Since TypeScript 2.7, we can use the `in` operator as a type guard to narrow down a given type, as demonstrated by the following example:

```
    interface Cat {
        meow(): void;
    }


    interface Dog {
        woof(): void;
    }
```

```
function doSomething(obj: Cat | Dog) {
    if ("meow" in obj) {
        obj.meow(); // OK
    } else {
        obj.woof(); // OK
    }
}
```

Control flow analysis

TypeScript includes a feature known as control flow analysis that is used to identify the type of a variable, based on the execution flow of a program. This feature allows TypeScript to have more precise type inference capabilities.

The following example defines a function that takes two arguments, and the type of one of them (named value) is the union type of number and array of number:

```
function increment(
   incrementBy: number, value: number | number[]
) {
  if (Array.isArray(value)) {
    // value must be an array of number
    return value.map(value => value + incrementBy);
  } else {
    // value is a number
    return value + incrementBy;
  }
}

increment(2, 2); // 4
increment(2, [2, 4, 6]); // [4, 6, 8]
```

Within the body of the function, we use an `if` statement to determine if the value variable is indeed an array of numbers or just a number. The type inference system will change the inferred type of the argument to match the correct type accordingly with the two paths of the `if...else` statement.

Control flow analysis improves the type checker's understanding of variable assignments and control flow statements, thereby greatly reducing the need for type guards.

Literal types

Literal types allow us to declare the exact value that a string Boolean or number must have. When we declare a variable using the `let` keyword, its value will be inferred as a primitive type:

```
let five = 5; // number
let falsy = false; // boolean
let shape = "rectangle"; // string
```

However, if we use the `const` keyword, the type is inferred as the actual assigned value:

```
const five = 5; // 5
const falsy = false; // false
const shape = "rectangle"; // rectangle
```

Literal types can be used in combination with union types, type guards, and type aliases with ease:

```
type ShapeKind = "square" | "rectangle" | "circle";
```

Literal types can be used in combination with type guards and the power of control flow analysis to narrow union types using a technique known as discriminated unions.

Discriminated unions

A discriminated union (also known as tagged unions or algebraic data types) is an advanced pattern that combines string literal types, union types, type guards, and types aliases.

Discriminated unions use a type guard to narrow union types based on tests of a discriminant property (a string literal type) and furthermore extend that capability to switch statements.

The following code snippet declares three types that share a string literal property named `kind`:

```
interface Cube {
    kind: "cube";
    size: number;
}


interface Pyramid {
```

```
    kind: "pyramid";
    width: number;
    length: number;
    height: number;
}

interface Sphere {
    kind: "sphere";
    radius: number;
}
```

We then declare the union type of the three types declared in the preceding code snippet:

```
type Shape = Cube | Pyramid | Sphere;

function volume(shape: Shape) {
    const PI = Math.PI;
    switch (shape.kind) {
        case "cube":
            return shape.size ** 3;
        case "pyramid":
            return (shape.width * shape.height * shape.length) / 3;
        case "sphere":
            return (4 / 3) * PI * (shape.radius ** 3);
    }
}
```

In the preceding function, the `switch` statement acts as a type guard. The type of shape is narrowed in each case clause, according to the value of the discriminant property, `kind`, thereby allowing the other properties of that variant to be accessed without a type assertion.

The never type

As described in the TypeScript documentation, the `never` type has the following characteristics:

- The `never` type is a subtype of and assignable to every type.
- No type is a subtype of or assignable to `never` (except `never` itself).
- In a function expression or arrow function with no return type annotation, if the function has no `return` statements or only `return` statements with expressions of type `never` and, if the end point of the function is not reachable (as determined by control flow analysis), the inferred return type for the function is `never`.

Working with Types

- In a function with an explicit never return type annotation, all `return` statements (if any) must have expressions of a type `never` and the end of the function must not be reachable.

In JavaScript, when a function doesn't explicitly return a value, it implicitly returns the value `undefined`. In TypeScript, the return type of such a function is inferred as void. When a function doesn't complete its execution (it throws an error or never finishes running at all), its return type is inferred as `never` by TypeScript:

```
function error(message: string): never {
    throw new Error(message);
}


// Type () => never
const sing = function() {
    while (true) {
        console.log("I will never return!");
    }
};
```

We can also encounter the `never` type when we reach impossible matches in discriminated unions:

```
function area(shape: Shape) {
    const PI = Math.PI;
    switch (shape.kind) {
        case "square": return shape.size * shape.size;
        case "rectangle": return shape.width * shape.height;
        case "circle": return PI * shape.radius * shape.radius;
        default:
            return shape; // never
    }
}
```

In the preceding code snippet, the default case will never be executed; therefore, the return type is inferred as the never type.

Enumerations

Enumerations allow us to define a set of named constants. Since the TypeScript 2.4 release, these named constant values can be string values. Originally, they could only be numeric values:

```
enum CardinalDirection {
    Up,
    Down,
    Left,
    Right
}
```

A common workaround to this limitation was the usage of union types of literal types:

```
type CardinalDirection =
    "North"
    | "East"
    | "South"
    | "West";


function move(distance: number, direction: CardinalDirection) {
    // ...
}

move(1,"North"); // Okay
move(1,"Nurth"); // Error!
```

Since the TypeScript 2.4 release, enumerations with string values are also supported:

```
enum CardinalDirection {
    Red = "North",
    Green = "East",
    Blue = "South",
    West = "West"
}
```

Object literals

Objects can be initialized using new `Object()`, `Object.create()`, or using the object literal notation, also known as initializer notation. An object initializer is a comma-delimited list of zero or more pairs of property names and values of an object, enclosed in curly braces:

```
let person = { name: "Remo", age: 28 };
```

The type inference system can automatically infer the type of object literals. The inferred type for the variable person declared in the preceding code snippet is `{ name: string, age: number }`. Alternatively, we can explicitly declare the type of an object literal:

```
interface User {
    name: string;
    age: number;
}

let person: User = { name: "Remo", age: 28 }; // OK
```

It is also possible to declare optional properties:

```
interface User {
    name: string;
    age?: number;
}

let person1: User = { name: "Remo", age: 28 }; // OK
let person2: User = { name: "Remo" }; // OK
```

> Please refer to Chapter 1, *Introducing TypeScript*, to learn more about the difference between the empty object type (`{}`), the Object (uppercase) type, and the object (lowercase) type.

Weak types

A weak type is an object literal type in which all properties are optional:

```
interface User {
    name?: string;
    age?: number;
}
```

TypeScript allows us to add a value with some or all the properties defined in the weak type, but it doesn't allow us to assign properties that are not part of the weak type:

```
let user1: User = { name: "Remo", age: 28 }; // OK
let user2: User = { firstName: "Remo", yearBorn: 28 }; // Error
```

The keyof operator

The `keyof` operator can be used to generate a union type of the properties of an object as string literal types:

```
interface User {
    name: string;
    age: number;
}

type userKeys = keyof User; // "name" | "age"
```

The `keyof` operator can be used in combination with other operators, such as the `typeof` operator, for example:

```
let person = { name: "Remo", age: "28" };

interface User {
    name: string;
    age: number;
}

type userKeys = keyof typeof person; // "name" | "age"
```

We will find out more about the `keyof` operator later in this chapter when we learn about lookup types.

Index signature

In JavaScript, we can access the properties of an object using the name of the object followed by a dot and the name of the property:

```
let foo: any = {};
foo.hello = 'World';
console.log(foo.hello); // World
```

Working with Types

However, it is also possible to access the properties of an object using the name of the object followed by the name of the property as a string wrapped by brackets:

```
let foo: any = {};
foo['hello'] = 'World';
console.log(foo['hello']); // World
```

This behavior can be declared using what is known as the index signature:

```
interface StringArray {
    [index: number]: string;
}

let myArray: StringArray = ["Bob", "Fred"];
let myStr: string = myArray[0];
```

As we can see in the preceding code snippet, the index signature allows us to specify the type of the value returned when we access a property using the brackets signature.

Local types

The TypeScript type system allows us to declare types (such as type aliases, classes, and interfaces) within the declaration of functions and methods. In the early releases of TypeScript, this was not allowed:

```
interface Person {
    name: string;
    age: number;
}

function makePerson(name: string, age: number): Person {

    // Local type
    class Person implements Person {
        constructor(
            public name: string,
            public age: number
        ) {}
    }

    return new Person(name, age);

}

let user = makePerson("Remo", 28);
```

Type casting

The TypeScript type system allows us to cast a given type using two different syntaxes:

```
var myObject: TypeA;
var otherObject: any;
myObject = <TypeA> otherObject; // Using <>
myObject = otherObject as TypeA; // Using as keyword
```

It is important to understand that the TypeScript casting does not affect the runtime type of the variables.

> Since Typescript 1.6, the default is `as`, because `<>` is ambiguous in `.tsx` files. We will learn more about `.tsx` files in Chapter 11, *Frontend Development with React and TypeScript*.

In general, it is recommended to avoid using type castings and prefer generic types instead.

Advanced features of the TypeScript type system

In this section, we are going to learn some advanced type system features such as generic types, mapped types, and lookup types.

Generic types

Generic types can help us avoid using type casting and increase the reusability of our code by allowing us to declare (`T`) when a function, class, or method is consumed, as opposed to when it is declared:

```
function deserialize<T>(json: string): T {
    return JSON.parse(json) as T;
}

interface User {
    name: string;
    age: number;
}

let user = deserialize<User>(`{"name":"Remo","age":28}`);
```

Working with Types

```
interface Rectangle {
    width: number;
    height: number;
}

let rectangle = deserialize<Rectangle>(`{"width":5,"height":8}`);
```

The preceding example declares a function named deserialize. The type returned by the function (T) is unknown at the point in which the function is declared. The function is then invoked on two occasions, and the type T becomes finally known (User and Rectangle).

> We will learn more about generic types in Chapter 4, *Object-Oriented Programming with TypeScript*.

Generic constraints

Sometimes, we don't need the concrete type required by a function, class, or method, but we know that such type must adhere to a certain set of rules.

For example, the following code snippet declares a generic function named isEquals. However, this time the type T has a constraint (T extends Comparable):

```
interface Comparable<T> {
    equals(value: T): boolean;
}

function isEqual<TVal, T extends Comparable<TVal>>(comparable: T, value: TVal) {
    return comparable.equals(value);
}
```

The constraint is used to ensure that all the types provided to isEqual as its generic type argument implement the Comparable interface:

```
interface RectangleInterface {
    width: number;
    height: number;
}

type ComparableRectangle = RectangleInterface & Comparable<RectangleInterface>;

class Rectangle implements ComparableRectangle {
```

```
    public width: number;
    public height: number;
    public constructor(width: number, height: number) {
        this.width = width;
        this.height = height;
    }
    public equals(value: Rectangle) {
        return value.width === this.width && value.height === this.height;
    }
};

interface CircleInterface {
    radious: number;
}

type ComparableCircle = CircleInterface & Comparable<CircleInterface>;

class Circle implements ComparableCircle {
    public radious: number;
    public constructor(radious: number) {
        this.radious = radious
    }
    public equals(value: CircleInterface): boolean {
        return value.radious === this.radious;
    }
}

const circle = new Circle(5);
const rectangle = new Rectangle(5, 8);

isEqual<RectangleInterface, ComparableRectangle>(rectangle, { width: 5, height: 8 });
isEqual<CircleInterface, ComparableCircle>(circle, { radius: 5 });
```

Mapped types

Mapped types are an advanced type feature that allows us to map the value of each of the properties of a type to a different type. For example, the following mapped type transforms the value of the properties of a given type to a string literal that matches the property name:

```
type Keyify<T> = {
    [P in keyof T]: P;
};
```

Working with Types

The following function takes an object and returns a new object in which all the properties have the same names, but their values are the names of the properties:

```
function getKeys<T>(obj: T): Keyify<T> {
    const keysArr = Object.keys(obj);
    const stringifyObj = keysArr.reduce((p, c, i, a) => {
        return {
            ...p,
            [c]: c
        };
    }, {});
    return stringifyObj as Keyify<T>;
}

interface User {
    name: string;
    age: number;
}

let user: User = { name: "Remo", age: 28 };
let keys = getKeys<User>(user);

keys.name; // "name"
keys.age; // "age"
```

TypeScript declares some commonly used mapped types for us:
```
// Make all properties in T optional
type Partial<T> = {
    [P in keyof T]?: T[P];
};


// Make all properties in T readonly
type Readonly<T> = {
    readonly [P in keyof T]: T[P];
};


// From T pick a set of properties K
type Pick<T, K extends keyof T> = {
    [P in K]: T[P];
}

// Construct a type with a set of properties K of type T
type Record<K extends string, T> = {
    [P in K]: T;
}
```

Lookup types

Lookup types are another advanced type system feature that allow us to combine the `keyof` operator with generic and object literals to create advanced type annotations. Let's look at an example:

```
function filterByProperty<T, K extends keyof T>(
    property: K, entities: T[], value: T[K]
) {
    return entities.filter(e => e[property] === value);
}
```

The preceding function takes two generic type arguments:

- `T` is the type of the items in the array passed as the first argument of the function.
- `K` is the name of the properties of `T`. This requirement is enforced by a generic constraint (extends `keyof T`).

The function also expects two arguments:

- An array of entities of type `T`.
- A value of type `T[K]`. The type `T[K]` represents the type of the value of the property `K` in the type `T`, and it is known as lookup type.

The preceding function can be used to filter the array of entities of type `T` by one of the properties of the type `T`:

```
interface User {
    surname: string;
    age: number;
}

const users = [
    { surname: "Smith", age: 28 },
    { surname: "Johnson", age: 55 },
    { surname: "Williams", age: 14 }
];

filterByProperty<User, "age">("age", users, 21);
filterByProperty<User, "surname">("surname", users, "Smith");
```

Working with Types

Mapped type modifiers

TypeScript 2.8 introduced a few operators that allow us to have a greater level of control over the definition of mapped types:

- We can use the `readonly` modifier to flag a property as immutable.
- We can use the `?` operator to flag a property as optional.
- We can use the `+` operator to apply a modifier, such as the `readonly` modifier, to a property in a type. We can also use the `+` operator with the `?` operator.
- We can use the `-` operator to apply a modifier, such as the `readonly` modifier to a property in a type. We can also use the `+` operator with the `?` operator.

We will now examine a few examples. The code snippet declares a mapped type that can be used to transform a type, `T`, into a new type that contains all the properties in `T` but is marked as both `readonly` and `optional`:

```
type ReadonlyAndPartial1<T> = {
    readonly [P in keyof T]?: T[P]
}
```

The following type declaration is identical to the one in the preceding code snippet:

```
type ReadonlyAndPartial2<T> = {
    +readonly [P in keyof T]+?: T[P];
}
```

The following type can be used to remove the `readonly` modifier from all the properties in a given type `T`:

```
type Mutable<T> = {
    -readonly [P in keyof T]: T[P]
}
```

We can apply the `Mutable` type to the following interface to generate a new type. The `abc` property is no longer immutable, but the `def` property is still optional:

```
interface Foo {
    readonly abc: number;
    def?: string;
}

type TotallyMutableFoo = Mutable<Foo>
```

[64]

Finally, the following code snippet declares a mapped type that can be used to remove the optional properties in a given type T:

```
type Required<T> = {
    [P in keyof T]-?: T[P];
}
```

Conditional types

Conditional mapped types are an advanced feature introduced in TypeScript 2.8. Previously in this chapter, we learned that we could use the `extends` keyword to declare generic constraints. When we declare a generic constraint, we are using the `extends` keyword as a kind of operator that allows us to check if a generic type (T) is a subtype of a given type. For example, the following code snippet declares two interfaces named Animal and Dog:

```
interface Animal {
    live(): void;
}
interface Dog extends Animal {
    woof(): void;
}
```

We then use the `extends` keyword as a conditional operator to generate a new type:

```
type Foo1 = Dog extends Animal ? number : string; // number
type Bar1 = RegExp extends Dog ? number : string; // string
```

Conditional types can be used to declare some complex types. For example, the Flatten function is a function that transforms a multi-dimensional array (`[][]`) into an array with only one dimension (`[]`). The type of the return of Flatten function is a conditional type, because it returns an array when a multidimensional array is provided and a number when an array with only one dimension is provided:

```
type Flatten<T> = T extends any[] ? T[number] : T;

type arr1 = number[];
type flattenArr1 = Flatten<arr1>; // number

type arr2 = number[][];
type flattenArr2 = Flatten<arr2>; // number[]
```

The infer keyword

In the preceding section, we have defined the `Flatten` type. However, this behavior was hardcoded to return a number when an array of one dimension is provided. This means that the `flatten` type only works as expected with arrays of numbers. Fortunately, since the TypeScript 2.8 release, we can use the `infer` keyword to overcome this limitation:

```
type TypedFlatten<T> = T extends Array<infer U> ? U : T;
```

The `infer` keyword can be used in other scenarios. For example, we can use it to infer the return type of a function:

```
type ReturnType<T extends (...args: any[]) => any> = T extends (...args:
any[]) => infer R ? R : any;

type func1 = () => number;
type returnOfFunc1 = ReturnType<func1>; // number
```

Built-in conditional types

In the preceding section, we have used the `ReturnType` type to extract the return type of a given function. The `ReturnType` type is included as a built-in type. TypeScript 2.8 includes many other types:

```
// Exclude from T those types that are assignable to U
type Exclude<T, U> = T extends U ? never : T;

// Extract from T those types that are assignable to U
type Extract<T, U> = T extends U ? T : never;

// string[] | number[]
type Foo2 = Extract<boolean | string[] | number[], any[]>;

// boolean
type Bar2 = Exclude<boolean | string[] | number[], any[]>;

// Exclude null and undefined from T
type NonNullable<T> = T extends null | undefined ? never : T;

//  Obtain the return type of a function type
type ReturnType<T extends (...args: any[]) => any> = T extends (...args:
any[]) => infer R ? R : any;
```

[66]

```
// Obtain the return type of a constructor function type
type InstanceType<T extends new (...args: any[]) => any> = T extends new
(...args: any[]) => infer R ? R : any;
```

The polymorphic this type

In JavaScript, the value of the `this` operator is determined by the way a function or method is invoked. In a method, the `this` operator usually points to the class instance.

The polymorphic `this` type is an improved version of the original type inference for the `this` operator that introduced the following behavior as documented by Anders Hejlsberg:

- The type of `this` in an expression within a nonstatic class or interface member is an instance of some class that derives from the containing class, as opposed to simply an instance of the containing class.
- The `this` keyword can be used in a type position within a nonstatic class or interface member to reference the type of this.
- When a class or interface is referenced as a type, all occurrences of the `this` type within the class (including those inherited from base classes) are replaced with the type itself.

This feature makes patterns such as fluent interfaces (https://en.wikipedia.org/wiki/Fluent_interface) much easier to express and implement, as we can see in the following example:

```
interface Person {
    name?: string;
    surname?: string;
    age?: number;
}

class PersonBuilder<T extends Person> {
    protected _details: T;
    public constructor() {
        this._details = {} as T;
    }
    public currentValue(): T {
        return this._details;
    }
    public withName(name: string): this {
        this._details.name = name;
        return this;
    }
```

Working with Types

```
    public withSurname(surname: string): this {
        this._details.surname = surname;
        return this;
    }
    public withAge(age: number): this {
        this._details.age = age;
        return this;
    }
}
```

> A fluent interface allows us to invoke multiple methods in an object by connecting them with dots, without having to write the object name each time.

Since the class methods return the `this` type, we can invoke multiple methods without having to write the class name multiple times:

```
let value1 = new PersonBuilder()
            .withName("name")
            .withSurname("surname")
            .withAge(28)
            .currentValue();
```

Since the class uses the `this` type, we can extend it and the new class can then provide a fluent interface that includes the base methods as well:

```
interface Employee extends Person {
    email: string;
    department: string;
}

class EmployeeBuilder extends PersonBuilder<Employee> {
    public withEmail(email: string) {
        this._details.email = email;
        return this;
    }
    public withDepartment(department: string) {
        this._details.department = department;
        return this;
    }
}

let value2 = new EmployeeBuilder()
    .withName("name")
    .withSurname("surname")
    .withAge(28)
```

```
        .withEmail("name.surname@company.com")
        .withDepartment("engineering")
        .currentValue();
```

> In Chapter 6, *Understanding the Runtime*, we will learn much more about the `this` operator.

Ambient declarations

The ambient declaration allows you to create a variable in your TypeScript code that will not be translated into JavaScript at compilation time. This feature was designed to make the integration with the existing JavaScript code and the **Document Object Model** (**DOM**) and **Browser Object Model** (**BOM**) easier. Let's look at an example:

```
customConsole.log("A log entry!");   // error
```

If you try to call the member log of an object named `customConsole`, TypeScript will let us know that the `customConsole` object has not been declared:

```
// Cannot find name 'customConsole'
```

This is not a surprise. However, sometimes we want to invoke an object that has not been defined, for example, the `console` or `window` objects:

```
console.log("Log Entry!");
const host = window.location.hostname;
```

When we access the DOM or BOM objects, we don't get an error because these objects have already been declared in a special TypeScript file known as **declaration files**. You can use the `declare` operator to create an ambient declaration.

In the following code snippet, we will declare an interface that is implemented by the `customConsole` object. We then use the `declare` operator to add the `customConsole` object to the scope:

```
interface ICustomConsole {
    log(arg: string) : void;
}
declare var customConsole : ICustomConsole;
```

Working with Types

> Interfaces are explained in greater detail in `Chapter 4`, *Object-Oriented Programming with TypeScript*.

We can then use the `customConsole` object without compilation errors:

```
customConsole.log("A log entry!"); // ok
```

TypeScript includes, by default, a file named `lib.d.ts` that provides interface declarations for the built-in JavaScript library as well as the DOM.

Declaration files use the file extension `.d.ts` and are used to increase the TypeScript compatibility with third-party libraries and runtime environments, such as Node.js or a browser.

> We will learn how to work with declaration files in `Chapter 5`, *Working with Dependencies*.

Type declarations – .d.ts

Sometimes, we will need to consume an existing JavaScript file, but we will not be able to migrate it to TypeScript. A common example of this scenario is when we consume a third-party JavaScript library.

If the library is open source, we could contribute to it by migrating it to TypeScript. However, sometimes, using TypeScript might not align with the preferences of the library authors, or the migration may require a significant amount of work. TypeScript solves this problem by allowing us to create special kinds of files known as type declarations or type definitions.

In the previous chapter, we learned that, by default, TypeScript includes a `lib.d.ts` file that provides interface declarations for the built-in JavaScript objects, as well as the DOM and BOM APIs.

The type definition files contain the type declarations of third-party libraries. These files facilitate the integration between the existing JavaScript libraries and TypeScript.

Chapter 2

To take advantage of all the TypeScript features while consuming a JavaScript library, we need to install the type definition file of such library. Fortunately, we don't need to create the type definition files by hand, because there is an open source project known as **DefinitelyTyped** that already contains some type definition files for many of the existing JavaScript libraries.

In the early days of TypeScript development, developers had to manually download and install the type definition files from the DefinitelyTyped project website, but those days are long gone and today we can use the node package manager (npm) to install and manage the type definition files required by our TypeScript application.

> We will learn how to work with declaration files in `Chapter 9`, *Automating Your Development Workflow*.

Summary

In this chapter, we learned about many of the features of the TypeScript type system. At this point, we should now have a good understanding of concepts such type inference, non-nullable types, structural typing, and control flow analysis.

In the next chapter, we will learn more about the usage of functions in TypeScript.

3
Working with Functions

In `Chapter 1`, *Introducing TypeScript*, we learned the basics of functions. Functions are the fundamental building blocks of any application in TypeScript, and they are powerful enough to deserve the dedication of an entire chapter to explore their potential.

In this chapter, we are going to learn how to work with functions in depth. The chapter is divided into two main sections. The first section starts with a quick recap of some basic concepts, and then moves on to some less commonly known features of functions and their use cases. The first section covers the following concepts:

- Function declarations and function expressions
- Function types
- Functions with optional parameters
- Functions with default parameters
- Functions with REST parameters
- Function overloading
- Specialized overloading signatures
- Function scope
- Immediately invoked functions
- Tag functions and tagged templates

The second section focuses on TypeScript's asynchronous programming capabilities and includes the following concepts:

- Callbacks and higher-order functions
- Arrow functions
- Callback hell
- Promises
- Generators
- Asynchronous functions (`async` and `await`)

Working with functions in TypeScript

This section focuses on the declaration and use of functions, parameters, and arguments.

Function declarations and function expressions

In the first chapter, we introduced the possibility of declaring functions with (named functions) or without (unnamed or anonymous functions) explicitly indicating their name, but we didn't mention that we were also using two different types of functions.

In the following example, the named function `greetNamed` is a **function declaration**, while `greetUnnamed` is a **function expression**. For now, please ignore the first two lines, which contain two `console.log` statements:

```
console.log(greetNamed("John")); // OK
console.log(greetUnnamed("John")); // Error

function greetNamed(name: string): string {
    return `Hi! ${name}`;
}

let greetUnnamed = function(name: string): string {
    return `Hi! ${name}`;
};
```

We might think that the preceding functions are identical, but they behave differently. The JavaScript interpreter can evaluate a function declaration as it is being parsed. On the other hand, the function expression is part of an assignment and will not be evaluated until the assignment has been completed.

> The main cause of the different behavior of these functions is a process known as **variable hoisting**. We will learn more about the variable hoisting process later in this chapter.

If we compile the preceding TypeScript code snippet into JavaScript and try to execute it in a web browser, we will observe that the first `console.log` call works. This is because JavaScript knows about the declaration function and can parse it before the program is executed.

However, the second alert statement will throw an exception, which indicates that `greetUnnamed` is not a function. The exception is thrown because the `greetUnnamed` assignment must be completed before the function can be evaluated.

Function types

We already know that it is possible to explicitly declare the type of an element in our application by using optional type annotations:

```
function greetNamed(name: string): string {
    return `Hi! ${name}`;
}
```

In the preceding function, we have specified the type of the parameter name (string) and its return type (string). Sometimes, we will need to not just specify the types of the function elements, but the function itself. Let's look at an example:

```
let greetUnnamed: (name: string) => string;

greetUnnamed = function(name: string): string {
    return `Hi! ${name}`;
};
```

In the preceding example, we have declared the `greetUnnamed` variable and its type. The `greetUnnamed` type is a function type that takes a string variable called `name` as its only parameter and returns a string after being invoked. After declaring the variable, a function, whose type must be equal to the variable type, is assigned to it.

We can also declare the `greetUnnamed` type and assign a function to it in the same line rather than declaring it in two separate lines as we did in the previous example:

```
let greetUnnamed: (name: string) => string = function(name: string): string
{
    return `Hi! ${name}`;
};
```

Just like in the previous example, the preceding code snippet also declares a variable, `greetUnnamed`, and its type. The `greetUnnamed` type is a function type that takes a string variable called `name` as its only parameter and will return a string after being invoked. We will assign a function to this variable in the same line in which it is declared. The type of the assigned function must match the type of the variable.

Working with Functions

> In the preceding example, we have declared the type of the `greetUnnamed` variable and then assigned a function as its value. The type of the function can be inferred from the assigned function, and for this reason, it is unnecessary to add a redundant type annotation. We have done this to help you understand this section, but it is important to mention that adding redundant type annotations can make our code harder to read, and it is considered bad practice.

Trailing commas in function arguments

Trailing commas are the commas that are used after the last argument of a function. Using a comma after the last parameter of a function can be useful because it is very common for programmers to forget to add a comma when they modify an existing function by adding additional parameters.

For example, the following function only takes one parameter and doesn't use trailing commas:

```
function greetWithoutTralingCommas(
    name: string
): string {
    return `Hi! ${name}`;
}
```

After some time, we might be required to add a parameter to the preceding function. A common mistake is to declare the new parameter and forget to add a comma after the first parameter:

```
function updatedGreetWithoutTralingCommas(
    name: string
    surname: string, // Error
): string {
    return `Hi! ${name} ${surname}`;
}
```

Using a trailing comma in the first version of the function could have helped us to prevent this common mistake:

```
function greetWithTralingCommas(
    name: string,
): string {
    return `Hi! ${name}`;
}
```

Using a trailing comma eliminates the possibility of forgetting the comma when adding a new argument:

```
function updatedGreetWithTralingCommas(
    name: string,
    surname: string,
): string {
    return `Hi! ${name} ${surname}`;
}
```

> TypeScript will throw an error if we forget a comma, so trailing commas are not needed as much as they are when working with JavaScript. Trailing commas are optional, but using them is considered a good practice by many JavaScript and TypeScript engineers.

Functions with optional parameters

Unlike JavaScript, the TypeScript compiler will throw an error if we attempt to invoke a function without providing the exact number and types of parameters that its signature declares. Let's look at a code sample to demonstrate this:

```
function add(foo: number, bar: number, foobar: number): number {
    return foo + bar + foobar;
}
```

The preceding function is called `add` and will take three numbers as parameters, named `foo`, `bar`, and `foobar`. If we attempt to invoke this function without providing exactly three numbers, we will get a compilation error indicating that the supplied parameters do not match the function's signature:

```
add(); // Error, expected 3 arguments, but got 0.
add(2, 2); // Error, expected 3 arguments, but got 2.
add(2, 2, 2); // OK, returns 6
```

Working with Functions

There are scenarios in which we might want to be able to call the function without providing all its arguments. TypeScript features optional parameters in functions to help us to increase the flexibility of our functions and overcome such scenarios.

We can indicate to the TypeScript compiler that we want a function's parameter to be optional by appending the ? character to its name. Let's update the previous function to transform the required `foobar` parameter into an optional parameter:

```
function add(foo: number, bar: number, foobar?: number): number {
    let result = foo + bar;
    if (foobar !== undefined) {
        result += foobar;
    }
    return result;
}
```

Note how we have changed the `foobar` parameter name to `foobar?`, and how we are checking the type of `foobar` inside the function to identify whether the parameter was supplied as an argument to the function or not. After implementing these changes, the TypeScript compiler will allow us to invoke the function without errors when we supply two or three arguments to it:

```
add(); // Error, expected 2-3 arguments, but got 0.
add(2, 2); // OK, returns 4
add(2, 2, 2); // OK, returns 6
```

It is important to note that the optional parameters must always be located after the required parameters in the function's parameter list.

Functions with default parameters

When a function has some optional parameters, we must check whether an argument has been passed to the function (just like we did in the previous example) to prevent potential errors.

There are some scenarios where it would be more useful to provide a default value for a parameter when it is not supplied than making it an optional parameter. Let's rewrite the `add` function (from the previous section) using the inline `if` structure:

```
function add(foo: number, bar: number, foobar?: number): number {
    return foo + bar + (foobar !== undefined ? foobar : 0);
}
```

There is nothing wrong with the preceding function, but we can improve its readability by providing a default value for the `foobar` parameter instead of using an optional parameter:

```
function add(foo: number, bar: number, foobar: number = 0): number {
    return foo + bar + foobar;
}
```

To indicate that a function parameter is optional, we need to provide a default value using the = operator when declaring the function's signature. After compiling the preceding code examples, the TypeScript compiler will generate an `if` structure in the JavaScript output to set a default value for the `foobar` parameter if it is not passed as an argument to the function:

```
function add(foo, bar, foobar) {
    if (foobar === void 0) { foobar = 0; }
    return foo + bar + foobar;
}
```

This is great because the TypeScript compiler generated the code necessary for us to prevent potential runtime errors.

> The `void 0` parameter is used by the TypeScript compiler to check whether a variable is undefined. While most developers use the undefined variable to perform this kind of check, most compilers use `void 0` because it will always evaluate as undefined. Checking against an undefined variable is less secure because its value could have been modified, as demonstrated by the following code snippet:
>
> ```
> function test() {
>     var undefined = 2; // 2
>     console.log(undefined === 2); // true
> }
> ```

Just like optional parameters, default parameters must always be located after any required parameters in the function's parameter list.

Working with Functions

Functions with REST parameters

We have learned how to use optional and default parameters to increase the number of ways that we can invoke a function. Let's return one more time to the previous example:

```
function add(foo: number, bar: number, foobar: number = 0): number {
    return foo + bar + foobar;
}
```

We have learned how to invoke the `add` function with two or three parameters, but what if we wanted to allow other developers to pass four or five parameters to our function? We would have to add two extra default or optional parameters. And what if we wanted to allow them to pass as many parameters as they need? The solution to this possible scenario is the use of REST parameters. The REST parameter syntax allows us to represent an indefinite number of arguments as an array:

```
function add(...foo: number[]): number {
    let result = 0;
    for (let i = 0; i < foo.length; i++) {
        result += foo[i];
    }
    return result;
}
```

As we can see in the preceding code snippet, we have replaced the function parameters `foo`, `bar`, and `foobar` with just one parameter named `foo`. Note that the name of the parameter `foo` is preceded by an ellipsis (a set of three periods—not the actual ellipsis character). A REST parameter must be of an array type or we will get a compilation error. We can now invoke the `add` function with as many parameters as we need:

```
add(); // 0
add(2); // 2
add(2, 2); // 4
add(2, 2, 2); // 6
add(2, 2, 2, 2); // 8
add(2, 2, 2, 2, 2); // 10
add(2, 2, 2, 2, 2, 2); // 12
```

Although there is no specific limit to the theoretical maximum number of arguments that a function can take, there are, of course, practical limits. These limits are entirely implementation-dependent and, most likely, will also depend on exactly how we are calling the function.

JavaScript functions have a built-in object called the `arguments` object. This object is available as a local variable named `arguments`. The `arguments` variable contains an object like an array that contains the arguments used when the function was invoked.

> The `arguments` object exposes some of the methods and properties provided by a standard array, but not all of them. Refer to the documentation at https://developer.mozilla.org/en-US/docs/Web/JavaScript/Reference/Functions/arguments to learn more about its peculiarities.

If we examine the JavaScript output, we will notice that TypeScript iterates the `arguments` object to add the values to the `foo` variable:

```
function add() {
    var foo = [];
    for (var _i = 0; _i < arguments.length; _i++) {
        foo[_i - 0] = arguments[_i];
    }
    var result = 0;
    for (var i = 0; i < foo.length; i++) {
        result += foo[i];
    }
    return result;
}
```

We can argue that this is an extra, unnecessary iteration over the function's parameters. Even though it is hard to imagine this extra iteration becoming a performance issue, if you think that this could be a problem for the performance of your application, you may want to consider avoiding the use of REST parameters and use an array as the only parameter of the function instead:

```
function add(foo: number[]): number {
    let result = 0;
    for (let i = 0; i < foo.length; i++) {
        result += foo[i];
    }
    return result;
}
```

The preceding function takes an array of numbers as its only parameter. The invocation API will be a little bit different from the REST parameters, but we will effectively avoid the extra iteration over the function's argument list:

```
add(); // Error, expected 1 arguments, but got 0.
add(2); // Error, '2' is not assignable to parameter of type 'number[]'.
add(2, 2); // Error, expected 1 arguments, but got 2.
```

Working with Functions

```
add(2, 2, 2); // Error, expected 1 arguments, but got 3.

add([]); // returns 0
add([2]); // returns 2
add([2, 2]); // returns 4
add([2, 2, 2]); // returns 6
```

Function overloading

Function overloading, or method overloading, is the ability to create multiple methods with the same name and a different number of parameters or types. In TypeScript, we can overload a function by specifying all function signatures (known as the **overload signatures**) of a function, followed by a signature (known as the **implementation signature**). Let's look at an example:

```
function test(name: string): string; // overloaded signature
function test(age: number): string; // overloaded signature
function test(single: boolean): string; // overloaded signature
function test(value: (string|number|boolean)): string { // implementation signature
    switch (typeof value) {
        case "string":
            return `My name is ${value}.`;
        case "number":
            return `I'm ${value} years old.`;
        case "boolean":
            return value ? "I'm single." : "I'm not single.";
        default:
            throw new Error("Invalid Operation!");
    }
}
```

As we can see in the preceding example, we have overloaded the function test three times by adding a signature that takes a string as its only parameter, another function that takes a number, and a final signature that takes a boolean as its unique parameter. It is important to note that all function signatures must be compatible; so if, for example, one of the signatures tries to return a number while another tries to return a string, we will get a compilation error:

```
function test(name: string): string;
function test(age: number): number; // Error
function test(single: boolean): string;
function test(value: (string|number|boolean)): string {
    switch (typeof value) {
        case "string":
```

```
            return `My name is ${value}.`;
        case "number":
            return `I'm ${value} years old.`;
        case "boolean":
            return value ? "I'm single." : "I'm not single.";
        default:
            throw new Error("Invalid Operation!");
    }
}
```

The implementation signature must be compatible with all the overloaded signatures, always be the last in the list, and take the any type or a union type as the type of its parameters.

Invoking the function providing arguments that don't match any of the types that are declared by the overload signatures will lead us to a compilation error:

```
test("Remo"); // returns "My name is Remo."
test(26); // returns "I'm 26 years old.";
test(false); // returns "I'm not single.";
test({ custom: "custom" }); // Error
```

Specialized overloading signature

We can use a specialized signature to create multiple methods with the same name and number of parameters, but a different return type. To create a specialized signature, we must indicate the type of function parameter using a string. The string literal is used to identify which of the function overloads is invoked:

```
interface Document {
    createElement(tagName: "div"): HTMLDivElement; // specialized
    createElement(tagName: "span"): HTMLSpanElement; // specialized
    createElement(tagName: "canvas"): HTMLCanvasElement; // specialized
    createElement(tagName: string): HTMLElement; // non-specialized
}
```

In the preceding example, we have declared three **specialized overloaded signatures** and one **nonspecialized signature** for the function named `createElement`.

Working with Functions

When we declare a specialized signature in an object, it must be assignable to at least one nonspecialized signature in the same object. This can be observed in the preceding example, as the `createElement` property belongs to a type that contains three specialized signatures, all of which are assignable to the nonspecialized signature in the type.

When writing overloaded declarations, we must list the nonspecialized signature last.

Function scope

Low-level languages, such as C, have low-level memory management features. In programming languages with a higher level of abstraction, such as TypeScript, values are allocated when variables are created and automatically cleared from memory when they are not used anymore. The process that cleans the memory is known as **garbage collection** and is performed by the JavaScript runtime garbage collector.

The garbage collector does a great job, but it is a mistake to assume that it will always prevent us from facing a memory leak. The garbage collector will clear a variable from the memory whenever the variable is out of the scope. It is important to understand how the TypeScript scope works, so we will now look at the life cycle of the variables.

Some programming languages use the structure of the program source code to determine what variables we are referring to (**lexical scoping**), while others use the runtime state of the program stack to determine what variable we are referring to (**dynamic scoping**). The majority of modern programming languages use lexical scoping (including TypeScript). Lexical scoping tends to be dramatically easier to understand for both humans and analysis tools than dynamic scoping.

While in most lexical-scoped programming languages, variables are scoped to a block (a section of code delimited by curly braces `{}`), in TypeScript (and JavaScript), variables are scoped to a function, as demonstrated by the following code snippet:

```
function foo(): void {
    if (true) {
        var bar: number = 0;
    }
    console.log(bar);
}

foo(); // 0
```

The preceding function named `foo` contains an `if` structure. We have declared a numeric variable named `bar` inside the `if` structure, and later, we have attempted to show the value of the `bar` variable using the `log` function.

We might think that the preceding code sample would throw an error in the fifth line because the `var` variable should be out of the scope when the `log` function is invoked. However, if we invoke the `foo` function, the `log` function will be able to display the `bar` variable without errors because all the variables inside a function will be in the scope of the entire function body, even if they are inside another block of code (except a function block).

This might seem confusing, but it is easy to understand once we know that at runtime, all the variable declarations are moved to the top of a function before the function is executed. This behavior is known as **hoisting**.

> TypeScript is compiled to JavaScript and then executed—this means that a TypeScript application is a JavaScript application at runtime, and for this reason, when we refer to the TypeScript runtime, we are talking about the JavaScript runtime. We will learn in depth about the runtime in Chapter 6, *Understanding the Runtime*.

Before the preceding code snippet is executed, the runtime will move the declaration of the `bar` variable to the top of our function:

```
function foo() {
    var bar;
    if (true) {
        bar = 0;
    }
    console.log(bar);
}

foo(); // 0
```

This explains why it is possible to use a variable before it is declared. Let's look at an example:

```
function foo(): void {
    bar = 0;
    var bar: number;
    console.log(bar);
}

foo(); // 0
```

Working with Functions

In the preceding code snippet, we have declared a `foo` function, and in its body, we have assigned the value 0 to a variable named `bar`. At this point, the variable has not been declared. In the second line, we are declaring the variable `bar` and its type. In the last line, we are displaying the value of `bar` using the alert function.

Because declaring a variable anywhere inside a function (except another function) is equivalent to declaring it at the top of the function, the `foo` function is transformed into the following at runtime:

```
function foo(): void {
    var bar: number;
    bar = 0;
    console.log(bar);
}

foo(); // 0
```

Because developers with a background in programming languages with block scope, such as Java or C#, are not used to the function scope, it is one of the most criticized characteristics of JavaScript. The people in charge of the development of the ECMAScript 6 specification are aware of this, and as a result, they have introduced the keywords `let` and `const`.

The `let` keyword allows us to set the scope of a variable to a block (`if`, `while`, `for`, and so on) rather than a function. We can update the first example in this section to showcase how `let` works:

```
function foo(): void {
    if (true) {
        let bar: number = 0;
        bar = 1;
    }
    console.log(bar); // Error
}
```

The `bar` variable is now declared using the `let` keyword, and as a result, it is only accessible inside the `if` block. The variable is not hoisted to the top of the `foo` function and cannot be accessed by the `alert` function outside the `if` statement.

While variables defined with `const` follow the same scope rules as variables declared with `let`, they can't be reassigned:

```
function foo(): void {
    if (true) {
        const bar: number = 0;
        bar = 1; // Error
    }
    alert(bar); // Error
}
```

If we attempt to compile the preceding code snippet, we will get an error because the `bar` variable is not accessible outside the `if` statement (just like when we used the `let` keyword), and a new error will occur when we try to assign a new value to the `bar` variable. The second error occurs because it is not possible to assign a new value to a constant variable once the variable has already been initialized.

> Variables declared with the `const` keyword cannot be reassigned, but are not immutable. When we say that a variable is immutable, we means that it cannot be modified. We will learn more about immutability in Chapter 7, *Functional Programming with TypeScript*.

Immediately invoked functions

An **immediately invoked function expression** (**IIFE**) is a design pattern that produces a lexical scope using function scoping. An IIFE can be used to avoid variable hoisting from within blocks, or to prevent us from polluting the global scope—for example:

```
let bar = 0; // global

(function() {
    let foo: number = 0; // In scope of this function
    bar = 1; // Access global scope
    console.log(bar); // 1
    console.log(foo); // 0
})();

console.log(bar); // 1
console.log(foo); // Error
```

In the preceding example, we have wrapped the declaration of a variable (`foo`) with an IIFE. The `foo` variable is scoped to the IIFE function and is not available in the global scope, which explains the error that is thrown when we try to access it on the last line.

Working with Functions

The `bar` variable is a global. Therefore, it can be accessed from both the inside and the outside of the IIFE function.

We can also pass a variable to the IIFE to have better control over the creation of variables outside its scope:

```
let bar = 0; // global
let topScope = window;

(function(global: any) {
    let foo: number = 0; // In scope of this function
    console.log(global.bar); // 0
    global.bar = 1; // Access global scope
    console.log(global.bar); // 1
    console.log(foo); // 0
})(topScope);

console.log(bar); // 1
console.log(foo); // Error
```

Furthermore, IIFE can help us to simultaneously allow public access to methods while retaining privacy for variables defined within the function. Let's look at an example:

```
class Counter {
    private _i: number;
    public constructor() {
        this._i = 0;
    }
    public get(): number {
        return this._i;
    }
    public set(val: number): void {
        this._i = val;
    }
    public increment(): void {
        this._i++;
    }
}

let counter = new Counter();
console.log(counter.get()); // 0
counter.set(2);
console.log(counter.get()); // 2
counter.increment();
console.log(counter.get()); // 3
console.log(counter._i); // Error: Property '_i' is private
```

We have defined a class named `Counter`, which has a private numeric attribute named `_i`. The class also has methods to get and set the value of the private `_i` property.

> By convention, TypeScript and JavaScript developers usually name private variables with names preceded by an underscore (_).

We have also created an instance of the `Counter` class and invoked the `set`, `get`, and `increment` methods to observe that everything is working as expected. If we attempt to access the `_i` property in an instance of `Counter`, we will get an error because the variable is `private`.

If we compile the preceding TypeScript code (only the class definition) and examine the generated JavaScript code, we will see the following:

```
var Counter = (function() {
    function Counter() {
        this._i = 0;
    }
    Counter.prototype.get = function() {
        return this._i;
    };
    Counter.prototype.set = function(val) {
        this._i = val;
    };
    Counter.prototype.increment = function() {
        this._i++;
    };
    return Counter;
})();
```

This generated JavaScript code will work perfectly in most scenarios, but if we execute it in a browser and try to create an instance of `Counter` and access its `_i` property, we will not get any errors because TypeScript will not generate runtime private properties for us. Sometimes we will need to write our classes in such a way that some properties are private at runtime—for example, if we release a library that will be used by JavaScript developers.

We can also use IIFE to simultaneously allow public access to methods while retaining privacy for variables defined within the function:

```
var Counter = (function() {
    var _i: number = 0;
    function Counter() {
        //
```

Working with Functions

```
    }
    Counter.prototype.get = function() {
        return _i;
    };
    Counter.prototype.set = function(val: number) {
        _i = val;
    };
    Counter.prototype.increment = function() {
        _i++;
    };
    return Counter;
})();
```

In the preceding example, everything is almost identical to the TypeScript's generated JavaScript, except now the variable `_i` is an object in the `Counter` closure instead of a property of the `Counter` class.

> Closures are functions that refer to independent (free) variables. In other words, the function defined in the closure *remembers* the environment (variables in the scope) in which it was created. We will discover more about closures in Chapter 6, *Understanding the Runtime*.

If we run the generated JavaScript output in a browser and try to invoke the `_i` property directly, we will notice that the property is now private at runtime:

```
let counter = new Counter();
console.log(counter.get()); // 0
counter.set(2);
console.log(counter.get()); // 2
counter.increment();
console.log(counter.get()); // 3
console.log(counter._i); // undefined
```

> In some cases, we will need to have precise control over scope and closures, and our code will end up looking much more like JavaScript. As long as we write our application components (classes, modules, and so on) to be consumed by other TypeScript components, we will rarely have to worry about implementing runtime private properties. We will look in depth at the TypeScript runtime in Chapter 6, *Understanding the Runtime*.

Tag functions and tagged templates

In TypeScript, we can use template strings such as the following:

```
let name = "remo";
let surname = "jansen";
let html = `<h1>${name} ${surname}</h1>`;
```

We can use a template string to create a special kind of function known as a **tag function**.

We can use a tag function to extend or modify the standard behavior of template strings. When we apply a tag function to a template string, the template string becomes a tagged template.

We are going to implement a tag function named `htmlEscape`. To use a tag function, we must use the name of the function followed by a template string:

```
let html = htmlEscape `<h1>${name} ${surname}</h1>`;
```

A tag template must return a string and take the following arguments:

- A `TemplateStringsArray` that contains all the static literals in the template string (`<h1>` and `</h1>` in the preceding example) is passed as the first argument.

> The `TemplateStringsArray` type is declared by the `lib.d.ts` file. We will learn more about the `lib.d.ts` file in Chapter 9, *Automating Your Development Workflow*.

- A REST parameter is passed as the second parameter. The REST parameter contains all the values in the template string (`name` and `surname`, in the preceding example).

The signature of a tag function looks as follows:

```
tag(literals: TemplateStringsArray, ...placeholders: any[]): string;
```

Let's implement the `htmlEscape` tag function:

```
function htmlEscape(literals: TemplateStringsArray, ...placeholders: any[])
{
    let result = "";
    for (let i = 0; i < placeholders.length; i++) {
        result += literals[i];
        result += placeholders[i]
            .replace(/&/g, "&amp;")
```

```
            .replace(/"/g, "&quot;")
            .replace(/'/g, "'")
            .replace(/</g, "&lt;")
            .replace(/>/g, "&gt;");
    }
    result += literals[literals.length - 1];
    return result;
}
```

We can then invoke the function as follows:

```
let html = htmlEscape `<h1>${name} ${surname}</h1>`;
```

The template string contains values and literals. The `htmlEscape` function iterates through them and ensures that the HTML code is escaped in the values to avoid possible code injection attacks.

The main benefit of using a tagged function is that it allows us to create custom template string processors.

Asynchronous programming in TypeScript

Now that we have seen how to work with functions, we will explore how we can use them, together with some native APIs, to write asynchronous applications.

Callbacks and higher-order functions

In TypeScript, functions can be passed as arguments to another function. Functions can also be returned by another function. A function passed to another as an argument is known as a **callback**. Functions that accept functions as parameters (callbacks) or return functions are known as **higher-order functions**.

Callbacks are usually anonymous functions. They can be declared before they are passed to the higher-order function, as demonstrated by the following example:

```
var foo = function() { // callback
  console.log("foo");
}

function bar(cb: () => void) { // higher order function
  console.log("bar");
  cb();
}
```

```
bar(foo); // prints "bar" then prints "foo"
```

However, callbacks are declared inline, at the same point at which they are passed to the higher-order function, as demonstrated by the following example:

```
bar(() => {
  console.log("foo");
}); // prints "bar" then prints "foo"
```

Arrow functions

In TypeScript, we can declare a function using a `function` expression or an arrow function. An arrow function has a shorter syntax than a function expression, and lexically binds the value of the `this` operator.

The `this` operator behaves a little differently in TypeScript and JavaScript compared to other popular programming languages. When we define a class in TypeScript, we can use the `this` operator to refer to the class. Let's look at an example:

```
class Person {
    private _name: string;
    constructor(name: string) {
        this._name = name;
    }
    public greet() {
        console.log(`Hi! My name is ${this._name}`);
    }
}

let person = new Person("Remo");
person.greet(); // "Hi! My name is Remo"
```

We have defined a `Person` class that contains a property of a string type called `name`. The class has a constructor and a `greet` method. We have created an instance named `person` and invoked the `greet` method, which uses the `this` operator internally to access the `_name` property. Inside the `greet` method, the `this` operator points to the object that encloses the `greet` method.

We must be careful when using the `this` operator, because in some scenarios it can point to the wrong value. Let's add an extra method to the previous example:

```
class Person {
    private _name: string;
    constructor(name: string) {
```

Working with Functions

```
        this._name = name;
    }
    public greet() {
        alert(`Hi! My name is ${this._name}`);
    }
    public greetDelay(time: number) {
        setTimeout(function() {
            alert(`Hi! My name is ${this._name}`); // Error
        }, time);
    }
}
```

In the `greetDelay` method, we perform an almost identical operation to the one performed by the `greet` method. This time, the function takes a parameter named `time`, which is used to delay the `greet` message.

To delay a message, we use the `setTimeout` function and a callback. As soon as we define an anonymous function (the callback), the `this` keyword changes its value and starts pointing to the anonymous function, which explains why the TypeScript compiler will throw an error.

As mentioned, an arrow function expression lexically binds the value of the `this` operator. This means that it allows us to add a function without altering the value of the `this` operator. Let's replace the function expression from the previous example with an arrow function:

```
class Person {
    private _name: string;
    constructor(name: string) {
        this._name = name;
    }
    public greet() {
        alert(`Hi! My name is ${this._name}`);
    }
    public greetDelay(time: number) {
        setTimeout(() => {
            alert(`Hi! My name is ${this._name}`); // OK
        }, time);
    }
}

let person = new Person("Remo");
person.greet(); // "Hi! My name is Remo"
person.greetDelay(1000); // "Hi! My name is Remo"
```

Chapter 3

By using an arrow function, we can ensure that the `this` operator still points to the `Person` instance and not to the `setTimeout` callback. If we execute the `greetDelay` function, the name property will be displayed as expected.

The following piece of code is generated by the TypeScript compiler. When compiling an arrow function, the TypeScript compiler will generate an alias for the `this` operator named `_this`. The alias is used to ensure that the `this` operator points to the right object:

```
Person.prototype.greetDelay = function (time) {
  var _this = this;
  setTimeout(function () {
    alert("Hi! My name is " + _this._name);
  }, time);
};
```

> We will look at the `this` operator in depth in Chapter 6, *Understanding the Runtime*.

Callback hell

We have learned that callbacks and higher-order functions are two powerful and flexible JavaScript and TypeScript features. However, the use of callbacks can lead to a maintainability issue known as **callback hell**.

We are now going to write an example to showcase callback hell. We are going to write three functions with the same behavior, named `doSomethingAsync`, `doSomethingElseAsync`, and `doSomethingMoreAsync`:

```
function doSomethingAsync(
    arr: number[],
    success: (arr: number[]) => void,
    error: (e: Error) => void
) {
    setTimeout(() => {
        try {
            let n = Math.ceil(Math.random() * 100 + 1);
            if (n < 25) {
                throw new Error("n is < 25");
            }
            success([...arr, n]);
        } catch (e) {
            error(e);
```

```
        }
    }, 1000);
}

function doSomethingElseAsync(
    arr: number[],
    success: (arr: number[]) => void,
    error: (e: Error) => void
) {
    setTimeout(() => {
        try {
            let n = Math.ceil(Math.random() * 100 + 1);
            if (n < 25) {
                throw new Error("n is < 25");
            }
            success([...arr, n]);
        } catch (e) {
            error(e);
        }
    }, 1000);
}

function doSomethingMoreAsync(
    arr: number[],
    success: (arr: number[]) => void,
    error: (e: Error) => void
) {
    setTimeout(() => {
        try {
            let n = Math.ceil(Math.random() * 100 + 1);
            if (n < 25) {
                throw new Error("n is < 25");
            }
            success([...arr, n]);
        } catch (e) {
            error(e);
        }
    }, 1000);
}
```

The preceding functions simulate an asynchronous operation by using the `setTimeout` function. Each function takes a success callback, which is invoked if the operation is successful, and an error callback, which is invoked if something goes wrong.

In real-world applications, asynchronous operations usually involve some interaction with hardware (for example, filesystems, networks, and so on). The interactions are known as **input/output** (**I/O**) operations. I/O operations can fail for many different reasons (for example, we get an error when we try to interact with the filesystem to save a new file and there is not enough space available on the hard disk).

The preceding functions generate a random number and throw an error if the number is lower than 25; we do this to simulate potential I/O errors.

The preceding functions add the random number to an array that is passed as an argument to each of the functions. If no errors take place, the result of the final function (doSomethingMoreAsync) should be an array with three random numbers.

Now that the three functions have been declared, we can try to invoke them in order. We are going to use callbacks to ensure that doSomethingMoreAsync is invoked after doSomethingElseAsync, and doSomethingElseAsync is invoked after doSomethingAsync:

```
doSomethingAsync([], (arr1) => {
    doSomethingElseAsync(arr1, (arr2) => {
        doSomethingMoreAsync(arr2, (arr3) => {
            console.log(
                `
                doSomethingAsync: ${arr3[0]}
                doSomethingElseAsync: ${arr3[1]}
                doSomethingMoreAsync: ${arr3[2]}
                `
            );
        }, (e) => console.log(e));
    }, (e) => console.log(e));
}, (e) => console.log(e));
```

The preceding example used a few nesting callbacks. The use of these kinds of nested callbacks is known as **callback hell** because they can lead to the following maintainability issues:

- Making the code harder to follow and understand
- Making the code harder to maintain (refactor, reuse, and so on)
- Making exception handling more difficult

Working with Functions

Promises

After seeing how the use of callbacks can lead to some maintainability problems, we are now going to learn about promises and how they can be used to write better asynchronous code. The core idea behind promises is that a promise represents the result of an asynchronous operation. A promise must be in one of the following three states:

- **Pending**: The initial state of a promise.
- **Fulfilled/resolved**: The state of a promise representing a successful operation. The terms "fulfilled" and "resolved" are both commonly used to refer to this state.
- **Rejected**: The state of a promise representing a failed operation.

Once a promise is fulfilled or rejected, its state can never change again. Let's look at the basic syntax of a promise:

```
function foo() {
    return new Promise<string>((fulfill, reject) => {
        try {
            // do something
            fulfill("SomeValue");
        } catch (e) {
            reject(e);
        }
    });
}

foo().then((value) => {
    console.log(value);
}).catch((e) => {
    console.log(e);
});
```

> A `try...catch` statement is used here to showcase how we can explicitly fulfill or reject a promise. The `try...catch` statement is not needed for a `Promise` function because when an error is thrown in a promise callback, the promise will automatically be rejected.

The preceding code snippet declares a function named `foo` that returns a promise. The promise contains a method named `then`, which accepts a function to be invoked when the promise is fulfilled. Promises also provide a method named `catch`, which is invoked when a promise is rejected.

Promises will not be recognized by the TypeScript compiler if we are targeting ES5, because the promises API is part of ES6. We can solve this by enabling the `es2015.promise` type using the `lib` option in the `tsconfig.json` file. Note that enabling this option will disable some types that are included by default and therefore break some of the examples. You will be able to solve the problems by including the `dom` and `es5` types, as well as by using the `lib` option in the `tsconfig.json` file:

```
"lib": [
    "es2015.promise",
    "dom",
    "es5",
    "es2015.generator", // new
    "es2015.iterable" // new
]
```

We will learn more about the `lib` setting in Chapter 9, *Automating Your Development Workflow*.

We are now going to rewrite the `doSomethingAsync`, `doSomethingElseAsync`, and `doSomethingMoreAsync` functions that we wrote during the callback hell example, using promises instead of callbacks:

```
function doSomethingAsync(arr: number[]) {
    return new Promise<number[]>((resolve, reject) => {
        setTimeout(() => {
            try {
                let n = Math.ceil(Math.random() * 100 + 1);
                if (n < 25) {
                    throw new Error("n is < 25");
                }
                resolve([...arr, n]);
            } catch (e) {
                reject(e);
            }
        }, 1000);
    });
}

function doSomethingElseAsync(arr: number[]) {
    return new Promise<number[]>((resolve, reject) => {
        setTimeout(() => {
            try {
                let n = Math.ceil(Math.random() * 100 + 1);
                if (n < 25) {
                    throw new Error("n is < 25");
                }
```

Working with Functions

```
            resolve([...arr, n]);
        } catch (e) {
            reject(e);
        }
    }, 1000);
    });
}

function doSomethingMoreAsync(arr: number[]) {
    return new Promise<number[]>((resolve, reject) => {
        setTimeout(() => {
            try {
                let n = Math.ceil(Math.random() * 100 + 1);
                if (n < 25) {
                    throw new Error("n is < 25");
                }
                resolve([...arr, n]);
            } catch (e) {
                reject(e);
            }
        }, 1000);
    });
}
```

We can chain the promises that are returned by each of the preceding functions using the promises API:

```
doSomethingAsync([]).then((arr1) => {
    doSomethingElseAsync(arr1).then((arr2) => {
        doSomethingMoreAsync(arr2).then((arr3) => {
            console.log(`
                doSomethingAsync: ${arr3[0]}
                doSomethingElseAsync: ${arr3[1]}
                doSomethingMoreAsync: ${arr3[2]}
            `);
        });
    });
}).catch((e) => console.log(e));
```

Chapter 3

The preceding code snippet is a little bit better than the one used in the callback example because we only needed to declare one exception handler instead of three exception handlers. This is possible because errors are propagated through the chain of promises.

The preceding example has introduced some improvements. However, the promises API allows us to chain promises in a much less verbose way:

```
doSomethingAsync([])
    .then(doSomethingElseAsync)
    .then(doSomethingMoreAsync)
    .then((arr3) => {
        console.log(
            `
            doSomethingAsync: ${arr3[0]}
            doSomethingElseAsync: ${arr3[1]}
            doSomethingMoreAsync: ${arr3[2]}
            `
        );
    }).catch((e) => console.log(e));
```

The preceding code is much easier to read and follow than the one used during the callback examples, but this is not the only reason to prefer promises over callbacks. Using promises also gives us better control over the execution flow of operations. Let's look at a couple of examples.

The promises API includes a method named `all`, which allows us to execute a series of promises in parallel and get all the results of each of the promises at once:

```
Promise.all([
    new Promise<number>((resolve) => {
        setTimeout(() => resolve(1), 1000);
    }),
    new Promise<number>((resolve) => {
        setTimeout(() => resolve(2), 1000);
    }),
    new Promise<number>((resolve) => {
        setTimeout(() => resolve(3), 1000);
    })
]).then((values) => {
    console.log(values); // [ 1 ,2, 3]
});
```

Working with Functions

The promises API also includes a method named race, which allows us to execute a series of promises in parallel and get the result of the first promise resolved:

```
Promise.race([
    new Promise<number>((resolve) => {
        setTimeout(() => resolve(1), 3000);
    }),
    new Promise<number>((resolve) => {
        setTimeout(() => resolve(2), 2000);
    }),
    new Promise<number>((resolve) => {
        setTimeout(() => resolve(3), 1000);
    })
]).then((fastest) => {
    console.log(fastest); // 3
});
```

We can use many different types of asynchronous flow control when working with promises:

- **Concurrent**: The tasks are executed in parallel (like in the Promise.all example)
- **Race**: The tasks are executed in parallel, and only the result of the fastest promise is returned
- **Series**: A group of tasks is executed in sequence, but the preceding tasks do not pass arguments to the next task
- **Waterfall**: A group of tasks is executed in sequence, and each task passes arguments to the next task (like in the example that preceded the Promise.all and Promise.race examples)
- **Composite**: This is any combination of the preceding concurrent, series, and waterfall approaches

Covariant checking in callback parameters

TypeScript 2.4 changed the way the type system behaves internally to improve the error detection in nested callbacks and promises:

> *TypeScript's checking of callback parameters is now covariant concerning immediate signature checks. Previously it was bivariant, which could sometimes let incorrect types through. Basically, this means that callback parameters and classes that contain callbacks are checked more carefully, so TypeScript will require stricter types in this release. This is particularly true of Promises and Observables due to the way in which their APIs are specified.*

In TypeScript versions before 2.4, the following example was considered valid, and no errors were thrown:

```
declare function someFunc(
    callback: (
    nestedCallback: (error: number, result: any) => void
    ) => void
): void;

someFunc(
    (
        nestedCallback: (e: number) => void // Error
    ) => {
        nestedCallback(1);
    }
);
```

In TypeScript versions following the 2.4 release, we need to add the complete signature of `nestedCallback` to solve this error:

```
someFunc(
    (
        nestedCallback: (e: number, result: any) => void // OK
    ) => {
        nestedCallback(1, 1);
    }
);
```

Thanks to the internal change in the TypeScript type system, the following error is also detected:

```
let p: Promise<number> = new Promise((res, rej) => {
    res("error"); // Error
});
```

Before TypeScript 2.4, the preceding promise would have been inferred as `Promise<{}>` because we forgot to add the generic `<number>` argument when we created an instance of the `Promise` class. The `error` string would then have been considered a valid instance of `{}`.

This is a clear example of why it is recommended that you upgrade TypeScript regularly. Each new version of TypeScript introduces new features that are able to detect new errors for us.

Working with Functions

Generators

If we invoke a function in TypeScript, we can assume that once the function starts running, it will always run to completion before any other code can run. However, a new kind of function that may be paused in the middle of execution—one or many times—and resumed later, allowing other code to run during these paused periods, has recently been added to the ECMAScript specification. These new kinds of functions are known as **generators**.

A generator represents a sequence of values. The interface of a `generator` object is just an **iterator**. An iterator implements the following interface:

```
interface Iterator<T> {
  next(value?: any): IteratorResult<T>;
  return?(value?: any): IteratorResult<T>;
  throw?(e?: any): IteratorResult<T>;
}
```

The `next()` function can be invoked until it runs out of values.

We can define a generator by using the `function` keyword followed by an asterisk (*). The `yield` keyword is used to stop the execution of the function and return a value. Let's look at an example:

```
function *foo() {
    yield 1;
    yield 2;
    yield 3;
    yield 4;
    return 5;
}

let bar = foo();
bar.next(); // Object {value: 1, done: false}
bar.next(); // Object {value: 2, done: false}
bar.next(); // Object {value: 3, done: false}
bar.next(); // Object {value: 4, done: false}
bar.next(); // Object {value: 5, done: true}
bar.next(); // Object { done: true }
```

> Note that some additional types are required by generators if you are targeting ES5. You will need to add `es2015.generator` and `es2015.iterable` to your `tsconfig.json` file:

```
"lib": [
    "es2015.promise",
    "dom",
    "es5",
    "es2015.generator", // new
    "es2015.iterable" // new
]
```

> We will learn more about the `lib` setting in Chapter 9, *Automating Your Development Workflow*.

As we can see, the preceding iterator has five steps. The first time we call `next`, the function will be executed until it reaches the first `yield` statement, and then it will return the value 1 and stop the execution of the function until we invoke the generator's `next` method again. As we can see, we are now able to stop the function's execution at a given point. This allows us to write infinite loops without causing a stack overflow, as demonstrated in the following example:

```
function* foo() {
let i = 1;
    while (true) {
        yield i++;
    }
}

let bar = foo();
bar.next(); // Object {value: 1, done: false}
bar.next(); // Object {value: 2, done: false}
bar.next(); // Object {value: 3, done: false}
bar.next(); // Object {value: 4, done: false}
bar.next(); // Object {value: 5, done: false}
bar.next(); // Object {value: 6, done: false}
bar.next(); // Object {value: 7, done: false}
```

The generator will open possibilities for synchronicity, as we can call the generator's `next` method after an asynchronous event has occurred.

Asynchronous functions – async and await

Asynchronous functions are a TypeScript feature that arrived with the TypeScript 1.6 release. Developers can use the `await` keyword to wait for the function results without blocking the normal execution of the program.

Using asynchronous functions helps to increase the readability of a piece of code when compared with the use of promises or callbacks, but technically, we can achieve the same features using both promises and synchronous code.

Let's take a look at a basic `async/await` example:

```
let p = Promise.resolve(3);

async function fn(): Promise<number> {
    let i = await p; // 3
    return 1 + i; // 4
}

fn().then((r) => console.log(r)); // 4
```

The preceding code snippet declares a promise named `p`. This promise is the piece of code whose execution we will wait for. While waiting, the program execution will not be blocked because JavaScript allows us to wait for an asynchronous function named `fn` without blocking it. As we can see, the `fn` function is preceded by the `async` keyword, which is used to indicate to the compiler that it is an asynchronous function.

Inside the function, the `await` keyword is used to suspend execution until the promise `p` is fulfilled or rejected. As we can see, the syntax is less verbose and cleaner than it would have been if we used the promises API or callbacks.

The `fn` function returns a promise at runtime because it is an `async` function. This should explain why we need to use the `then` callback to invoke it at the end of the code snippet.

The following code snippet showcases how we can declare an asynchronous function named `invokeTaskAsync`. The asynchronous function uses the `await` keyword to wait for the result of the `doSomethingAsync`, `doSomethingElseAsync`, and `doSomethingMoreAsync` functions that we declared during the promises example:

```
async function invokeTaskAsync() {
    let arr1 = await doSomethingAsync([]);
    let arr2 = await doSomethingElseAsync(arr1);
    return await doSomethingMoreAsync(arr2);
}
```

The `invokeTaskAsync` function is asynchronous, and therefore, it will return a promise at runtime. This means that we can use the promises API to await a result or catch potential errors respectively:

```
invokeTaskAsync().then((result) => {
    console.log(
        `
        doSomethingAsync: ${result[0]}
        doSomethingElseAsync: ${result[1]}
        doSomethingMoreAsync: ${result[2]}
        `
    );
}).catch((e) => {
    console.log(e);
});
```

We can also define asynchronous IIFE as a convenient way to use the `async` and `await` keywords:

```
(async () => {
    try {
        let arr1 = await doSomethingAsync([]);
        let arr2 = await doSomethingElseAsync(arr1);
        let arr3 = await doSomethingMoreAsync(arr2);
        console.log(
            `
            doSomethingAsync: ${arr3[0]}
            doSomethingElseAsync: ${arr3[1]}
            doSomethingMoreAsync: ${arr3[2]}
            `
        );
    } catch (e) {
        console.log(e);
    }
})();
```

Using an async IIFE is very useful because it is very common to not be able to use the `await` keyword outside of a function—for example, in the entry point of an application. We can use the async IIFE to overcome this limitation:

```
(async () => {
    await main();
})();
```

Asynchronous generators

We have already learned about the interface that is implemented by all iterators:

```
interface Iterator<T> {
  next(value?: any): IteratorResult<T>;
  return?(value?: any): IteratorResult<T>;
  throw?(e?: any): IteratorResult<T>;
}
```

However, we haven't yet learned about the interface that is implemented by all asynchronous iterators:

```
interface AsyncIterator<T> {
  next(value?: any): Promise<IteratorResult<T>>;
  return?(value?: any): Promise<IteratorResult<T>>;
  throw?(e?: any): Promise<IteratorResult<T>>;
}
```

An asynchronous iterator returns a promise every time we invoke the `next` method. The following code snippet demonstrates how asynchronous iterators can be very useful when used in conjunction with asynchronous functions:

```
let counter = 0;

function doSomethingAsync() {
    return new Promise<number>((r) => {
        setTimeout(() => {
            counter += 1;
            r(counter);
        }, 1000);
    });
}

async function* g1() {
    yield await doSomethingAsync();
    yield await doSomethingAsync();
    yield await doSomethingAsync();
}

let i = g1();
i.next().then((n) => console.log(n)); // 1
i.next().then((n) => console.log(n)); // 2
i.next().then((n) => console.log(n)); // 3
```

Some additional types are required by asynchronous iterators if we are targeting ES5. You will need to add `esnext.asynciterable` to your `tsconfig.json` file. We are also going to need to enable an additional setting in our `tsconfig.json` to provide full support for iterables (for example, using `for...of` control flow statements, the spread operator or object destructuring) when targeting ES3 or ES5:

```
"lib": [
"es2015.promise",
"dom",
"es5",
"es2015.generator",
"es2015.iterable",
"esnext.asynciterable" // new
]
```

We will learn more about the `lib` setting in Chapter 9, *Automating Your Development Workflow*.

Asynchronous iteration (for await...of)

We can use the new `for...await...of` expression to iterate and await each of the promises returned by an asynchronous iterator:

```
async function func() {
    for await (const x of g1()) {
        console.log(x);
    }
}
```

Delegating to another generator (yield*)

We can use the `yield*` expression to delegate from one generator to another. The following code snippet defines two generator functions named `g1` and `g2`. The `g2` generator uses the `yield*` expression to delegate the iteration to the iterator created by `g1`:

```
function* g1() {
    yield 2;
    yield 3;
    yield 4;
}
```

```
function* g2() {
    yield 1;
    yield* g1();
    yield 5;
}

var iterator1 = g2();

console.log(iterator1.next()); // {value: 1, done: false}
console.log(iterator1.next()); // {value: 2, done: false}
console.log(iterator1.next()); // {value: 3, done: false}
console.log(iterator1.next()); // {value: 4, done: false}
console.log(iterator1.next()); // {value: 5, done: false}
console.log(iterator1.next()); // {value: undefined, done: true}
```

The `yield*` expression can also be used to delegate the iteration to iterables, such as arrays:

```
function* g2() {
    yield 1;
    yield* [2, 3, 4];
    yield 5;
}

var iterator = g2();

console.log(iterator.next()); // {value: 1, done: false}
console.log(iterator.next()); // {value: 2, done: false}
console.log(iterator.next()); // {value: 3, done: false}
console.log(iterator.next()); // {value: 4, done: false}
console.log(iterator.next()); // {value: 5, done: false}
console.log(iterator.next()); // {value: undefined, done: true}
```

Summary

In this chapter, we have learned how to work with functions in depth. We started with a quick recap of some basic concepts and then moved on to some lesser-known function features and use cases.

Once we learned how to work with functions, we focused on the use of callbacks, promises, and generators to take advantage of the asynchronous programming capabilities of TypeScript.

In the next chapter, we will look at how to work with classes, interfaces, and other object-oriented programming features of the TypeScript programming language.

4
Object-Oriented Programming with TypeScript

In the previous chapter, we learned how to work with functions and how to take advantage of some asynchronous programming APIs. In this chapter, we are going to learn how to implement TypeScript applications using the **object-oriented programming** (**OOP**) paradigm. We are going to learn about the following topics:

- Classes
- Association, aggregation, and composition
- Inheritance
- Mixins
- Generic classes
- Generic constraints
- Interfaces
- The SOLID principles

Classes

We should already be familiar with the basics of TypeScript classes, as we have declared some of them in previous chapters. We will now look at some details and OOP concepts through examples. Let's start by declaring a simple class:

```
class Person {
    public name: string;
    public surname: string;
    public email: string;
    public constructor(
        name: string, surname: string, email: string
    ) {
```

Object-Oriented Programming with TypeScript

```
        this.email = email;
        this.name = name;
        this.surname = surname;
    }
    public greet() {
        console.log("Hi!");
    }
}
```

We use classes to represent the type of an object or entity. A **class** is composed of a name, **properties** (also known as **attributes**), and **methods**. Both methods and properties are known as **members**. Class properties are used to describe the object's characteristics, while class methods are used to describe its behavior.

The class in the preceding example is named `Person` and contains three attributes or properties (`name`, `surname`, and `email`) and two methods (`constructor` and `greet`).

A **constructor** is a special method used by the `new` keyword to create **instances** (also known as **objects**) of our class. We have declared a variable named `me`, which holds an instance of the `Person` class. The `new` keyword uses the `Person` class's constructor to return an object whose type is `Person`:

```
const person = new Person(
    "Remo",
    "Jansen",
    "remo.jansen@wolksoftware.com"
);
```

Strict property initialization

Since the release of TypeScript 2.7, a compile-time error will be thrown if strict mode is enabled and we forget to initialize one of the properties of a class. For example, the following class initializes the property named `height` using a method, and the property named `width` using its constructor. TypeScript knows that if an instance of the class is created, a value will be assigned to the `width` property. However, it has no way to ensure that a value is assigned to the `height` property. If strict mode is enabled, an error will be thrown:

```
class Rectangle {

    public width: number;
    public height: number; // Error
```

```
    public constructor(width: number) {
        this.width = width;
    }

    public setHeight(height: number) {
        this.height = height;
    }
}
```

We can use the ! operator to let TypeScript know that we don't want an error to be thrown:

```
class Rectangle {

    public width: number;
    public height!: number; // OK

    public constructor(width: number) {
        this.width = width;
    }

    public setHeight(height: number) {
        this.height = height;
    }

}
```

It is very common to encounter this compilation error when we define a class without a constructor:

```
class Rectangle {
    public width: number; // Error
    public height: number; // Error
}
```

We can use the ! operator to solve the compile-time error when we don't want to define a constructor:

```
class Rectangle {
    public width!: number; // OK
    public height!: number; // OK
}
```

Object-Oriented Programming with TypeScript

Alternatively, we can initialize the properties with a default value:

```
class Rectangle6 {
    public width: number = 0; // OK
    public height: number = 0; // OK
}
```

Inheritance

One of the most fundamental OOP features is its capability to extend existing classes. This feature is known as **inheritance** and allows us to create a new class (child class) that inherits all the properties and methods from an existing class (parent class). Child classes can include additional properties and methods that are not available in the parent class.

We are going to use the `Person` class that we declared in the preceding section as the parent class of a child class named `Teacher`. We can extend the parent class (`Person`) by using the reserved keyword `extends`:

```
class Teacher extends Person {
    public teach() {
        console.log("Welcome to class!");
    }
}
```

The `Teacher` class will inherit all the attributes and methods from its parent class. However, we have also added a new method named `teach` to the `Teacher` class.

If we create instances of the `Person` and `Teacher` classes, we will be able to see that both instances share the same attributes and methods except for the `teach` method, which is only available for the instance of the `Teacher` class:

```
const person = new Person(
    "Remo",
    "Jansen",
    "remo.jansen@wolksoftware.com"
);

const teacher = new Teacher(
    "Remo",
    "Jansen",
    "remo.jansen@wolksoftware.com"
);

person.greet(); // "Hi!"
```

```
teacher.greet(); // "Hi!"
person.teach(); // Error
teacher.teach(); // "Welcome to class!"
```

Depth of the inheritance tree (DIT)

We can also declare a new class that inherits from a class, which is already inheriting from another class. In the following code snippet, we declare a class called `SchoolPrincipal` that `extends` the `Teacher` class, which extends the `Person` class:

```
class SchoolPrincipal extends Teacher {
    public manageTeachers() {
        return console.log(
            `We need to help our students!`
        );
    }
}
```

If we create an instance of the `SchoolPrincipal` class, we will be able to access all the properties and methods from its parent classes (`SchoolPrincipal`, `Teacher`, and `Person`):

```
const principal = new SchoolPrincipal(
    "Remo",
    "Jansen",
    "remo.jansen@wolksoftware.com"
);

principal.greet(); // "Hi!"
principal.teach(); // "Welcome to class!"
principal.manageTeachers(); // "We need to help our students!"
```

> It is **not recommended to have too many levels in the inheritance tree**. A class situated too deeply in the inheritance tree will be relatively complex to develop, test, and maintain.

Unfortunately, we don't have a specific rule that we can follow when we are unsure whether we should increase the **depth of the inheritance tree (DIT)**.

We should use inheritance in such a way that it helps us to reduce the complexity of our application and not the opposite. We should try to keep the DIT between zero and four because a value greater than four would compromise encapsulation and increase complexity.

Access modifiers

TypeScript allows us to restrict the access to the properties and methods of a class using the `public`, `private`, and `protected` keywords.

The public access modifier

If we use the `public` modifier, the method or property can be accessed by other objects. The following example redeclares the `Person` and `Teacher` classes that we have used in the preceding section. It is important to note that the `public` access modifier is used in all the properties of the class, but for this example, we are going to pay special attention to the property named `email`:

```
class Person {
    public name: string;
    public surname: string;
    public email: string;
    public constructor(
        name: string, surname: string, email: string
    ) {
        this.email = email;
        this.name = name;
        this.surname = surname;
    }
    public greet() {
        console.log("Hi!");
    }
}

class Teacher extends Person {
    public teach() {
        console.log("Welcome to class!");
    }
}
```

If we create an instance of both the `Person` and `Teacher` classes, we will be able to confirm that the `email` property can be accessed by both instances and by an external object such as the `console` object:

```
const person = new Person(
    "Remo",
    "Jansen",
    "remo.jansen@wolksoftware.com"
);
const teacher = new Teacher(
    "Remo",
    "Jansen",
    "remo.jansen@wolksoftware.com"
);

console.log(person.email);  // ""remo.jansen@wolksoftware.com"
console.log(teacher.email); // ""remo.jansen@wolksoftware.com"
```

The private access modifier

If we use the `private` modifier, the method or property can only be accessed by the object that owns them.

The following example redeclares, once more, the classes that we declared in the preceding example, but uses the `private` access modifier instead of the `public` modifier. The example also adds a couple of extra methods to the classes to demonstrate the implications of using a `private` access modifier:

```
class Person {
    public name: string;
    public surname: string;
    private _email: string;
    public constructor(
        name: string, surname: string, email: string
    ) {
        this._email = email;
        this.name = name;
        this.surname = surname;
    }
    public greet() {
        console.log("Hi!");
    }
    public getEmail() {
        return this._email;
```

Object-Oriented Programming with TypeScript

```
        }
    }

    class Teacher extends Person {
        public teach() {
            console.log("Welcome to class!");
        }
        public shareEmail() {
            console.log(`My email is ${this._email}`); // Error
        }
    }
```

If we create an instance of both the `Person` and `Teacher` classes, we will be able to observe that the `getEmail` method, which belongs to the `Person` instance, can access the `private` property. However, the `private` property, `email`, cannot be accessed from the method named `shareEmail`, which is declared by the derived `Teacher` class. Also, other objects (such as the `console` object) cannot access the `private` property. This code snippet confirms that the `email` property can only be accessed by the instances of the `Person` class:

```
    const person = new Person(
        "Remo",
        "Jansen",
        "remo.jansen@wolksoftware.com"
    );

    const teacher = new Teacher(
        "Remo",
        "Jansen",
        "remo.jansen@wolksoftware.com"
    );

    console.log(person._email); // Error
    console.log(teacher._email); // Error
    teacher.getEmail();
```

We can update the `Teacher` class to use the public `getEmail` method instead of trying to access the `private` property directly:

```
    class Teacher extends Person {
        public teach() {
            console.log("Welcome to class!");
        }
        public shareEmail() {
            console.log(`My email is ${this.getEmail()}`); // OK
        }
    }
```

The protected access modifier

If we use the `protected` modifier, the method or property can only be accessed by the object that owns them or instances of the derived classes.

The following example declares, once more, the classes that we declared in the preceding examples, but uses the `protected` access modifier instead of the `public` modifier:

```
class Person {
    public name: string;
    public surname: string;
    protected _email: string;
    public constructor(
        name: string, surname: string, email: string
    ) {
        this._email = email;
        this.name = name;
        this.surname = surname;
    }
    public greet() {
        console.log("Hi!");
    }
}

class Teacher extends Person {
    public teach() {
        console.log("Welcome to class!");
    }
    public shareEmail() {
        console.log(`My email is ${this._email}`);
    }
}
```

If we create an instance of both the `Person` and `Teacher` classes, we will be able to observe that the `protected` property, `email`, can be accessed from the method named `shareEmail`, which is declared by the derived `Teacher` class. However, other objects (such as the `console` object) cannot access the `private` property. This code snippet confirms that the `email` property can only be accessed by the instances of the `Person` class or derived classes, but it cannot be accessed by other objects:

```
const person = new Person(
    "Remo",
    "Jansen",
    "remo.jansen@wolksoftware.com"
);
```

```
const teacher = new Teacher(
    "Remo",
    "Jansen",
    "remo.jansen@wolksoftware.com"
);

console.log(person._email); // Error
console.log(teacher._email); // Error
teacher.shareEmail(); // "My email is remo.jansen@wolksoftware.com"
```

Parameter properties

In TypeScript, when we declare a class, we can define its properties and initialize some or all of the properties using the class constructor:

```
class Vector {
    private x: number;
    private y: number;
    public constructor(x: number, y: number) {
        this.x = x;
        this.y = y;
    }
}
```

However, we can use an alternative syntax, which allows us to declare the properties and initialize them using the class constructor in a less verbose way. We only need to remove the property declarations and its initialization, and add access modifiers to the arguments of the constructor of the class.

The preceding code snippet declares a class with an identical behavior to the following class. However, it uses the parameter properties syntax:

```
class Vector {
    public constructor(
        private x: number,
        private y: number
    ) {}
}
```

Class expressions

We can use two different APIs to declare a class. The first one is the class declaration syntax that we used during the preceding section. The second one is an alternative syntax known as a class expression.

The following code snippet redeclares the `Person` class that we declared in the preceding section using the class expression syntax:

```
const Person = class {
    public constructor(
        public name: string,
        public surname: string,
        public email: string
    ) {}
    public greet() {
        console.log("Hi!");
    }
};
```

There are no differences between the creation of an instance of a class declared using the class expression syntax and one declared using the class declaration syntax:

```
const person = new Person(
    "Remo",
    "Jansen",
    "remo.jansen@wolksoftware.com"
);
```

Static members

We can use the `static` keyword to enable the usage properties and methods in a class without needing to create an instance of it:

```
class TemperatureConverter {
    public static CelsiusToFahrenheit(
        celsiusTemperature: number
    ) {
        return (celsiusTemperature * 9 / 5) + 32;
    }
    public static FahrenheitToCelsius(
        fahrenheitTemperature: number
    ) {
```

Object-Oriented Programming with TypeScript

```
        return (fahrenheitTemperature - 32) * 5 / 9;
    }
}
```

As we can observe in the preceding code snippet, the `TemperatureConverter` class has two static methods named `CelsiusToFahrenheit` and `FahrenheitToCelsius`. We can invoke these methods without creating an instance of the `TemperatureConverter` class:

```
let fahrenheit = 100;
let celsius = TemperatureConverter.FahrenheitToCelsius(fahrenheit);
fahrenheit = TemperatureConverter.CelsiusToFahrenheit(celsius);
```

When a method or property is not static, we refer to it as an instance method or an instance property. It is possible to declare classes that have both static and instance methods or properties:

```
class Vector3 {

    public static GetDefault() {
        return new Vector3(0, 0, 0);
    }

    public constructor(
        private _x: number,
        private _y: number,
        private _z: number
    ) {}

    public length() {
        return Math.sqrt(
            this._x * this._x +
            this._y * this._y +
            this._z * this._z
        );
    }

    public normalize() {
        let len = 1 / this.length();
        this._x *= len;
        this._y *= len;
        this._z *= len;
    }

}
```

The preceding class declares a vector in a 3D space. The vector class has instance methods to calculate the length of the vector and to normalize it (change its length to 1 without changing its direction). We can create instances of the class using the class constructor and the `new` keyword:

```
const vector2 = new Vector3(1, 1, 1);
vector2.normalize();
```

However, the class also has a static method named `GetDefault`, which can be used to create a default instance:

```
const vector1 = Vector3.GetDefault();
vector1.normalize();
```

Optional members

We can define optional class properties and methods by appending the ? character at the end of the name of a property or method. This behavior is like the behavior that we observed in Chapter 3, *Working with Functions*, when we learned how to use the ? character to declare optional arguments in a function.

The following code snippet defines a class named `Vector` with an optional property named `z`. When we define a `Vector` instance using numeric values for the properties `x` and `y`, the `Vector` has two dimensions. When we define a `Vector` instance using numeric values for the properties `x`, `y`, and `z`, the `Vector` has three dimensions:

```
class Vector {
    public constructor(
        public x: number,
        public y: number,
        public z?: number
    ) {}

    public is3D() {
        return this.z !== undefined;
    }

    public is2D() {
        return this.z === undefined;
    }
}
```

Object-Oriented Programming with TypeScript

The following code snippet declares a `Vector` instance using only two constructor arguments. As a result, the optional property, z, will be `undefined`:

```
const vector2D = new Vector(0, 0);
vector2D.is2D(); // true
vector2D.is3D(); // false

const lenght1 = Math.sqrt(
    vector2D.x * vector2D.x +
    vector2D.y * vector2D.y +
    vector2D.z * vector2D.z // Error
);
```

The following code snippet declares a `Vector` instance using three constructor arguments. As a result, the optional property, z, will be defined:

```
const vector3D = new Vector(0, 0, 0);
vector3D.is2D(); // false
vector3D.is3D(); // true

const lenght2 = Math.sqrt(
    vector3D.x * vector3D.x +
    vector3D.y * vector3D.y +
    ((vector3D.z !== undefined) ? (vector3D.z * vector3D.z) : 0) // OK
);
```

Read-only properties

The `readonly` keyword is a modifier that can be applied to the properties of a class. When a property declaration includes a `readonly` modifier, assignments to the property can only take place as part of the declaration or in a constructor in the same class.

The following example showcases how the `readonly` modifier prevents assignments to the x, y, and z properties:

```
class Vector3 {

    public constructor(
        public readonly x: number,
        public readonly y: number,
        public readonly z: number
    ) {}

    public length() {
        return Math.sqrt(
```

```
            this.x * this.x +
            this.y * this.y +
            this.z * this.z
        );
    }

    public normalize() {
        let len = 1 / this.length();
        this.x *= len; // Error
        this.y *= len; // Error
        this.z *= len; // Error
    }
}
```

We can fix the compilation errors in the preceding code snippet by modifying the `normalize` method so that it returns a new vector (instead of modifying the original vector):

```
class Vector3 {

    public constructor(
        public readonly x: number,
        public readonly y: number,
        public readonly z: number
    ) {}

    public length() {
        return Math.sqrt(
            this.x * this.x +
            this.y * this.y +
            this.z * this.z
        );
    }

    public normalize() {
        let len = 1 / this.length();
        return new Vector3(
            this.x * len, // OK
            this.y * len, // OK
            this.z * len  // OK
        );
    }

}
```

Object-Oriented Programming with TypeScript

Method overriding

Sometimes, we will need a child class to provide a specific implementation of a method that is already provided by its parent class. We can use the reserved keyword `super` for this purpose.

We are going to use, once more, the `Person` and `Teacher` classes declared during the *Inheritance* section in this chapter.

Imagine that we want to add a new attribute to list the teacher's subjects, and we want to be able to initialize this attribute through the teacher constructor. We are going to use the `super` keyword to explicitly reference the parent class constructor inside the child class constructor:

```
class Person {
    public constructor(
        public name: string,
        public surname: string,
        public email: string
    ) {}
    public greet() {
        console.log("Hi!");
    }
}

class Teacher extends Person {
    public constructor(
        name: string,
        surname: string,
        email: string,
        public subjects: string[]
    ) {
        super(name, surname, email);
        this.subjects = subjects;
    }
    public greet() {
        super.greet();
        console.log("I teach " + this.subjects.join(" & "));
    }
    public teach() {
        console.log("Welcome to class!");
    }
}
```

We have also used the `super` keyword to extend an existing method, such as `greet`. This OOP language feature that allows a subclass or child class to provide a specific implementation of a method that is already provided by its parent classes is known as **method overriding**.

At this point, we can create an instance of the `Person` and `Teacher` classes to observe their differences:

```
const person = new Person(
    "Remo",
    "Jansen",
    "remo.jansen@wolksoftware.com"
);

const teacher = new Teacher(
    "Remo",
    "Jansen",
    "remo.jansen@wolksoftware.com",
    ["math", "physics"]
);

person.greet();  // "Hi!"
teacher.greet(); // "Hi! I teach math & physics"
person.teach();  // Error
teacher.teach(); // "Welcome to class!"
```

Generic classes

In the previous chapter, we learned how to work with generic functions. Now, we will look at how to work with generic classes.

Just like with generic functions, generic classes can help us to avoid the duplication of code. Let's look at an example:

```
class User {
    public name!: string;
    public surname!: string;
}
```

Object-Oriented Programming with TypeScript

We have declared a class named `User` with two properties named `name` and `password`. We will now declare a class named `UserQueue`. A queue is a data structure that we can use to store a list of items. Items can be added at the end of the list and removed from the beginning of the list. For this reason, a queue is considered a **first-in-first-out** (**FIFO**) data structure. The `UserQueue` class doesn't use generics:

```
class UserQueue {
    private _items: User[] = [];
    public push(item: User) {
        this._items.push(item);
    }
    public pop() {
        return this._items.shift();
    }
    public size() {
        return this._items.length;
    }
}
```

> Please note the array shift method removes the first element from an array and returns that removed element.

Once we have finished declaring the `UserQueue` class, we can create an instance and invoke the `push` and `pop` methods to add and remove items, respectively:

```
const userQueue = new UserQueue();
userQueue.push({ name: "Remo", surname: "Jansen" });
userQueue.push({ name: "John", surname: "Smith" });
const remo = userQueue.pop();
const john = userQueue.pop();
```

If we also need to create a new queue with items of a different type, we could end up duplicating a lot of code that looks almost identical:

```
class Car {
    public manufacturer!: string;
    public model!: string;
}

class CarQueue {
    private _items: Car[] = [];
    public push(item: Car) {
        this._items.push(item);
    }
```

[128]

```
    public pop() {
        return this._items.shift();
    }
    public size() {
        return this._items.length;
    }
}

const carQueue = new CarQueue();
carQueue.push({ manufacturer: "BMW", model: "M3" });
carQueue.push({ manufacturer: "Tesla", model: "S" });
const bmw = carQueue.pop();
const tesla = carQueue.pop();
```

If the number of entities grows, we will continue to repeatedly duplicate code. We could use the any type to avoid this problem, but then we would be losing the type checks at compile time:

```
class Queue {
    private _items: any[] = [];
    public push(item: any) {
        this._items.push(item);
    }
    public pop() {
        return this._items.shift();
    }
    public size() {
        return this._items.length;
    }
}
```

A much better solution is to create a generic queue:

```
class Queue<T> {
    private _items: T[] = [];
    public push(item: T) {
        this._items.push(item);
    }
    public pop() {
        return this._items.shift();
    }
    public size() {
        return this._items.length;
    }
}
```

The generic queue code is identical to `UserQueue` and `CarQueue`, except for the type of the `items` property. We have replaced the hardcoded reference to the `User` and `Car` entities and replaced them with the generic type `T`. We can now declare as many kinds of queues as we might need without duplicating a single line of code:

```
class User {
    public name!: string;
    public surname!: string;
}

const userQueue = new Queue<User>();
userQueue.push({ name: "Remo", surname: "Jansen" });
userQueue.push({ name: "John", surname: "Smith" });
const remo = userQueue.pop();
const john = userQueue.pop();

class Car {
    public manufacturer!: string;
    public model!: string;
}

const carQueue = new Queue<Car>();
carQueue.push({ manufacturer: "BMW", model: "M3" });
carQueue.push({ manufacturer: "Tesla", model: "S" });
const bmw = carQueue.pop();
const tesla = carQueue.pop();
```

Generic constraints

Sometimes, we might need to restrict the use of a generic class. For example, we can add a new feature to the generic queue. The new feature is going to validate the entities before they are added to the queue.

One possible solution would be to use the `typeof` operator to identify the type of the generic type parameter `T` within a generic class or function:

```
class User {
    public name!: string;
    public surname!: string;
}

class Car {
    public manufacturer!: string;
    public model!: string;
}
```

```
class Queue<T> {
    private _items: T[] = [];
    public push(item: T) {
        if (item instanceof User) {
            if (
                item.name === "" ||
                item.surname === ""
            ) {
                throw new Error("Invalid user");
            }
        }
        if (item instanceof Car) {
            if (
                item.manufacturer === "" ||
                item.model === ""
            ) {
                throw new Error("Invalid car");
            }
        }
        this._items.push(item);
    }
    public pop() {
        return this._items.shift();
    }
    public size() {
        return this._items.length;
    }
}

const userQueue = new Queue<User>();
userQueue.push({ name: "", surname: "" }); // Runtime Error
userQueue.push({ name: "Remo", surname: "" }); // Runtime Error
userQueue.push({ name: "", surname: "Jansen" }); // Runtime Error

const carQueue = new Queue<Car>();
carQueue.push({ manufacturer: "", model: "" }); // Runtime Error
carQueue.push({ manufacturer: "BMW", model: "" }); // Runtime Error
carQueue.push({ manufacturer: "", model: "M3" }); // Runtime Error
```

The problem is that we will have to modify our Queue class to add extra logic with each new kind of entity. We will not add the validation rules into the Queue class because a generic class should not know the type used as the generic type.

A better solution is to add a method named `validate` to the entities. The method will throw and exception if the entity is invalid:

```
class Queue<T> {
    private _items: T[] = [];
    public push(item: T) {
        item.validate(); // Error
        this._items.push(item);
    }
    public pop() {
        return this._items.shift();
    }
    public size() {
        return this._items.length;
    }
}
```

The preceding code snippet throws a compilation error because we can use the generic repository with any type, but not all types have a method named `validate`. Fortunately, this issue can easily be resolved by using a generic constraint. Constraints will restrict the types that we can use as the generic type parameter `T`. We are going to declare a constraint, so only the types that implement an interface named `Validatable` can be used with the generic method. Let's start by declaring the `Validatable` interface:

```
interface Validatable {
    validate(): void;
}
```

Now, we can proceed to implement the interface. In this case, we must implement the `validate` method:

```
class User implements Validatable {
    public constructor(
        public name: string,
        public surname: string
    ) {}
    public validate() {
        if (
            this.name === "" ||
            this.surname === ""
        ) {
            throw new Error("Invalid user");
        }
    }
}
```

```
class Car implements Validatable {
    public constructor(
        public manufacturer: string,
        public model: string
    ) {}
    public validate() {
        if (
            this.manufacturer === "" ||
            this.model === ""
        ) {
            throw new Error("Invalid car");
        }
    }
}
```

Now, let's declare a generic repository and add a type constraint so that only types that implement the `Validatable` interface are accepted:

```
class Queue<T extends Validatable> {
    private _items: T[] = [];
    public push(item: T) {
        item.validate();
        this._items.push(item);
    }
    public pop() {
        return this._items.shift();
    }
    public size() {
        return this._items.length;
    }
}
```

> Even though we have used an interface, we used the `extends` keyword and not the `implements` keyword to declare the constraint in the preceding example. There is no special reason for that. This is just the way the TypeScript constraint's syntax works.

At this point, we should be ready to see the new validation feature in action:

```
const userQueue = new Queue<User>();
userQueue.push(new User("", "")); // Error
userQueue.push(new User("Remo", "")); // Error
userQueue.push(new User("", "Jansen")); // Error

const carQueue = new Queue<Car>();
carQueue.push(new Car("", "")); // Error
carQueue.push(new Car("BMW", "")); // Error
carQueue.push(new Car("", "M3")); // Error
```

If we attempt to use a class that doesn't implement the Validatable as the generic parameter T, we will get a compilation error.

Multiple types in generic type constraints

We can only refer to one type when declaring a generic type constraint. Let's imagine that we need a generic class to be constrained, so it only allows types that extend the following two interfaces:

```
interface Foo {
    doSomething(): void;
}

interface Bar {
    doSomethingElse(): void;
}
```

We may think that we can define the required generic constraint as follows:

```
class Example1<T extends Foo, Bar> {
    private prop!: T;
    public doEverything() {
        this.prop.doSomething();
        this.prop.doSomethingElse(); // error
    }
}
```

[134]

However, this code snippet will throw a compilation error. We cannot specify multiple types when declaring a generic type constraint. However, we can work around this issue by using `Foo` and `Bar` in a superinterface:

```
interface FooBar extends Foo, Bar {}
```

`Foo` and `Bar` are now superinterfaces because they are the parent interfaces of the `FooBar` interface. We can then declare the constraint using the new `FooBar` interface:

```
class Example2<T extends FooBar> {
    private prop!: T;
    public doEverything() {
        this.prop.doSomething();
        this.prop.doSomethingElse();
    }
}
```

The new operator in generic types

To create a new object within a generic piece of code, we need to use the constructor function of the type. This means that instead of using `t: T` as follows:

```
function factory<T>(t: T) {
    return new t(); // Error
}
```

We should use `t: { new(): T; }`, as follows:

```
function factory<T>(t: { new(): T }) {
    return new t();
}

class Foo {
    public name!: "foo";
}

class Bar {
    public name!: "bar";
}

const foo = factory<Foo>(Foo);
const bar = factory<Bar>(Bar);
```

Object-Oriented Programming with TypeScript

Association, aggregation, and composition

In OOP, classes can have a relationship with each other. In this section, we are going to talk about three different types of relationships between classes.

Association

We call **association** those relationships whose objects have an independent life cycle where there is no ownership of the objects. Let's take a look at an example of a teacher and a student. Multiple students can be associated with a single teacher, and a single student can be associated with multiple teachers, but both have independent life cycles (both can create and delete independently). So, when a teacher leaves the school, we don't need to delete any students, and when a student leaves the school, we don't need to delete any teachers:

Teacher
+ students: Student[]
+ teach(): void

Student
+ teachers: Teacher[]
+ learn(): void

Aggregation

We call **aggregation** those relationships whose objects have an independent life cycle, but there is ownership, and child objects cannot belong to another parent object. Let's take an example of a cell phone and a cell phone battery. A single battery can belong to a phone, but if the phone stops working, and we delete it from our database, the phone battery will not be deleted because it may still be functional. So, in aggregation, while there is ownership, objects have their life cycle:

CellPhone
+ battery: CellBaterry
+ ring(number : int): void

CellBattery
+ remainingEnergy: int
+ charge(): void

Composition

We use the term **composition** to refer to relationships whose objects don't have an independent life cycle, and if the parent object is deleted, all child objects will also be deleted.

Let's take an example of the relationship between questions and answers. Single questions can have multiple answers, and answers cannot belong to multiple questions. If we delete questions, answers will automatically be deleted.

Objects with a dependent life cycle (answers in the example) are known as **weak entities**.

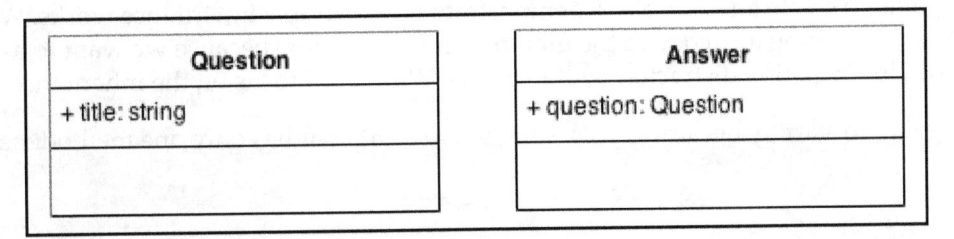

Question
+ title: string

Answer
+ question: Question

Sometimes, it can be a complicated process to decide if we should use association, aggregation, or composition. This difficulty is caused in part because aggregation and composition are subsets of association, which means they are specific cases of association:

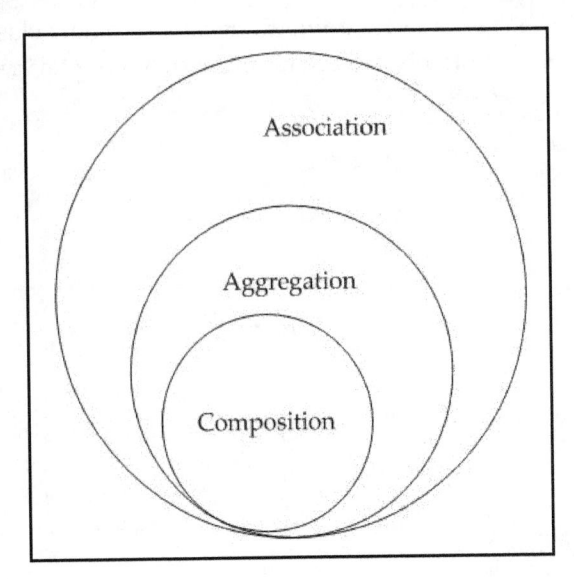

It is also important to mention that, in general, we should try to **use composition over inheritance** whenever it is possible. Inheritance tightly couples derived classes to their respective base classes and it can become a maintainability issue over time. Composition can lead to much less tightly coupled code than inheritance.

Mixins (multiple inheritance)

Sometimes, we will find scenarios in which it would be useful to be able to declare a class that inherits from two or more classes simultaneously (known as **multiple inheritance**).

We are going to create an example to demonstrate how multiple inheritance works. We are going to avoid adding any code to the methods in this example because we want to avoid the possibility of getting distracted by the details. We should focus on the inheritance tree.

We are going to start by declaring a class named `Animal` that has only one method, named `eat`:

```
class Animal {
  eat() {
    // ...
  }
}
```

After declaring the `Animal` class, we are going to declare two new classes named `WingedAnimal` and `Mammal`. Both classes are inherited from the `Animal` class:

```
class Mammal extends Animal {
    public breath() {
        // ...
    }
}

class WingedAnimal extends Animal {
    public fly() {
        // ...
    }
}
```

Now that we have our classes ready, we are going to try to implement a class named `Bat`. Bats are mammals and have wings. This means that we need to create a new class named `Bat`, which will extend both the `Mammal` and `WingedAnimal` classes. We might think that this seems logical, however, if we attempt to do this, we will encounter a compilation error:

```
// Error: Classes can only extend a single class.
class Bat extends WingedAnimal, Mammal {
    // ...
}
```

This error is thrown because TypeScript doesn't support multiple inheritance. This means that a class can only extend one class. Most OOP languages such as C# or TypeScript do not support multiple inheritance because it can potentially increase the complexity of applications and lead to a well-defined problem known as the diamond problem.

The diamond problem

Sometimes, a class inheritance diagram can take a diamond-like shape (as seen in the following diagram). This kind of class inheritance diagram can potentially lead us to a design issue known as the **diamond problem**:

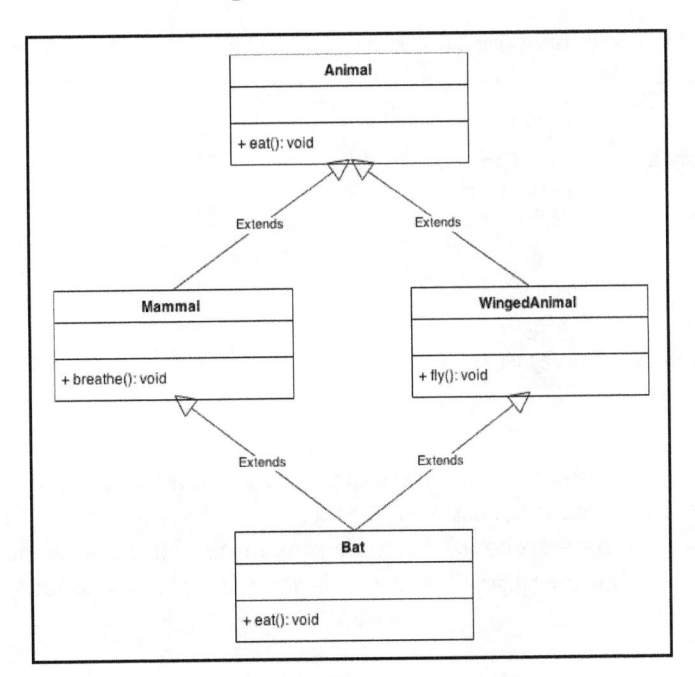

If multiple inheritance was allowed and we encounter an inheritance tree with a diamond shape, we would not face any problems while using a method that is exclusive to only one of the classes in the inheritance tree:

```
var bat = new Bat();
bat.fly(); // OK
bat.eat();// OK
bat.breath();// OK
```

The problem takes place when we try to invoke one of the `Bat` class's parent methods, and it is unclear or ambiguous which of the parent's implementations of that method should be invoked. For example, if we could add a method named move to both the `Mammal` and the `WingedAnimal` classes and try to invoke it from an instance of `Bat`, we would get an ambiguous call error.

Implementing mixins

Now that we know why multiple inheritance can be potentially dangerous, we will introduce a feature known as **mixins**. Mixins are an alternative to multiple inheritance with some limitations.

We are going to re-declare the `Mammal` and `WingedAnimal` classes to showcase how to work with mixins:

```
class Mammal {
    public breath(): string {
        return "I'm alive!";
    }
}

class WingedAnimal {
    public fly(): string {
        return "I can fly!";
    }
}
```

The two classes presented in the preceding example are not much different from the ones that we declared in the preceding sections. We have added some logic to the `breath` and `fly` methods, so we can have some values to help us understand this demonstration. It is also important to note that the `Mammal` and `WingedAnimal` classes no longer extend the `Animal` class.

The `Bat` class needs some important additions. We are going to use the `reserved` keyword `implements` to indicate that `Bat` will implement the functionality declared in the `Mammal` and `WingedAnimal` classes. We are also going to add the signature of each of the methods that the `Bat` class will implement:

```
class Bat implements Mammal, WingedAnimal {
    public eat!: () => string;
    public breath!: () => string;
    public fly!: () => string;
}
```

We need to copy the following function somewhere in our code to be able to apply mixins:

```
function applyMixins(derived: any, bases: any[]) {
    bases.forEach(base => {
        const props = Object.getOwnPropertyNames(base.prototype);
        props.forEach(name => {
            if (name !== "constructor") {
                derived.prototype[name] = base.prototype[name];
            }
        });
    });
}
```

> The preceding function is a well-known pattern and can be found in many books and online references, including the official *TypeScript Handbook*. Don't worry if you don't fully understand it at this point because it uses some concepts (such as An iterator is a behavioral design pattern which porotypes) that will not be covered until Chapter 6, *Understanding the Runtime*.

This function iterates each property of the parent classes (contained in an array named `bases`) and copies the implementation to a child class (`derived`). We only need to declare this function once in our entire application. Once we have done it, we can use it as follows:

```
applyMixins(Bat, [Mammal, WingedAnimal]);
```

The child class (`Bat`) will then contain each of the properties and methods of the two parent classes (`WingedAnimal` and `Mammal`):

```
const bat = new Bat();
bat.breath(); // "I'm alive!"
bat.fly(); // "I can fly!"
```

Object-Oriented Programming with TypeScript

As we said at the beginning of this section, mixins have some limitations:

- The first limitation is that we can only inherit the properties and methods from one level in the inheritance tree. This explains why we removed the `Animal` class before applying the mixins.
- The second limitation is that if two or more of the parent classes contain a method with the same name, the method that is going to be inherited will be taken from the last class passed in the `bases` array to the `applyMixins` function.

We will now see an example that presents both of these limitations.

To show the first limitation, we will re-declare the `Animal` class:

```
class Animal {
  public eat(): string {
    return "I need food!";
  }
}
```

We will then declare the `Mammal` and `WingedAnimal` classes, but this time, they will extend the `Animal` class:

```
class Mammal extends Animal {
    public breath() {
        return "I'm alive!";
    }
    public move() {
        return "I can move like a mammal!";
    }
}

class WingedAnimal extends Animal {
    public fly() {
        return "I can fly!";
    }
    public move() {
        return "I can move like a bird!";
    }
}
```

We will then declare again the `Bat` class. This class will implement both the `Mammal` and `WindgedAnimal` classes:

```
class Bat implements Mammal, WingedAnimal {
    public eat!: () => string;
    public breath!: () => string;
    public fly!: () => string;
    public move!: () => string;
}
```

We are ready to invoke the `applyMixins` function. Notice how we pass `Mammal` before `WingedAnimal` in the array:

```
applyMixins(Bat, [Mammal, WingedAnimal]);
```

We can now create an instance of `Bat`, and we will be able to observe that the `eat` method has not been inherited from the `Animal` class due to the first limitation:

```
const bat = new Bat();
bat.eat(); // Error: bat.eat is not a function
```

Each of the parent class's methods has been inherited without issues:

```
bat.breath(); // I'm alive!
bat.fly();    // I can fly!"
```

The `move` method has issues because according to the second limitation, only the implementation of the last parent class passed to the `applyMixins` method will be implemented. In this case, the implementation is inherited from the `WingedAnimal` class:

```
bat.move(); // I can move like a bird
```

To finalize, we will see the effect of switching the order of the parent classes when invoking the `applyMixins` method. Notice how we have passed `WingedAnimal` before `Mammal` in the array:

```
applyMixins(Bat2, [WingedAnimal, Mammal]);
const bat = new Bat2();
bat.eat();       // Error: not a function
bat.breathe();   // I'm alive!
bat.fly();       // I can fly!
bat.move()       // I can move like a mammal
```

Iterables

An iterator is a behavioral design pattern that is common in OOP. An iterator is an object that implements an interface such as the following one:

```
interface Iterator<T> {
    next(value?: any): IteratorResult<T>;
    return?(value?: any): IteratorResult<T>;
    throw?(e?: any): IteratorResult<T>;
}
```

The preceding interface allows us to retrieve the items available in a collection. The iterator result allows us to know if we have reached the last item in the collection and to access the values in the collection:

```
interface IteratorResult<T> {
    done: boolean;
    value: T;
}
```

We can create custom iterators by implementing the `IterableIterator` interface. We will need to implement the next method and a method named `Symbol.iterator`:

```
class Fib implements IterableIterator<number> {

  protected fn1 = 0;
  protected fn2 = 1;

  public constructor(protected maxValue?: number) {}

  public next(): IteratorResult<number> {
    let current = this.fn1;
    this.fn1 = this.fn2;
    this.fn2 = current + this.fn1;
    if (this.maxValue && current <= this.maxValue) {
      return {
        done: false,
        value: current
      };
    } else {
      return {
        done: true,
        value: 0
      };
    }
  }
```

```
    public [Symbol.iterator](): IterableIterator<number> {
        return this;
    }

}
```

We can use brackets to define the name of a property or method using the value of a variable as the name of the method or property. In this case, the `Symbol.iterator` is used as the name of the method. The `Symbol` iterator contains the unique string `@@iterator`. This name is a special name for a method because whenever an object needs to be iterated (such as at the beginning of a `for...of` loop), its `@@iterator` method is called with no arguments, and the returned iterator is used to obtain the values to be iterated.

After declaring the class, we can create instances and iterate their values:

```
let fib = new Fib(5);

fib.next(); // { done: false, value: 0 }
fib.next(); // { done: false, value: 1 }
fib.next(); // { done: false, value: 1 }
fib.next(); // { done: false, value: 2 }
fib.next(); // { done: false, value: 3 }
fib.next(); // { done: false, value: 5 }
```

The preceding iterable never stops returning values, but we can also declare an instance with a fixed number of items and iterate the items using a `for...of` loop:

```
let fibMax21 = new Fib(21);

for (let num of fibMax21) {
    console.log(num); // Prints fibonacci sequence 0 to 21
}
```

Object-Oriented Programming with TypeScript

> Note that some additional types are required by asynchronous iterators if we are targeting ES5 or ES3. You will need to add `esnext.asynciterable` to your `tsconfig.json` file. We are also going to need to enable an additional setting in our `tsconfig.json` to provide full support for iterables (for example, using `for...of` control flow statements, the spread operator or object destructuring) when targeting ES3 or ES5:
> ```
> "lib": [
>             "es2015.promise",
>             "dom",
>             "es5",
>             "es5",
>             "es2015.generator",
>             "es2015.iterable",
>             "esnext.asynciterable" // new
> ]
> ```
> You might also need a recent version of Node.js as the preceding example will not work in old versions of Node.js. We will learn more about the `lib` setting in Chapter 9, *Automating Your Development Workflow*.

Abstract classes

Abstract classes are base classes that can be extended by other classes. The `abstract` keyword is used to define abstract classes as well as abstract methods within an abstract class:

```
abstract class Department {

    constructor(public name: string) {
    }

    public printName(): void {
        console.log("Department name: " + this.name);
    }

    public abstract printMeeting(): void; // must be implemented in derived classes
}
```

The methods in an abstract class that are preceded by the `abstract` keyword cannot contain an implementation and must be implemented by the derived classes.

Abstract methods may look like interface methods. However, an abstract class may contain implementation details for some of its members:

```
class AccountingDepartment extends Department {

    public constructor() {
        super("Accounting and Auditing"); // constructors in derived
classes must call super()
    }

    public printMeeting(): void {
        console.log("The Accounting Department meets each Monday at 10
am.");
    }

    public generateReports(): void {
        console.log("Generating accounting reports...");
    }
}
```

It is not possible to create an instance of an abstract class:

```
// OK: Create a reference to an abstract type
let department: Department;

// Error: cannot create an instance of an abstract class
department = new Department();

// OK: Create and assign a non-abstract subclass
department = new AccountingDepartment();
department.printName();
department.printMeeting();

// Error: Method doesn't exist on declared abstract type
department.generateReports();
```

Interfaces

Interfaces are probably the feature that you will miss the most while developing large-scale web applications with JavaScript if you have a background in object-oriented statically-typed programming languages such as Java or C#.

Object-Oriented Programming with TypeScript

Traditionally, in OOP, we say that a class can extend only one class and implement one or more interfaces. An interface can implement one or more interfaces and cannot extend another class or interface. Wikipedia's definition of interfaces in OOP is as follows:

> *"In object-oriented languages, the term interface is often used to define an abstract type that contains no data or code, but defines behaviors as method signatures."*

In TypeScript, interfaces don't strictly follow this definition. The two main differences are that in TypeScript:

- An interface can extend a class
- An interface can define data and behaviors as opposed to only behaviors

For example, we can define an interface named `Weapon`:

```
interface Weapon {
    tryHit(fromDistance: number): boolean;
}
```

The `Weapon` interface defines the behavior shared by all weapons (a weapon can be used to try to hit an enemy, but each kind of weapon has a different range). However, the interface does not define the details of each if its implementations (the specific range of each kind of weapon).

Implementing an interface can be understood as signing a contract. An interface is a contract, and when we sign it (implement it), we must follow its rules. The interface rules are the signatures of the methods and properties, and we must implement them:

```
class Katana implements Weapon {
    public tryHit(fromDistance: number) {
        return fromDistance <= 2;
    }
}

class Shuriken implements Weapon {
    public tryHit(fromDistance: number) {
        return fromDistance <= 15;
    }
}
```

The two preceding classes implement the methods defined by the `Weapon` interface. Both classes share the same public API but have different internal implementations. We will see many more examples of interfaces through the rest of this chapter.

SOLID principles, encapsulation, and polymorphism

In the early days of software development, developers used to write code with procedural programming languages. In procedural programming languages, the programs follow a top-to-bottom approach, and the logic is wrapped with functions.

New styles of computer programming, such as modular programming or structured programming, emerged when developers realized that procedural computer programs could not provide them with the desired level of abstraction, maintainability, and reusability.

The development community created a series of recommended practices and design patterns to improve the level of abstraction and reusability of procedural programming languages, but some of these guidelines required a certain level of expertise. To facilitate adherence to these guidelines, a new style of computer programming known as **object-oriented programming** (OOP) was created.

Developers quickly noticed some common OOP mistakes and came up with five rules that every OOP developer should follow to create a system that is easy to maintain and extend over time. These five rules are known as the SOLID principles. SOLID is an acronym introduced by Michael Feathers. Each of the characters in the acronym represents one of the following principles:

- **Single responsibility principle** (SRP): This principle states that a software component (function, class, or module) should focus on one unique task (have only one responsibility).
- **Open/closed principle** (OCP): This principle states that software entities should be designed with application growth (new code) in mind (be open to extension), but that application growth should require as few changes to the existing code as possible (be closed for modification).
- **Liskov substitution principle** (LSP): This principle states that we should be able to replace a class in a program with another class if both classes implement the same interface. After replacing the class, no other changes should be required, and the program should continue to work as it did originally.

- **Interface segregation principle (ISP):** This principle states that we should split interfaces that are very large (general-purpose interfaces) into smaller and more specific ones (many client-specific interfaces) so that clients will only need to know about the methods that are of interest to them.
- **Dependency inversion principle (DIP):** This principle states that entities should depend on abstractions (interfaces) as opposed to depending on concretion (classes).

In this chapter, we are going to learn how to write TypeScript code that adheres to these principles so that our applications are easy to maintain and extend over time.

SOLID – the single responsibility principle

All our classes should adhere to the **single responsibility principle** (**SRP**). The `Person` class declared during the very first example in this chapter represents a person, including all of their characteristics (attributes) and behaviors (methods). We are going to modify the preceding class by adding an `email` as validation logic:

```
class Person {
    public name: string;
    public surname: string;
    public email: string;
    public constructor(
        name: string, surname: string, email: string
    ) {
        this.surname = surname;
        this.name = name;
        if (this.validateEmail(email)) {
            this.email = email;
        } else {
            throw new Error("Invalid email!");
        }
    }
    public validateEmail(email: string) {
        const re = /S+@S+.S+/;
        return re.test(email);
    }
    public greet() {
        console.log(
            `Hi! I'm ${this.name},
            you can reach me at ${this.email}`
        );
    }
}
```

When an object doesn't follow the SRP and it knows too much (has too many properties) or does too much (has too many methods), we say that the object is a God object. The `Person` class here is a God object because we have added a method named `validateEmail` that is not related to the `Person` class's behavior.

Deciding which attributes and methods should or should not be part of a class is a relatively subjective decision. If we spend some time analyzing our options, we should be able to identify ways to improve the design of our classes.

We can refactor the `Person` class by declaring an `Email` class, which is responsible for email validation, and use it as an attribute in the `Person` class:

```
class Email {
    public static validateEmail(email: string) {
        const re = /S+@S+.S+/;
        return re.test(email);
    }
}
```

Now that we have an `Email` class, we can remove the responsibility of validating the emails from the `Person` class and update its `email` attribute to use the `Email` type instead of string:

```
class Person {
    public name: string;
    public surname: string;
    public email: string;
    public constructor(
        name: string, surname: string, email: string
    ) {
        if (Email.validateEmail(email) === false) {
            throw new Error("Invalid email!");
        }
        this.email = email;
        this.name = name;
        this.surname = surname;
    }
    public greet() {
        console.log(
            `Hi! I'm ${this.name},
            you can reach me at ${this.email.toString()}`
        );
    }
}
```

Object-Oriented Programming with TypeScript

Making sure that a class has a single responsibility makes it easier to see what it does and how we can extend/improve it.

Encapsulation

We can further improve our `Person` and `Email` classes declared in the previous section by increasing the level of abstraction of our classes. For example, when we use the `Email` class, we don't need to be aware of the existence of the `validateEmail` method; this method could be invisible from outside the `Email` class. As a result, the `Email` class would be much simpler to understand.

When we increase the level of abstraction of an object, we can say that we are encapsulating some logic. Encapsulation is also known as **information hiding**. For example, the `Email` class allows us to use emails without having to worry about email validation because the class will deal with it for us. We can make this clearer by using access modifiers (`public` or `private`) to flag all the class attributes and methods that we want to abstract from the use of the `Email` class as `private`:

```
class Email {
    private _email: string;
    public constructor(email: string) {
        if (this._validateEmail(email)) {
            this._email = email;
        } else {
            throw new Error("Invalid email!");
        }
    }
    public toString(): string {
        return this._email;
    }
    private _validateEmail(email: string) {
        const re = /S+@S+.S+/;
        return re.test(email);
    }
}

class Person {
    public name: string;
    public surname: string;
    public email: Email;
    public constructor(
        name: string, surname: string, email: Email
    ) {
        this.email = email;
```

[152]

```
        this.name = name;
        this.surname = surname;
    }
    public greet() {
        console.log(
            `Hi! I'm ${this.name},
             you can reach me at ${this.email.toString()}`
        );
    }
}
```

We can then simply use the `Email` class without needing to explicitly perform any kind of validation:

```
let person: Person = new Person(
    "Remo",
    "Jansen",
    new Email("remo.jansen@wolksoftware.com")
);
```

SOLID – the open/closed principle

The **open/closed principle** (**OCP**) recommends that we design our classes and methods in a way that enables us to extend their behavior (open for extension) in the future without modifying their current behavior (closed for modification).

The following code snippet is not great because it does not adhere to the open/closed principle:

```
class Rectangle {
    public width!: number;
    public height!: number;
}

class AreaCalculator {
    public area(shapes: Rectangle[] ) {
        return shapes.reduce(
            (p, c) => {
                return p + (c.height * c.width);
            },
            0
        );
    }
}
```

Object-Oriented Programming with TypeScript

The preceding code does not adhere to the open/closed principle because if we need to extend our program to also support circles, we will need to modify the existing `AreaCalculator` class:

```
class Circle {
    public radius!: number;
}

class AreaCalculator {
    public area(shapes: Array<Rectangle|Circle>) {
        return shapes.reduce(
            (p, c) => {
                if (c instanceof Rectangle) {
                    return p + (c.width * c.height);
                } else {
                    return p + (c.radius * c.radius * Math.PI);
                }
            },
            0
        );
    }
}
```

A better solution is to add the area calculation as a method of the shapes so that when we add a new shape (extension), we don't need to change the existing `AreaCalculator` class (modification):

```
abstract class Shape {
    public abstract area(): number;
}

class Rectangle extends Shape {
    public width!: number;
    public height!: number;
    public area() {
        return this.width * this.height;
    }
}

class Circle implements Shape {
    public radius!: number;
    public area() {
        return (this.radius * this.radius * Math.PI);
    }
}

class AreaCalculator {
```

```
    public area(shapes: Shape[]) {
        return shapes.reduce(
            (p, c) => p + c.area(),
            0
        );
    }
}
```

The second approach follows the second SOLID principle, the open/closed principle, as we can create new entities, and the generic repository will continue to work (open for extension), but no additional changes to it will be required (closed for modification).

Polymorphism

Polymorphism is the ability to present the same interface for differing underlying forms (data types). Polymorphism is often referred to as the third pillar of object-oriented programming, after encapsulation and inheritance.

Polymorphism is what enabled us to implement the LSP in the preceding section:

```
class AreaCalculator {
    public area(shapes: Shape[]) {
        return shapes.reduce(
            (p, c) => p + c.area(),
            0
        );
    }
}
```

Objects of the derived class (`Circle` and `Rectangle`) may be treated as objects of a base class (`Shape`) in places such as method parameters (such as the `area` method). Base classes may define and implement abstract methods, and derived classes can override them, which means they provide their definition and implementation.

SOLID – the Liskov substitution principle

The **Liskov substitution principle** (LSP) states, *Subtypes must be substitutable for their base types.* Let's look at an example to understand what this means.

[155]

We will declare a class named `PersistanceService`, the responsibility of which is to persist some object into some sort of storage. We will start by declaring the following interface:

```
interface PersistanceServiceInterface {
    save(value: string): string;
}
```

After declaring the `PersistanceServiceInterface` interface, we can implement it. We will use cookies as the storage for the application's data:

```
function getUniqueId() {
    return Math.random().toString(36).substr(2, 9);
}

class CookiePersitanceService implements PersistanceServiceInterface {
    public save(value: string): string {
        let id = getUniqueId();
        document.cookie = `${id}=${value}`;
        return id;
    }
}
```

We will continue by declaring a class named `FavouritesController`, which has a dependency on `PersistanceServiceInterface`:

```
class FavouritesController {
    private _persistanceService: PersistanceServiceInterface;
    public constructor(persistanceService: PersistanceServiceInterface) {
        this._persistanceService = persistanceService;
    }
    public saveAsFavourite(articleId: string) {
        return this._persistanceService.save(articleId);
    }
}
```

We can finally create an instance of `FavouritesController` and pass an instance of `CookiePersitanceService` via its constructor:

```
const favController1 = new FavouritesController(
    new CookiePersitanceService()
);
```

The LSP allows us to replace a dependency with another implementation if both implementations are based in the same base type; so, if we decide to stop using cookies as storage and use the HTML5 local storage API instead, we can declare a new implementation:

```
class LocalStoragePersitanceService implements PersistanceServiceInterface
{
    public save(value: string): string {
        const id = getUniqueId();
        localStorage.setItem(`${id}`, value);
        return id;
    }
}
```

We can then replace it without having to add any changes to the `FavouritesController` controller class:

```
const favController = new FavouritesController(
    new LocalStoragePersitanceService()
);
```

SOLID – the interface segregation principle

Interfaces are used to declare how two or more software components cooperate and exchange information with each other. This declaration is known as an **application programming interface** (**API**). In the previous example, our interface was `PersistanceServiceInterface`, and it was implemented by the classes `LocalStoragePersitanceService` and `CookiePersistanceService`. The interface was consumed by the `FavouritesController` class, so we say that this class is a client of the `PersistanceServiceInterface` API.

The **interface segregation principle** (**ISP**) states that no client should be forced to depend on methods it does not use. To adhere to the ISP, we need to keep in mind that when we declare the API (how two or more software components cooperate and exchange information with each other) of our application's components, the declaration of many client-specific interfaces is better than the declaration of one general-purpose interface. Let's look at an example.

Object-Oriented Programming with TypeScript

If we design an API to control all the elements in a vehicle (engine, radio, heating, navigation, and lights), we could have one general-purpose interface, that allows us to control every single element of the vehicle:

```
interface VehicleInterface {
    getSpeed(): number;
    getVehicleType(): string;
    isTaxPayed(): boolean;
    isLightsOn(): boolean;
    isLightsOff(): boolean;
    startEngine(): void;
    accelerate(): number;
    stopEngine(): void;
    startRadio(): void;
    playCd(): void;
    stopRadio(): void;
}
```

If a class has a dependency (client) in the `VehicleInterface` interface but it only wants to use the radio methods, we would be facing a violation of the ISP because, as we have already seen, a client shouldn't be forced to depend on methods it does not use.

The solution is to split the `VehicleInterface` interface into many client-specific interfaces so that our class can adhere to the ISP by depending only on the `RadioInterface` interface:

```
interface VehicleInterface {
    getSpeed(): number;
    getVehicleType(): string;
    isTaxPayed(): boolean;
    isLightsOn(): boolean;
}

interface LightsInterface {
    isLightsOn(): boolean;
    isLightsOff(): boolean;
}

interface RadioInterface {
    startRadio(): void;
    playCd(): void;
    stopRadio(): void;
}

interface EngineInterface {
    startEngine(): void;
    accelerate(): number;
```

```
    stopEngine(): void;
}
```

SOLID – the dependency inversion principle

The **dependency inversion** (**DI**) principle states, *Depend upon abstractions. Do not depend upon concretions.* In the LSP, we implemented a class named `FavouritesController`. In the example, it was possible to replace an implementation of `PersistanceServiceInterface` with another without having to perform any additional change to `FavouritesController`.

We followed the DI principle, as `FavouritesController` has a dependency upon `PersistanceServiceInterface` (abstraction):

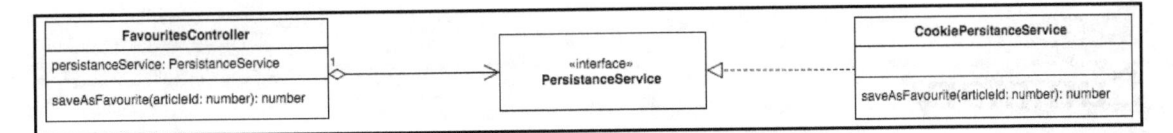

FavouritesController
persistanceService: PersistanceService
saveAsFavourite(articleId: number): number

«interface»
PersistanceService

CookiePersistanceService
saveAsFavourite(articleId: number): number

The preceding can be implemented as follows:

```
class FavouritesController {
    private _persistanceService: PersistanceServiceInterface;
    public constructor(persistanceService: PersistanceServiceInterface) {
        this._persistanceService = persistanceService;
    }
    public saveAsFavourite(articleId: string) {
        return this._persistanceService.save(articleId);
    }
}
```

Rather than `FavouritesController` having a dependency on `LocalStoragePersitanceService` or `CookiePersitanceService` (concretions) directly:

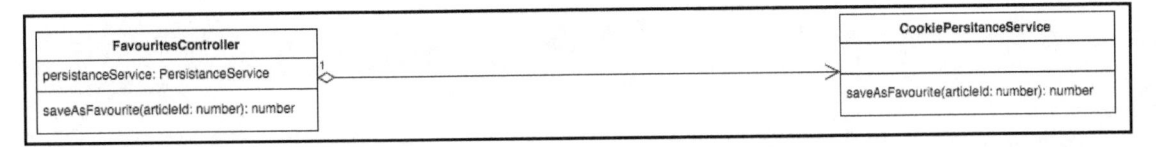

FavouritesController
persistanceService: PersistanceService
saveAsFavourite(articleId: number): number

CookiePersistanceService
saveAsFavourite(articleId: number): number

The preceding can be implemented as follows:

```
class FavouritesController {
    private _persistanceService: CookiePersitanceService;
    public constructor(persistanceService: CookiePersitanceService) {
        this._persistanceService = persistanceService;
    }
    public saveAsFavourite(articleId: string) {
        return this._persistanceService.save(articleId);
    }
}
```

If we compare the two diagrams, we will notice that the direction arrow that links the dependent and the dependency has been inverted thanks to the introduction of the interface (abstraction). This should help us to understand why this principle is known as the dependency inversion principle.

Summary

In this chapter, we have learned how to work with classes and interfaces in depth. We were able to make our application more maintainable by using techniques such as encapsulation and dependency inversion. In the next chapter, we will learn how to work with dependencies.

5
Working with Dependencies

In the previous chapter, we learned how to work with classes and interfaces. We also learned about the SOLID principles and other object-oriented programming best practices. In this chapter, we will learn how to work with dependencies. The first part of the chapter will focus on the usage of modules. The second part of the chapter will focus on the management of dependencies in object-oriented programming.

We are going to cover the following topics:

- Third-party dependencies
- Internal modules
- External modules
- Asynchronous module definition (AMD)
- CommonJS modules
- ES6 modules
- Browserify and universal module definition (UMD)
- Circular dependencies
- Dependency injection

Third-party dependencies

Third-party dependencies are usually open source libraries created by third-party organizations or independent software engineers. Third-party dependencies are external modules and can be imported using their name instead of a relative or absolute path.

Package management tools

Package management tools are used for dependency management so that we no longer have to download and manage our application's dependencies manually.

The rise and fall of package management tools

The TypeScript ecosystem has experienced the rise and fall of many package managers over the past few years. This generated some confusion in the early days of TypeScript but, fortunately, today we have a much more stable ecosystem.

Some notable package managers in the TypeScript history include tsd, typings, npm, bower, yarn, and turbo. Some package managers, such as tsd, typings, and bower, are not recommended anymore, and others, such as yarn or turbo, are relatively new and not as widely adopted as npm. The recommended package manager at the time of writing is npm.

npm

The **Node Package Manager** (**npm**) was originally developed as the default Node.js package management tool, but today it is used by many other tools.

npm uses a configuration file, named `package.json`, to store references to all the dependencies installed in our project. Originally, npm was usually only used to install backend dependencies, but today it is used to install any dependencies. This includes the following:

- Backend dependencies
- Frontend dependencies
- Development tools
- TypeScript type definitions

Before we install any packages, we should add a `package.json` file to our project. We can do this by executing the following command:

```
npm init
```

> Please note that we must install Node.js to be able to use the npm command.

Chapter 5

The `npm init` command will ask for some basic information about our project, including its name, version, description, entry point, test command, Git repository, keywords, author, and license.

> Refer to the official npm documentation at `https://docs.npmjs.com/files/package.json` if you are unsure about the purpose of some of the `package.json` fields mentioned earlier.

The `npm` command will then show us a preview of the `package.json` file that is about to be generated, and ask for our final confirmation.

If you would like to skip the questions and generate the file using the default settings, you can use the `npm init` command together with the `--yes` flag:

```
npm init --yes
```

After creating the project's `package.json` file, we will use the `npm install` command to install our first dependency.

The `npm install` command takes as arguments the name of one or multiple dependencies separated by a single space, and the scope of the installation.

The scope can be the following:

- Global dependency
- Dependency at development time (for example, testing frameworks, compilers, and so on)
- Dependency at runtime (for example, a web framework, database ORMs, and so on)

We will use the `tslint` npm package to check the style of our TypeScript code, so let's install it as a development dependency (using the `--save-dev` argument):

```
npm install tslint --save-dev
```

To install a global dependency, we will use the `-g` argument:

```
npm install webpack-dev-server -g
```

Working with Dependencies

> We might need administrative privileges to install packages with global scope in our development environment.
> Also note that npm will not add any entries to our `package.json` when installing packages with a global scope, but is important that we manually add the right dependencies to the `devDependencies` section in `package.json` to guarantee that the continuous integration build server will resolve all our project's dependencies correctly.

To install a runtime dependency, use the `--save` argument:

```
npm install react --save
```

> Please note that `react` is a module that can be used to create user interfaces.

Once we have installed some dependencies in the `package.json` file, the contents should look like the following:

```
{
  "name": "repository-name",
  "version": "1.0.0",
  "description": "example",
  "main": "index.html",
  "scripts": {
    "test": "echo \"Error: no test specified\" && exit 1"
  },
  "repository": {
    "type": "git",
    "url": "https://github.com/username/repository-name.git"
  },
  "keywords": [
    "typescript",
    "demo",
    "example"
  ],
  "author": "Name Surname",
  "contributors": [],
  "license": "MIT",
  "bugs": {
    "url": "https://github.com/username/repository-name/issues"
  },
  "homepage": "https://github.com/username/repository-name",
  "engines": {},
  "dependencies": {
```

Chapter 5

```
    "react": "16.2.0"
  },
  "devDependencies": {
    "tslint": "5.9.1"
  }
}
```

> Some fields in the `package.json` file must be configured manually. To learn more about the available `package.json` configuration fields, visit `https://docs.npmjs.com/files/package.json`.
> The versions of the npm packages used throughout this book may have been updated since its publication. Refer to the package documentation at `https://npmjs.com` to find out potential incompatibilities and learn about new features.
> If you are using one of the modern versions of npm, installing a module will also generate a file named `package-lock.json`. This file describes the exact dependency tree that was generated, such that subsequent installations can generate identical trees, regardless of intermediate dependency updates.

All the npm packages will be saved in the `node_modules` directory. It is recommended to avoid saving the `node_modules` directory into source control (for example, a Git repository).

The next time we set up our development environment, we will need to download all our dependencies again, but to do so, we will only need to execute the `npm install` command without any additional parameters:

npm install

The package manager (npm) will then search for the `package.json` file and install all the dependencies listed in it.

> We can use the npm search engine at `https://www.npmjs.com` to find potential modules that could be useful for our application.

Working with Dependencies

We can check whether the dependencies of our project are outdated using the `npm outdated` command.

We have learned how to use npm to manage the dependencies of a project. However, npm is more than a package manager, because it also allows us to create commands to perform some custom automation tasks, for example, to release a version of our application or run some automated tests. We will learn more about this feature later in `Chapter 9`, *Automating Your Development Workflow*.

Type definitions

The TypeScript support for existing JavaScript libraries is achieved thanks to the declaration of the public interface, or API, of the library. The declaration of the public interface of a third-party module is known as **type definition**.

When we install an npm module, we can face a few different scenarios.

Modules with native support for TypeScript

Some third-party dependencies feature built-in support for TypeScript. For example, an example of a module with native support for TypeScript is the InversifyJS module. In this case, installing the npm module is enough, because the module includes the required type definitions:

```
npm install inversify --save
```

Modules with external support for TypeScript

Some third-party dependencies do not feature built-in support for TypeScript, but type definitions are available in a separate npm module. An example of a module with external support for TypeScript is the `react` module. In this case, installing the npm module is not enough, because it doesn't include the required type definitions. We can solve this by installing the npm module which contains the missing type definitions:

```
npm install react --save
npm install @types/react --save-dev
```

The TypeScript team has developed an automated process that publishes all the available open source type definitions under one unique organization on the npm public registry. The organization is named `@types`, and the type definitions use the name of the module that they are defining.

Modules with no support for TypeScript

Some third-party dependencies don't feature built-in support for TypeScript, and type definitions are not available in a separate npm. In this case, installing the npm module is not enough, because it doesn't include the required type definitions. We can solve this by creating our type definitions.

Unfortunately, the process of creating our type definitions is not something that can be systematically described and requires a bit of experience, but we are going to try to explain the main complexities around it.

Let's pretend that we need to write custom type definition for the `react-side-effect` npm module, which is not the case because the type definitions are available already, but we will use it as an example.

The first thing that we need to do is to install the package that is missing the type definitions:

```
npm install react-side-effect --save
```

Then we need to open the `package.json` contained inside the `react-side-effect` module. Each npm module contains a `package.json` file, so it should be located at the following path:

```
/node_modules/react-side-effect/package.json
```

If we examine the `package.json` file, we should be able to find the `main` field. The `main` field describes the entry point of the npm module. The `main` field in the `package.json` of the `react-side-effect` npm module looks as follows:

```
"main": "lib/index.js"
```

We need to open that file and find which elements are exported by the module and how they are exported. This is the complicated part: we need to navigate through the source code and identify the exported elements and the kind of exports. The `lib/index.js` file only exports a function named `withSideEffect`:

```
module.exports = function withSideEffect // ...
```

Working with Dependencies

At this point, we can create a file named `external.d.ts` and add the following type definitions:

```
declare module "react-side-effect" {
    declare const withSideEffect: any;
    export = withSideEffect;
}
```

> Please note that we have used the following:
> `export = withSideEffect;`
>
> We have used this kind of module export because that is the kind of export that we can see in the library's source code.
> Sometimes we will see a module export like the following:
> `export default withSideEffect;`
>
> Or one like the following:
> `export { withSideEffect };`
>
> We need to ensure that our type definition file uses the same kind of export that is used in the library. We will learn more about the different kinds of exports later in this chapter.

The preceding code snippet declares a module named react-side-effect. The module exports an entity named `withSideEffect` with type `any`. The preceding type definitions should be enough to be able to import the module:

```
import * as withSideEffect from "react-side-effect";
```

But if we do so, we will get an error:

```
Module '"react-side-effect"' resolves to a non-module entity and cannot be imported using this construct.
```

Unfortunately, the only way to fix this is by adding an extra namespace, as described at https://github.com/Microsoft/TypeScript/issues/5073:

```
declare module "react-side-effect" {
    declare const withSideEffect: any;
    namespace withSideEffect {};
    export = withSideEffect;
}
```

[168]

At this point, we can import the module without errors, but the type of `withSideEffect` is `any`. We can solve this by examining the source code and spending some time trying to figure out the signature of the function. If we do so, we will end up with something like the following:

```
declare module "react-side-effect" {

    import React = __React;

    function withSideEffect(
        reducePropsToState: (propsList: any[]) => any,
        handleStateChangeOnClient: (state: any) => any,
        mapStateOnServer?: (state: any) => any
    ): ClassDecorator;

    class ElementClass extends React.Component<any, any> {}

    interface ClassDecorator {
        <T extends (typeof ElementClass)>(component:T): T;
    }

    namespace withSideEffect {};

    export = withSideEffect;
}
```

> Please note that it is highly recommended to share your type definitions with the TypeScript community at https://github.com/DefinitelyTyped/DefinitelyTyped.

The ECMAScript specification type definitions (lib.d.ts)

The TypeScript compiler automatically includes type definitions for the ECMAScript version that we are targeting. For example, if we target ES5, we will not be able to access the Promise API, because it is part of the ES6 specification:

```
const p = Promise.resolve(1); // Error
```

However, TypeScript allows us to import the type definitions for a proposal instead of an entire ECMAScript specification. For example, we can target ES5 and use the Promise API by adding the following to our `tsconfig.json` file:

```
"lib": ["es5", "dom", "es2015.promise"]
```

The preceding setting is indicating to the TypeScript compiler that we want it to import the type definitions for the entire ECMAScript 5 specification, the **document object model** (**DOM**) and the Promise API.

External TypeScript helpers (tslib)

As we already know, TypeScript allows us to use features of the upcoming ECMAScript specifications. TypeScript uses a series of helper functions to implement some of these features at runtime. The following are some of the helper functions generated by TypeScript:

- `__extends` for inheritance
- `__assign` for object spread properties
- `__rest` for object rest properties
- `__decorate`, `__param`, and `__metadata` for decorators
- `__awaiter` and `__generator` for `async/await`

If one of these helpers is required, TypeScript will generate it at compilation time. However, this can be a problem, because the helper is generated in all of the files that require it, which can lead to a lot of duplicated code.

We can use the following compilation settings to solve this problem:

- The `noEmitHelpers` flag will prevent TypeScript from emitting the helper functions
- The `importHelpers` flag will emit the code necessary to import the helpers from the `tslib` npm module instead of emitting the helper functions

The `tslib` module contains the declaration of all the required TypeScript helpers. We can install the `tslib` module using npm, as follows:

```
npm install tslib --save
```

This way, the helper functions are only declared once (by the `tslib` module).

Internal modules (module and namespace)

We can use the `module` and `namespace` keywords to define internal modules. TypeScript originally allowed us to use the `module` keyword to declare internal modules, but it was later deprecated in favor of the `namespace` keyword.

> Internal modules (`namespaces`) can be used to encapsulate certain elements of an application and to provide our code with a better organization. However, **we should try to avoid them and favor external modules over namespaces**. External modules should be our preferred option because they are required by some tools that allow us to optimize certain aspects of our application. External modules will be covered in detail later in this chapter.

We can use namespaces to group interfaces, classes, and objects that are somehow related. For example, we could wrap all our application models inside an internal module named `Models`:

```
namespace Models {
  export class UserModel {
    // ...
  }
}
```

All entities contained by a `namespace` are private by default. We can use the `export` keyword to declare what parts of our `namespace` we wish to make public.

Nested internal modules

We can nest one `namespace` inside another as follows:

```
namespace App {
    export namespace Models {
        export class UserModel {
            // ...
        }
        export class TalkModel {
            // ...
        }
    }
}
```

[171]

Working with Dependencies

In the preceding example, we have declared a namespace named `App`, and inside it, we have declared a public namespace named `Models`, which contains two public classes: `UserModel` and `TalkModel`.

We can then access the namespace entities by indicating the full namespace name:

```
const user = new App.Models.UserModel();
const talk = new App.Models.TalkModel();
```

Cross-file internal modules

TypeScript allows us to declare internal modules across multiple files. If an internal module becomes too big, it can be divided into multiple files to increase its maintainability. If we take the preceding example, we could add more contents to the internal module named `App` by referencing it in a new file.

Let's create a new file, named `validation.ts`, and add the following code to it:

```
namespace App {
    export namespace Validation {
        export class UserValidator {
            // ...
        }

        export class TalkValidator {
            // ...
        }
    }
}
```

We can then access the namespace entities declared in both files by indicating the full namespace name:

```
const userModel = new App.Models.UserModel();
const talkModel = new App.Models.TalkModel();
const userValidator = new App.Validation.UserValidator();
const talkValidator = new App.Validation.TalkValidator();
```

Even though the namespaces `Models` and `Validation` are declared in two different files, we can access them through the `App` namespace.

Chapter 5

Namespace names can contain periods. For example, instead of nesting the internal modules (validation and models) inside the `app` module, we could have used periods in the `validation` and `models` internal module names:

```
namespace App.Validation {
  // ...
}
namespace App.Models {
  // ...
}
```

Internal module aliases

The `import` keyword can be used within an internal module to provide an alias for another module, as follows:

```
import TalkValidator = app.validation.TalkValidator;
const talkValidator2 = new TalkValidator();
```

Compiling internal modules

Once we have finished declaring our internal modules, we can decide whether we want to compile each one into JavaScript or whether we prefer to concatenate all the files into one single file.

We can use the `--out` flag to compile all the input files into a single JavaScript output file:

```
tsc --out output.js input.ts
```

The compiler will automatically order the output file based on the reference tags present in the files. We can then import our files or file using an HTML `<script>` tag.

External modules

TypeScript also has the concept of an external module. JavaScript versions before ECMAScript 6 (ES6) don't include native support for external modules. Developers were forced to develop custom module loaders, and the open source community tried to come up with improved solutions over the years. As a result, today, there are several types of module loaders, and each one of them supports at least one module definition syntax.

Working with Dependencies

> In general, we can assume that when someone talks about a module, without explicitly specifying whether they are talking about an internal or external module, they are referring to an external module.

Module loaders and module definition syntaxes

The main difference between using modules (instead of namespaces or internal modules) is that after declaring all our modules, we will not import them using an HTML `<script>` tag. Using the `<script>` tag is not recommended, because web browsers "halt" (or "freeze") simultaneous downloads and rendering of the page when they encounter and load the contents of a `<script>` tag.

> We will discover more about network performance in `Chapter 13`, *Application Performance*.

External modules avoid loading the modules of our application using the `<script>` and use a module loader instead. A **module loader** is a tool that allows us to have better control over the module loading process. This allows us to perform tasks such as loading files asynchronously or combining multiple modules into a single highly optimized file.

Several module definition syntaxes have been proposed over the years by different open source projects due to the lack of native support for external modules in JavaScript:

Module definition syntax	Notes
AMD	Introduced by the RequireJS module loader
CommonJS	Introduced by Node.js
UMD	Supports both AMD and UMD
SystemJS	Introduced by Angular 2, supports multiple syntaxes
ES6 modules	Introduced by the ECMAScript 6 specification

We can also encounter a wide variety of module loaders:

Module loader	Module definition syntax	Notes
RequireJS	AMD	RequireJS was the very first mainstream module loader for JavaScript applications
Browserify	CommonJS	CommonJS modules were introduced by the original Node.js module system, but today Node.js supports ES6 modules natively
SystemJS	Supports multiple module definition syntaxes	Supports multiple module definition syntaxes
Native	ES6	Modern JavaScript engines can support ES6 modules natively

External modules at design time and runtime

TypeScript adds a layer of choice, because it allows us to choose which module definition syntax we want to use at design time and which one we want to use at runtime. In a landscape with so many options, it is very easy to feel overwhelmed and confused.

Fortunately, only two module definition syntaxes are available at design time in TypeScript, and one of them is considered deprecated:

- The legacy external module syntax (deprecated)
- The ES6 module syntax (recommended)

> It is also possible to use other module definition syntaxes at runtime, such as the AMD or the UMD syntaxes, but the TypeScript compiler will not try to compile them into the selected module definition output.

Working with Dependencies

TypeScript allows us to choose which kind of module definition syntax will be used at runtime:

- ES6
- CommonJS
- AMD
- SystemJS
- UMD

We can indicate our preference by using the `--module` flag when compiling, as follows:

```
tsc --module commonjs main.ts    // use CommonJS
tsc --module amd main.ts         // use AMD
tsc --module umd main.ts         // use UMD
tsc --module system main.ts      // use SytemJS
```

It is important to understand that the kind of module definition syntax used at design time and the one used at runtime can be different.

Since the release of TypeScript 1.5, it has been recommended to use the ECMAScript 6 module definition syntax, because it is based on the ECMAScript specification, which is considered a standard. Additionally, if we are planning to run our TypeScript application in a modern JavaScript engine, we will be able to use the ECMAScript 6 module definition syntax at both design time and runtime.

We will now look at each of the available module definition syntaxes.

ES6 modules (runtime and design time)

TypeScript 1.5 introduced support for the ES6 module syntax. The following code snippet defines an external module using the ES6 module syntax:

```
class UserModel {
  // ...
}
export { UserModel };
```

We don't need to use the `namespace` keyword to declare an ES6 module, but we must use the `export` keyword. We can use the `export` keyword at the bottom of the module or when an entity is declared:

```
export class TalkModel {
  // ...
}
```

We can also export an entity using an alias:

```
class UserModel {
  // ...
}
export { UserModel as User }; // UserModel exported as User
```

An export declaration exports all meanings of a name:

```
interface UserModel {
  // ...
}

class UserModel {
  // ...
}
export { UserModel }; // Exports both interface and function
```

To import a module from another module, we must use the `import` keyword as follows:

```
import { UserModel } from "./models";
```

The `import` keyword creates a variable for each imported component. In the preceding code snippet, a new variable named `UserModel` is declared, and its value contains a reference to the `UserModel` class, which is declared and exported by the imported module (the `model.ts` file).

We can use the `export` keyword to export multiple entities, as follows:

```
class UserValidator {
  // ...
}

class TalkValidator {
  // ...
}

export { UserValidator, TalkValidator };
```

Working with Dependencies

Furthermore, we can use the `import` keyword to import multiple entities from a single module, as follows:

```
import { UserValidator, TalkValidator } from "./validation.ts"
```

Finally, we can also use the `default` keyword to declare the default entity to be imported when no explicit entities are imported:

```
export default UserValidator;
```

We can then import the default export as follows:

```
import UserValidator from "./validation.ts"
```

> ES6 modules work natively on modern JavaScript engines, but if you are targeting a JavaScript engine that doesn't support ES6 modules, you will need to use a tool such as webpack to enable backward compatibility with previous JavaScript engines.

Legacy external modules (design time only)

Before TypeScript 1.5, external modules were declared using a specific design-time syntax. However, once compiled into JavaScript, modules were transformed into AMD, CommonJS, UMD, or SystemJS modules.

We should **try to avoid using the legacy external module syntax and use the new ES6 syntax instead**. However, we will take a quick look at the external module syntax, because it is still possible to face it sometimes in old applications and documentation.

To export a module using the legacy external module syntax, we need to use the `export` keyword. We can apply the `export` keyword directly to a class or interface as follows:

```
export class User {
  // ...
}
```

We can also use the `export` keyword on its own by assigning to it the value that we desire to export:

```
class User {
  // ...
}
export = User;
```

External modules can be compiled into any of the available module definition syntaxes (AMD, CommonJS, SystemJS, or UMD).

The legacy external module syntax `import` statements look as follows:

```
import User = require("./user_class");
```

AMD modules (runtime only)

If we compile the external module that we defined in the ES6 modules section into an AMD module (using the flag `--compile amd`), we will generate the following AMD module:

```
define(["require", "exports"], function (require, exports) {
    var UserModel = (function () {
        function UserModel() {
        }
        return UserModel;
    })();
    return UserModel;
});
```

The `define` function takes an array as its first argument. This array contains a list of the names of the module dependencies. The second argument is a callback that will be invoked once all the module dependencies have been loaded. The callback takes each of the module dependencies as its parameters and contains all the logic from our TypeScript component. Notice how the return type of the callback matches the components that we declared as public by using the `export` keyword.

TypeScript will throw a compilation error because the `define` function is not declared. We can solve this problem by installing the RequireJS type definitions:

npm install --save @types/requirejs

The AMD module can then be loaded using the RequireJS module loader as follows:

```
require(["./models"], function(models) {
    const user = new models.UserModel();
});
```

As we can observe, AMD modules use two different functions to define modules (`define`) and consume modules (`require`). Usually, the application entry point uses the require function to load all the required dependencies.

[179]

Working with Dependencies

> We will not discuss AMD and RequireJS further in this book, but if you want to learn more about it, you can do so by visiting http://requirejs.org/docs/start.html.

CommonJS modules (runtime only)

If we compile the external module that we defined in the ES6 modules section into an CommonJS module (using the flag `--compile commonjs`), we will obtain the following CommonJS module:

```
var UserModel = (function () {
    function UserModel() {
      //...
    }
    return UserModel;
})();
module.exports = UserModel;
```

As we can see in the preceding code snippet, the CommonJS module definition syntax is almost identical to that of the legacy external module syntax. The main difference is the usage of the `module` object and its `exports` property instead of the `exports` keyword.

The preceding CommonJS module can be loaded natively by a Node.js application using the `import` keyword and the `require` function:

```
import UserModel = require('./UserModel');
const user = new UserModel();
```

However, if we attempt to use the `require` function in a web browser, an exception will be thrown because the `require` function is undefined. We can easily solve this problem by using Browserify. Browserify is a module loader that allows us to use CommonJS modules in a web browser.

> If you need more information about Browserify, visit the official documentation at https://github.com/substack/node-browserify#usage.

[180]

UMD modules (runtime only)

If we want to release a JavaScript library or framework, we will need to compile our TypeScript application into both CommonJS and AMD modules, as well as compile in a way that it can be used by developers who don't want to use a module loader.

The web development community has developed the following code snippet to help us to achieve UMD support:

```
(function (root, factory) {
  if (typeof exports === 'object') {
    // CommonJS
    module.exports = factory(require('b'));
  } else if (typeof define === 'function' && define.amd) {
    // AMD
    define(['b'], function (b) {
      return (root.returnExportsGlobal = factory(b));
    });
  } else {
    // Global Variables
    root.returnExportsGlobal = factory(root.b);
  }
}(this, function (b) {
  // Your actual module
  return {};
}));
```

The preceding code snippet is great, but we want to avoid manually adding it to every single module in our application. Fortunately, there are a few options available to achieve UMD support with ease.

The first option is to use the flag `--compile umd` to generate one UMD module for each module in our application. The second option is to create one single UMD module that will contain all the modules in the application using a module loader such as Browserify.

> Refer to the official Browserify project website at http://browserify.org/ to learn more about Browserify. Refer to the `Browserify-standalone` option to learn more about the generation of one unique optimized file.

Working with Dependencies

SystemJS modules (runtime only)

While UMD gives you a way to output a single module that works in both AMD and CommonJS, SystemJS will allow you to use ES6 modules closer to their native semantics without requiring an ES6-compatible browser engine.

SystemJS was introduced by Angular 2.0, which is a popular web application development framework.

> Refer to the official SystemJS project website at `https://github.com/systemjs/systemjs` to learn more about SystemJS.
>
> There is a free list of common module mistakes available online at `http://www.typescriptlang.org/Handbook#modules-pitfalls-of-modules`.

Modules summary

We can summarize all the preceding details using the following comparison table:

Module syntax	Design-time support	Module loader runtime support	Native runtime support	Optimization tool support	Recommended
Legacy internal modules	Yes	No	Yes (via closures)	No	No
Namespaces	Yes	No	Yes (via closures)	No	No
ES6	**Yes**	**Yes**	**Yes**	**Yes**	**Yes**
Legacy external modules	Yes	Yes	No	Yes	No
AMD	No	Yes	No	Yes	No
CommonJS	No	Yes	No	Yes	No
UMD	No	Yes	No	Yes	No
SystemJS	No	Yes	No	Yes	No

As we can see, **the recommended solution going forward is the usage of ES6 modules**. If you are targeting a JavaScript engine that doesn't support ES6 modules, you will need to use a tool such as webpack to enable backward compatibility with previous JavaScript engines.

> We will learn more about Webpack in `Chapter 9`, *Automating Your Development Workflow*.

Managing dependencies in OOP

We have learned how to work with application dependencies and third-party dependencies. We will now learn about the dependency inversion and extend what we learned in the previous chapter about the dependency inversion principle.

Dependency injection versus dependency inversion

Many articles use the terms *dependency injection* and *dependency inversion* as if their meanings were identical, but they are two very different concepts.

The following example declares a class named `Ninja` and a class named `Katana`. The `Ninja` class has a dependency on the class `Katana`:

```
class Katana {
    public tryHit(fromDistance: number) {
        return fromDistance <= 2;
    }
}

class Ninja {
    public constructor(
        private _katana: Katana
    ) {}
    public fight(fromDistance: number) {
        return this._katana.tryHit(fromDistance);
    }
}
```

Working with Dependencies

After declaring the preceding classes, we can inject an instance of `Katana` into the `Ninja` class:

```
const ninja = new Ninja(new Katana());
ninja.fight(2); // true
ninja.fight(5); // false
```

The preceding code snippet implements the dependency injection design pattern because we are injecting a dependency (`Katana`) into the `Ninja` class. However, we are not implementing the dependency inversion principle because the `Ninja` class has a direct dependency on the `Katana` class.

The relationship between the `Ninja` class and the `Katana` class can be represented using the following diagram:

Ninja → Katana

The following code snippet declares an interface named `Weapon`, which is then implemented by the `Katana` class. This time, the `Ninja` class has a dependency on the `Weapon` interface instead of the `Katana` class:

```
interface Weapon {
    try Hit(fromDistance: number): boolean;
}

class Katana implements Weapon {
    public tryHit(fromDistance: number) {
        return fromDistance <= 2;
    }
}

class Ninja {
    public constructor(
        private _weapon: Weapon
    ) {}
    public fight(fromDistance: number) {
        return this._weapon.tryHit(fromDistance);
    }
}
```

After declaring the preceding classes, we can inject an instance of Katana into the Ninja class:

```
const ninja = new Ninja(new Katana());
ninja.fight(2); // true
ninja.fight(5); // false
```

The preceding code snippet implements the dependency injection design pattern because we are injecting a dependency (Katana) into the Ninja class. It also implements the dependency inversion principle because the Ninja class does not have a direct dependency on the Katana class.

This time, the relationship between the classes can be represented using the following:

Ninja → Weapon ← Katana

As we can see, the arrow that represents the relationship between the Ninja and the Katana classes has been inverted. This explains the name of the dependency inversion principle.

The dependency inversion principle is important because it makes our code easier to maintain by reducing the level of coupling between the entities in our application. For example, if we rename the Katana class, we will not need to change the Ninja class. This means that the Katana and the Ninja classes are fully independent of each other.

Inversion of control containers

An **inversion of control** (**IoC**) container is a kind of tool that acts as a *smart factory*. An IoC container can be used to create instances of a class. If the class has some dependencies, the IoC container will be able to use dependency injection to cover the need for them. We say that the factory is *smart* because it can create dependencies based on matching conditions in the execution context and it can also control the life cycle of the instances that it creates.

When we use an IoC container, we are *losing control* of the creation of class instances, and the injection of dependencies and the IoC container will take control of these aspects of our application. This fact should explain the meaning of the term *inversion of control*.

InversifyJS basics

InversifyJS is an IoC container for TypeScript applications. InversifyJS can be used to implement the dependency inversion principle.

To use InversifyJS, we need to install it using npm as follows:

```
npm install inversify reflect-metadata --save
```

We can then import some of the entities declared by `inversify` and `reflect-metadata` as follows:

```
import { Container, inject, injectable } from "inversify";
import "reflect-metadata";
```

The following code snippet adds an annotation to the `Ninja` class using the `inject` decorator:

```
interface Weapon {
    tryHit(fromDistance: number): boolean;
}

@injectable()
class Katana implements Weapon {
    public tryHit(fromDistance: number) {
        return fromDistance <= 2;
    }
}

@injectable()
class Ninja {
    public constructor(
        @inject("Weapon") private _weapon: Weapon
    ) {}
    public fight(fromDistance: number) {
        return this._weapon.tryHit(fromDistance);
    }
}
```

To create an instance of `Ninja` using InversifyJS, we need to create an instance of the `Container` class and declare what is known as **type binding**. A type binding is a link between a type and an implementation of that type. The following code snippet declares two type bindings. The first type binding links the type `Weapon` with the implementation `Katana`. The second type binding links the type `Ninja` to itself:

```
const container = new Container();
container.bind<Weapon>("Weapon").to(Katana);
container.bind<Ninja>("Ninja").to(Ninja);
```

We can then create instances of the `Ninja` class using the container. The container uses the annotation to identify that the `Ninja` class has a dependency on the `Weapon` type. The container then creates an instance of the `Katana` class and is injected into the `Ninja` class because it knows that the `Katana` class is a valid implementation of the `Weapon` interface:

```
const ninja = container.get<Ninja>("Ninja");
ninja.fight(2); // true
ninja.fight(5); // false
```

InversifyJS also allows us to control the life cycle of the dependencies. For example, we can configure the `Katana` type binding to make all instances a single shared instance (singleton):

```
container.bind<Weapon>("Weapon").to(Katana).inSingletonScope();
```

We can also configure complex runtime constraints, which will determine how dependencies are resolved. For example, we could have two implementations of `Weapon` that are injected in different circumstances:

```
container.bind<Weapon>("Weapon").to(Katana)
        .whenInjectedInto(Samurai);

container.bind<Weapon>("Weapon").to(Shuriken)
        .whenInjectedInto(Ninja);
```

Circular dependencies

A circular dependency is an issue that we can encounter when working with multiple components and dependencies. Sometimes it is possible to reach a point in which one component (A) has a dependency on a second component (B), which depends on the first component (A). In the following diagram, each node is a component, and we can observe that the nodes **circular1.ts** and **circular2.ts** (in red) have a circular dependency. The nodes without dependencies are displayed in green, and those with dependencies but no issues are displayed in blue:

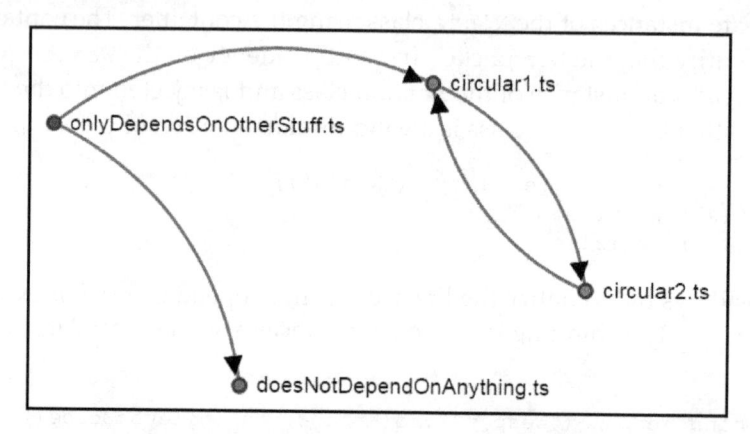

The circular dependencies don't necessarily need to involve just two components. We can encounter scenarios in which a component depends on another component, which depends on other components, and some of the components in the dependency tree end up pointing to one of their parent components in the tree. InversifyJS will throw a runtime exception if a circular dependency is detected.

Summary

In this chapter, we learned the basics about managing third-party dependencies. We also learned the differences between internal and external modules, and each of the main kinds of modules in each of these categories.

We also learned how to work with dependencies in object-oriented programming. Finally, we learned how to implement dependency injection and how to work with IoC containers.

In the next chapter, we will learn about the TypeScript/JavaScript runtime.

6
Understanding the Runtime

After reading this book, you will probably be eager to start a new project to put into practice everything that you have learned so far. At this point, you should be able to write a small web application using TypeScript and resolve the potential design-time issues that you might encounter.

However, as your new project grows, and you develop more complex features, you might encounter some runtime issues. This chapter should provide you with the missing knowledge that will help you to resolve runtime issues.

We have only briefly mentioned the TypeScript runtime in the preceding chapters, but depending on your background, you may already know a lot about it, because the TypeScript runtime is the JavaScript runtime.

TypeScript is only used at design time; the TypeScript code is then compiled into JavaScript and finally executed at runtime. The JavaScript runtime oversees the execution of the JavaScript code. It is important to understand that we will never execute TypeScript code and we will always execute JavaScript code; for this reason, when we refer to the TypeScript runtime, we will, in fact, be talking about the JavaScript runtime.

When we compile our TypeScript code, we will generate JavaScript code, which will be executed on the server side or the client side. It is then that we may encounter some challenging runtime issues.

In this chapter, we will cover the following topics:

- The execution environment
- The event loop
- The `this` operator
- Prototypes
- Closures

Let's start by learning about the execution environment.

The execution environment

The execution environment is one of the first things that we must think about before we can start developing a TypeScript application. Once we have compiled our TypeScript code into JavaScript, it can be executed in many different environments. While most of those environments will be part of a web browser such as Chrome, Internet Explorer, or Firefox, we might also want to be able to run our code on the server side or in a desktop application in environments such as Node.js, RingoJS, or Electron.

It is important to keep in mind that there are some variables and objects available at runtime that are environment-specific. For example, we could create a library and access the `document.layers` variable. While `document` is part of the W3C **Document Object Model** (**DOM**) standard, the layers property is only available in Internet Explorer and is not part of the W3C DOM standard.

The W3C defines the DOM as follows:

> "The Document Object Model is a platform- and language-neutral interface that will allow programs and scripts to dynamically access and update the content, structure, and style of documents. The document can be further processed, and the results of that processing can be incorporated back into the presented page".

Similarly, we can also access a set of objects known as the **Browser Object Model** (**BOM**) from a web browser runtime environment. The BOM consists of the objects `navigator`, `history`, `screen`, `location`, and `document`, which are properties of the `window` object.

We need to keep in mind that the DOM is only available in web browsers. If we want to run our application in a web browser, we will be able to access the DOM and BOM. However, in environments such as Node.js or RingoJS, these APIs will not be available since they are standalone JavaScript environments completely independent of a web browser. We can also find other objects in the server-side environments (such as `process.stdin` in Node.js) that will not be available if we attempt to execute our code in a web browser.

We also need to keep in mind the existence of multiple versions of these JavaScript environments. In some cases, we will have to support multiple browsers and multiple versions of Node.js. The recommended practice when dealing with this problem is to add conditional statements that check for the availability of features rather than the availability of an environment or version.

> A really good library is available that can help us to implement feature detection when developing for web browsers. The library is called **Modernizr** and can be downloaded at `http://modernizr.com/`.

Understanding the event loop

The TypeScript runtime (JavaScript) has a concurrency model based on an **event loop**. This model is quite different from the model in other languages, such as C or Java. Before we focus on the event loop itself, we must understand some runtime concepts.

What follows is a visual representation of some important runtime concepts: heap, stack, queue, and frame:

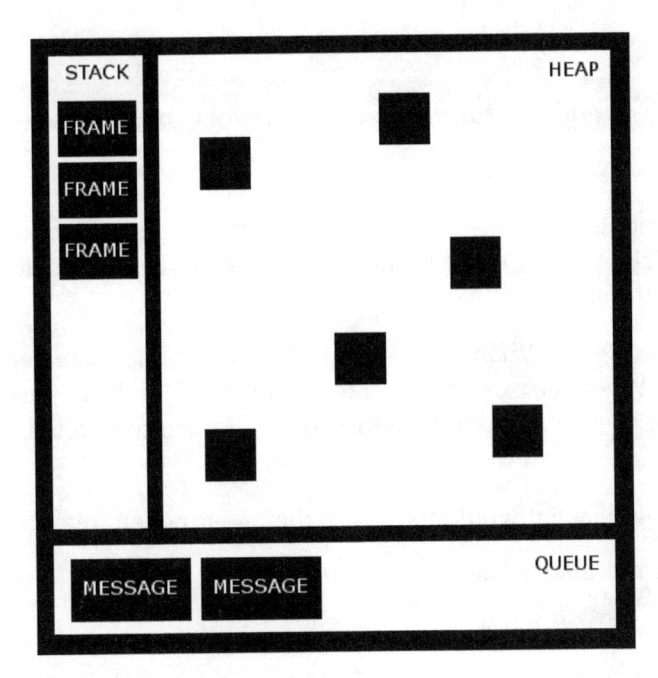

We will now look at the role of each of these concepts.

Frames

A frame is a sequential unit of work. In the preceding diagram, the frames are represented by the blocks inside the stack.

When a function is invoked in JavaScript, the runtime creates a frame in the stack. The frame holds that function's arguments and local variables. When the function returns, the frame is removed from the stack. Let's look at an example:

```
function foo(a: number): number {
    const value = 12;
    return value + a;
}

function bar(b: number): number {
    const value = 4;
    return foo(value * b);
}
```

After declaring the `foo` and `bar` functions, we will invoke the `bar` function:

```
bar(21);
```

When `bar` is executed, the runtime will create a new frame containing the arguments of `bar` and all its local variables (value). The frame (represented as blocks inside the stack) is then added to the top of the stack.

Internally, `bar` invokes `foo`. When `foo` is invoked, a new frame is created and allocated to the top of the stack. When the execution of `foo` is finished (`foo` has returned), the top frame is removed from the stack. When the execution of `bar` is also completed, it is removed from the stack as well.

Now, let's try to imagine what would happen if the `foo` function invoked the `bar` function:

```
function foo(a: number): number {
    const value = 12;
    return bar(value + a);
}

function bar(b: number): number {
    const value = 4;
    return foo(value * b);
}
```

We would create a never-ending function call loop. With each function call, a new frame would be added to the stack, and eventually there would be no more space in the stack, and an error would be thrown. Most software engineers are familiar with this error, known as a *stack overflow* error.

Stack

The stack contains sequential steps (frames). A stack is a data structure that represents a simple **last-in-first-out** (**LIFO**) collection of objects. Therefore, when a frame is added to the stack, it is always added to the top of the stack.

Since the stack is a LIFO collection, the event loop processes the frames stored in it from top to bottom. The dependencies of a frame are added to the top of it in the stack to ensure that all the dependencies of each of the frames are met.

Queue

The queue contains a list of messages waiting to be processed. Each message is associated with a function. When the stack is empty, a message is taken out of the queue and processed. The processing consists of calling the associated function and adding the frames to the stack. The message processing ends when the stack becomes empty again.

In the previous runtime diagram, the blocks inside the queue represent the messages.

Heap

The heap is a memory container that is not aware of the order of the items stored in it. The heap contains all the variables and objects currently in use. It may also contain frames that are currently out of scope but have not yet been removed from memory by the garbage collector.

The event loop

Concurrency is the ability for two or more operations to be executed simultaneously. The runtime execution takes place on one single thread, which means that we cannot achieve real concurrency.

Understanding the Runtime

The event loop follows a run-to-completion approach, which means that it will process a message from beginning to end before any other message is processed.

Every time a function is invoked, a new message is added to the queue. If the stack is empty, the function is processed (the frames are added to the stack).

When all the frames have been added to the stack, the stack is cleared from top to bottom. At the end of the process, the stack is empty, and the next message is processed.

> Web workers can perform background tasks in a different thread. They use a separated queue, heap, and stack.

One of the advantages of the `event loop` is that the execution order is quite predictable and easy to follow. Another important advantage of the `event loop` approach is that it features non-blocking I/O. This means that when the application is waiting for an input and output (I/O) operation to finish, it can still process other things, such as user input.

A disadvantage of this approach is that, if a message (function) takes too long to complete, the application becomes unresponsive. A good practice to follow is to make message processing short and, if possible, split one message into several messages.

The this operator

In JavaScript, the `this` operator behaves a little differently compared to other languages. The value of the `this` operator is often determined by the way a function is invoked. Its value cannot be set by assignment during execution, and it may be different each time a function is invoked.

> The `this` operator also has some differences when using the strict mode and non-strict mode. To learn more about the strict mode, refer to `https://developer.mozilla.org/en-US/docs/Web/JavaScript/Reference/Strict_mode`.

The this operator in the global context

In the global context, the `this` operator will always point to the global object. In a web browser, the `window` object is the global object:

```
console.log(this === window); // true
this.a = 37;
console.log(window.a); // 37
console.log(window.document === this.document); // true
console.log(this.document === document); // true
console.log(window.document === document); // true
```

> The preceding example is a JavaScript example, not a TypeScript example.

The this operator in a function context

The value of `this` inside a function depends on how the function is invoked. If we simply invoke a function in non-strict mode, the value of `this` within the function will point to the global object as follows:

```
function f1() {
  return this;
}
f1() === window; // true
```

> All examples in this sub section (that is, the `this` operator in a function context) are JavaScript examples, not TypeScript examples.

However, if we invoke a function in strict mode, the value of `this` within the function's body will point to `undefined` as follows:

```
console.log(this); // global (window)

function f2() {
  "use strict";
  return this; // undefined
}

console.log(f2()); // undefined
```

Understanding the Runtime

```
console.log(this); // window
```

> ECMAScript 5's strict mode is a way to opt in to a restricted variant of JavaScript. You can learn more about the strict mode at `https://developer.mozilla.org/en-US/docs/Web/JavaScript/Reference/Strict_mode`.

However, the value of the `this` operator inside a function invoked as an instance method points to the instance. In other words, the value of the `this` operator within a function that is part of a class points to that class:

```
const person = {
  age: 37,
  getAge: function() {
    return this.age; // this points to the instance (person)
  }
};
console.log(person.getAge()); // 37
```

In the preceding example, we have used object literal notation to define an object named p, but the same applies when declaring objects using prototypes:

```
function Person() {}
Person.prototype.age = 37;
Person.prototype.getAge = function () {
  return this.age;
}
const person = new Person();
person.age;      // 37
person.getAge(); // 37
```

When a function is used as a constructor (with the `new` keyword), the `this` operator points to the object being constructed:

```
function Person() { // function used as a constructor
  this.age = 37;
}
const person = new Person();
console.log(person.age); // logs 37
```

The call, apply, and bind methods

All functions inherit the `call`, `apply`, and `bind` methods from `Function.prototype`. We can use these methods to set the value of `this`.

The `call` and `apply` methods are almost identical; both methods allow us to invoke a function and set the value of the `this` operator within the function. The main difference between `call` and `apply` is that, while `apply` lets us invoke the function with arguments as an array, `call` requires the function parameters to be listed explicitly.

> A useful mnemonic is *A (apply) for an array and C (call) for a comma.*

Let's look at an example. We will start by declaring a class named `Person`. This class has two properties (`name` and `surname`) and one method (`greet`). The `greet` method uses the `this` operator to access the `name` and `surname` instance properties:

```
class Person {

  public name: string;
  public surname: string;
  public constructor(name: string, surname: string) {
    this.name = name;
    this.surname = surname;
  }

  public greet(city: string, country: string) {
    // we use the "this" operator to access name and surname
    let msg = `Hi, my name is ${this.name} ${this.surname}.`;
    msg += `I'm from ${city} (${country}).`;
    console.log(msg);
  }

}
```

After declaring the `Person` class, we will create an instance:

```
const person = new Person("remo", "Jansen");
```

If we invoke the `greet` method, it will work as expected:

```
person.greet("Seville", "Spain");
```

Alternatively, we can invoke the method using the `call` and `apply` functions. We have supplied the `person` object as the first parameter of both functions because we want the `this` operator (inside the `greet` method) to take person as its value:

```
person.greet.call(person, "Seville", "Spain");
person.greet.apply(person, ["Seville", "Spain"]);
```

Understanding the Runtime

If we provide a different value to be used as the value of `this`, we will not be able to access the `name` and `surname` properties within the `greet` function:

```
person.greet.call(null, "Seville", "Spain");
person.greet.apply(null, ["Seville", "Spain"]);
```

The two preceding examples may seem useless, because the first one invoked the function directly and the second one caused unexpected behavior. The `apply` and `call` methods make sense only when we want the `this` operator to take a different value when a function is invoked:

```
const valueOfThis = { name : "Anakin", surname : "Skywalker" };
person.greet.call(valueOfThis, "Mos espa", "Tatooine");
person.greet.apply(valueOfThis, ["Mos espa", "Tatooine"]);
```

The `bind` method can be used to set the value of the `this` operator (within a function), regardless of how it is invoked.

When we invoke a function's `bind` method, it returns a new function with the same body and scope as the original function, but the `this` operator (within the body function) is permanently bound to the first argument of `bind`, regardless of how the function is being used.

Let's look at an example. We will start by creating an instance of the `Person` class that we declared in the previous example:

```
const person = new Person("Remo", "Jansen");
```

Then, we can use bind to set the `greet` function to be a new function with the same scope and body:

```
const greet = person.greet.bind(person);
```

If we try to invoke the `greet` function using `bind` and `apply`, just like we did in the previous example, we will be able to observe that, this time, the `this` operator will always point to the object instance regardless of how the function is invoked:

```
greet.call(person, "Seville", "Spain");
greet.apply(person, ["Seville", "Spain"]);
// Hi, my name is Remo Jansen. I'm from Seville Spain.

greet.call(null, "Seville", "Spain");
greet.apply(null, ["Seville", "Spain"]);
// Hi, my name is Remo Jansen. I'm from Seville Spain.
```

```
const valueOfThis = { name: "Anakin", surname: "Skywalker" };
greet.call(valueOfThis, "Mos espa", "Tatooine");
greet.apply(valueOfThis, ["Mos espa", "Tatooine"]);
// Hi, my name is Remo Jansen. I'm from Mos espa Tatooine.
```

Once we bind an object to a function with `bind`, we cannot override it:

```
const valueOfThis = { name: "Anakin", surname: "Skywalker" };
const greet = person.greet.bind(valueOfThis);
greet.call(valueOfThis, "Mos espa", "Tatooine");
greet.apply(valueOfThis, ["Mos espa", "Tatooine"]);
// Hi, my name is Remo Jansen. I'm from Mos espa Tatooine.
```

> Using the `bind`, `apply`, and `call` methods is often discouraged because it can lead to confusion. Modifying the default behavior of the `this` operator can lead to unexpected results. Remember to use these methods only when strictly necessary and to document your code properly to reduce the risk caused by potential maintainability issues.

Prototypes

When we compile a TypeScript program, all classes and objects become JavaScript objects. However, sometimes we may encounter an unexpected behavior at runtime, even if the compilation was completed without errors. To be able to identify and understand the cause of this behavior, we need a good understanding of the JavaScript runtime. One of the main concepts that we need to understand is how inheritance works at runtime.

The runtime inheritance system uses a prototypal inheritance model. In a prototypal inheritance model, objects inherit from objects, and there are no classes available. However, we can use prototypes to simulate classes. Let's see how it works.

At runtime, every JavaScript object has an internal property called prototype. The value of the prototype attribute is an object, which contains some attributes (data) and methods (behavior).

Understanding the Runtime

In TypeScript, we can use a class-based inheritance system:

```
class Person {

    public name: string;
    public surname: string;
    public age: number = 0;

    public constructor(name: string, surname: string) {
        this.name = name;
        this.surname = surname;
    }

    public greet() {
        let msg = `Hi! my name is ${this.name} ${this.surname}`;
        msg += `I'm ${this.age}`;
    }

}
```

We have defined a class named `Person`. At runtime, this class is declared using prototypes instead of classes:

```
var Person = (function() {
    function Person(name, surname) {
        this.age = 0;
        this.name = name;
        this.surname = surname;
    }
    Person.prototype.greet = function() {
        let msg = "Hi! my name is " + this.name +
                  " " + this.surname;
        msg += "I'm " + this.age;
    };
    return Person;
})();
```

The preceding code is emitted by TypeScript when we target ES5. The `class` keyword is supported by ES6 at runtime, but it is syntactic sugar. In computer science, syntactic sugar is syntax within a programming language that is designed to make things easier to read or to express. This means that the `class` keyword is just a helper to make our lives as software engineers easier and, internally, prototypes are always used.

Chapter 6

The TypeScript compiler wraps the object definition (we will not refer to it as a class definition because, technically, it is not a class) with an **immediately invoked function expression** (**IIFE**). Inside the IIFE, we can find a function named `Person`. If we examine the function and compare it with the TypeScript class, we will notice that it takes the same parameters that the class constructor takes in the TypeScript class. This function is used to create new instances of the `Person` class.

After the constructor, we can see the definition of the `greet` method. As we can see, the `prototype` attribute is used to attach the `greet` method to the `Person` class.

Instance properties versus class properties

Because JavaScript is a dynamic programming language, we can add properties and methods to an instance of an object at runtime, and they don't need to be part of the object (class) itself. Let's look at an example:

```
function Person(name, surname) {
      // instance properties
      this.name = name;
      this.surname = surname;
}
const person = new Person("Remo", "Jansen");
person.age = 27;
```

We have defined a constructor function for an object named `person`, which takes two variables (`name` and `surname`) as arguments. Then, we have created an instance of the `Person` object and added a new property named `age` to it. We can use a `for...in` statement to check the properties of `person` at runtime:

```
for(let property in person) {
   console.log("property: " + property + ", value: '" +
   person[property] + "'");
}
// property: name, value: 'remo'
// property: surname, value: 'jansen'
// property: age, value: 27
// property: greet, value: 'function (city, country) {
//       let msg = "Hi, my name is " + this.name + " " +
 //this.surname;
//       msg += "nI'm from " + city + " " + country;
//       console.log(msg);
//    }'
```

[201]

Understanding the Runtime

All these properties are **instance properties** because they hold a value for each new instance. If, for example, we create a new instance of `Person`, both instances will hold their own values:

```
let person2 = new Person("John", "Wick");
person2.name; // "John"
person1.name; // "Remo"
```

We have defined these instance properties using the `this` operator, because when a function is used as a constructor (with the `new` keyword), the `this` operator is bound to the new object being constructed.

This also explains why we can alternatively define instance properties through the object's prototype:

```
Person.prototype.name = name;    // instance property
Person.prototype.name = surname; // instance property
```

We can also declare class-level properties and methods (also known as static properties). The main difference is that the values of class properties and methods are shared between all instances of an object.

Class properties are often used to store static values:

```
function MathHelper() {
  /* ... */
}

// class property
MathHelper.PI = 3.14159265359;
```

Class methods are also often used as utility functions that perform calculations upon supplied parameters and return a result:

```
function MathHelper() { /* ... */ }

// class property
MathHelper.PI = 3.14159265359;

// class method
MathHelper.areaOfCircle = function(radius) {
   return radius * radius * MathHelper.PI;
}
```

In the preceding example, we have accessed a class attribute (`PI`) from a class method (`areaOfCircle`). We can access class properties from instance methods, but we cannot access instance properties or methods from class properties or methods. We can demonstrate this by declaring `PI` as an instance property instead of a class property:

```
function MathHelper() {
  // instance property
  this.PI = 3.14159265359;
}
```

If we then attempt to access `PI` from a class method, it will be undefined:

```
// class method
MathHelper.areaOfCircle = function(radius) {
   return radius * radius * this.PI;  // this.PI is undefined
}

MathHelper.areaOfCircle(5); // NaN
```

We are not supposed to access class methods or properties from instance methods, but there is a way to do it. We can achieve it by using the prototype's constructor property as demonstrated in the following example:

```
function MathHelper () { /* ... */ }

// class property
MathHelper.PI = 3.14159265359;

// instance method
MathHelper.prototype.areaOfCircle = function(radius) {
    return radius * radius * this.constructor.PI;
}

const math = new MathHelper ();
console.log(MathHelper.areaOfCircle(5)); // 78.53981633975
```

We can access the `PI` class property from the `areaOfCircle` instance method using the prototype's constructor property, because this property returns a reference to the object's constructor.

Inside `areaOfCircle`, the `this` operator returns a reference to the object's prototype:

```
this === MathHelper.prototype
```

Understanding the Runtime

The value of `this.constructor` is equal to `MathHelper.prototype.constructor` and, therefore, `MathHelper.prototype.constructor` is equal to `MathHelper`.

Prototypal inheritance

We might be wondering how the `extends` keyword works. Let's create a new TypeScript class, which inherits from the `Person` class, to understand it:

```
class SuperHero extends Person {
    public superpower: string;
    public constructor(
        name: string,
        surname: string,
        superpower: string
    ) {
        super(name, surname);
        this.superpower = superpower;
    }
    public userSuperPower() {
        return `I'm using my ${this.superpower}`;
    }
}
```

The preceding class is named `SuperHero` and extends the `Person` class. It has one extra attribute (`superpower`) and method (`useSuperPower`). If we compile the code, we will notice the following piece of code:

```
var __extends = this.__extends || function (d, b) {
    for (var p in b) if (b.hasOwnProperty(p)) d[p] = b[p];
    function __() { this.constructor = d; }
    __.prototype = b.prototype;
    d.prototype = new __();
};
```

> Please note that the preceding code snippet is slightly more complicated in TypeScript 2.8. We will use the code from the previous versions here because it contains fewer conditions and is easier to understand.

This piece of code is generated by TypeScript. Even though it is a small piece of code, it showcases almost every concept contained in this chapter, and understanding it can be quite challenging.

Before the function expression is evaluated for the first time, the `this` operator points to the global object, which does not contain a method named __extends. This means that the __extends variable is undefined.

When the function expression is evaluated for the first time, the value of the function expression (an anonymous function) is assigned to the __extends property in the global scope.

TypeScript generates the function expression one time for each TypeScript file containing the `extends` keyword. However, the function expression is only evaluated once (when the __extends variable is undefined). This behavior is implemented by the conditional statement in the first line:

```
var __extends = this.__extends || function (d, b) { // ...
```

The first time this line of code is executed, the function expression is evaluated. The value of the function expression is an anonymous function, which is assigned to the __extends variable in the global scope. Because we are in the global scope, `var __extends` and `this.__extends` refer to the same variable at this point.

When a new file is executed, the __extends variable is already available in the global scope, and the function expression is not evaluated. This means that the value of the function expression is only assigned to the __extends variable once, even if the snippet is executed multiple times.

Let's focus now on the __extends variable (the anonymous function):

```
function (d, b) {
    for (var p in b) if (b.hasOwnProperty(p)) d[p] = b[p];
    function __() { this.constructor = d; }
    __.prototype = b.prototype;
    d.prototype = new __();
}
```

This function takes two arguments, named d and b. When we invoke it, we should pass a derived object constructor (d) and a base object constructor (b).

The first line inside the anonymous function iterates each class property and method from the base class and creates their copy in the derived class:

```
for (var p in b) if (b.hasOwnProperty(p)) d[p] = b[p];
```

Understanding the Runtime

> When we use a `for...in` statement to iterate an instance of an object to a, it will iterate the object's instance properties. However, if we use a `for...in` statement to iterate the properties of an object's constructor, the statement will iterate its class properties. In the preceding example, the `for...in` statement is used to inherit the object's class properties and methods. To inherit the instance properties, we will copy the object's prototype.

The second line declares a new constructor function named __, and inside it, the `this` operator is used to access its prototype:

```
function __() { this.constructor = d; }
```

The prototype contains a special property named `constructor`, which returns a reference to the object's constructor. The function named __ and `this.constructor` are pointing to the same variable at this point. The value of the derived object constructor (d) is then assigned to the __ constructor.

In the third line, the value of the prototype object from the base object constructor is assigned to the prototype of the __ object constructor:

```
__.prototype = b.prototype;
```

In the last line, `new __()` is invoked, and the result is assigned to the derived class (d) prototype. By performing all these steps, we can invoke the following:

```
var instance = new d();
```

Upon doing so, we will get an object that contains all the properties from both the derived class (d) and the base class (b). Furthermore, any instance objects constructed by the derived constructor (d) will be instances of the derived class while inheriting both the class and instance properties and methods from the base class (b).

We can see the function in action by examining the runtime code that defines the `SuperHero` class:

```
var SuperHero = (function (_super) {
    __extends(SuperHero, _super);
    function SuperHero(name, surname, superpower) {
        _super.call(this, name, surname);
        this.superpower = superpower;
    }
    SuperHero.prototype.userSuperPower = function () {
        return "I'm using my " + superpower;
```

[206]

```
    };
    return SuperHero;
})(Person);
```

We can see an IIFE here again. This time, the IIFE takes the `Person` object constructor as the argument. Inside the function, we will refer to this argument using the name `_super`. Inside the IIFE, the `__extends` function is invoked and the `SuperHero` (derived class) and `_super` (base class) arguments are passed to it.

In the next line, we can find the declaration of the `SuperHero` object constructor and the `useSuperPower` function. We can use `SuperHero` as an argument of `__extend` before it is declared because function declarations are hoisted to the top of the scope.

> Function expressions are not hoisted. When we assign a function to a variable in a function expression, the variable is hoisted, but its value (the function itself) is not hoisted.

Inside the `SuperHero` constructor, the base class (`Person`) constructor is invoked using the `call` method:

```
_super.call(this, name, surname);
```

As we discovered previously in this chapter, we can use `call` to set the value of the `this` operator in a function context. In this case, we are passing the `this` operator, which points to the instance of `SuperHero` being created:

```
function Person(name, surname) {
    // this points to the instance of SuperHero being created
    this.name = name;
    this.surname = surname;
}
```

The prototype chain and property shadowing

When we try to access a property or a method of an object, the runtime will search for that property or method in the object's properties and methods. If it is not found, the runtime will continue searching through the object's inherited properties by navigating the entire inheritance tree. Because a derived object is linked to its base object through the `prototype` property, we refer to this inheritance tree as **the prototype chain**.

Understanding the Runtime

Let's look at an example. We will declare two simple TypeScript classes named `Base` and `Derived`:

```
class Base {
    public method1() { return 1; }
    public method2() { return 2; }
}

class Derived extends Base {
    public method2() { return 3; }
    public method3() { return 4; }
}
```

Now we will examine the JavaScript code generated by TypeScript:

```
var Base = (function () {
    function Base() {
    }
    Base.prototype.method1 = function () { return 1; };
    Base.prototype.method2 = function () { return 2; };
    return Base;
})();
var Derived = (function (_super) {
    __extends(Derived, _super);
    function Derived() {
        _super.apply(this, arguments);
    }
    Derived.prototype.method2 = function () { return 3; };
    Derived.prototype.method3 = function () { return 4; };
    return Derived;
})(Base);
```

We can then create an instance of the `Derived` class:

```
var derived = new Derived();
```

If we try to access the method named `method1`, the runtime will find it in the instance's properties:

```
console.log(derived.method1); // 1
```

The instance also has an own property named `method2` (with value 2), but there is also an inherited property named `method2` (with value 3). The object's property (`method2` with value 3) prevents the access to the `prototype` property (`method2` with value 2). This is known as **property shadowing**:

```
console.log(derived.method2); // 3
```

The instance does not have an own property named `method3`, but it has a property named `method3` in its prototype:

```
console.log(derived.method3); // 4
```

Neither the instance nor the objects in the prototype chain (the `Base` class) have a property named `method4`:

```
console.log(derived.method4); // error
```

Accessing the prototype of an object

Prototypes can be accessed in three different ways:

- `Person.prototype`
- `Object.getPrototypeOf(person)`
- `person.__proto__`

> The use of `__proto__` is controversial and has been discouraged by many experienced software engineers. It was never originally included in the ECMAScript language specification, but modern browsers decided to implement it anyway. Today, the `__proto__` property has been standardized in the ECMAScript 6 language specification and will be supported in the future, but it is still a slow operation that should be avoided if performance is a concern.

Understanding the Runtime

The new operator

We can use the `new` operator to generate an instance of `Person`:

```
const person = new Person("remote", "Jansen");
```

When we use the new operator, the runtime creates a new object that inherits from the `Person` class prototype.

Closures

Closures are one of the most powerful features available at runtime, but they are also one of the most misunderstood. The Mozilla developer network defines closures as follows:

> *"Closures are functions that refer to independent (free) variables. In other words, the function defined in the closure 'remembers' the environment in which it was created".*

We understand independent (free) variables as variables that persist beyond the lexical scope from which they were created. Let's look at an example:

```
function makeArmy() {
    const shooters = [];
    for (let i = 0; i < 10; i++) {
        const shooter = () => { // a shooter is a function
            console.log(i); // which should display it's number
        };
        shooters.push(shooter);
    }
    return shooters;
}
```

> The preceding example is a JavaScript example, not a TypeScript example.

We have declared a function named `makeArmy`. Inside the function, we have created an array of functions named `shooters`. Each function in the `shooters` array will display a number, the value of which was set from the variable `i` inside a `for` statement. We will now invoke the `makeArmy` function:

```
const army = makeArmy();
```

Chapter 6

The variable `army` should now contain the array of the function's `shooters`. However, we will notice a problem if we execute the following piece of code:

```
army[0](); // 10 (expected 0)
army[5](); // 10 (expected 5)
```

The preceding code snippet does not work as expected because we made one of the most common mistakes related to closures. When we declared the `shooter` function inside the `makeArmy` function, we created a closure without being aware of it.

The reason for this is that the functions assigned to `shooter` are closures; they consist of the function definition and the captured environment from the `makeArmy` function's scope. We have created ten closures, but all of them the same environment. By the time the `shooter` functions are executed, the loop has run its course, and the `i` variable (shared by all the closures) has been left pointing to the last entry (`10`).

One solution, in this case, is to use more closures:

```
function makeArmy() {
    const shooters = [];
    for (let i = 0; i < 10; i++) {
        ((index: number) => {
            const shooter = () => {
                console.log(index);
            };
            shooters.push(shooter);
        })(i);
    }
    return shooters;
}

const army = makeArmy();
army[0](); // 0
army[5](); // 5
```

> The preceding example is a TypeScript example, not a JavaScript example.

This works as expected. Rather than the shooter functions sharing a single environment, the immediately invoked function creates a new environment for each one in which `i` refers to the corresponding value.

[211]

Understanding the Runtime

Static variables powered by closures

In the previous section, we learned that when a variable in a closure context is shared between multiple instances of a class, the variable behaves like a static variable.

We will now see how we can create variables and methods that behave like a static variables. Let's start by declaring a TypeScript class named `Counter`:

```
class Counter {
    private static _COUNTER = 0;
    public increment() {
        this._changeBy(1);
    }
    public decrement() {
        this._changeBy(-1);
    }
    public value() {
        return Counter._COUNTER;
    }
    private _changeBy(val: number) {
        Counter._COUNTER += val;
    }
}
```

> The preceding example is a TypeScript example, not a JavaScript example.

The preceding class contains a static member named `_COUNTER`. The TypeScript compiler transforms it into the resultant code:

```
var Counter = (function () {
    function Counter() {
    }
    Counter.prototype._changeBy = function (val) {
        Counter._COUNTER += val;
    };
    Counter.prototype.increment = function () {
        this._changeBy(1);
    };
    Counter.prototype.decrement = function () {
        this._changeBy(-1);
    };
    Counter.prototype.value = function () {
        return Counter._COUNTER;
```

```
    };
    Counter._COUNTER = 0;
    return Counter;
})();
```

> The preceding example is a JavaScript example, not a TypeScript example.

As we can observe, the static variable is declared by the TypeScript compiler as a class property (as opposed to an `instance` property). The compiler uses a class property because class properties are shared across all instances of a class. The problem is that the private variable is not private at runtime.

Alternatively, we could write some JavaScript (remember that all valid JavaScript is valid TypeScript) code to emulate static properties at runtime using closures:

```
var Counter = (function() {

    // closure context
    let _COUNTER = 0;

    function changeBy(val) {
        _COUNTER += val;
    }
    function Counter() {};
    // closure functions
    Counter.prototype.increment = function() {
      changeBy(1);
    };
    Counter.prototype.decrement = function() {
      changeBy(-1);
    };
    Counter.prototype.value = function() {
      return _COUNTER;
    };
    return Counter;
})();
```

> The preceding example is a JavaScript example, not a TypeScript example.

Understanding the Runtime

The preceding code snippet declares a class named `Counter`. The class has some methods used to increment, decrement, and read the variable named `_COUNTER`. The `_COUNTER` variable itself is not part of the object prototype.

All the instances of the `Counter` class will share the same context, which means that the context (the variable `counter` and the function `changeBy`) will behave as a singleton.

> The singleton pattern requires an object to be declared as a static variable to avoid the need to create its instance whenever it is required. The object instance is, therefore, shared by all the components in the application. The singleton pattern is frequently used in scenarios where it is not beneficial, introducing unnecessary restrictions in situations where a unique instance of a class is not required and introduces global state into an application.

Now we know how to use closures to emulate static variables:

```
let counter1 = new Counter();
let counter2 = new Counter();
console.log(counter1.value()); // 0
console.log(counter2.value()); // 0
counter1.increment();
counter1.increment();
console.log(counter1.value()); // 2
console.log(counter2.value()); // 2 (expected 0)
counter1.decrement();
console.log(counter1.value()); // 1
console.log(counter2.value()); // 1 (expected 0)
```

Private members powered by closures

In the previous section, we learned that closures can access variables that persist beyond the lexical scope from which they were created. These variables are not part of the function prototype or body, but they are part of the function context.

Because there is no way we can directly invoke the function context, the context variables and methods can be used to emulate private members at runtime. The main advantage of using closures to emulate private members (instead of the TypeScript private access modifier) is that closures will prevent access to private members at runtime.

Chapter 6

TypeScript avoids emulating private properties at runtime because the compiler will throw an error at compilation time if we attempt to access a private member. TypeScript avoids the use of closures to emulate private members to improve the application performance. If we add or remove an access modifier to or from one of our classes, the resultant JavaScript code will not change at all. This means that the private members of a class (at design time) become public members at runtime.

However, it is possible to use closures to emulate private properties at runtime. Let's look at an example:

```
function makeCounter() {

    // closure context
    let _COUNTER = 0;

    function changeBy(val: number) {
        _COUNTER += val;
    }

    class Counter {
        public increment() {
            changeBy(1);
        }
        public decrement() {
            changeBy(-1);
        }
        public value() {
            return _COUNTER;
        }
    }
}
```

> The preceding example is a TypeScript example, not a JavaScript example.

The preceding class is almost identical to the class that we previously declared to demonstrate how to emulate static variables at runtime using closures.

Understanding the Runtime

This time, a new closure context is created every time we invoke the `makeCounter` function, so each new instance of `Counter` will remember an independent context (`counter` and `changeBy`):

```
let counter1 = makeCounter();
let counter2 = makeCounter();
console.log(counter1.value()); // 0
console.log(counter2.value()); // 0
counter1.increment();
counter1.increment();
console.log(counter1.value()); // 2
console.log(counter2.value()); // 0 (expected 0)
counter1.decrement();
console.log(counter1.value()); // 1
console.log(counter2.value()); // 0 (expected 0)
```

Since the context cannot be accessed directly, we can say that the variable `counter` and the `changeBy` function are private members:

```
console.log(counter1.counter); // undefined
counter1.changeBy(2); // changeBy is not a function
console.log(counter1.value()); // 1
```

Summary

In this chapter, we have acquired a better understanding of the runtime, which allows us not only to resolve runtime issues with ease but also to be able to write better TypeScript code. A deep understanding of closures and prototypes will allow us to develop some complex features that would have not been possible to develop without this knowledge.

In the next chapter, we will learn about the **functional programming** (**FP**) paradigm.

7
Functional Programming with TypeScript

JavaScript has been a multi-paradigm programming language since its inception back in 1995. It allows us to take advantage of an object-oriented programming style, but it also allows us to take advantage of a **functional programming** (**FP**) style. The same can be said about TypeScript. However, TypeScript is even better suited to FP than JavaScript because, as we will learn in this chapter, static type systems and type inference are very important in FP languages, such as the ML family of programming languages.

The JavaScript and TypeScript ecosystems have experienced a significant increase in interest in FP over the last 3 or 4 years. I believe that the cause of this increase in interest is the success of React. React is a library used to build user interfaces developed by Facebook, which is highly influenced by some core FP concepts.

We will learn more about React toward the end of this book, but, for now, we will focus on learning how to use some basic FP techniques with TypeScript on its own and with some small FP libraries such as `Immutable.js` and `Ramda`.

In this chapter, you will learn about the following:

- Pure functions
- Side effects
- Immutability
- Function arity
- Higher-order functions
- Function composition
- Function partial application
- Currying and Pointfree style
- Pipes and sequences
- Category theory

FP concepts

FP receives its name from the way we build applications when we use it as our preferred programming paradigm.

In a programming paradigm such as object-oriented programming, the main building blocks that we use to create an application are objects (objects are declared using classes). However, in FP we use functions as the main building block in our applications.

Each new programming paradigm introduces a series of concepts and ideas associated with it. Some of these concepts are universal and are also of interest while learning a different programming paradigm. In object-oriented programming, we have concepts such as inheritance, encapsulation, and polymorphism. In FP we have concepts such as higher-order functions, function partial application, immutability, and referential transparency. We will try to learn about some of these concepts in this chapter.

Michael Feathers, the author of the SOLID acronym and many other well-known software engineering principles, once wrote:

> "Object-oriented programming makes code understandable by encapsulating moving parts. Functional Programming makes code understandable by minimizing moving parts."

The preceding quote mentions *moving parts*; we should understand these moving parts as state changes (also known as state mutations). In object-oriented programming, we use encapsulation to prevent objects from being aware of the state mutations of other objects. In FP we try to avoid dealing with a mutable state instead of encapsulating it. FP reduces the number of places in which state changes take place within an application and tries to move these places into the boundaries of the application to try to keep application's core stateless.

A mutable state is bad because it makes the behavior of our code harder to predict. Take, for example, the following function:

```
function isIndexPage() {
    return window.location.pathname === "/";
}
```

The preceding code snippet declared a function named `isIndexPage`. This function can be used to check whether the current page is the root page in a web application based on the current path.

The path is some data that changes all the time, so we can consider it a piece of state. If we try to predict the result of invoking the `isIndexPage`, we will need to know the current state. The problem is that we could wrongly assume that the state has not changed since the last known state. We can solve this problem by transforming the function into a pure function, as we will learn in the following section.

Pure functions

FP introduces some concepts and principles that will help us to improve the predictability of our code. Let's look at one of these core concepts: **pure functions**.

A function can be considered pure when it returns a value computed using only the arguments passed to it. Also, a pure function avoids mutating its arguments or any other external variables. As a result, a pure function always returns the same value given the same arguments, independently of when it is invoked.

The `isIndexPage` function declared in the preceding section is not a pure function because it accesses the `pathname` variable and it has not been passed as an argument to the function. We can transform the preceding function into a pure function by rewriting it as follows:

```
function isIndexPage(pathname: string) {
    return pathname === "/";
}
```

Even though this is a basic example, we can easily perceive that the newer version is much easier to predict. Pure functions help us to make our code easier to understand, maintain, and test.

Imagine that we wanted to write a unit test for the impure version of the `isIndexPage` function. We would encounter some problems when trying to test because the function uses the `window.location` object. We could overcome this issue using a mocking framework, but it would add a lot of complexity to our unit tests just because we didn't use a pure function.

On the other hand, testing the pure version of the `isIndexPage` function would be straightforward:

```
function shouldReturnTrueWhenPathIsIndex() {
    let expected = true;
    let result = isIndexPage("/");
    if (expected !== result) {
        throw new Error(`Expected ${expected} to equals ${result}`);
    }
}

function shouldReturnFalseWhenPathIsNotIndex() {
    let expected = false;
    let result = isIndexPage("/someotherpage");
    if (expected !== result) {
        throw new Error(`Expected ${expected} to equals ${result}`);
    }
}
```

Now that we understand how FP helps us to write better code by avoiding state mutations, we can learn about side effects and referential transparency.

Side effects

In the preceding section, we learned that a pure function returns a value that can be computed using only the arguments passed to it. A pure function also avoids mutating its arguments or any other external variable that is not passed to the function as an argument. In FP terminology, it is common to say that a pure function is a function that has no side effects. This means that when we invoke a pure function, we can expect that the function is not going to interfere (via a state mutation) with any other component in our application.

Some programming languages, such as Haskell, can ensure that an application is free of side effects using its type system. TypeScript has fantastic interoperability with JavaScript, but the downside of this, compared to a more isolated language such as Haskell, is that the type system is not able to guarantee that our application is free of side effects.

> If you like the idea of your JavaScript applications being free of side effects, you can try open source projects such as https://github.com/bodil/eslint-config-cleanjs. The project is an ESLint configuration that aims to restrict you to a subset of JavaScript that is as close to an idealized pure functional language as possible. Unfortunately, at the time of writing, there were no similar tools available that were specifically designed for TypeScript.

Referential transparency

Referential transparency is another concept closely related to pure functions and side effects. A function is pure when it is free of side effects. An expression is said to be referentially transparent when it can be replaced with its corresponding value without changing the application's behavior.

A pure function is a referentially transparent expression. An expression that is not referentially transparent is known as referentially opaque.

Immutability

Immutability refers to the inability to change the value of a variable after a value has been assigned to it. Purely FP languages include immutable implementations of common data structures. For example, when we add an element to an array, we are mutating the original array. However, if we use an immutable array, and we try to add a new element to it, the original array will not be mutated, and we will add the new item to a copy of it.

In JavaScript and TypeScript, we can use the `Immutable.js` library to enjoy immutable data structures.

Functions as first-class citizens

It is common to find mentions of functions as *first-class citizens* in FP literature. We say that a function is a *"first-class citizen"* when it can do everything that a variable can do. This means that functions can be passed to other functions as an argument or to be returned by another function. Functions can also be assigned to variables. Both JavaScript and TypeScript treat functions as *"first-class citizens"*.

Lambda expressions

Lambda expressions are just expressions that can be used to declare anonymous functions (functions without a name). Before the ES6 specification, the only way to assign a function as a value to a variable was using a function expression:

```
const log = function(arg: any) { console.log(arg); };
```

Functional Programming with TypeScript

The ES6 specification introduced the arrow function syntax:

```
const log = (arg: any) => console.log(arg);
```

> Please refer to Chapter 3, *Working with Functions,* and Chapter 6, *Understanding the Runtime,* to learn more about arrow functions and function expressions.

Function arity

The arity of a function is the number of arguments that the function takes. A unary function is a function that only takes one argument:

```
function isNull<T>(a: T|null) {
    return (a === null);
}
```

Unary functions are very important in FP because they facilitate the usage of the function composition pattern.

> We will learn more about the function composition pattern later in this chapter.

A **binary function** is a function that takes two arguments:

```
function add(a: number, b: number) {
    return a + b;
}
```

Functions with two or more arguments are also important because some of the most common FP patterns and techniques (for example, partial application and currying) have been designed to transform functions that allow multiple arguments into unary functions.

> We will learn more about partial application and currying later in this chapter.

There are also functions with three (**ternary function**) or more arguments. However, functions that accept a variable number of arguments, known as **variadic functions**, are particularly interesting in FP:

```
function addMany(...numbers: number[]) {
    numbers.reduce((p, c) => p + c, 0);
}
```

Higher-order functions

A higher-order function is a function that does at least one of the following:

- Takes one or more functions as arguments
- Returns a function as its result

Higher-order functions are one of the most powerful tools that we can use to write JavaScript in an FP style. Let's see some examples.

The following code snippet declares a function named `addDelay`. The function creates a new function that waits a given number of microseconds before printing a message in the console. The function is considered a higher-order function because it takes a function as one of its arguments:

```
function addDelay(msg: string, ms: number) {
    return () => {
        setTimeout(() => {
            console.log(msg);
        }, ms);
    };
}

const delayedSayHello = addDelay("Hello world!", 500);
delayedSayHello(); // Prints "Hello world!" (after 500 ms)
```

The following code snippet declares a function named `addDelay`. The function adds a delay in microseconds to the execution of another function that is passed as an argument. The function is considered a higher-order function because it returns a function:

```
function addDelay(func: () => void, ms: number) {
    setTimeout(() => {
        func();
    }, ms);
}
```

Functional Programming with TypeScript

```
function sayHello() {
    console.log("Hello world!");
}

addDelay(sayHello, 500); // Prints "Hello world!" (after 500 ms)
```

The following code snippet declares a function named `addDelay`. The function creates a new function that adds a delay in microseconds to the execution of another function that is passed as an argument. The function is considered a higher-order function because it takes a function as an argument and returns a function:

```
function addDelay(func: () => void, ms: number) {
    return () => {
        setTimeout(() => {
            func();
        }, ms);
    };
}

function sayHello() {
    console.log("Hello world!");
}

const delayedSayHello = addDelay(sayHello, 500);
delayedSayHello(); // Prints "Hello world!" (after 500 ms)
```

Higher-order functions are an effective technique to abstract a solution for a common problem. The preceding example demonstrates how we can use a higher-order function (`addDelay`) to add a delay to another function (`sayHello`). This allows us to abstract the delay functionality and keep the `sayHello` function or other functions agnostic of the implementation details of the delay functionality.

The benefits of FP

Writing TypeScript code using an FP style has many benefits, among which we can highlight the following:

- **Testable code**: If we try to write our functions pure functions, we will be able to write unit tests extremely easily.
- **Code is easy to reason about**: FP can seem hard to understand for developers with a lack of experience in FP. However, when an application is implemented correctly using the FP paradigm, the results are very small functions (often one-line functions) and very declarative APIs that can be reasoned about with ease.

- **Concurrency**: Most of our functions are stateless, and our entities are mostly stateless. We push state out of the core of our application, which makes our applications much more likely to be able to support many concurrent operations and be more scalable.
- **Caching**: Strategies for caching results become much simpler when we can predict the output of a function given its arguments.

Is TypeScript a FP language?

The answer to this question is yes, but only partially. TypeScript is a multi-paradigm programming language and, as a result, it includes many influences from both object-oriented programming languages and FP languages.

However, if we focus on TypeScript as an FP language, we can observe that it is not a purely FP language because, for example, the TypeScript compiler doesn't enforce our code to be free of side effects.

Not being a purely FP language should not be interpreted as something negative. TypeScript provides us with an extensive set of features and allows us to take advantage of some of the best features of both the world of object-oriented programming languages and the world of FP languages.

FP techniques

Now that we have learned about the most common FP concepts, it is time to learn about the most common FP techniques and patterns.

Composition

Functional composition is a technique or pattern that allows us to combine multiple functions to create a more complex function.

The following code snippet declares a function used to trim a string and a function used to transform a piece of text in uppercase text:

```
const trim = (s: string) => s.trim();
const capitalize = (s: string) => s.toUpperCase();
```

Functional Programming with TypeScript

We can create a function that performs both the preceding operations by composing them:

```
const trimAndCapitalize = (s: string) => capitalize(trim(s));
```

The variable `trimAndCapitalize` is a function that invokes the `trim` function using `s` as its argument and passes its return to the `capitalize` function. We can invoke the `trimAndCapitalize` function as follows:

```
trimAndCapitalize("   hello world   "); // "HELLO WORLD"
```

The composition of two functions `f(x)` and `g(x)` is defined as `f(g(x))`, and that is exactly what we have done in the `trimAndCapitalize` function. However, such a behavior can be abstracted using a higher-order function:

```
const compose = <T>(f: (x: T) => T, g: (x: T) => T) => (x: T) => f(g(x));
```

We can then use the preceding function to compose two given functions:

```
const trimAndCapitalize = compose(trim, capitalize);
```

We can invoke the `trimAndCapitalize` function as follows:

```
trimAndCapitalize("   hello world   "); // "HELLO WORLD"
```

One important thing to note is that the result of the `g` function is passed as the argument of the `f` function. This means that `f` can only take one argument (it must be a unary function), and its type must match the return type of the `g` function. A more correct definition of the `compose` function would be something like the following:

```
const compose = <T1, T2, T3>(
    f: (x: T2) => T3,
    g: (x: T1) => T2
) => (x: T1) => f(g(x));
```

We can also compose `composed` functions:

```
const composed1 = compose(func1, func2);
const composed2 = compose(func1, func2);
const composed3 = compose(composed1, composed2);
```

Alternatively, we can declare a higher-order function to compose three functions in one call:

```
const compose3 = <T1, T2, T3, T4>(
    f: (x: T3) => T4,
    g: (x: T2) => T3,
    h: (x: T1) => T2
) => (x: T1) => f(g(h(x)));
```

We can also create a helper that allows us to compose an unlimited number of functions:

```
const compose = (...functions: Array<(arg: any) => any>) =>
    (arg: any) =>
        functions.reduce((prev, curr) => {
            return curr(prev);
        }, arg);
```

Functional composition is an extremely powerful technique, but it can be hard to put into practice in certain scenarios, for example, when our functions are not unary functions. However, there are other techniques that can help in those scenarios.

> Please note that the entire example is included in the companion source code.

Partial application

Partial application is an FP technique that allows us to pass the arguments required by a function at different points in time.

This technique can feel like a weird idea at first glance because most software engineers are used to the idea of applying (also known as invoking) a function at one unique point in time (complete application), as opposed to applying a function at multiple points in time (partial application).

The following code snippet implements a function that doesn't support partial application and invokes it (providing all the required arguments) at one single point in time:

```
function add(a: number, b: number) {
    return a + b;
}

const result = add(5, 5); // All arguments are provided at the same time
console.log(result); // 10
```

Functional Programming with TypeScript

The following code snippet implements the preceding function as a higher-order function to allow us to provide the required arguments at different points in time:

```
function add(a: number) {
    return (b: number) => {
        return a + b;
    };
}
const add5 = add(5); // The 1st argument is provided
const result = add5(5); // The 2nd argument is provided later
console.log(result); // 10
```

As we can see in the preceding code snippet, the first and the second arguments are provided at a different point in time. However, it cannot be considered an example of function partial application because the two functions are unary functions, and we have provided one argument at a time.

We can also write a function that allows both its complete and partial application:

```
function add(a: number, b?: number) {
    if (b !== undefined) {
        return a + b;
    } else {
        return (b2: number) => {
            return a + b2;
        };
    }
}

const result1 = add(5, 5); // All arguments are
console.log(result1); // 10

const add5 = add(5) as (b: number) => number; // The 1st passed
const result2 = add5(5); // The 2nd argument is passed later
console.log(result2); // 10
```

The preceding example can be considered an example of partial application because we can apply the function with all its arguments (complete application) or some of them (partial application).

Now that we know how function partial application works, let's focus on why it is useful. In the preceding *Composition* section, we learned how to compose two functions named `trim` and `capitalize` into a third function named `trimAndCapitalize`:

```
const trim = (s: string) => s.trim();
const capitalize = (s: string) => s.toUpperCase();
const trimAndCapitalize = compose(trim, capitalize);
```

Function composition works very well with unary functions but not so well with binary or ternary functions. We are going to declare the following function to demonstrate this:

```
const replace = (s: string, f: string, r: string) => s.split(f).join(r);
```

The preceding function can be used to replace a substring in given string. Unfortunately, the function cannot be used with compose with ease because it is not a unary function:

```
const trimCapitalizeAndReplace = compose(trimAndCapitalize, replace); // Error
```

However, we can implement the function in a way that allows us to apply the function partially:

```
const replace = (f: string, r: string) =>
(s: string) =>
s.split(f).join(r);
```

We can then use the compose function without problems:

```
const trimCapitalizeAndReplace = compose(
    trimAndCapitalize,
    replace("/", "-")
);
trimCapitalizeAndReplace(" 13/feb/1989 "); <// "13-FEB-1989"
```

Thanks to our knowledge of function partial application, we can use compose with ease, without having to worry about the arity of the functions. However, enabling partial application requires a significant amount of manual boilerplate. In the next section, we will learn how an FP technique known as currying can help us to solve this problem.

> Please note that the entire example is included in the companion source code.

Currying

Currying is an FP technique that allows us to use partial application without having to worry about partial application while we write our functions. Currying is the process of taking a function that takes multiple arguments and transforming it into a chain of unary functions:

```
function curry2<T1, T2, T3>(fn: (a: T1, b: T2) => T3) {
    return (a: T1) => (b: T2) => fn(a, b);
}
```

The preceding function is a higher-order function that allows us to abstract our functions from the partial application functionality:

```
function add(a: number, b: number) {
    return a + b;
}

const curriedAdd = curry2(add);
const add5 = curriedAdd(5);
const addResult = add5(5);
console.log(addResult); // 10
```

The `curry2` function allows us to transform a binary function into two unary functions. The `curry2` function is a higher-order function and can be used with any binary function. For example, in the preceding code snippet, we passed the add function to the `curry2` function, but the following example passes the multiply function to the `curry2` function instead:

```
function multiply(a: number, b: number) {
    return a * b;
}

const curriedMultiply = curry2(multiply);
const multiplyBy5 = curriedMultiply(5);
const multiplyResult = multiplyBy5(5);
console.log(multiplyResult); // 25
```

In the preceding *Partial application* section, we learned how to use partial application to use compose with functions that are not unary. We declared the following function named `replace` and then passed it to the `compose` function:

```
const replace = (f: string, r: string) =>
    (s: string) =>
        s.split(f).join(r);

const trimCapitalizeAndReplace = compose(
```

```
        trimAndCapitalize,
        replace("/", "-")
);
```

We can declare a function named `curry3` that transforms a ternary function into a chain of three unary functions:

```
function curry3<T1, T2, T3, T4>(fn: (a: T1, b: T2, c: T3) => T4) {
    return (a: T1) => (b: T2) => (c: T3) => fn(a, b, c);
}
```

We can then use the `curry3` function to rewrite the `replace` function in a way that is agnostic of the function partial application implementation details:

```
const replace = (s: string, f: string, r: string) =>
    s.split(f).join(r);

const curriedReplace = curry3(replace);

const trimCapitalizeAndReplace = compose(
    trimAndCapitalize,
    curriedReplace("/")("-")
);
```

> Please note that the entire example is included in the companion source code.

Pipes

A pipe is a function or operator that allows us to pass the output of a function as the input of another. JavaScript and TypeScript don't support piles natively (as an operator), but we can implement our pipes using the following function:

```
const pipe = <T>(...fns: Array<(arg: T) => T>) =>
    (value: T) => fns.reduce((acc, fn) => fn(acc), value);
```

We are going to use the `curry3`, `trim`, `capitalize`, and `replace` functions that we declared previously in this chapter:

```
const trim = (s: string) => s.trim();
const capitalize = (s: string) => s.toUpperCase();

const replace = curry3(
```

```
        (s: string, f: string, r: string) => s.split(f).join(r)
);
```

We can then use the pipe function to declare a new function:

```
const trimCapitalizeAndReplace = pipe(
    trim,
    capitalize,
    replace("/")("-")
);
trimCapitalizeAndReplace("   13/feb/1989   "); // "13-FEB-1989"
```

The `pipe` function ensures that the output of the `trim` function is passed to the `capitalize` function. The return of the `capitalize` function is then passed to the `replace` function, which has been already partially applied.

There is an official proposal to add a new operator to JavaScript known as the pipeline operator (`|>`). This operator will allow us to implement a pipe as follows:

```
const result = "   13/feb/1989   "
    |> trim
    |> capitalize
    |> replace("/")("-");
```

> Please refer to the pipeline operator proposal: https://github.com/tc39/proposal-pipeline-operator. Please note that the entire example is included in the companion source code.

Pointfree style

Tacit programming, also known as **pointfree style**, is a programming style in which function declarations do not declare the arguments (or *points*) on which they operate.

The following code snippet declares a few functions that are used to determine whether a person is eligible to vote in elections:

```
interface Person {
    age: number;
    birthCountry: string;
    naturalizationDate: Date;
}

const OUR_COUNTRY = "Ireland";
```

```
const wasBornInCountry = (person: Person) =>
    person.birthCountry === OUR_COUNTRY;

const wasNaturalized = (person: Person) =>
    Boolean(person.naturalizationDate);

const isOver18 = (person: Person) =>
    person.age >= 18;

const isCitizen = (person: Person) =>
    wasBornInCountry(person) || wasNaturalized(person);

const isEligibleToVote = (person: Person) =>
    isOver18(person) && isCitizen(person);

isEligibleToVote({
    age: 27,
    birthCountry: "Ireland",
    naturalizationDate: new Date(),
});
```

The preceding code snippet didn't use any of the FP techniques that we have already learned in this chapter. The following code snippet implements an alternative solution for the same problem, using techniques such as partial application. This code snippet declares two functions named `both` and `either` that can be used to determine whether a variable matches the requirements specified by some or both functions, provided to these functions:

```
const either = <T1>(
    funcA: (a: T1) => boolean,
    funcB: (a: T1) => boolean
) => (arg: T1) => funcA(arg) || funcB(arg);

const both = <T1>(
    funcA: (a: T1) => boolean,
    funcB: (a: T1) => boolean
) => (arg: T1) => funcA(arg) && funcB(arg);

interface Person {
    age: number;
    birthCountry: string;
    naturalizationDate: Date;
}

const OUR_COUNTRY = "Ireland";

const wasBornInCountry = (person: Person) =>
    person.birthCountry === OUR_COUNTRY;
```

Functional Programming with TypeScript

```
const wasNaturalized = (person: Person) =>
    Boolean(person.naturalizationDate);

const isOver18 = (person: Person) =>
    person.age >= 18;

// Pointfree style
const isCitizen = either(wasBornInCountry, wasNaturalized);
const isEligibleToVote = both(isOver18, isCitizen);

isEligibleToVote({
    age: 27,
    birthCountry: "Ireland",
    naturalizationDate: new Date(),
});
```

As we can see, the functions `isCitizen` and `isEligibleToVote` take some functions as arguments, but they don't mention which data they expect as arguments. For example, we could write the following:

```
const isCitizen = (person: Person) =>
    wasBornInCountry(person) || wasNaturalized(person);
```

However, we could write the following instead:

```
const isEligibleToVote = both(isOver18, isCitizen);
```

This style, in which we avoid referencing the function arguments, is known as pointfree style, and it has some advantages over more conventional function declaration styles:

- It makes programs simpler and more concise. This isn't always a good thing, but it can be.
- It makes algorithms easier to understand by focusing only on the functions being combined; we get a better sense of what's going on without the data arguments getting in the way.
- It forces us to think more about the how the data is used than about which data is being used.
- It helps us think about our functions as generic building blocks that can work with different kinds of data, rather than thinking about them as operations on a kind of data.

> Please note that the entire example is included in the companion source code.

Recursion

A function that calls itself is known as a **recursive function**. The following function is a recursive function that allows us to calculate the factorial of a given number n. The factorial is the product of all positive integers less than or equal to n:

```
const factorial = (n: number): number =>
(n === 0) ? 1 : (n * factorial(n - 1));
```

We can invoke the preceding function as follows:

```
factorial(5); // 120
```

Category theory

FP has a reputation for being difficult to learn and understand because of its mathematical background. FP languages and design patterns are influenced by concepts that originated in many different mathematical fields. However, we can highlight **category theory** as one of the most significant fields of influence. We can think about category theory as an alternative to set theory, which defines the theory behind a series of data structures or objects known as **algebraic data types**.

There are many algebraic data types, and understanding all their properties and rules that they must implement requires a significant amount of time and effort. The following diagram illustrates the relationships between some of the most common algebraic data types:

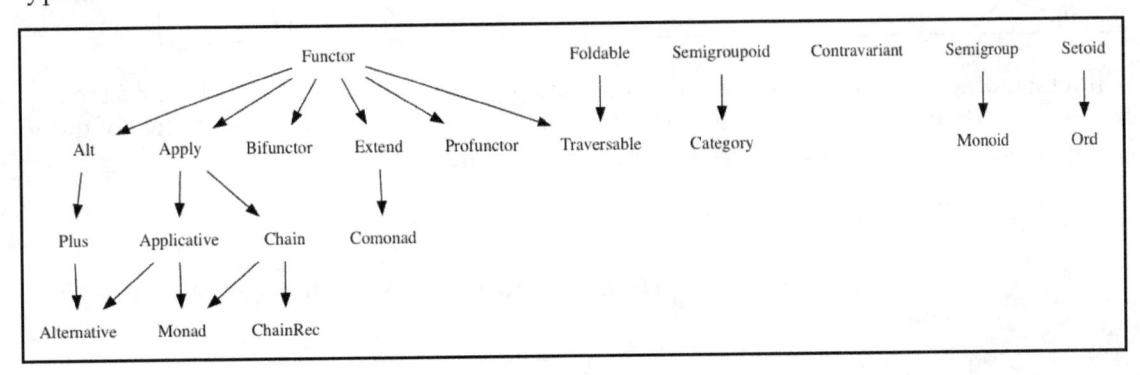

The arrows in the diagram indicate that a given algebraic data type must implement the specification of some other algebraic data types. For example, the `Monad` type must implement the specifications of the `Applicative` and `Chain` types.

The open source project `fantasy - land` declares a specification for some of these algebraic data types, while the open source project `ramda - fantasy` implements the specifications in a way that is compatible with `Ramda`, which is a popular FP library that we will explore later in this chapter.

The algebraic data type specifications can be implemented in many ways. For example, the fnctor specification can be implemented by a `Maybe` or an `Either` data type. Both types implement the `Functor` specification but can also implement other specifications, such as the monad or the applicative specification.

The following table describes which specifications (listed in the top row) are implemented by one of the algebraic data type implementations (left row) in the `ramda - fantasy` project:

Name	Setoid	Semigroup	Functor	Applicative	Monad	Foldable	ChainRec
Either	✓	✗	✓	✓	✓	✗	✓
Future	✗	✗	✓	✓	✓	✗	✓
Identity	✓	✗	✓	✓	✓	✗	✓
IO	✗	✗	✓	✓	✓	✗	✓
Maybe	✓	✓	✓	✓	✓	✓	✓
Reader	✗	✗	✓	✓	✓	✗	✗
Tuple	✓	✓	✓	✗	✗	✗	✗
State	✗	✗	✓	✓	✓	✗	✓

Understanding category theory and all these data types and specifications is beyond the scope of this book. However, in this chapter, we are going to learn the basics of two of the most common algebraic data types: the `Functor` and the `Monad`.

> Please refer to the `fantasy - land` project at `https://github.com/fantasyland/fantasy-land` and the `ramda - fantasy` project at `https://github.com/ramda/ramda-fantasy` to learn more about algebraic data types.

Functor

A `Functor` is an object that holds a value and implements a method named `map`. The following code snippet declares a class named `Container`. This class can be considered a `Functor`:

```
class Container<T> {
    private _value: T;
    public constructor(val: T) {
        this._value = val;
    }
    public map<TMap>(fn: (val: T) => TMap) {
        return new Container<TMap>(fn(this._value));
    }
}
```

We can use the container as follows:

```
let double = (x: number) => x + x;
let container = new Container(3);
let container2 = container.map(double);
console.log(container2); // { _value: 6 }
```

At this point, it might feel like a `Functor` is not very useful because we have implemented the most basic version possible. The next two sections implement two functors known as `Maybe` and `Either`. These two functors are much more useful and should demonstrate that functors are a powerful tool.

Applicative

An `Applicative` is a `Functor` that implements a method named `of`:

```
class Container<T> {
    public static of<TVal>(val: TVal) {
        return new Container(val);
    }
    private _value!: T;
    public constructor(val: T) {
        this._value = val;
    }
    public map<TMap>(fn: (val: T) => TMap) {
        return new Container<TMap>(fn(this._value));
    }
}
```

Functional Programming with TypeScript

We can use the `Applicative` as follows:

```
let double = (x: number) => x + x;
let container = Container.of(3);
let container2 = container.map(double);
console.log(container2); // { _value: 6 }
```

> Please note that the entire example is included in the companion source code.

Maybe

The following `Maybe` data type is a `Functor` and an `Applicative`, which means it contains a value and implements the map method. The main difference with the preceding implementation of `Functor` is that in the `Maybe Functor`, the value contained by the data type is optional:

```
class MayBe<T> {
    public static of<TVal>(val?: TVal) {
        return new MayBe(val);
    }
    private _value!: T;
    public constructor(val?: T) {
        if (val) {
            this._value = val;
        }
    }
    public isNothing() {
        return (this._value === null || this._value === undefined);
    }
    public map<TMap>(fn: (val: T) => TMap) {
        if (this.isNothing()) {
            return new MayBe<TMap>();
        } else {
            return new MayBe<TMap>(fn(this._value));
        }
    }
}
```

As we can see in the preceding implementation of the `map` method, the mapping function is only applied if the `Maybe` data type contains a value.

To demonstrate how to use the `Maybe` type and why it is useful, we are going to declare a function to fetch the latest TypeScript news in www.reddit.com:

```
interface New {
    subreddit: string;
    id: string;
    title: string;
    score: number;
    over_18: boolean;
    url: string;
    author: string;
    ups: number;
    num_comments: number;
    created_utc: number;
}

interface Response {
    kind: string;
    data: {
        modhash: string;
        whitelist_status: boolean|null;
        children: Array<{ kind: string, data: New }>;
        after: string|null;
        before: string|null;
    };
}

async function fetchNews() {
    return new Promise<MayBe<Response>>((resolve, reject) => {
        const url = "https://www.reddit.com/r/typescript/new.json";
        fetch(url)
            .then((response) => {
                return response.json();
            }).then((json) => {
                resolve(new MayBe(json));
            }).catch(() => {
                resolve(new MayBe());
            });
    });
}
```

The preceding code snippet uses the fetch API to send an HTTP request. This is an asynchronous operation, which explains why the snippet creates a promise instance. When the operations are completed successfully, the response is returned as a `Maybe` instance. When the operations are completed unsuccessfully, an empty `Maybe` instance is returned.

Functional Programming with TypeScript

The following code snippet demonstrates how we can use the `fetchNews` function:

```
(async () => {

    const maybeOfResponse = await fetchNews();

    const maybeOfNews = maybeOfResponse
        .map(r => r.data)
        .map(d => d.children)
        .map(children => children.map(c => c.data));

    maybeOfNews.map((news) => {
        news.forEach((n) => console.log(`${n.title} - ${n.url}`));
        return news;
    });

})();
```

The preceding code snippet uses `fetchNews` to fetch a list of posts about TypeScript from Reddit. If the request is completed successfully, the `fetchNews` function returns the HTTP response wrapped in a `MayBe` instance. We then use the `map` method to find the list of posts within the response. The nice thing about using a `MayBe` instance is that mapping logic is only executed if there is an actual response, so we don't need to worry about potential null or undefined errors.

> Please note that the preceding example uses some browser APIs, which means that we need to add `dom` to the `lib` field in our `tsconfig.json` file. This will prevent compilation errors such as Cannot find name *console*. Please note that the entire example is included in the companion source code.

Either

The `Either` algebraic data type is the union of the `Just` and `Nothing` types:

```
type Either<T1, T2> = Just<T1> | Nothing<T2>;
```

The `Just` type is a `Functor` used to represent a non-nullable value:

```
class Nothing<T> {
    public static of<TVal>(val?: TVal) {
        return new Nothing(val);
    }
    private _value: T|undefined;
    public constructor(val?: T) {
```

```
            this._value = val;
        }
        public map<TMap>(fn: (val: T) => TMap) {
            if (this._value !== undefined) {
                return new Nothing<TMap>(fn(this._value));
            } else {
                return new Nothing<TMap>(this._value as any);
            }
        }
    }
```

The `Nothing` type represents the lack of a value:

```
    class Just<T> {
        public static of<TVal>(val: TVal) {
            return new Just(val);
        }
        private _value: T;
        public constructor(val: T) {
            this._value = val;
        }
        public map<TMap>(fn: (val: T) => TMap) {
            return new Just<TMap>(fn(this._value));
        }
    }
```

The following code snippet is an implementation of the `fetchNews` function that we declared in the preceding section. The main difference this time is that we will return an instance of `Just` if the HTTP request is completed successfully and an instance of `Nothing` if the HTTP request is not completed successfully:

```
    interface New {
        subreddit: string;
        id: string;
        title: string;
        score: number;
        over_18: boolean;
        url: string;
        author: string;
        ups: number;
        num_comments: number;
        created_utc: number;
    }

    interface Response {
        kind: string;
        data: {
```

```
                modhash: string;
                whitelist_status: boolean|null;
                children: Array<{ kind: string, data: New }>;
                after: string|null;
                before: string|null;
        };
}

async function fetchNews() {
        return new Promise<Either<Response, Error>>((resolve, reject) => {
            const url = "https://www.reddit.com/r/typescript/new.json";
            fetch(url)
                .then((response) => {
                    return response.json();
                }).then((json) => {
                    resolve(new Just(json));
                }).catch((e) => {
                    resolve(new Nothing(e));
                });
        });
}
```

If we try to use map on an Either instance, we will get a compilation error:

```
(async () => {

    const maybeOfResponse = await fetchNews();

    maybeOfResponse.map(r => r.message)
    // Error:
    // Cannot invoke an expression whose type lacks a call signature.
    // Type
    // (<TMap>(fn: (val: Response) => TMap) => Just<TMap>) |
    // (<TMap>(fn: (val: Error) => TMap) => Nothin<TMap>'
    // has no compatible call signatures.

})();
```

We can use a type guard to ensure that we are accessing a Nothing instance when the request fails and a Just instance if the request was completed without errors:

```
(async () => {

    const maybeOfResponse = await fetchNews();

    if (maybeOfResponse instanceof Nothing) {

        maybeOfResponse
```

```
            .map(r => r.message)
            .map(msg => {
                console.log(`Error: ${msg}`);
                return msg;
            });
    } else {
        const maybeOfNews = maybeOfResponse.map(r => r.data)
            .map(d => d.children)
            .map(children => children.map(c => c.data));

        maybeOfNews.map((news) => {
            news.forEach((n) => console.log(`${n.title} - ${n.url}`));
            return news;
        });
    }
})();
```

The good thing about using Either is that the compiler forces us to use a type guard. This means that using an Either can lead to increased type safety when dealing with potential failures in operations.

> Please note that the entire example is included in the companion source code.

Monad

We are going to finish our introduction to algebraic data types by learning about monads. A `Monad` is a `Functor`, but it also implements the `Applicative` and `Chain` specifications.

We can transform the previously declared `Maybe` data type into a `Monad` by adding two extra methods named `join` and `chain`:

```
class MayBe<T> {
    public static of<TVal>(val?: TVal) {
        return new MayBe(val);
    }
    private _value!: T;
    public constructor(val?: T) {
        if (val) {
            this._value = val;
```

```
            }
        }
        public isNothing() {
            return (this._value === null || this._value === undefined);
        }
        public map<TMap>(fn: (val: T) => TMap) {
            if (this.isNothing()) {
                return new MayBe<TMap>();
            } else {
                return new MayBe<TMap>(fn(this._value));
            }
        }
        public join() {
            return this.isNothing() ? Nothing.of(this._value) : this._value;
        }
        public chain<TMap>(fn: (val: T) => TMap) {
            return this.map(fn).join();
        }
    }
```

The `MayBe` data type was already a `Functor` and an `Applicative`, but now it is also a `Monad`. The following code snippet showcases how we can use it:

```
let maybeOfNumber = MayBe.of(5);

maybeOfNumber.map((a) => a * 2);
// MayBe { value: 10 }

maybeOfNumber.join();
// 5

maybeOfNumber.chain((a) => a * 2);
// 10

let maybeOfMaybeOfNumber = MayBe.of(MayBe.of(5));
// MayBe { value: MayBe { value: 5 } }

maybeOfMaybeOfNumber.map((a) => a.map(v => v * 2));
// MayBe { value: MayBe { value: 10 } }

maybeOfMaybeOfNumber.join();
// MayBe { value: 5 }

maybeOfMaybeOfNumber.chain((a) => a.map(v => v * 2));
// MayBe { value: 10 }
```

The preceding code snippet demonstrates how the `join` and `chain` methods work. As we can see, they are very useful when we have a `Functor` of a `Functor`, and we want to access the contained value. The `chain` method is just a one-step shortcut for the two operations, `join` and `map`.

> Please note that the entire example is included in the companion source code.

Real-world FP

In this section, we are going to explore some open source libraries that can be useful while working in a real-world FP application.

Immutable.js

As we have learned in this chapter, one of the main ideas in FP is minimizing the number of places in which state is mutated in our application. However, in JavaScript, objects are not immutable, which we can lead us to mutate the application's state by mistake. For example, we could try to sort an array using the following function:

```
function sort(arr: number[]) {
    return arr.sort((a, b) => b - a);
}
```

The preceding function could lead to issues because the `sort` method mutates the original array. This example is a demonstration of what is known as an implicit mutation. We mutated the application's state, but we didn't do it explicitly. `Immutable.js` helps us to make all the mutations in our application explicit.

We can install `immutable` using `npm`:

```
npm install --save immutable
```

No type definitions are required because they are already included in the `immutable` package.

The following code snippet demonstrates how to transform objects into immutable objects and how to work with them. The immutable API includes methods such as `set`, `mergeDeep`, or `updateIn` that allow us to work with basic objects and nested objects:

```
Import * as immutable from "immutable";

const map1 = immutable.Map({ a: 1, b: 2, c: 3 });
const map2 = map1.set("b", 50);
console.log(`${map1.get("b")} vs.${map2.get("b")}`);
// 2 vs. 50

const nested = immutable.fromJS({ a: { b: { c: [ 3, 4, 5 ] } } });

const nested2 = nested.mergeDeep({ a: { b: { d: 6 } } });
// Map { a: Map { b: Map { c: List [ 3, 4, 5 ], d: 6 } } }

console.log(nested2.getIn([ "a", "b", "d" ]));
// 6

const nested3 = nested2.updateIn(
    [ "a", "b", "d" ],
    (value: string) => value + 1
);

console.log(nested3);
// Map { a: Map { b: Map { c: List [ 3, 4, 5 ], d: 7 } } }

const nested4 = nested3.updateIn(
    [ "a", "b", "c" ],
    (list: number[]) => list.push(6)
);

console.log(nested4);
// Map { a: Map { b: Map { c: List [ 3, 4, 5, 6 ], d: 7 } } }
```

> Please note that the entire example is included in the companion source code.

These immutable objects cannot be mutated. The methods return new copies of the original objects, instead of mutating them. Immutable uses some smart algorithms and data structures to share some memory between objects and to be as efficient as possible when comparing them.

Ramda

In a real-world application, we don't need to create our own our FP utilities (for example, compose or curry functions). We can use existing JavaScript libraries that already implement these helpers and many others. One of these libraries is Ramda.

We can install Ramda using npm:

```
npm install --save ramda
npm install --save-dev @types/ramda
```

Ramda includes helper functions to implement function composition, currying, and many more FP techniques, and its API is influenced by the pointfree style.

The following code snippet re-implements the example that we used earlier in this chapter in the *Currying* section but uses the Ramda implementations of compose and currying, instead of using custom implementations:

```
import * as R from "ramda";const trim = (s: string) => s.trim();
const capitalize = (s: string) => s.toUpperCase();
const trimAndCapitalize = R.compose(trim, capitalize);

const replace = (s: string, f: string, r: string) =>
    s.split(f).join(r);

const curriedReplace = R.curry(replace);
const trimCapitalizeAndReplace = R.compose(
    trimAndCapitalize,
    curriedReplace("/")("-")
);

trimAndCapitalizeReplace("   13/feb/1989    "); // "13-FEB-1989"
```

> Please note that the entire example is included in the companion source code.

React and MobX

Earlier in the chapter, we learned that FP reduces the number of places in which state changes take place within an application and tries to move these places into the boundaries of the application to try to keep application's core stateless.

`React` and `MobX` are two popular open source libraries that can be used to build user interfaces. These libraries are highly influenced by FP and try to prevent state mutations by using pure functions and immutable objects (powered by libraries such as `Immutable.js`). However, state mutations must take place at some point. That is the main role of `MobX`, a library that allows us to manage the state in a `React` application.

In a `MobX` application, a new state should only be generated within one of the application's components, known as a `Store`. This is a very clear example of an FP architecture because it pushes all the state mutations in the entire application to one unique location.

> Please refer to `Chapter 11`, *Frontend Development with React and TypeScript*, to learn more about `React` and `MobX`.

Summary

We started this chapter by learning some of the main FP concepts, including concepts such as pure functions, higher-order functions, and immutability.

We also learned some of the main FP techniques, including techniques such as functional composition, function partial application, and currying.

Later, we learned what category theory is and how to work with some algebraic data types.

Finally, we learned about some FP libraries that can help us to put some of these techniques and concepts into practice in a real-world application.

In the next chapter, we will learn how to work with decorators.

8
Working with Decorators

In this chapter, we are going to learn about annotations and decorators—the two new features based on the future ECMAScript 7 specification, but we can use them today with TypeScript 1.5 or higher. You will learn about the following topics:

- Annotations and decorators
- The reflection metadata API
- The decorator factory

Prerequisites

The TypeScript features in this chapter require TypeScript 1.5 or higher and the following options to be enabled in the `tsconfig.json` file:

```
"experimentalDecorators": true,
"emitDecoratorMetadata": true
```

> As indicated by the experimental decorators compilation flag, the decorator's API is considered experimental. This doesn't mean that it is not ready for production usage. It means that the decorator API is subject to potential breaking changes in the future.

We are also going to need a polyfill for the `reflect-metadata` API. We need a polyfill because most JavaScript engines don't support this API yet. We can expect that, in the long term, this polyfill will not be required but, currently, we can use the `reflect-metadata` npm module:

```
npm install reflect-metadata
```

Working with Decorators

> The `reflect-metadata` version was 0.1.12 at the time of writing. Please note that the examples are included in the companion source code. The examples can be executed with ts node. For example, the first example included in the companion source code can be executed as follows:
> `ts-node chapters/chapter_08/01_class_decorator.ts`

Annotations versus decorators

Annotations are a way to add metadata to class declarations. The metadata can then be used by libraries and other development tools, such as inversion of control containers. The annotations API was originally proposed by the Google AtScript team, but annotations are not a standard. However, decorators are a proposed standard for the ECMAScript specification, to annotate and modify classes and properties at design time. Annotations and decorators are pretty much the same:

> "Annotations and decorators are nearly the same thing. From a consumer perspective, we have exactly the same syntax. The only thing that differs is that we don't have control over how annotations are added as metadata to our code. A decorator is rather an interface to build something that ends up as annotation. Over a long term, however, we can just focus on decorators, since those are a real proposed standard. AtScript is TypeScript and TypeScript implements decorators".
> – Pascal Precht, The Difference between Annotations and Decorators

We are going to use the following class to showcase how to work with decorators:

```
class Person {

    public name: string;
    public surname: string;

    public constructor(name: string, surname: string) {
        this.name = name;
        this.surname = surname;
    }

    public saySomething(something: string): string {
        return `${this.name} ${this.surname} says: ${something}`;
    }

}
```

There are four types of decorators that can be used to annotate: classes, properties, methods, and parameters.

The class decorators

The official TypeScript decorator proposal defines a class decorator as follows:

> *A class decorator function is a function that accepts a constructor function as its argument, and returns either undefined, the provided constructor function, or a new constructor function. Returning undefined is equivalent to returning the provided constructor function.*
>
> *– Ron Buckton, Decorators Proposal - TypeScript*

A class decorator is used to modify the constructor of a class in some way. If the class decorator returns `undefined`, the original constructor remains the same. If the decorator returns, the return value will be used to override the original class constructor. The following type declares the signature of a class decorator:

```
declare type ClassDecorator = <TFunction extends Function>(target: TFunction) => TFunction | void;
```

> Please note that this signature is subject to change in future releases of TypeScript. Please refer to the `lib.d.ts` file in the TypeScript source code at https://github.com/Microsoft/TypeScript/blob/master/lib/lib.d.ts to find the current signature.

We are going to create a class decorator named `logClass`. We can start by defining the decorator as follows:

```
function logClass(target: any) {
    // ...
}
```

The preceding class decorator does not have any logic yet, but we can already apply it to a class. To apply a decorator, we need to use the at (@) symbol:

```
@logClass
class Person {
    public name: string;
    public surname: string;
    //...
```

Working with Decorators

If we compile the preceding code snippet into JavaScript, a function named `__decorate` will be generated by the TypeScript compiler. We are not going to examine the internal implementation of the `__decorate` function, but we need to understand that it is used to apply a decorator at runtime because the decorator syntax is not supported natively by JavaScript. We can see it in action by examining the JavaScript code that is generated when we compile the decorated `Person` class mentioned previously:

```javascript
var Person = /** @class */ (function () {
    function Person(name, surname) {
        this.name = name;
        this.surname = surname;
    }
    Person.prototype.saySomething = function (something) {
        return this.name + " " + this.surname + " says: " + something;
    };
    Person = __decorate([
        logClass
    ], Person);
    return Person;
}());
```

As we can see in the preceding code snippet, the `Person` class is declared, but it is then passed to the `__decorate` function. The value returned by the `__decorate` function is re-assigned to the `Person` class. Now that we know how the class decorator will be invoked, let's implement it:

```typescript
function logClass<TFunction extends Function>(target: TFunction) {

    // save a reference to the original constructor
    const originalConstructor = target;

    function logClassName(func: TFunction) {
        console.log("New: " + func.name);
    }

    // a utility function to generate instances of a class
    function instanciate(constructor: any, ...args: any[]) {
        return new constructor(...args);
    }

    // the new constructor behaviour
    const newConstructor = function(...args: any[]) {
        logClassName(originalConstructor);
        return instanciate(originalConstructor, ...args);
    };
```

```
    // copy prototype so instanceof operator still works
    newConstructor.prototype = originalConstructor.prototype;

    // return new constructor (will override original)
    return newConstructor as any;
}
```

The class decorator takes the constructor of the class being decorated as its only argument. This means that the argument (named `target`) is the constructor of the `Person` class. The decorator starts by creating a copy of the class constructor, then it defines a utility function (named `instanciate`) that can be used to generate instances of a class. Decorators are used to add some extra logic or metadata to the decorated element. When we try to extend the functionality of a function (methods or constructors), we need to wrap the original function with a new function, which contains the additional logic and invokes the original function. In the preceding decorator, we added extra logic to log in the console, the name of the class when a new instance is created. To achieve this, a new class constructor (named `newConstructor`) was declared. The new constructor invokes a function named `logClassName`, which implements the additional logic and uses the `instanciate` function to invoke the original class constructor. At the end of the decorator, the prototype of the original constructor function is copied to the new constructor function to ensure that the `instanceof` operator continues to work when it is applied to an instance of the decorated class. Finally, the new constructor is returned, and it is used to override the original class constructor. After decorating the class constructor, a new instance is created:

```
const me = new Person("Remo", "Jansen");
```

On doing so, the following text appears in the console:

```
"New: Person"
```

The method decorators

The official TypeScript decorator proposal defines a method decorator as follows:

> *"A method decorator function is a function that accepts three arguments: The object that owns the property, the key for the property (a string or a symbol), and optionally the property descriptor of the property. The function must return either undefined, the provided property descriptor, or a new property descriptor. Returning undefined is equivalent to returning the provided property descriptor".*
> *— Ron Buckton, Decorators Proposal - TypeScript*

Working with Decorators

The method decorator is like the class decorator, but it is used to override a method, as opposed to using it to override the constructor of a class. The following type declares the signature of a method decorator:

```
declare type MethodDecorator = <T>(target: Object, propertyKey: string |
symbol, descriptor: TypedPropertyDescriptor<T>) =>
TypedPropertyDescriptor<T> | void;
```

> Please note that this signature is subject to change in future releases of TypeScript. Please refer to the `lib.d.ts` file in the TypeScript source code at https://github.com/Microsoft/TypeScript/blob/master/lib/lib.d.ts to find the current signature.

The method decorator takes as arguments the class being decorated (target), the name of the method being decorated, and a `TypePropertyDescriptor` of the property being decorated. A property descriptor is an object used to describe the properties of a class. A property descriptor contains the following properties:

```
interface TypedPropertyDescriptor<T> {
    enumerable?: boolean;
    configurable?: boolean;
    writable?: boolean;
    value?: T;
    get?: () => T;
    set?: (value: T) => void;
}
```

> Note that a property descriptor is an object that can be obtained by invoking the `Object.getOwnPropertyDescriptor()` method. You can learn more at https://developer.mozilla.org/en-US/docs/Web/JavaScript/Reference/Global_Objects/Object/getOwnPropertyDescriptor.

If the method decorator returns a property descriptor, the returned value will be used to override the property descriptor of the method. Let's declare a method decorator named `logMethod` without any behavior for now:

```
function logMethod(target: any, key: string, descriptor: any) {
    // ...
}
```

[254]

Chapter 8

We can apply the decorator to one of the methods in the `Person` class:

```
class Person {

    public name: string;
    public surname: string;

    public constructor(name: string, surname: string) {
        this.name = name;
        this.surname = surname;
    }

    @logMethod
    public saySomething(something: string): string {
        return `${this.name} ${this.surname} says: ${something}`;
    }

}
```

If we compile the preceding code snippet into JavaScript, we will be able to observe that the method decorator is invoked using the following arguments:

- The prototype (`Person.prototype`) of the class that contains the method being decorated
- The name of the method (`saySomething`) being decorated
- The property descriptor of the method being decorated is `Object.getOwnPropertyDescriptor(Person.prototype, saySomething)`

Now that we know the value of the decorator parameters, we can proceed to implement it:

```
function logMethod(
    target: any,
    key: string,
    descriptor: TypedPropertyDescriptor<any>
) {

    // save a reference to the original method
    const originalMethod = descriptor.value;

    function logFunctionCall(method: string, args: string, result: string)
    {
        console.log(`Call: ${method}(${args}) => ${result}`);
    }

    // editing the descriptor/value parameter
    descriptor.value = function(this: any, ...args: any[]) {
```

[255]

Working with Decorators

```
        // convert method arguments to string
        const argsStr = args.map((a: any) => {
            return JSON.stringify(a);
        }).join();

        // invoke method and get its return value
        const result = originalMethod.apply(this, args);

        // convert result to string
        const resultStr = JSON.stringify(result);

        // display in console the function call details
        console.log();
        console.log(`Call: ${key}(${argsStr}) => ${resultStr}`);

        // return the result of invoking the method
        return result;
    };

    // return edited descriptor
    return descriptor;
}
```

Just like we did when we implemented the class decorator, we start by creating a copy of the element being decorated. Instead of accessing the method via the class prototype (`target[key]`), we will access it via the property descriptor (`descriptor.value`). We then create a new function that will replace the method being decorated. The new function invokes the original method but also contains some additional logic used to log in the console, the method name, and the value of its arguments every time it is invoked. After applying the decorator to the method, the method name and arguments will be logged in the console when it is invoked:

```
const person = new Person("Michael", "Jackson");
person.saySomething("Annie, are you ok?");
```

On doing so, the following text appears in the console:

```
Call: saySomething("Annie, are you ok?") => "Michael Jackson says: Annie, are you ok?"
```

The property decorators

The official TypeScript decorators proposal defines a method property as follows:

> *A property decorator function is a function that accepts two arguments: The object that owns the property and the key for the property (a string or a symbol). A property decorator does not return.*
>
> —Ron Buckton, Decorators Proposal - TypeScript

The following type declares the signature of a property decorator:

```
declare type PropertyDecorator = (target: Object, propertyKey: string | symbol) => void;
```

> Please note that this signature is subject to change in future releases of TypeScript. Please refer to the `lib.d.ts file` in the TypeScript source code at https://github.com/Microsoft/TypeScript/blob/master/lib/lib.d.ts to find the current signature.

A property decorator is really like a method decorator. The main differences are that a property decorator doesn't return a value and that the third parameter (the property descriptor is missing) is not passed to the property decorator. Let's create a property decorator named `logProperty` to see how it works:

```
function logProperty(target: any, key: string) {
    // ...
}
```

We can use it in one of the `Person` class's properties as follows:

```
class Person {

    @logProperty
    public name: string;

    @logProperty
    public surname: string;

    public constructor(name: string, surname: string) {
        this.name = name;
        this.surname = surname;
    }

    public saySomething(something: string): string {
        return `${this.name} ${this.surname} says: ${something}`;
    }
```

Working with Decorators

```
    }
```

As we have been doing so far, we are going to implement a decorator that will override the decorated property with a new property that will behave exactly as the original one, but will perform an additional task—logging the property value in the console whenever it changes:

```
function logProperty(target: any, key: string) {

    // property value
    let _val = target[key];

    function logPropertyAccess(acces: "Set" | "Get", k: string, v: any) {
        console.log(`${acces}: ${k} => ${v}`);
    }

    // property getter
    const getter = function() {
        logPropertyAccess("Get", key, _val);
        return _val;
    };

    // property setter
    const setter = function(newVal: any) {
        logPropertyAccess("Set", key, newVal);
        _val = newVal;
    };

    // Delete property. The delete operator throws
    // in strict mode if the property is an own
    // non-configurable property and returns
    // false in non-strict mode.
    if (delete target[key]) {
        Object.defineProperty(target, key, {
            get: getter,
            set: setter,
            enumerable: true,
            configurable: true
        });
    }
}
```

In the preceding decorator, we created a copy of the original property value and declared two functions: `getter` (invoked when we change the value of the property) and `setter` (invoked when we read the value of the property) respectively. The method decorator returned a value used to override the element being decorated. Because the property decorator doesn't return a value, we can't override the property being decorated, but we can replace it. We have manually deleted the original property (using the `delete` keyword) and created a new property using the `Object.defineProperty` function and the previously declared getter and setter functions. After applying the decorator to the `name` property, we will be able to observe any changes to its value in the console:

```
const person = new Person("Michael", "Jackson");
// Set: name => Michael
// Set: surname => Jackson

person.saySomething("Annie, are you ok?");
// Get: name => Michael
// Get: surname => Jackson
```

The parameter decorators

The official decorators proposal defines a parameter decorator as follows:

> *"A parameter decorator function is a function that accepts three arguments: The object that owns the method that contains the decorated parameter, the property key of the property (or undefined for a parameter of the constructor), and the ordinal index of the parameter. The return value of this decorator is ignored".*
>
> *- Ron Buckton, Decorators Proposal - TypeScript*

The following type declares the signature of a parameter decorator:

```
declare type ParameterDecorator = (target: Object, propertyKey: string | symbol, parameterIndex: number) => void;
```

> Please note that this signature is subject to change in future releases of TypeScript. Please refer to the `lib.d.ts` file in the TypeScript source code at https://github.com/Microsoft/TypeScript/blob/master/lib/lib.d.ts to find the current signature.

Working with Decorators

The main difference between the preceding decorators and the parameter decorators is that we cannot use a parameter decorator to extend the functionality of a given class. Let's create a parameter decorator named `addMetadata` to see how it works:

```
function addMetadata(target: any, key: string, index: number) {
    // ...
}
```

We can apply the parameter decorator to a parameter as follows:

```
@logMethod
public saySomething(@addMetadata something: string): string {
    return `${this.name} ${this.surname} says: ${something}`;
}
```

The parameter decorator doesn't return, which means that we will not be able to override the original method that takes the parameter being decorated as an argument. We can use parameter decorators to link some metadata to the class being decorated. In the following implementation, we will add an array named `log_${key}_parameters` as a class property, where `key` is the name of the method that contains the parameter being decorated:

```
function addMetadata(target: any, key: string, index: number) {
    const metadataKey = `_log_${key}_parameters`;
    if (Array.isArray(target[metadataKey])) {
        target[metadataKey].push(index);
    } else {
        target[metadataKey] = [index];
    }
}
```

To allow more than one parameter to be decorated, we check whether the new field is an array. If the new field is not an array, we create and initialize the new field to be a new array containing the index of the parameter being decorated. If the new field is an array, the index of the parameter being decorated is added to the array. A parameter decorator is not useful on its own; it needs to be used with a method decorator, so the parameter decorator adds the metadata, and the method decorator reads it:

```
@readMetadata
public saySomething(@addMetadata something: string): string {
    return `${this.name} ${this.surname} says: ${something}`;
}
```

The following method decorator works like the method decorator that we implemented previously in this chapter, but it will read the metadata added by the parameter decorator, and instead of displaying all the arguments passed to the method in the console when it is invoked, it will only log the ones that have been decorated:

```
function readMetadata(target: any, key: string, descriptor: any) {

    const originalMethod = descriptor.value;

    descriptor.value = function(...args: any[]) {

        const metadataKey = `_log_${key}_parameters`;
        const indices = target[metadataKey];

        if (Array.isArray(indices)) {

            for (let i = 0; i < args.length; i++) {

                if (indices.indexOf(i) !== -1) {
                    const arg = args[i];
                    const argStr = JSON.stringify(arg);
                    console.log(`${key} arg[${i}]: ${argStr}`);
                }
            }
        }

        return originalMethod.apply(this, args);

    };

    return descriptor;
}
```

If we apply the `saySomething` method:

```
const person = new Person("Remo", "Jansen");
person.saySomething("hello!");
```

The `readMetadata` decorator will display the value of the parameters and which indices were added to the metadata (class property named `_log_saySomething_parameters`) in the console by the `addMetadata` decorator:

```
saySomething arg[0]: "hello!"
```

> Note that in the previous example, we used a class property to store some metadata. However, this is not recommended practice. Later in this chapter, you will learn how to use the `reflection-metadata` API; this API has been designed specifically to generate and read metadata, and it is, therefore, recommended to use it when we need to work with decorators and metadata.

Decorators with arguments

We can use a special kind of decorator factory to allow developers to configure the behavior of a decorator. For example, we could pass a string to a class decorator as follows:

```
@logClass("option")
class Person {
// ...
```

To be able to pass some parameters to a decorator, we need to wrap the decorator with a function. The wrapper function takes the options of our choice and returns a decorator:

```
function logClass(option: string) {
    return function(target: any) {
        // class decorator logic goes here
        // we have access to the decorator parameters
        console.log(target, option);
    };
}
```

This can be applied to all the kinds of decorators that you learned in this chapter.

> It is very important to **avoid using an arrow function as the inner function** to prevent potential problems with the `this` operator at runtime.

The reflect metadata API

We have learned that decorators can be used to modify and extend the behavior of a class's methods or properties. While this is a very good way to get to understand decorator in depth, **it is not recommended to use a decorator to modify and extend the behavior of a class**. Instead, we should try to use decorators to add metadata to the class being decorated. The metadata can then be consumed by other tools.

> The recommendation to avoid using a decorator to modify and extend the behavior of a class could be reverted in the future if the TypeScript team implements a future known as *decorator mutation*. You can learn more about the status of the decorator mutation proposal at `https://github.com/Microsoft/TypeScript/issues/4881`.

The possibility of adding metadata to a class might not seem useful or exciting, but in my opinion, it is one of the greatest things that has happened to JavaScript in the past few years. As we already know, TypeScript only uses types at design time. However, some features, such as dependency injection, runtime type assertions, reflection, and automated mocking during testing are not possible when the type information is not available at runtime. The lack of type information at runtime is not a problem anymore because we can use decorators to generate metadata and that metadata can contain the required type information. The metadata can then be processed at runtime. When the TypeScript team started to think about the best possible way to allow developers to generate type information metadata, they reserved a few special decorator names for this purpose. The idea was that when an element was decorated using these reserved decorators, the compiler would automatically add the type's information to the element being decorated. The reserved decorators were the following:

> "TypeScript compiler will honor special decorator names and will flow additional information into the decorator factory parameters annotated by these decorators.
>
> @type - The serialized form of the type of the decorator target
> @returnType - The serialized form of the return type of the decorator target if it is a function type, undefined otherwise
> @parameterTypes - A list of serialized types of the decorator target's arguments if it is a function type, undefined otherwise
> @name - The name of the decorator target "
>
> *– Decorators brainstorming by Jonathan Turner*

Shortly after, the team TypeScript decided to use the reflection metadata API (one of the proposed ES7 features) instead of the reserved decorators. The idea is almost identical, but instead of using the reserved decorator names, we will use some reserved metadata keys to retrieve the metadata using the reflection metadata API. The TypeScript documentation defines three reserved metadata keys:

- *Type metadata uses the metadata key design:type.*

Working with Decorators

- *Parameter type metadata uses the metadata key design: paramtypes.*
- *Return type metadata uses the metadata key design: returntype.*

- Issue #2577 - TypeScript Official Repository at GitHub.com

We will now learn how we to use the reflection metadata API. We need to start by installing the `reflect-metadata` npm module:

```
npm install reflect-metadata
```

> We don't need to install type definitions for the `reflect-metadata` npm module because it includes the type definitions.

We can then import the `reflect-metadata` npm module as follows:

```
import "reflect-metadata";
```

> The `reflect-metadata` module **should be imported only once in your entire application** because the `Reflect` object is meant to be a global singleton.

If you try to use some of the `reflect-metadata` API from a TypeScript in which the `reflect-metadata` module is not imported, you will need to add the following option to your `tsconfig.json` file:

```
"types": [
  "reflect-metadata"
]
```

We can then create a class for testing purposes. We are going to get the type of one of the class properties at runtime. We are going to decorate the class using a `property` decorator named `logType`:

```
class Demo1 {
    @logType
    public attr1: string;
    public constructor(attr1: string) {
        this.attr1 = attr1;
    }
}
```

[264]

We need to invoke the `Reflect.getMetadata()` method using the `design:type` as the metadata key. The metadata value will be returned as a function. For example, for the type string, the `function String(){}` function is returned. We can use the `function.name` property to get the type as a string:

```
function logType(target: any, key: string) {
    const type = Reflect.getMetadata("design:type", target, key);
    console.log(`${key} type: ${type.name}`);
}
```

If we compile the preceding code and run the resulting JavaScript code in a web browser, we will be able to see the type of the `attr1` property in the console:

`'attr1 type: String'`

> Remember that to run this example, the `reflect-metadata` library must be imported as follows:
> `import "reflect-metadata";`

We can apply the other reserved metadata keys similarly. Let's create a method with many parameters to use the `design:paramtypes` reserved metadata key to retrieve the types of the parameters:

```
class Foo {}
interface FooInterface {}

class Demo2 {
    @logParamTypes
    public doSomething(
        param1: string,
        param2: number,
        param3: Foo,
        param4: { test: string },
        param5: FooInterface,
        param6: Function,
        param7: (a: number) => void
    ): number {
        return 1;
    }
}
```

Working with Decorators

This time, we will use the `design:paramtypes` reserved metadata key. We are querying the types of multiple parameters, so the types will be returned as an array by the `Reflect.getMetadata()` function:

```
function logParamTypes(target: any, key: string) {
    const types = Reflect.getMetadata(
        "design:paramtypes",
        target,
        key
    );
    const s = types.map((a: any) => a.name).join();
    console.log(`${key} param types: ${s}`);
}
```

If we compile and run the preceding code in a web browser, we will be able to see the types of the parameters in the console:

```
'doSomething param types: String, Number, Foo, Object, Object, Function, Function'
```

The types are serialized and follow some rules. We can see that functions are serialized as function, and object literals (`{test : string}`) and interfaces are serialized as object. The following table showcases how different types are serialized:

Type	Serialized
void	Undefined
string	String
number	Number
boolean	Boolean
symbol	Symbol
any	Object
enum	Number
Class C{}	C
Object literal {}	Object
interface	Object

[266]

> Note that some developers have required the possibility of accessing the type of interfaces and the inheritance tree of a class via metadata. This feature is known as **complex type serialization** and is not available at the time of writing.

To conclude, we are going to create a method with a return type and use the `design:returntype` reserved metadata key to retrieve the types of the return type:

```
class Demo3 {
    @logReturntype
    public doSomething2(): string {
        return "test";
    }
}
```

Just like in the two previous decorators, we need to invoke the `Reflect.getMetadata()` function passing the `design:returntype` reserved metadata key:

```
function logReturntype(target: any, key: string) {
    const returnType = Reflect.getMetadata(
        "design:returntype",
        target,
        key
    );
    console.log(`${key} return type: ${returnType.name}`);
}
```

If we compile and run the preceding code in a web browser, we will be able to see the types of the return type in the console:

```
'doSomething2 return type: String'
```

The decorator factory

The official decorators proposal defines a decorator factory as follows:

> *A decorator factory is a function that can accept any number of arguments, and must return one of the types of decorator function.*
>
> *- Ron Buckton, Decorators Proposal - TypeScript*

Working with Decorators

We have learned to implement class, property, method, and parameter decorators. However, in most cases, we will consume decorators, not implement them. For example, in `InversifyJS`, we use the `@injectable` decorator to declare that a class will be injected into other classes, but we don't need to implement the `@injectable` decorator. We can use the decorator factory to make decorators easier to consume. Let's consider the following code snippet:

```
@logClass
class Person {

    @logProperty
    public name: string;

    @logProperty
    public surname: string;

    public constructor(name: string, surname: string) {
        this.name = name;
        this.surname = surname;
    }

    @readMetadata
    public saySomething(@addMetadata something: string): string {
        return `${this.name} ${this.surname} says: ${something}`;
    }
}
```

The problem with the preceding code is that we, as developers, need to know that the `logMethod` decorator can only be applied to a method. This might seem trivial because the decorator name used (`logMethod`) makes it easier for us. A better solution is to enable developers to use a decorator named `@log` without having to worry about using the right kind of decorator:

```
@log
class Person {

    @log
    public name: string;

    @log
    public surname: string;

    public constructor(name: string, surname: string) {
        this.name = name;
        this.surname = surname;
    }
```

```
    @log
    public saySomething(@log something: string): string {
        return `${this.name} ${this.surname} says: ${something}`;
    }
}
```

We can achieve this by creating a decorator factory. A decorator factory is a function that can identify what kind of decorator is required and return it:

```
function decoratorFactory(
    classDecorator: Function,
    propertyDecorator: Function,
    methodDecorator: Function,
    parameterDecorator: Function
) {
    return function (this: any, ...args: any[]) {
        const nonNullableArgs = args.filter(a => a !== undefined);
        switch (nonNullableArgs.length) {
            case 1:
                return classDecorator.apply(this, args);
            case 2:
                // break instead of return as property
                // decorators don't have a return
                propertyDecorator.apply(this, args);
                break;
            case 3:
                if (typeof args[2] === "number") {
                    parameterDecorator.apply(this, args);
                } else {
                    return methodDecorator.apply(this, args);
                }
                break;
            default:
                throw new Error("Decorators are not valid here!");
        }
    };
}
```

As we can observe in the preceding code snippet, the decorator factory is a factory of decorators. The generated decorator uses the number and type of arguments passed to the decorator to identify the required kind of decorator that is appropriate for each case. The decorator factory can be used to create a universal decorator as follows:

```
const log = decoratorFactory(
    logClass,
    logProperty,
    readMetadata,
    addMetadata
);
```

Summary

In this chapter, we learned how to consume and implement the four available types of decorators (class, method, property, and parameter). We used decorators to mutate the original classes to understand how they work but we also learned that we **should avoid using decorators to mutate the prototype of a class**. We also learned how to create a decorator factory to abstract developers from the decorator types when they are consumed, how to pass configuration to a decorator, and how to use the reflection metadata API to access type information at runtime. As we have already mentioned, decorators in TypeScript are still an experimental feature, which doesn't mean that they are not ready for their usage in production systems but that their public API might be subject to breaking changes in the future. Please note that the future TypeScript releases will document how to get around these potential breaking changes if they end up happening. In the following chapter, we will learn how to configure an advanced TypeScript development workflow.

9
Automating Your Development Workflow

In the previous chapters, we learned about the main elements of the TypeScript syntax and the main features of its type system. Over the next few chapters, we will focus on the TypeScript tools and other elements of its ecosystem.

In this chapter, we are going to learn how to use some tools to automate our development workflow. These tools will help us to reduce the amount of time that we usually spend in some trivial and repetitive tasks.

In this chapter, we will learn about the following topics:

- Source control tools
- Package management tools
- Task runners
- Module bundlers
- Test automation and test coverage
- Integration tools
- Scaffolding tools

A modern development workflow

Developing a web application with high-quality standards has become a time-consuming activity. If we want to achieve a great user experience, we will need to ensure that our applications can run as smoothly as possible on many different web browsers, devices, internet connection speeds, and screen resolutions. Furthermore, we will need to spend a lot of our time working on quality assurance and performance optimization tasks.

As software engineers, we should try to minimize the time we spend on trivial and repetitive tasks. This might sound familiar as we have been doing this for years. We started by writing build scripts (such as makefiles) or automated tests and today, in a modern web development workflow, we use many tools to literally try to automate as many tasks as we can. These tools can be categorized into the following groups:

- Source control tools
- Package managers tools
- Task runners
- Module bundlers
- Test runners
- Continuous integration (CI) tools
- Scaffolding tools

Prerequisites

We are about to learn how to automate many tasks in our development workflow; however, before that, we need to install a few tools in our development environment.

Node.js

Node.js is a platform built on V8 (Google's open source JavaScript engine). Node.js allows us to run JavaScript outside a web browser. We can write backend and desktop applications using TypeScript and Node.js.

Even if we are planning to write backend applications, we are going to need Node.js because many of the tools used in this chapter are Node.js applications.

If you didn't install Node.js in the previous chapters, you could visit `https://nodejs.org/en/download/` to download the installer for your operating system.

Visual Studio Code

Visual Studio Code is an open source editor developed by Microsoft. The open source community around this editor is really active and has developed many plugins and themes. We can download Visual Studio Code from `https://code.visualstudio.com/download`.

We can additionally visit the Visual Studio extensions panel (the fifth icon on the left-hand side of the screen) to browse and install an extension or theme.

> Visual Studio Code is open source, and it is available for Linux, OS X, and Windows, so it will suit most readers. If you want to work with Visual Studio, you will be able to find the extension to enable TypeScript support in Visual Studio at `https://visualstudiogallery.msdn.microsoft.com/2d42d8dc-e085-45eb-a30b-3f7d50d55304`.

Git and GitHub

Toward the end of this chapter, we will learn how to configure a CI service. The CI service will observe changes in our application's code and ensure that the changes don't break the application.

To be able to observe the changes in the code, we will need to use a source control system. There are a few source control systems available. Some of the most widely used ones are Subversion, Mercurial, and Git.

Source control systems have many benefits, among which we can highlight the following:

- Source control tools enable multiple developers to work on a source file without any work being potentially lost by one developer overriding previous changes.
- Source control tools allow us to track and audit the changes in our source code. These features can be really useful, for example, when trying to find out when a new bug was introduced.

While working through the examples in this chapter, we will perform some changes to the source code. We will use Git and GitHub to manage these changes.

We need to visit `http://git-scm.com/downloads` to download the Git installer. We can then visit `https://github.com/` to create a GitHub account.

> A GitHub account will offer a few different subscription plans. The free plan offers everything we need to follow the examples in this book.

Automating Your Development Workflow

Companion source code

The companion source code for this book can be found online at `https://github.com/remojansen/LearningTypeScript`. The source code for this chapter includes a small example with the following directory architecture:

```
├── gulpfile.js
├── index.html
├── package-lock.json
├── package.json
├── src
│   ├── calculator.ts
│   ├── main_server.ts
├── main_browser.ts
│   └── operations
│       ├── add.ts
│       ├── pow.ts
│       └── validation.ts
├── test
│   ├── add.test.ts
│   ├── calculator.test.ts
│   ├── pow.test.ts
│   └── validation.test.ts
├── tsconfig.json
├── tslint.json
└── webpack.config.js
```

There are two main files, named `main_server.ts` and `main_browser.ts`. Both files are located under the `src` directory. These files create an instance of a class named `Calculator` and use it to perform some operations. The result of the operations is logged in the console:

```
import chalk from "chalk";
import { Calculator } from "./calculator";

const calculator = new Calculator();

const addResult = calculator.calculate("add", 2, 3);
console.log(chalk.green(`2 + 3 = ${addResult}`));

const powResult = calculator.calculate("pow", 2, 3);
console.log(chalk.green(`2 + 3 = ${powResult}`));
```

> The `main_browser.ts` file displays the results inside an HTML element instead of displaying them in the console. The `main_browser.ts` file also imports a `.scss` file to demonstrate how we can work with `.css` and `.scss` files, with Webpack.

The `Calculator` class can perform different kinds of mathematical operations and is defined in the `calculator.ts` file, which is located under the `src` directory:

```typescript
import { add } from "./operations/add";
import { pow } from "./operations/pow";

interface Operation {
    name: string;
    operation(a: number, b: number): number;
}

export class Calculator {
    private readonly _operations: Operation[];
    public constructor() {
        this._operations = [
            { name: "add", operation: add },
            { name: "pow", operation: pow }
        ];
    }
    public calculate(operation: string, a: number, b: number) {
        const opt = this._operations.filter((o) => o.name === operation)[0];
        if (opt === undefined) {
            throw new Error(`The operation ${operation} is not available!`);
        } else {
            return opt.operation(a, b);
        }
    }
}
```

The `Calculator` class can only perform two operations. Each operation is defined on its own file under the `operations` directory. The `add` operation is defined in the `add.ts` file and looks as follows:

```typescript
import { isNumber } from "./validation";

export function add(a: number, b: number) {
    isNumber(a);
    isNumber(b);
    return a + b;
}
```

The `pow` operation is defined in the `pow.ts` file and looks as follows:

```
import { isNumber } from "./validation";

export function pow(base: number, exponent: number) {
    isNumber(base);
    isNumber(exponent);
    let result = base;
    for (let i = 1; i < exponent; i++) {
        result = result * base;
    }
    return result;
}
```

Finally, the `isNumber` validation function looks as follows:

```
export function isNumber(a: number) {
    if (typeof a !== "number") {
        throw new Error(`${a} must be a number!`);
    }
}
```

We are going to use these files during the rest of this chapter, which means that we might need to come back to them later to fully understand the rest of the contents of this chapter.

Source control tools

Now that we have installed Git and created a GitHub account, we will use GitHub to create a new code repository. A repository is a central file storage location. It is used by the source control systems to store multiple versions of files. While a repository can be configured on a local machine for a single user, it is often stored on a server, which can be accessed by multiple users.

To create a new repository on GitHub, log in to your GitHub account and click on the link to create a new repository, which you can find in the top-right corner of the screen:

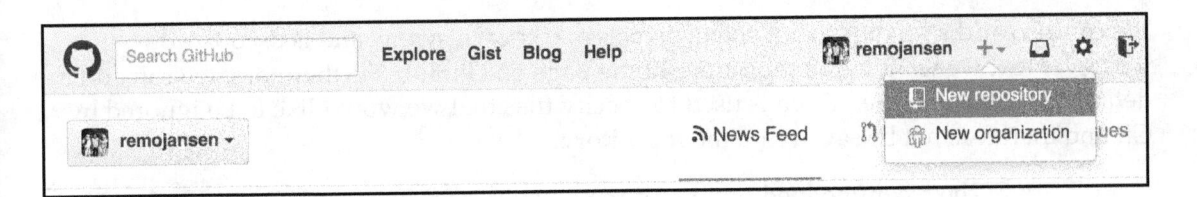

A form similar to the one in the following screenshot will then be displayed on screen:

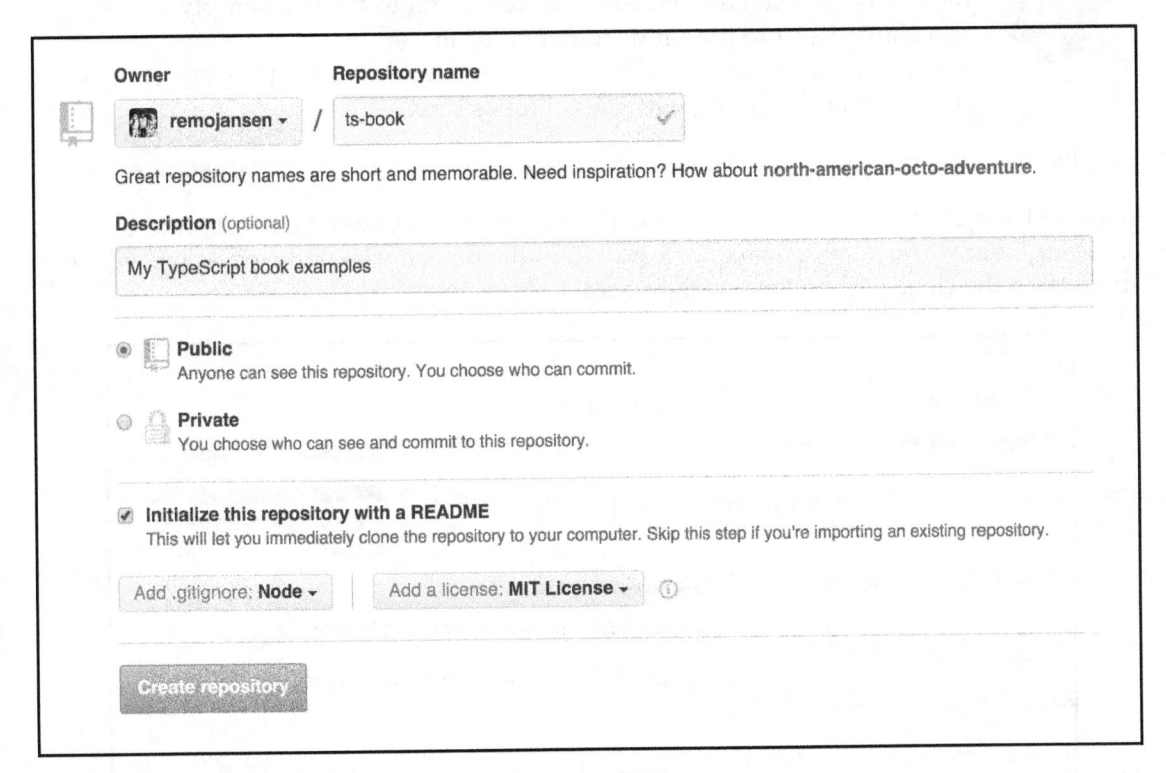

This form contains some fields that allow us to set the repository's name, description, and some privacy settings.

> Please note that you will need a paid GitHub account if you want to use a private repository.

Automating Your Development Workflow

We can also add a `README.md` file, which uses markdown syntax and is used to add whatever text we want to the repository home page on GitHub. Furthermore, we can add a default `.gitignore` file, which is used to specify files that we would like to be ignored by Git and therefore not be saved into the repository.

> The recommended option for the default `.gitignore` file is `Node`. We will use GitHub throughout this book. However, if you want to use a local repository, you can use the Git `init` command to create an empty repository. Refer to the Git documentation at http://git-scm.com/docs/git-init to learn more about the `git init` command and working with a local repository.

Last, but not less important, we can also select a software license to cover our source code.

Once we have created the repository, we will visit our profile page on GitHub, find the repository that we have just created, and visit it. In the repository's home page, we will be able to find the clone URL in the top-right corner of the page:

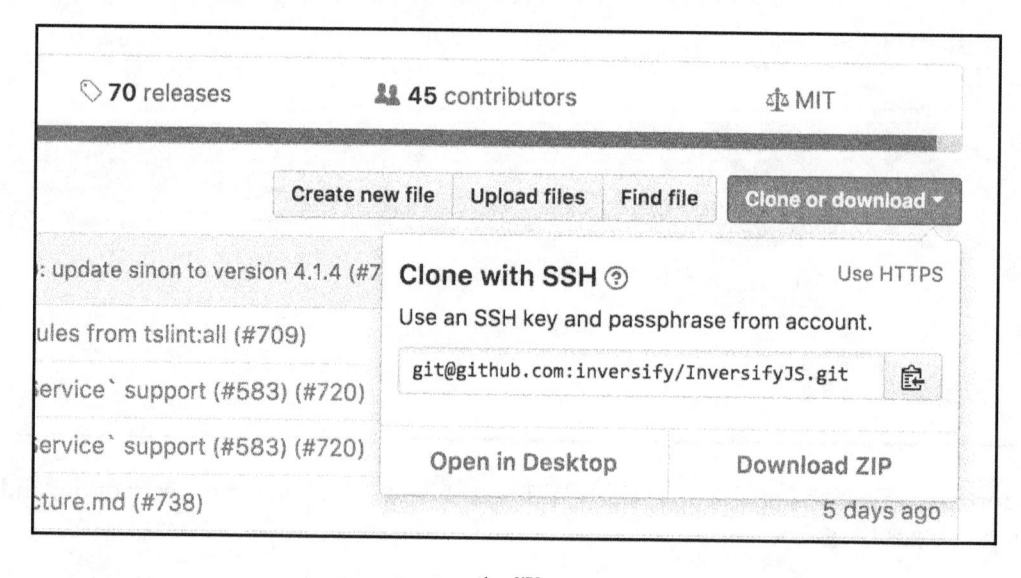

clone URL

We need to copy the repository's clone URL, open a console, and use the URL as an argument of the following command:

```
git clone https://github.com/user-name/repository-name.git
```

[278]

> Sometimes the Windows **command-line interface** (**CLI**) is not able to find the Git and Node commands. The easiest way to get around this issue is to use the Git console (installed with Git) rather than using the Windows command line. If you want to use the Windows console, you will need to manually add the Git and Node installation paths to the Windows PATH environment variable. If you are working with OS X or Linux, the default CLI should work fine. Also, note that we will use the Unix path syntax in all the examples.

The command's output should look similar to the following:

```
Cloning into 'repository-name'...
remote: Counting objects: 3, done.
remote: Compressing objects: 100% (3/3), done.
remote: Total 3 (delta 2), reused 0 (delta 0), pack-reused 0
Unpacking objects: 100% (3/3), done.
Checking connectivity... done.
```

We can then move into the repository's directory using the change directory command (`cd`) and use the `git status` command to check the local repository status. The command's output should look similar to the following:

```
cd repository-name
git status
On branch master
Your branch is up-to-date with 'origin/master'.
nothing to commit, working directory clean
```

The `git status` command is telling us that there are no changes in our working directory. Let's open the repository folder in Visual Studio Code and create a new file called `gulpfile.js`. Now, run the `git status` command again, and we should see some new untracked files:

```
On branch master
Your branch is up-to-date with 'origin/master'.
Untracked files:
  (use "git add <file>..." to include in what will be committed)
    gulpfile.js
nothing added to commit but untracked files present (use "git add" to track)
```

> The project explorer in Visual Studio Code displays the files using a color code to help us to identify whether a file is new (green), has been removed (red), or has changed (yellow) since our last commit.

Automating Your Development Workflow

When we make some changes, such as adding a new file or changing an existing file, we need to execute the `git add` command to indicate that we want to add that change to a snapshot:

```
git add gulpfile.js
git status
On branch master
Your branch is up-to-date with 'origin/master'.
Changes to be committed:
  (use "git reset HEAD <file>..." to unstage)
    new file:   gulpfile.js
```

Now that we have staged the content we want to snapshot, we have to run the `git commit` command to actually record the snapshot. Recording a snapshot requires a commentary field, which can be provided using the `git commit` command together with the `-m` argument:

```
git commit -m "added the new gulpfile.js"
```

> **TIP**
> To run the preceding command you need to configure your GitHub email/username on the Terminal. You can use any one of the following commands to configure your GitHub account on the Terminal:
> `git config --global user.email "you@example.com"`
> `git config --global user.name "Your Name"`

If everything goes well, the command output should be similar to the following:

```
[master 2a62321] added the new file gulpfile.js
 1 file changed, 1 insertions(+)
 create mode 100644 gulpfile.js
```

To share the commit with the other developers, we need to push our changes to the remote repository. We can do this by executing the `git push` command:

```
git push
```

The `git push` command will ask for our GitHub username and password and then send the changes to the remote repository. If we visit the repository's page on GitHub, we will be able to find the recently created file. We will return to GitHub later in this chapter to configure our CI server.

[280]

> If we are working with a large team, we might encounter some file conflicts when attempting to push some changes to the remote repository. Resolving a file conflict is out of the scope of this book; however, if you need further information about Git, you will find an extensive user manual at `https://www.kernel.org/pub/software/scm/git/docs/user-manual.html`.

Package management tools

Package management tools are used for dependency management, so that we no longer have to manually download and manage our application's dependencies. We are not going to cover package management tools in this chapter because we have already covered them in `Chapter 5`, *Working with Dependencies*.

The TypeScript compiler

Now that we have learned how to use `npm`, we can install TypeScript using the following command:

```
npm install typescript -g
```

The TypeScript compiler will then become available in our CLI as a command named `tsc`. We can check the version of TypeScript installed in our machine using the following command:

```
tsc -v
```

The TypeScript compiler accepts many more options. For example, we can use the `--target` or `-t` option to select which version of JavaScript we would like to target as the compilation output:

```
tsc --target es6
```

Alternatively, we can create a `tsconfig.json` file to set the desired compilation settings. We can also use the TypeScript compiler to autogenerate a `tsconfig.json` file with default settings using the following command:

```
tsc --init
```

Automating Your Development Workflow

After creating a `tsconfig.json` file, you can pass it to the TypeScript compiler using the `--project` or `-p` option:

```
tsc -p tsconfig.json
```

> Please refer to the official TypeScript documentation at https://www.typescriptlang.org/docs/handbook/compiler-options.html if you wish to learn more about the available compilation options.

Linting tools

The following tool is a code linting tool. A linting tool helps us to enforce certain code styling rules in our code base. For example, in a large development team, it is very common to have long discussions about the code styling.

The term *code styling* refers to certain cosmetic elements of our code, such as using spaces or tabs. However, sometimes the code styling involves certain rules that are not purely cosmetic and are intended to make our code more maintainable. A good example of this would be a code styling rule that enforces using trailing commas.

Code styling guidelines and rules are great but enforcing them can take a significant amount of human effort. We would have to review every single code change to make sure that the code contributions respect our code styling rules.

The main goal of a linting tool is to automate the enforcement of the code styling rules.

In the TypeScript world, the leading linting tool is **tslint**. We can install `tslint` using `npm`:

```
npm install -g tslint
```

We then need to create a `tslint.json` file. This file contains the configuration that allows us to enable and disable certain styling rules. The following code snippet is an example of a `tslint.json` file:

```
{
    "extends": "tslint:all",
    "rules": {
      "array-type": [true, "array"],
      "ban-types": false,
      "comment-format": false,
      "completed-docs": false,
      "cyclomatic-complexity": false,
```

```
        "interface-name": false,
        "linebreak-style": false,
        "max-classes-per-file": false,
        "max-file-line-count": false,
        "max-line-length": [true, 140],
        "member-ordering": false,
        "newline-before-return": false,
        "no-any": false,
        "no-empty-interface": false,
        "no-floating-promises": false,
        "no-import-side-effect": false,
        "no-inferred-empty-object-type": false,
        "no-magic-numbers": false,
        "no-namespace": false,
        "no-null-keyword": false,
        "no-parameter-properties": false,
        "no-submodule-imports": false,
        "no-unbound-method": false,
        "no-unnecessary-class": false,
        "no-unnecessary-qualifier": false,
        "no-unsafe-any": false,
        "no-reference": false,
        "no-void-expression": false,
        "only-arrow-functions": false,
        "prefer-function-over-method": false,
        "prefer-template": false,
        "promise-function-async": false,
        "space-before-function-paren": false,
        "strict-boolean-expressions": false,
        "strict-type-predicates": false,
        "switch-default": false,
        "trailing-comma": false,
        "typedef": false,
        "variable-name": false
    }
}
```

After creating the tslint.json file, we can check our source code using the following command:

```
tslint --project tsconfig.json -c tslint.json ./**/*.ts
```

The preceding command is not really convenient. We can use `npm scripts` to create a more convenient command, named `lint`:

```
"scripts": {
  "lint": "tslint --project tsconfig.json -c tslint.json ./**/*.ts"
}
```

We can then run `tslint` using the following `npm` command:

```
npm run lint
```

Working with npm scripts

The `package.json` file contains a field named `scripts`. This field can contain multiple entries, and each entry is used to create a command. A command can execute any kind of custom logic.

When we create the `package.json` file using the `npm init` command, the default command is not implemented:

```
"scripts": {
    "test": "echo "Error: no test specified" && exit 1"
},
```

In a real-world scenario, we would have multiple commands as in the following example:

```
{
  "name": "repository-name",
  "version": "1.0.0",
  "description": "example",
  "main": "index.html",
  "scripts": {
    "start": "node ./src/index.js",
    "test": "gulp test",
    "lint": "tslint -c tslint.json ./**/*.ts"
  },
  "repository": {
    "type": "git",
    "url": "https://github.com/username/repository-name.git"
  },
```

Some commands, such as the `test`, `install`, or `start` commands, are considered standard commands. You can execute a standard command by using the `npm` command followed by the name of the standard command:

```
npm test
npm start
```

For the commands that are not considered standard, we need to use the `npm` command followed by the `run` command and the name of the command:

```
npm run lint
```

> Please refer to the npm documentation at `https://docs.npmjs.com` to learn more about all the npm features.

Gulp

Two of the most popular JavaScript task runners are Grunt and Gulp. The main difference between Gulp and Grunt is that while in Grunt we work using files as the input and output of our tasks, in Gulp we work with streams and pipes.

Grunt is configured using some configuration fields and values. However, Gulp prefers code over configuration. This approach makes the Gulp configuration somehow more minimalist and easy to read.

> In this book, we will work with Gulp; however, if you want to learn more about Grunt, you can do so at `http://gruntjs.com/`.

To gain a good understanding of Gulp, we are going to configure some tasks.

Let's start by installing `gulp` using `npm`:

```
npm install gulp -g
```

Automating Your Development Workflow

Then let's create a JavaScript file named `gulpfile.js` inside the root folder of our project, which should contain the following piece of code:

```
let gulp = require("gulp");

gulp.task("hello", function() {
    console.log("Hello Gulp!");
});
```

And, finally, run `gulp`:

gulp hello

> Please note that we installed Gulp using the `-g` flag because we are going to invoke the `gulp` command directly from the command-line interface. However, if we are planning to use `npm scripts`, we should install Gulp and any other dependencies as project dependencies using the `--save-dev` flag instead. Note that using global (`-g`) dependencies is not recommended. Also, note that we must execute this command from the location in which the `gulpfile.js` file is located.

We have created our first Gulp task, which is named `hello`. When we run the `gulp` command, it will automatically try to search for the `gulpfile.js` in the current directory, and once found, it will try to find the `hello` task. If everything worked as expected, we should see an output similar to the following in our CLI:

Using gulpfile
Starting 'hello'...
Hello Gulp!
Finished 'hello' after 255 μs

We will now add a second task, which will use the `gulp-tslint` plugin to check whether our TypeScript code follows a series of recommended practices.

We need to install the plugin with `npm`:

npm install tslint gulp-tslint -g

We can then load the plugin in our `gulpfile.js` file and add a new task:

```
let tslint = require("tslint");
let gulpTslint = require("gulp-tslint");

gulp.task("lint", function() {
```

[286]

```
    let program = tslint.Linter.createProgram("./tsconfig.json");
    return gulp.src([
        "src/**/**.ts",
        "test/**/**.test.ts"
    ])
    .pipe(gulpTslint({
        formatter: "stylish",
        program
    }))
    .pipe(gulpTslint.report());
});
```

We have named the new task `lint`. Let's take a look at the operations performed by the `lint` task, step by step:

1. The `gulp src` function will read the files with the file extension `.ts` located in the `src` directory and its subdirectories. We are also fetching all the files with the file extension `.test.ts` in the directory located in `test` and its subdirectories.
2. Many plugins allow us to indicate files to be ignored by adding the exclamation symbol (`!`) before a path. For example, the path `!path/*.d.ts` will ignore all files with the extension `.d.ts`.
3. The `pipe` function is used to pass the output stream of the `src` as the input of the `gulpTslint` function.
4. Finally, we use the output of the `tslint` function as the input of the `report` function.

Now that we have added the `lint` task, we will modify the `gulpfile.js` file to add one more task, named `default`:

```
gulp.task("default", ["hello", "lint"]);
```

The default task can be used to invoke both the `hello` and `lint` tasks. When we define a `gulp` task, we invoke the `task` function with two arguments. The first argument is the task name. The second argument can take a function that defines a task or an array containing a list of subtasks.

Controlling the gulp task execution order

We will now learn how to control the order in which the tasks are executed. If we try to execute the default, the `hello` and `lint` tasks will be executed in parallel because the subtasks are executed in parallel by default.

Sometimes we will need to run our tasks in a certain order. Controlling the execution order of our tasks can be challenging since in Gulp all the tasks are asynchronous by default.

However, there are three ways to make a task synchronous.

Passing in a callback to the task definition function

All we need to do is to pass a callback function to the task definition function as follows:

```
gulp.task("sync", function (cb) {
    // We used setTimeout here to illustrate an async operation
    setTimeout(function () {
        console.log("Hello Gulp!");
        cb(); // note the cb usage here
    }, 1000);
});
```

Returning a promise

All we need to do is to use a promise as the return of the task definition function as follows:

```
gulp.task("sync", function () {
    return new Promise((resolve) => {
        setTimeout(function () {
            console.log("Hello Gulp!");
            resolve();
        }, 1000);
    });
});
```

Returning a stream

All we need to do is to use a stream as the return of the task definition function. This is simple because the pipe operator returns a stream:

```
gulp.task("sync", function () {
    return gulp.src([
        "src/**/**.ts"
    ])
    .pipe(somePlugin({}))
    .pipe(somePlugin ());
});
```

Now that we have some synchronous tasks, we can use them as a subtask of a new task named `async`:

```
gulp.task("async", ["sync1", "sync2"], function () {
    // This task will not start until
    // the sync tasks are completed!
    console.log("Done!");
});
```

As we can see in the preceding code snippet, it is also possible to define a task that has some subtasks. However, if the complexity of our build process increases, we can end up with a very difficult to follow task dependency graph. Fortunately, we can install the `run-sequence` Gulp plugin via `npm`, which will allow us to have better control over the task execution order:

```
let runSequence = require('run-sequence');

gulp.task('default', function(cb) {
    runSequence(
        'lint',                          // lint
        ['tsc', 'tsc-tests'],            // compile
        ['bundle-js','bundle-test'],     // optimize
        'karma'                          // test
        'browser-sync',                  // serve
        cb                               // callback
    );
});
```

The preceding code snippet will run in the following order:

1. `lint`
2. `tsc` and `tsc-tests` in parallel
3. `bundle-js` and `bundle-test` in parallel
4. `karma`
5. `browser-sync`

> The Gulp development team announced plans to improve the management of the task execution order without the need of external plugins. Refer to the Gulp documentation at `https://github.com/gulpjs/gulp/` to learn more about it.

Webpack

As we already know, when we compile our TypeScript code, the compiler will generate a JavaScript file for each existing TypeScript file. If we run the application in a web browser, these files won't be really useful on their own because the only way to use them would be to create an individual HTML `script` tag for each one of them.

However, this would be highly inconvenient and inefficient because each `script` tag will translate into a round trip between the web browser and the server serving the JavaScript files. Using `script` tags is also slower than using Ajax calls because `script` tags can prevent the browser from rendering.

> Please note that in a modern web browser, we can make some of the `script` tags asynchronous but it is not always an option. Please refer to https://developers.google.com/web/fundamentals/performance/critical-rendering-path/adding-interactivity-with-javascript to learn more about asynchronous scripts.

Fortunately, there are a few potential solutions for this problem:

- **Load the files using AJAX calls**: We can use a tool to load each of the JavaScript files on demand using AJAX calls. This approach is known as asynchronous module loading. To follow this approach, we will need to use Require.js and change the configuration of the TypeScript compiler to use the asynchronous module definition (AMD) notation.
- **Bundle all the files into one unique file and load it using a script tag**: We can use a tool to trace the application modules and dependencies and generate a highly optimized single file, which will contain all the application modules. To follow this approach, we will need to use a tool, such as Webpack or Browserify and change the configuration of the TypeScript compiler to use the correct module syntax (usually CommonJS).
- **Hybrid approach**: We can follow a hybrid approach by creating a highly optimized bundle that contains the minimum number of files required by the application to be able to work. Additional files are then loaded on demand using AJAX calls when they are required by the application users.

> Please refer to `Chapter 5`, *Working with Dependencies*, to learn more about modules.

In this chapter, we are going to focus on the second approach. We will create a highly optimized module bundler using Webpack. Creating a highly optimized application bundle usually involves multiple steps; Webpack can perform each of these tasks but it is not really designed to be used as a task runner. We can install Webpack using npm:

```
npm install webpack --save-dev
```

We are also going to install a few extra modules required by this example:

```
npm install awesome-typescript-loader css-loader extract-text-webpack-plugin node-sass resolve-url-loader sass-loader style-loader --save-dev
```

Most of these modules are Webpack plugins and their dependencies. We need them because we are going to use them in our Webpack configuration file.

We can configure Webpack by creating a file named `webpack.config.js` in the root directory of our project. The following code section displays the entire content of the Webpack configuration file used by the companion source code of this chapter.

The `webpack.config.js` file is importing some dependencies:

```
const { CheckerPlugin, TsConfigPathsPlugin } = require("awesome-typescript-loader");
const webpack = require("webpack");
const ExtractTextPlugin = require("extract-text-webpack-plugin");
```

Then, we declare three variables:

- The `corePlugins` variable is an array that contains the configuration of Webpack plugins that are used in development builds and production builds
- The `devPlugins` variable is an array that contains the configuration of Webpack plugins used in development builds only
- The `prodPlugins` variable is an array that contains the configuration of Webpack plugins used in production builds only

Each of the plugins requires some specific configuration. For example, the `ExtractTextPlugin` is used to extract our CSS code from the main application bundle:

```
const corePlugins = [
    new CheckerPlugin(),
    new webpack.DefinePlugin({
        "process.env.NODE_ENV": JSON.stringify(process.env.NODE_ENV || "development")
    }),
    new ExtractTextPlugin({
```

[291]

Automating Your Development Workflow

```
            filename: "[name]main.css",
            allChunks: true
        })
    ];

    const devPlugins = [];

    const prodPlugins = [
        new webpack.optimize.UglifyJsPlugin({
            output: { comments: false }
        })
    ];

    const isProduction = process.env.NODE_ENV === "production";
    const plugins = isProduction ? corePlugins.concat(prodPlugins) :
    corePlugins.concat(devPlugins);
```

The configuration file uses the environment variable `NODE_ENV` determine whether we are running a development build or a production build. The production build uses the `uglify` plugin, but it is not used by the development build.

We then use the `uglify` plugin to minimize the output size. The reduced file size will reduce the application loading time but will make it harder to debug. Fortunately, we can generate source maps to facilitate the debugging process. The source maps are generated by the `source-map-loader` plugin.

> Uglify removes all line breaks and whitespaces and reduces the length of some variable names. Source map files allow us to map the source code of the reduced file to its original code while debugging. A source map provides a way of mapping code within a compressed file back to its original position in a source file. This means we can easily debug an application even after its assets have been optimized. The Chrome and Firefox developer tools both ship with built-in support for source maps.

At this point, we define the application's entry point. We use an object as a map to define an entry point, which means that we can define multiple entry points. Each entry point is transformed into a `bundle.js` file that will be stored under a directory named `public`.

As we can see in the rest of the `webpack.config.js` file, we have appended a forward slash to the name of the application's entry point. We have also used a special syntax to use the name of the entry point as part of the name of the output files (for example, `[name]bundle.js`). This is a trick that we can use to generate a unique folder for each of the output bundles.

Finally, the file declares the configuration for some of the plugins, such as the TypeScript plugin or the `sass` plugin:

```
module.exports = {
    entry: {
        "calculator_app/": "./src/main_browser.ts"
    },
    devServer: {
        inline: true
    },
    output: {
        filename: "[name]bundle.js",
        path: __dirname + "/public",
        publicPath: "/public"
    },
    devtool: isProduction ? "source-map" : "eval-source-map",
    resolve: {
        extensions: [".webpack.js", ".ts", ".tsx", ".js"],
        plugins: [
            new TsConfigPathsPlugin({
                configFileName: "tsconfig.json"
            })
        ]
    },
    module: {
        rules: [
            {
                enforce: "pre",
                test: /.js$/,
                loader: "source-map-loader",
                exclude: [/node_modules/, /experimental/]
            },
            {
                test: /.(ts|tsx)$/,
                loader: "awesome-typescript-loader",
                exclude: [/node_modules/, /experimental/]
            },
            {
                test: /.scss$/,
                use: ExtractTextPlugin.extract({
                    fallback: "style-loader",
                    use: ["css-loader", "resolve-url-loader", "sass-loader"]
                })
            }
        ]
    },
```

[293]

Automating Your Development Workflow

```
    plugins: plugins
};
```

We can execute the Webpack bundling process using the following command:

webpack

> Please note that we must execute this command from the location in which the `gulpfile.js` file is located.

If everything went well, we should be able to see a new folder named `public`. The `public` folder should contain the following files:

```
public/
└── calculator_app
    ├── bundle.js
    └── main.css
```

The companion source code also includes a file named `index.html`. This file is the entry point of the frontend application that we just created:

```
<!doctype html>
<html lang="en">
  <head>
    <meta charset="utf-8">
    <link rel="stylesheet" href="./public/calculator_app/main.css">
    <title>Calculator</title>
  </head>
  <body>
    <div id="main"><!-- Content created by JavaScript --></div>
    <script src="./public/calculator_app/bundle.js"></script>
  </body>
</html>
```

This example should give us a good first impression about how to work with Webpack. The following section describes how we can use the Webpack development as a web server to access this application from a web browser.

> Please refer to the documentation at `https://webpack.js.org/concepts/` if you need additional information about webpack. It is also recommended to refer to the documentation of each of the plugins to learn more about the available configuration options. Some npm modules might require some additional tools. It is not very common, but some modules might require tools such as the gcc/g++ compilers and the Python interpreter to be installed in your development environment. Please refer to the documentation of your operating system online to learn how to install the gcc/g++ compilers and the Python interpreter if you encounter this kind of issue.

Webpack development server

The Webpack development server is a command-line utility that monitors our filesystem for changes and triggers the Webpack bundling process.

We can install the Webpack development server using npm:

```
npm install -g webpack-dev-server
```

We can then execute the webpack development server using the following command:

```
webpack-dev-server
```

The Webpack development server will then start watching our filesystem for changes. If a change is detected, it will automatically run the Webpack build process using the existing the `webpack.config.js` file.

The Webpack development server also starts a web server. The server is running on port 8080 by default.

> Please refer to the documentation at `https://github.com/webpack/webpack-dev-server` to learn more about the Webpack development server.

[295]

Unit testing and test coverage

Unit testing refers to the practice of testing certain functions and areas (units) of our code. This gives us the ability to verify that our functions work as expected.

> It is expected that the reader will have some understanding of the unit test process, but the contents exposed here will be covered at a much higher level of detail in Chapter 14, *Application Testing*.

At the beginning of this chapter, we included the most important parts of the application included in the companion source code for this chapter. The source code defined a calculator with support for two operations: pow and add.

The pow operation expects two numbers as its arguments and has two possible execution paths:

- The pow function will throw an exception if one of the two arguments provided is not a number
- The pow function will return a number if both arguments are valid numbers

Ideally, we will write a unit test of each of the execution paths of our function.

The following code snippet declares a couple of unit tests for the pow operation using two testing libraries, mocha and chai:

```
import { expect } from "chai";
import { pow } from "../src/operations/pow";

describe("Operation: pow", () => {

    it ("Should be able to calculate operation", () => {
        const result = pow(2, 3);
        expect(result).to.eql(8);
    });

    it ("Should throw if an invalid argument is provided", () => {
        const a: any = "2";
        const b: any = 3;
        const throws = () => pow(a, b);
        expect(throws).to.throw();
    });

});
```

The preceding code snippet groups all the tests related to the `pow` operation in what is known as a **test fixture**. A test fixture can be defined using the `describe` function and is just a group of test cases. A test case can be defined using the `it` functions and can contain one or more test assertions.

Our test assertions are defined using the `assert` function, which is part of the Chai library.

Both the `describe` and the `it` functions are global functions declared by Mocha. We don't need to import `Mocha` because it is imported as a global by our test runner configuration.

We can run the tests and generate a test coverage report using the following command:

```
nyc -x **/*.js --clean --all --require ts-node/register --extension .ts
-- mocha --timeout 5000 **/*.test.ts
```

The preceding command uses `nyc`, which is a tool used to generate test coverage reports. This tool uses `ts-node` and `mocha` to run the tests. This explains why we can run the test without compiling them and why we can use Mocha without importing it explicitly.

This command is not very convenient, but we can declare an `npm` command to solve this problem:

```
"scripts": {
    "nyc": "nyc -x **/*.js --clean --all --require ts-node/register --extension .ts -- mocha --timeout 5000 **/*.test.ts"
}
```

Please note that we need to install all these dependencies and their type definitions (when appropriate) using npm. We can then use the following npm command instead:

```
npm run nyc
```

Automating Your Development Workflow

The companion source code includes many more tests. The existing tests cover most of the possible execution paths of all the existing functions in the application but don't fully cover the `main_server.ts` file. This can be observed in the test coverage report generated by `nyc`:

```
Operation: add
  ✓ Should be able to calculate operation
  ✓ Should throw if an invalid argument is provided

Calculator
  ✓ Should be able to calculate operations
  ✓ Should throw if an invalid operation is provided

Operation: pow
  ✓ Should be able to calculate operation
  ✓ Should throw if an invalid argument is provided

isNumber
  ✓ Should be able to add calculate operation
  ✓ Should throw if an invalid argument is provided


8 passing (17ms)
```

File	% Stmts	% Branch	% Funcs	% Lines	Uncovered Lines
All files	91.76	100	100	91.03	
src	63.16	100	100	58.82	
calculator.ts	100	100	100	100	
main.ts	0	100	100	0	2,3,4,5,6,7,8
src/operations	100	100	100	100	
add.ts	100	100	100	100	
pow.ts	100	100	100	100	
validation.ts	100	100	100	100	
test	100	100	100	100	
add.test.ts	100	100	100	100	
calculator.test.ts	100	100	100	100	
pow.test.ts	100	100	100	100	
validation.test.ts	100	100	100	100	

Visual Studio Code

Visual Studio is a lightweight but powerful code editor with an extensive number of features. Learning all these features is out of the scope of this book because we could dedicate an entire book to cover them. However, we are going to dedicate a little bit of time to learning about two of the best features available in this code editor: quick fixes and the code debugger.

> It is recommended to read the Visual Studio Code user guide at `https://code.visualstudio.com/docs/editor/codebasics` to learn how to make the most of this IDE.

Quick fixes

Visual Studio Code can detect some errors and automatically fix them using a set of features known as *quick fixes*.

Visual Studio Code will display a bulb icon on the left-hand side of our code near some error. If we click on the bulb icon, Visual Studio Code will display all the available quick fixes. If we select one of the available quick fixes, Visual Studio Code will perform the necessary changes to solve the problem automatically:

```
1    interface Person {
2        doSometing(): string;
3    }
4    
5    class User implements Person {
6        Implement interface 'Person'
7    }
8
```

Debugging utilities

Before we can debug our application using Node.js, we need to configure a debugging task in Visual Studio Code. We need to select the debug panel and add a new configuration:

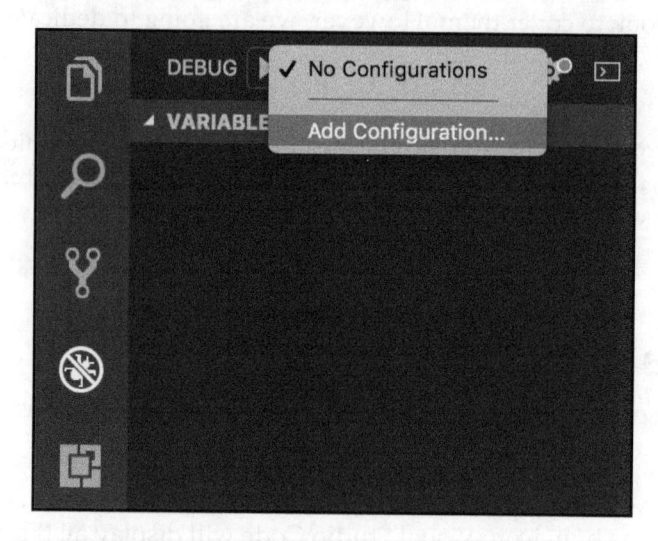

A panel with a few options will then be displayed. We need to select Node.js. If you want to run and debug the application using Docker, you will be able to do so as well but it is out of the scope of this book:

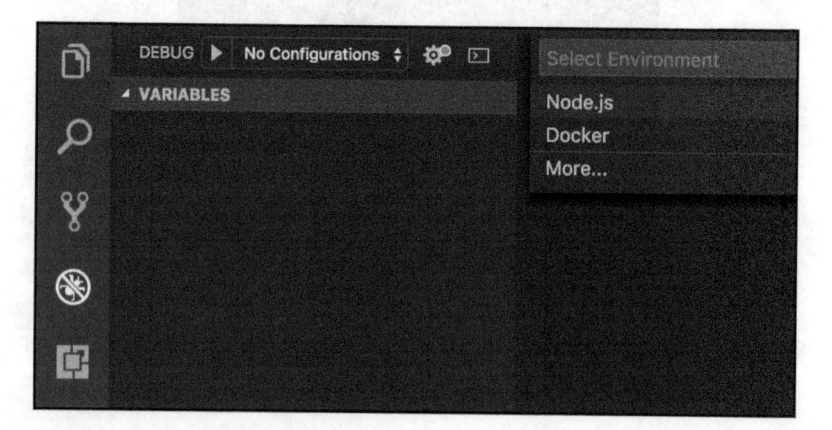

Selecting Node.js will create a folder named `.vscode` and a file named `launch.json`. This file allows us to define as many debugging tasks as we may need. A debug task declares the instructions required to debug our unit tests.

The configuration of the debugging task is different for each testing tool. In the example application, we have used `mocha`, which means that our debugging task will need to use the `mocha` binary and some arguments to start a debugging session.

The following configuration can be used to debug the tests in the example application:

```
{
    "version": "0.2.0",
    "configurations": [
        {
            "type": "node",
            "request": "launch",
            "name": "Debug Mocha Tests",
            "program": "${workspaceFolder}/node_modules/mocha/bin/_mocha",
            "args": [
                "--require",
                "ts-node/register",
                "-u",
                "tdd",
                "--timeout",
                "999999",
                "--colors",
                "${workspaceFolder}/test/**/*.test.ts"
            ],
            "internalConsoleOptions": "openOnSessionStart",
            "sourceMaps": true
        }
    ]
}
```

> Please note that the `.vscode` folder must be in the root of your project. The companion source code includes this folder under the chapter's folder instead of the root directory. If you want to try it, you will need to open the chapter's folder as the root directory with Visual Studio Code.

After creating and configuring the `launch.json` file, we can select the task that we just defined under the **DEBUG** panel and click on the *Play* button:

The test execution will be paused when a breakpoint is reached. We can set a breakpoint by clicking on the left-hand side of a line in our source code:

```typescript
import { expect } from "chai";
import { Calculator } from "../src/calculator";

describe("Calculator", () => {

    it ("Should be able to calculate operations", () => {
        const calculator = new Calculator();
        const addResult = calculator.calculate("add", 2, 3);
        expect(addResult).to.eql(5);
        const powResult = calculator.calculate("pow", 2, 3);
        expect(powResult).to.eql(8);
    });
```

The Visual Studio Code debugging panel allows us to examine the current execution context using the debugging panel available on the left-hand side of the screen. This panel contains a few subpanels:

- The variables panel allows us to see all the variables declared in the current execution context.
- The watch panel allows us to create a *watcher*. A watcher is just a filter that allows us to display the value of a variable of our choice.
- The call stack panel allows us to see the function call stack. We can click on the function in the call stack to navigate to the selected function.
- The breakpoints panel allows us to enable and disable the breakpoints that we have created, as well as to enable some generic ones (for example, uncaught exceptions):

Chapter 9

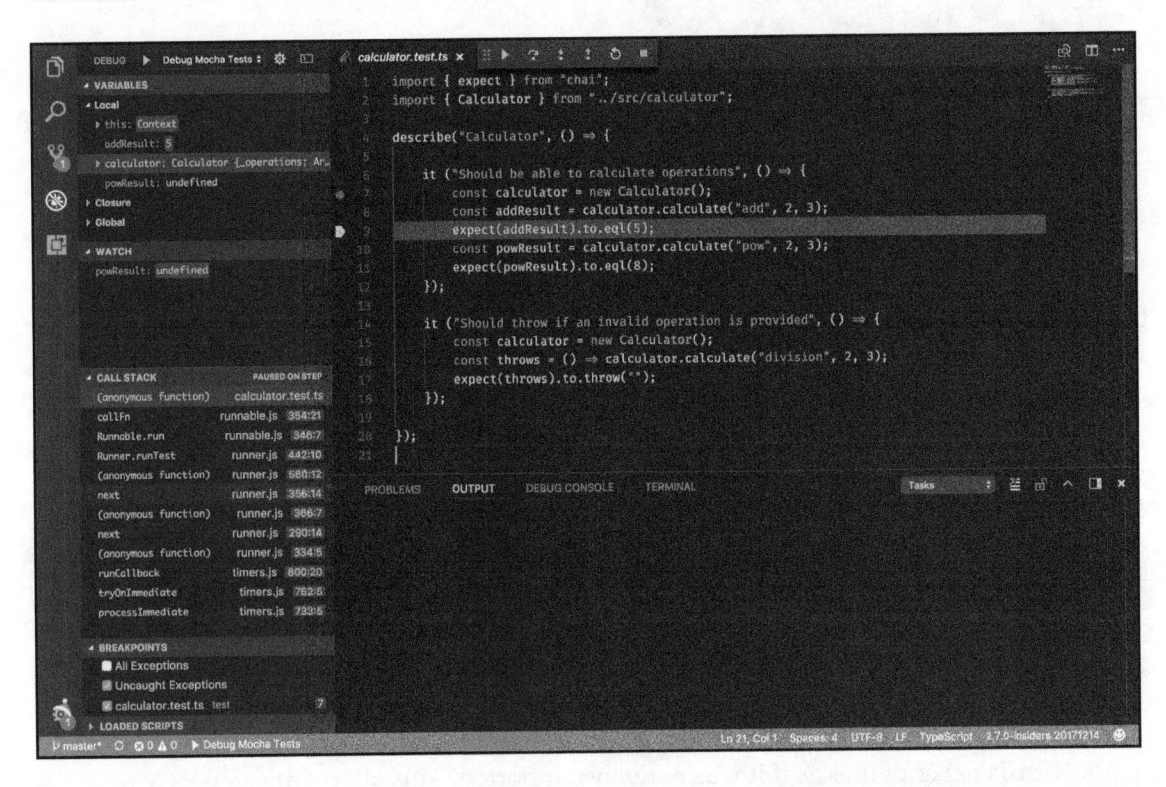

The execution panel located on the top of the screen allows us to control the execution of the test at our own pace.

Source control utilities

Visual Studio Code also allows us to interact with Git through a graphical user interface. To access the Git features, we need to click on the Git panel on the left-hand side of the screen.

[303]

Automating Your Development Workflow

The Git panel allows us to see the current changes. We can select changes to be committed (stag) or roll back the changes. We can then commit the changes by introducing a message and clicking on the approval icon located on the top right-hand side of the Git panel:

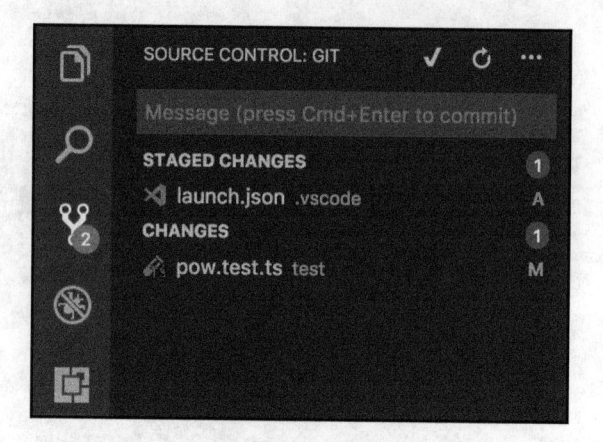

ts-node

The TypeScript community has developed an alternative version of Node.js that is able to work with TypeScript files as if it was natively supported. This alternative version of Node.js is known as `ts-node`.

The `ts-node` command allows us to execute TypeScript files without having to compile them first. We can execute a TypeScript file using the following command:

```
ts-node ./src/main_server.ts
```

The example application uses npm `scripts` to create a more convenient version of this command:

```
"scripts": {
  "ts-node": "ts-node ./src/main_server.ts"
}
```

The `npm` command can be executed as follows:

```
npm run ts-node
```

By default, the `ts-node` command tries to find the compilation setting in the `tsconfig.json` file and expects it to be located in the current directory.

[304]

The `ts-node` command is a very convenient tool when we want to try something without having to spend too much time configuring a tool such as Webpack.

It may feel like `ts-node` can execute TypeScript natively, but this is not the case. Our TypeScript code is first compiled and then executed using the Node.js binary. This means that using `ts-node` in a production Node.js application is not recommended because we will pay a performance penalty (the compilation time).

Continuous integration (CI) tools

CI is a development practice that helps to prevent potential integration issues. Software integration issues refer to the difficulties that may arise during the practice of combining individually tested software components into an integrated whole. Software is integrated when components are combined into subsystems or when subsystems are combined into products.

Components may be integrated after all are implemented and tested, as in a waterfall model or a big bang approach. On the other hand, CI requires developers to daily commit their code into a remote code repository. Each commit is then verified by an automated process, allowing teams to detect integration issues earlier.

In this chapter, we have learned how to create a code repository on GitHub and how to validate our application using unit tests and linting tools, but we haven't configured a CI server to observe our commits and run these validations accordingly.

We are going to use Travis CI as our CI server because it is highly integrated with GitHub and is free for open source projects and learning purposes. There are many other options when it comes to choosing a CI server, but exploring these options is out of the scope of this book.

To configure Travis CI, we need to visit `https://travis-ci.org` and log in using our GitHub credentials. Once we have logged in, we will be able to see a list of our public GitHub repositories and will also be able to enable the CI:

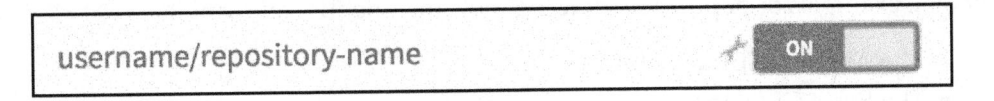

```
username/repository-name                    ON
```

Automating Your Development Workflow

To finish the configuration, we need to add a file named `travis.yml` to our application's root directory, which contains the Travis CI configuration:

```
language: node_js
node_js:
  - stable
```

> There are many other available Travis CI configuration options. Refer to http://docs.travis-ci.com/ to learn more about the available options.

After completing these two small configuration steps, Travis CI will be ready to observe the commits to our remote code repository.

We have used the configuration to indicate to Travis CI that our application is a Node.js application. The CI build for each potential kind of application can be highly customized, regardless of its technology stack.

However, in most cases, we will simply use the defaults set for a given kind of application. In the case of Node.js, Travis CI uses `npm install` and `npm test` as the default commands.

> If the build works in the local development environment, but fails in the CI server, we will have to check the build error log and try to figure out what went wrong. Chances are that the software versions in our environment will be ahead of the ones in the CI server and we will need to indicate to Travis CI that a dependency needs to be installed or updated. We can find the Travis CI documentation at http://docs.travis-ci.com/user/build-configuration/ to learn how to resolve this kind of issue.

Scaffolding tools

A scaffolding tool is used to autogenerate the project structure, building scripts, and much more. Some examples of popular scaffolding tools include the following:

- The Angular CLI
- The React CLI (create-react-app-typescript)
- Yeoman

[306]

These tools are designed to support many kinds of projects. The scaffolding tools will save us time by autogenerating some things for us, such as the webpack configuration or the `package.json` file.

It is highly recommended to spend some time reading the documentation of these tools to learn more about their existing customization options.

> Please note that you can learn more about the Angular CLI, the React CLI, and Yeoman at `https://cli.angular.io`, `https://github.com/wmonk/create-react-app-typescript`, and `http://yeoman.io` respectively. Please note that it is never a good idea to let a tool generate some code for us if we don't understand what that code does. While, in the future, you should consider using a tool to generate a new project, it is recommended to gain a good understanding of task and test runners before using a scaffolding tool.

Why does the command line win?

You may have noticed that during this chapter, we have used the CLI a lot instead of visual tools. We have used the command-line terminal to perform many kinds of tasks:

- Work with source control
- Install dependencies
- Run tasks
- Test our code
- Debug our code
- Create projects

The CLI has always been popular but I remember that, a few years ago, I used to do some of these things using Visual tools. For example, I remember running unit tests in .NET applications using a visual test runner for NUnit (a unit testing library for .NET applications). You might be wondering why we stopped using the visual tool and went back to the command line like in the early days?

I believe that the CLI wins for two main reasons:

- Our software development teams have become much more diverse
- Our software development methodologies have evolved toward automation

Our software teams are much more diverse today and, as a result, it is common to encounter teams composed of DevOps engineers who work with a Linux distribution, mobile software engineers who work on OS X, and web engineers who work on Windows.

The team members may use different operating systems, but they all follow the same process, and they share one unique development process. For example, if one of the members of the team wants to execute the unit tests, it would be possible to do so by executing a command in the OS console. We can go one step further and also use the same command as part of our CI build.

The CLI wins because it enables our development teams to share one unique set of development processes and practices.

Summary

In this chapter, we learned how to work with a long list of different development tools. It is impossible to cover so many tools in depth in one chapter, but now that we know the basics, it should be much easier to gradually dive deeper into more advanced use cases.

In the next chapter, we will learn about the development of backend applications with Node.js and TypeScript.

10
Node.js Development with TypeScript

Over the preceding chapters of this book, we have been using Node.js and some of the tools of its ecosystem, but we haven't developed a Node.js application. In this chapter, we are going to learn how to develop applications with Node.js. We are going to cover the following topics:

- The main characteristics of Node.js
- The main characteristics of the Node.js core API
- Server-side development with Node.js
- Developing REST APIs with Node.js

Understanding Node.js

Node.js is a JavaScript runtime built on Chrome's V8 JavaScript engine. Node.js is single-threaded and uses an event-driven, non-blocking I/O model that makes it lightweight and efficient.

Understanding non-blocking I/O

An input or output operation (I/O) is an operation that requires writing or reading from a physical source. This includes things such as saving a file into your hard disk or sending a file through the network.

In the past, operating systems only allowed us to perform I/O operations in what is known as a blocking model. In a **blocking model**, we can run an application in a thread, but when an I/O request takes place, the thread is blocked until the request is completed.

Web servers implemented using blocking I/O are not be able to handle multiple simultaneous connections using the same thread. For example, when an HTTP request arrives at the web server, it might need to perform some I/O operation (for example, reading from a database or talking to another server through the network) to provide the creator of the request with a response. If the web server uses one unique thread, it will be blocked until the I/O operation has been completed. As a result, if a second HTTP request hits the server, the server will not be able to handle it. The solution to this problem was to create a new thread for each HTTP request but this solution was not scalable because a single CPU cannot handle a very large number of threads and CPUs are one of the most expensive components of a server.

The following diagram represents the blocking I/O model:

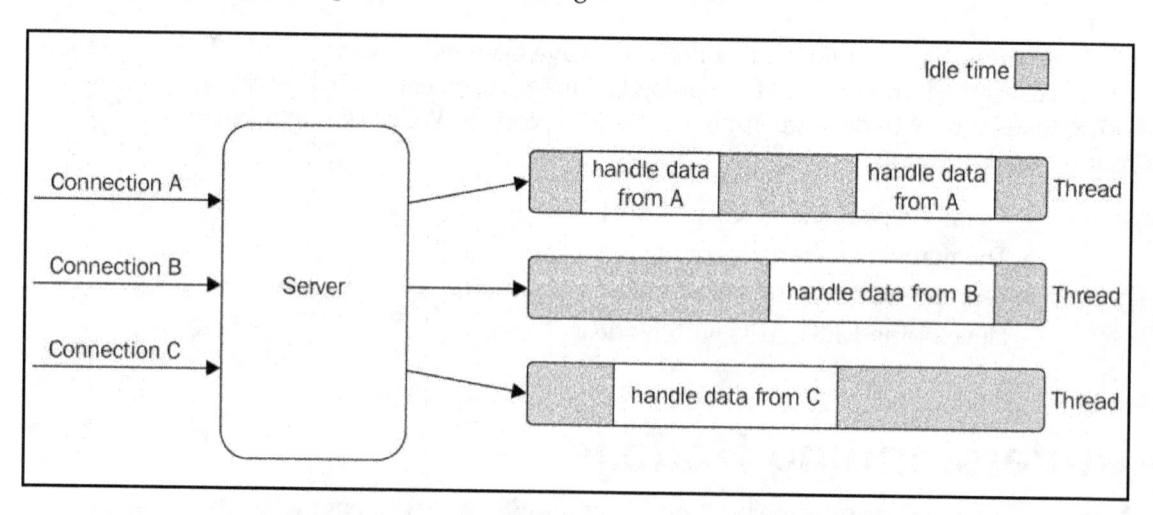

The non-blocking I/O model is the solution to the limitations of the blocking I/O model. In the non-blocking model, an I/O request doesn't block the main thread. Instead of that, the I/O events are collected and queued by a component known as the event demultiplexer. Node.js implements a pattern known as the reactor pattern, which combines the JavaScript event loop with the event demultiplexer.

The following diagram represents the interactions between the event loop and the event demultiplexer:

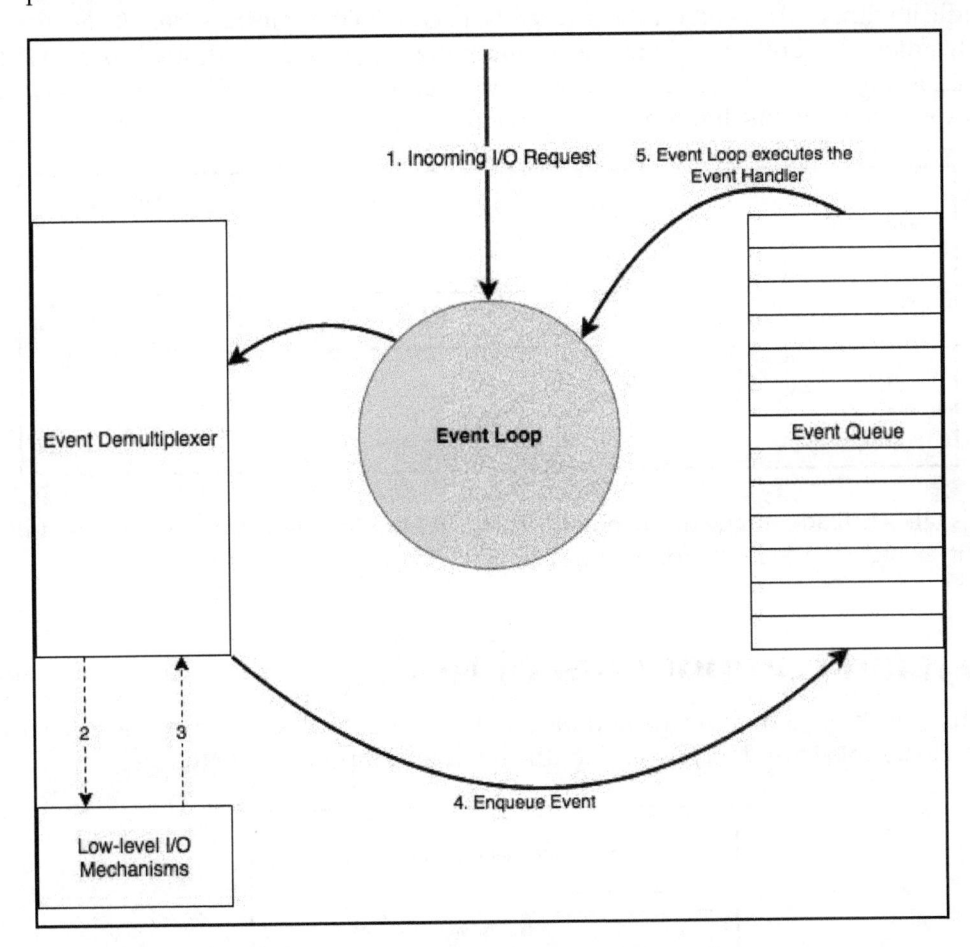

```
1. Incoming I/O Request        5. Event Loop executes the
                                   Event Handler

    Event Demultiplexer    Event Loop    Event Queue

         2    3
                           4. Enqueue Event
    Low-level I/O
    Mechanisms
```

The main idea behind it is to have a handler (which in Node.js is represented by a callback function) associated with each I/O operation. When the I/O operation is completed, an event is produced and consumed by the JavaScript event loop, which invokes the handler.

> Please refer to `Chapter 6`, *Understanding the Runtime*, to learn more about the JavaScript event loop and the way event handlers work.

If the web server uses one unique thread, it will not be blocked until the I/O operation has been completed. As a result, if a second HTTP request hits the server, the server will be able to handle it without the need for more threads. Each HTTP request creates I/O events and event handlers that are stored in memory, and if the server is hit by thousands of HTTP requests, it can still reach a limit. However, the level of concurrent HTTP requests is much higher than the previous limit imposed by the blocking I/O model:

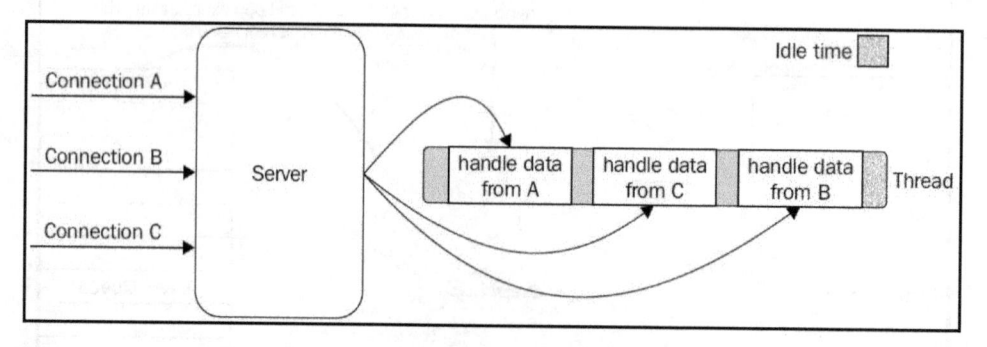

Node.js takes full advantage of the non-blocking I/O model and is fundamentally built on top of it, as we will see in the following section.

The main components of Node.js

Now that we understand how the non-blocking I/O model works, we are in a much better position to be able to understand each of the internal components of Node.js:

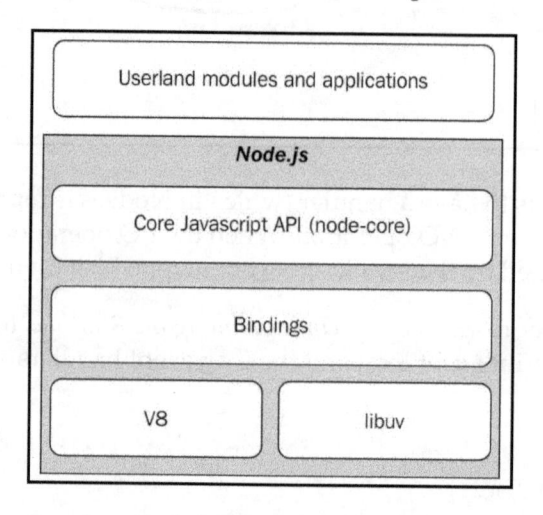

V8

V8 is the JavaScript engine originally developed for Google's Chrome. It is responsible for the parsing, interpretation, and execution of JavaScript.

> Please refer to the V8 documentation at `https://github.com/v8/v8/wiki` if you wish to learn more about it.

Libuv

Each operating system has its interface for the event demultiplexer and each I/O operation can behave quite differently depending on the type of the resource, even within the same OS. Libuv is a C library that makes Node.js compatible with all the major platforms and normalizes the non-blocking behavior of the different types of resource; libuv today represents the low-level I/O engine of Node.js.

> Please refer to the official libuv documentation at `https://libuv.org/` and `http://docs.libuv.org/en/v1.x/` if you wish to learn more.

Bindings

The bindings are a set of libraries that wrap the V8 and libuv public APIs in a way that allows us to consume them using JavaScript instead of C or C++ code.

The Node.js core API (node-core)

Node.js includes a set of core APIs to perform common operations, such as reading files, sending an HTTP request, or encrypting a text file. These APIs use V8 and libuv under the hood, but they don't talk to them directly, they do it through the bindings.

> Please note that we will learn more about the Node.js core APIs later in this chapter.

Node.js environment versus browser environment

The Node.js environment and the browser environment are not identical. For example, the environment in web browsers includes an API known as the **Document Object Model** (**DOM**) and an API known as the **Browser Object Model** (**BOM**). These APIs define APIs, such as the window object or the history API. However, these APIs are not available in the Node.js environment. The following table highlights some of the most significant differences between the environment Node.js and web browsers:

Feature	Node.js	Web browsers
DOM	No	Yes
BOM	No	Yes
Global variable is named window	No	Yes
Global variable is named global	Yes	No
The require function	Yes	No
Common JS modules	Yes	No
Access to sensitive resources (for example, the filesystem)	Yes	No

The Node.js ecosystem

In this section, we are going to explore the Node.js ecosystem. We are going to learn what Node.js has to offer us, and some significant code conventions are followed by its entire ecosystem.

The Node.js core API

The Node.js core API, also known as node-core, is a set of libraries that are part of Node.js and, as a result, are installed in our OS when we install Node.js. The Node.js core API includes the following modules:

- `assert`
- `async_hooks`
- `buffer`

Chapter 10

- `child_process`
- `cluster`
- `crypto`
- `dgram`
- `dns`
- `domain`
- `events`
- `fs`
- `http`
- `http2`
- `https`
- `net`
- `os`
- `path`
- `perf_hooks`
- `punycode`
- `querystring`
- `readline`
- `repl`
- `stream`
- `string_decoder`
- `tls`
- `tty`
- `url`
- `util`
- `v8`
- `vm`
- `zlib`

As we can see in the preceding list, there are modules to work with **Domain Name Servers** (**DNS**), working with HTTP requests (`http`), or reading and writing files to the hard disk (`fs`). Covering all these modules is out of the scope of this book. However, we are going to use some of them later in this chapter.

Node.js Development with TypeScript

> Please note that you can visit the official Node.js documentation at `https://nodejs.org/docs/` to learn all the details about each of the features available in each of the modules.

The style of the Node.js core API

Earlier in this chapter, we learned how the reactor pattern and the non-blocking I/O model are two of the most fundamental characteristics of Node.js. This should help us to understand why callbacks are used so extensively in the entire Node.js core API. As we can imagine, the core API has a direct impact on all the other modules. As a result, the entire Node.js ecosystem uses callbacks extensively.

Node.js not only uses callbacks extensively, but it also uses them in a very consistent way:

- Callbacks in Node.js are always the last argument of a function
- Callbacks in Node.js always take an error as the first argument

The following code snippet uses the filesystem API to read a text file. The `readFile` function showcases the two preceding rules in action:

```
import { readFile } from "fs";

readFile("./hello.txt", (err, buffer) => {
    console.log(buffer.toString());
});
```

There are a few new rules about Node.js callbacks:

- Errors are never thrown by a function that takes a callback. The errors should be passed to the callback instead.
- When we have nested callbacks, if an error takes place, it should be passed to the callback in the top level.

The following code snippet showcases both the preceding rules in action:

```
function readJson(
    fileName: string,
    callback: (err: Error|null, json?: any) => void
) {
    readFile(fileName, "utf-8", (err, buffer) => {
```

```
        if (err) {
            callback(err);
        }

        try {
            const parsed = JSON.parse(buffer);
            callback(null, parsed);
        } catch (innerErr) {
            callback(err);
        }
    });
}
```

Node.js uses callbacks because when it was originally implemented, promises, generators, and `async/await` were not available in V8. This seems unfortunate because, as TypeScript users, we know how much nicer is to use `async/await` instead of callbacks and promises.

Thanks to the consistency of the Node.js APIs, we can write a helper that takes a function implemented with a callback-based API and returns the same function implemented with a promise-based API. In fact, this function is part of the `util` core module and can be imported as follows:

```
import * as util from "util";
const promisify = util.promisify;
```

We can use the preceding helper function to transform the `readFile` function that we used during the previous example into a function that returns a promise. The new function is named `readFileAsync`. Now that the function returns a promise, we can use `async/await`:

```
import { readFile } from "fs";

const readFileAsync = promisify(readFile);

(async () => {
    const buffer = await readFileAsync("./hello.txt", "utf-8");
    console.log(buffer.toString());
})();
```

The following code snippet showcases how to transform the second example into the `async/await` style:

```
import { readFile } from "fs";

const { promisify } = require("util");
const readFileAsync = promisify(readFile);
```

```
async function readJson(fileName: string) {
    try {
        const buffer = await readFileAsync(fileName, "utf-8");
        const parsed = JSON.parse(buffer.toString());
        return parsed;
    } catch (err) {
        return err;
    }
}
```

In the future, Node.js will support promises in its core API natively but, for now, using the `promisify` helper is a good option.

The npm ecosystem

We have used npm previously in this book, and by now we should know how to use it well. The npm ecosystem is composed of thousands of external modules. We can use the official npm website at `https://www.npmjs.com/` to search for a package that might help us to complete a given task. Unlike the modules that are part of the core Node.js API, external `npm` modules need to be installed using `npm`:

`npm install react`

If the module is not recognized by TypeScript, we will also need to install its type definitions (if available):

`npm install @types/react`

> Please refer to `Chapter 13`, *Application Performance*, and `Chapter 9`, *Automating Your Development Workflow*, to learn more about other tools in the Node.js ecosystem, for example, the Node.js inspector, a tool that allows us to debug and analyze the performance of our Node.js applications.

Setting up Node.js

To set up Node.js on your machine, you will need to visit the official download page at `https://nodejs.org/en/download` and follow the instructions for your operating system.

If you are an OS X or Linux user, you can additionally install the **node version manager** (**nvm**) following the instructions at `https://github.com/creationix/nvm`. This tool allows us to install multiple versions of Node.js on the same machine and to switch between them in a matter of seconds. If you are a Windows user, you will need to install `https://github.com/coreybutler/nvm-windows` instead.

If we want to use one of the Node.js core API modules, all we need to do is to import it. We don't need to install an additional `npm` module. For example, the filesystem module can be used to read and write files and manage directories. If we want to use the filesystem API, all we need to do is to import the module as follows:

```
import * as fs from "fs";
```

However, TypeScript will not recognize the module by default because it is not part of the JavaScript specification. We can solve this problem by installing the Node.js type definitions:

`npm install @types/node`

Finally, you may want to install `ts-node` to be able to execute Node.js applications implemented with TypeScript without the need to compile them first. We can run a Node.js application or a TypeScript application using the following commands respectively:

`node app.js`

`ts-node app.ts`

Node.js development

In this section, we are going to look at a few small real-world examples of the usage of Node.js.

Working with the filesystem

We are going to implement a very small Node.js application. This application can be used as a search and replace tool. The result can be used as a command-line application and can be executed using the following command:

```
ts-node app.ts --files ./**/*.txt --find SOMETHING --replace SOMETHING_ELSE
```

The application will replace one word for another in all the matching files. We are going to use the core filesystem API (`fs`) and two external `npm` modules:

- `glob` is used to find files that match a given pattern
- `yargs` is used to parse command-line arguments

We need to install both packages and the corresponding type definition files:

```
npm install glob yargs --save
```

```
npm install @types/glob @types/yargs @types/node -save-dev
```

Let's look at the source code:

```typescript
import * as fs from "fs";

import * as yargs from "yargs";

import glob from "glob";

const { promisify } = require("util");
```

We are going to use the `promisify` function to transform some callback-based APIs into promise-based APIs:

```typescript
const globAsync = promisify(glob);

const readFileAsync = promisify(fs.readFile);

const writeFileAsync = promisify(fs.writeFile);
```

The following function reads the arguments from the command line:

```
function getCommandLineArguments() {
    const files = yargs.argv.files;

    if (!files) {
        throw new Error("Missing argument --files");
    }

    const find = yargs.argv.find;

    if (!find) {
        throw new Error("Missing argument --find");
    }

    const replace = yargs.argv.replace;

    if (!replace) {
        throw new Error("Missing argument --replace");
    }

    return {
        pattern: files,
        find: find,
        replace: replace
    };
};
```

The following function validates the command-line arguments:

```
function validateCommandLineArguments(args: any) {

    if (args.pattern === undefined) {

        throw new Error(`Invalid pattern ${args.pattern}`);

    }

    if (args.find === undefined) {

        throw new Error(`Invalid find ${args.find}`);

    }

    if (args.replace === undefined) {

        throw new Error(`Invalid replace ${args.replace}`);
```

        }

    }

The following function finds the path of files that match the `glob` pattern provided:

```
async function findMatchingFilesAsync(pattern: string) {
    const files = await globAsync(pattern);
    // We need to let TypeScript that files are an array
    return files as string[];
}
```

The following function is used to find a word in a file and replace it with a second word:

```
async function findAndReplaceAsync(
    file: string,
    find: string,
    replace: string
) {
    const buffer = await readFileAsync(file);
    const originalText = buffer.toString();
    // This is a quick way to replace a word in JavaScript
    const newText = originalText.split(find).join(replace);
    await writeFileAsync(file, newText, "utf8");
}
```

This function is the main function in the application and the application's entry point. It delegates work to all the previous functions:

```
async function runAsync() {
    // Read arguments
    const args = getCommandLineArguments();
```

Chapter 10

```
    // Validate arguments
    validateCommandLineArguments(args);

    // Find matching files
    const files = await findMatchingFilesAsync(args.pattern);

    // Find and replace
    files.forEach(async (file) => {
        await findAndReplaceAsync(file, args.find, args.replace);
    });
}
```

At this point, we can invoke the application's entry point:

```
(async () => {
    await runAsync();
})();
```

Working with databases

In this section, we are going to learn how to interact with a database from a Node.js application using a TypeScript library known as TypeORM. TypeORM is an **object-relational mapping** (**ORM**) library. An ORM is a tool that allows us to use objects and methods to interact with a database instead of using one of the flavors of the SQL programming language.

We are going to need a Postgres database server running in our development environment before we can implement an example. There are multiple ways to get a server up and running, but we are going to use Docker. Docker is a virtualization service that allows us to run software in standalone virtual machines known as containers. A Docker container is an instance of a Docker image. We are going to start by installing the Docker community edition by following the instructions at the official Docker installation guide, which can be found at `https://docs.docker.com/install`, and we will then run the following command to download the Docker Postgres image:

```
docker pull postgres:9.5
```

We can use the following command to see all the installed images:

```
docker images
```

Node.js Development with TypeScript

We also need to set some environment variables. The following should work if you are using Bash as your command line:

```
export DATABASE_USER=postgres

export DATABASE_PASSWORD=secret

export DATABASE_HOST=localhost

export DATABASE_PORT=5432

export DATABASE_DB=demo
```

> Please note that if you are using Windows, you will need to use the `setx` command instead of the `export` command to declare an environment variable. You can learn more about the `setx` command at https://docs.microsoft.com/en-us/windows-server/administration/windows-commands/setx.

At this point, we can run a container using the Postgres image. The following command runs the container using the environment variables that we declared in the preceding step:

```
docker run --name POSTGRES_USER -p "$DATABASE_PORT":"$DATABASE_PORT"

-e POSTGRES_PASSWORD="$DATABASE_PASSWORD"

-e POSTGRES_USER="$DATABASE_USER"

-e POSTGRES_DB="$DATABASE_DB"

-d postgres
```

We can run the following command to see all the Docker containers on our machine:

```
docker ps -a
```

If everything went well, you should see something like the following in your console:

```
CONTAINER ID   IMAGE      COMMAND                CREATED        STATUS         PORTS                    NAMES
3d2288e4acc1   postgres   "docker-entrypoint..." 42 minutes ago Up 42 minutes  0.0.0.0:5432->5432/tcp   POSTGRES_USER
```

If you need to start again, you can stop and remove the Docker container using the following commands respectively:

```
docker stop $containerId

docker rm $containerId
```

> Please note that we are not going to go into more details about Docker because it is out of the scope of this book. Please refer to the official Docker documentation at `https://docs.docker.com` if you need additional help.

At this point, we should have a Postgres server running as a Docker container. We also need to install some `npm` modules:

```
npm install reflect-metadata pg typeorm
```

> The `pg` module is used by TypeORM to connect to the Postgres database. The `reflect-metadata` is used by TypeORM to read and write metadata. It is very important to import the `reflect-metadata` module only once in our entire application.

The following code snippet uses TypeORM to declare an entity named `Movie`. The `Movie` entity will be mapped into a database table by TypeORM. The example also creates a database connection and a `Movie` repository. We finally use the repository instance to insert a new movie into the movie table and to read the movies in the table that match the year 1977:

```
import "reflect-metadata";

import {
    Entity,
    getConnection,
    createConnection,
    PrimaryGeneratedColumn,
    Column
} from "typeorm";

@Entity()
class Movie {
    @PrimaryGeneratedColumn()
    public id!: number;
    @Column()
    public title!: string;
    @Column()
    public year!: number;
}

const entities = [
    Movie
];
```

```
const DATABASE_HOST = process.env.DATABASE_HOST || "localhost";
const DATABASE_USER = process.env.DATABASE_USER || "";
const DATABASE_PORT = 5432;
const DATABASE_PASSWORD = process.env.DATABASE_PASSWORD || "";
const DATABASE_DB = "demo";

(async () => {
    const conn = await createConnection({
        type: "postgres",
        host: DATABASE_HOST,
        port: DATABASE_PORT,
        username: DATABASE_USER,
        password: DATABASE_PASSWORD,
        database: DATABASE_DB,
        entities: entities,
        synchronize: true
    });

    const getRepository = (entity: Function) => conn.getRepository(entity);
    const movieRepository = conn.getRepository(Movie);

    // INSERT INTO movies
    // VALUES ('Star Wars: Episode IV - A New Hope', 1977)
    await movieRepository.save({
        title: "Star Wars: Episode IV - A New Hope",
        year: 1977
    });

    // SELECT * FROM movies WHERE year=1977
    const aMovieFrom1977 = await movieRepository.findOne({
        year: 1977
    });

    if (aMovieFrom1977) {
        console.log(aMovieFrom1977.title);
    }
})();
```

> The repository design pattern uses classes to encapsulate the data access logic and the mapping between the database and the domain entities. You can learn more about the repository pattern at https://msdn.microsoft.com/en-us/library/ff649690.aspx.

Finally, we can run the example using `ts-node`:

```
ts-node app.ts
```

> Please note that the environment variables and the Postgres server must be configured correctly for this example to work.

Working with REST APIs

In this section, we are going to learn how to implement some REST APIs using Node.js.

Hello world (http)

The `http` module allows us to perform tasks in relation to the HTTP protocol. The following code snippet showcases how we can use the `http` module to implement very minimal implantation of a web server:

```
import * as http from "http";
const hostname = "127.0.0.1";
const port = 3000;

const server = http.createServer((req, res) => {
    res.statusCode = 200;
    res.setHeader("Content-Types", "text/plain");
    res.end("Hello world!");
});

server.listen(port, hostname, () => {
    console.log(`Server running at http://${hostname}:${port}/`);
});
```

We have created a web server that will listen to all the HTTP requests. The `http` module allows us to implement our web HTTP server, but its level of abstraction is very low. In a real-world application, we would prefer something with a higher level of abstraction, something that, for example, doesn't require us to set the response status code by hand. There are multiple frameworks for Node.js that can provide us with a higher level of abstraction over the HTTP protocol. In the following section, we are going to learn how to use one of them: Express.js.

Hello world (Express.js)

Express.js is a framework designed for the implementation of server-side web applications. To use Express with TypeScript, we are going to need the following `npm` modules:

```
npm install @types/node @types/express -save-dev
```

```
npm install express --save
```

The following example implements an application with a behavior almost identical to the application that we implemented in the preceding section, but this time we use Express.js instead of the `http core` module:

```
import express from "express";

const port = 3000;
const app = express();

app.get("/", (req, res) => {
    res.send("Hello World!");
});

app.listen(port, () => {
    console.log(`Server running at http://127.0.0.1:${port}/`);
});
```

As we can see, even in an example as simple as the preceding one, with Express, sometimes we don't need to take care of some low-level details, such as setting up the response status code.

Routing with Express

In the preceding section, we learned how to declare a route; however, as our application grows, we are going to need to implement some route organization strategy. Express allows us to create multiple router instances and nest them as a tree-like data structure. The following code snippet demonstrates how to create two routers that deal with two different kinds of entities (`movies` and `directors`); the two routers are then used by the Express application:

```
import express from "express";

const moviesRouter = express.Router();

// URL "/api/v1/movies" + "/"
moviesRouter.get("/", (req, res) => {
```

```
        res.send("Hello from movies!");
});

const directorsRouter = express.Router();

// URL "/api/v1/directors" + "/"
directorsRouter.get("/", (req, res) => {
    res.send("Hello from directors!");
});

const port = 3000;
const app = express();

app.use("/api/v1/movies", moviesRouter);
app.use("/api/v1/directors", directorsRouter);

app.listen(port, () => {
    console.log(`Server running at http://127.0.0.1:${port}/`);
});
```

When we run the preceding example, two routes are available:

- http://localhost:3000/api/v1/directors
- http://localhost:3000/api/v1/directors

Express middleware

Express also allows us to declare a middleware function. A middleware function allows us to implement cross-cutting concerns. A cross-cutting concern is a requirement that affects the entire application or a subset of it. Common examples of cross-cutting concerns are logging and authorization.

A middleware function takes the current request and response as arguments together with a function known as next:

```
const middlewareFunction = (
    req: express.Request,
    res: express.Response,
    next: express.NextFunction
) => {
    next();
};
```

We can chain middleware functions, and the `next` function is what communicates to Express that the middleware has finished its task and the next middleware can be invoked. When no more middleware functions are available, the route handler is invoked.

The following code snippet declares two middleware functions. The first middleware function (`timerMiddleware`) is invoked once for each HTTP request that hits the server. The second middleware function (`loggerMiddleware`) is invoked once for each HTTP request that hits the `http://localhost:3000` endpoint:

```
import express from "express";

const port = 3000;
const app = express();

const timerMiddleware = (
    req: express.Request,
    res: express.Response,
    next: express.NextFunction
) => {
    console.log(`Time: ${Date.now()}`);
    next();
};

const loggerMiddleware = (
    req: express.Request,
    res: express.Response,
    next: express.NextFunction
) => {

    console.log(`URL: ${req.url}`);
    next();
};

// Application level middleware
app.use(timerMiddleware);

// Route level middleware
app.get("/", loggerMiddleware, (req, res) => {
    res.send("Hello World!");
});

app.listen(port, () => {
    console.log(`Server running at http://127.0.0.1:${port}/`);
});
```

When we execute the preceding example, the following route becomes available: `http://localhost:3000`. When an HTTP request hits the preceding URL, the response is `Hello world!` and the console displays the output generated by both middleware functions previously declared:

```
URL: /
Time: 1520354128960
```

Architecting Node.js application – the MVC design pattern

Architecting Node.js applications is a very extensive topic that could take an entire book on its own. However, we are going to cover one of the most commonly used design patterns, the **Model-View-Controller** (**MVC**) design pattern, defined as follows by MSDN:

The MVC framework includes the following components:

- `Models`: Model objects are the parts of the application that implement the logic for the application's data domain. Often, model objects retrieve and store model state in a database. For example, a `Product` object might retrieve information from a database, operate on it, and then write updated information back to a Products table in a database. In small applications, the model is often a conceptual separation instead of a physical one. For example, if the application only reads a dataset and sends it to the view, the application does not have a physical model layer and associated classes. In that case, the dataset takes on the role of a model object.
- `Views`: Views are the components that display the application's **user interface** (**UI**). Typically, this UI is created from the model data. An example would be an edit view of a Products table that displays text boxes, drop-down lists and checks boxes based on the current state of a `Product` object.
- `Controllers`: Controllers are the components that handle user interaction, work with the model, and ultimately select a view to render that displays UI. In an MVC application, the view only displays information; the controller handles and responds to user input and interaction. For example, the controller handles query-string values and passes these values to the model, which in turn might use these values to query the database.

The MVC design pattern can be implemented in both the backend and the frontend. However, in this section, we are going to implement it in the backend.

> Please note that to be able to run this example without problems, you must first install all dependencies using `npm install` from the `chapter_10` folder in the companion source code. Then you can open `09_mvc`.

Model

Our model is going to be composed of two layers. We are going to implement an entity and a repository. The entity is implemented using TypeORM:

```
import {
    Entity,
    PrimaryGeneratedColumn,
    Column
} from "typeorm";

@Entity()
export class Movie {
    @PrimaryGeneratedColumn()
    public id!: number;
    @Column()
    public title!: string;
    @Column()
    public year!: number;
}
```

Repository

The repository is also implemented with TypeORM:

```
import { getConnection } from "typeorm";

import { Movie } from "../entities/movie";

export function getRepository() {
    const conn = getConnection();
    const movieRepository = conn.getRepository(Movie);
    return movieRepository;
}
```

Controller

The controller uses the model (entity + repository) and it is implemented using the Express routing techniques that we explored earlier in this chapter.

We are going to declare routes to get all movies, filter movies by year, and create a new movie. The example also uses `req.params` to access the request parameter year.

It is important to note that we can use the `get` method to declare a route handler for an HTTP GET request, while we can use the `post` method to declare a route handler for an HTTP POST request:

```
import { Router } from "express";

import { getRepository } from "../repositories/movie_repository";

const movieRouter = Router();
movieRouter.get("/", function (req, res) {
    const movieRepository = getRepository();
    movieRepository.find().then((movies) => {
        res.json(movies);
    }).catch((e: Error) => {
        res.status(500);
        res.send(e.message);
    });
});

movieRouter.get("/:year", function (req, res) {
    const movieRepository = getRepository();
    movieRepository.find({
        year: req.params.year
    }).then((movies) => {
        res.json(movies);
    }).catch((e: Error) => {
        res.status(500);
        res.send(e.message);
    });
});

movieRouter.post("/", function (req, res) {
    const movieRepository = getRepository();
    const newMovie = req.body;
    if (
        typeof newMovie.title !== "string" ||
        typeof newMovie.year !== "number"
    ) {
        res.status(400);
        res.send(`Invalid Movie!`);
    }

    movieRepository.find(newMovie).then((movie) => {
        res.json(movie);
```

```
    }).catch((e: Error) => {
        res.status(500);
        res.send(e.message);
    });
});

export { movieRouter };
```

Database

In our repository, we have used the `getConnection` function from TypeORM. Before we can invoke this function, we need to ensure that a connection has been created. The following function is used later to create a database connection:

```
import { createConnection } from "typeorm";

import { Movie } from "./entities/movie";

export async function getDbConnection() {
    const DATABASE_HOST = process.env.DATABASE_HOST || "localhost";
    const DATABASE_USER = process.env.DATABASE_USER || "";
    const DATABASE_PORT = 5432;
    const DATABASE_PASSWORD = process.env.DATABASE_PASSWORD || "";
    const DATABASE_DB = "demo";

    const entities = [
        Movie
    ];

    const conn = await createConnection({
        type: "postgres",
        host: DATABASE_HOST,
        port: DATABASE_PORT,
        username: DATABASE_USER,
        password: DATABASE_PASSWORD,
        database: DATABASE_DB,
        entities: entities,
        synchronize: true
    });

    return conn;

}
```

View

Because we are implementing REST services, we don't have a data presentation layer. The REST API can be completely decoupled from the web user interface. We will not learn how to implement the presentation layer in this chapter because this topic is going to be covered in the upcoming chapters.

Index

The index file is the application's entry point. The entry point creates a new Express app and a database connection. It then connects the controller routes to the Express app and launches the web server:

```
import "reflect-metadata";

import express from "express";

import { getDbConnection } from "./db";

import { movieRouter } from "./controllers/movie_controller";

(async () => {
    await getDbConnection();
    const port = 3000;
    const app = express();
    app.use("/api/v1/movies", movieRouter);
    app.listen(port, () => {
        console.log(`Server running at http://127.0.0.1:${port}/`)
    });
})();
```

Controllers and routing with inversify-express-utils

Earlier in this book, we learned about dependency injection and dependency inversion with InversifyJS. In this section, we are going to learn how to use InversifyJS together with Express, using a helper npm module known as `inversify-express-utils`. We are going to need to install `inversify` and `inversify-express-utils`:

```
npm install inversify inversify-express-utils
```

Node.js Development with TypeScript

> Please note that to be able to run this example without problems, you must first install all dependencies using `npm install` from the `chapter_10` folder in the companion source code. Then you can open the `10_inversify_express_utils` folder.

Model, repository, database, and view

We can reuse 100% of the code used for the model, repository, database, and view in the preceding example.

Types

We need to declare some identifiers required for the InversifyJS type bindings. If you don't know what a type binding is, you should go back to Chapter 5, *Working with Dependencies*, to learn the basics about InversifyJS. We are going to declare a binding for the `MovieRepository` class:

```
export const TYPE = {
    MovieRepository: Symbol("MovieRepository")
};
```

Controller

The InversifyJS Express utils allow us to declare controllers using what is known as declarative routing. Instead of declaring `Router` instances, we can annotate a controller class using some decorators. The metadata generated by the decorators is later used by the InversifyJS express utils to generate the `Router` instances for us.

The following example uses the following decorators:

- `@controller(path)`: It is used to declare the path of a router
- `@inject(type)`: It is used to inject dependencies into a class
- `@httpGet(subpath)`: It is used to declare a route handler for HTTP GET requests
- `@httpPost(subpath)`: It is used to declare a route handler for HTTP POST requests
- `@response()`: It is used to pass the response object to a route handler as an argument

- `@requestParam(paramName)`: It is used to pass a request parameter to a route handler as an argument
- `@requestBody()`: It is used to pass the request body to a route handler as an argument

Another interesting feature of the InversifyJS Express utils is that we can use `async` methods. InversifyJS will automatically detect whether our methods are `async` and use `await` when necessary:

```
import express from "express";

import { inject } from "inversify";

import {
    controller,
    httpGet,
    httpPost,
    response,
    requestParam,
    requestBody
} from "inversify-express-utils";

import { Repository } from "typeorm";

import { Movie } from "../entities/movie";

import { TYPE } from "../constants/types";

@controller("/api/v1/movies")
export class MovieController {
    private readonly _movieRepository: Repository<Movie>;
    public constructor(
        @inject(TYPE.MovieRepository) movieRepository: Repository<Movie>
    ) {
        this._movieRepository = movieRepository;
    }
    @httpGet("/")
    public async get(
        @response() res: express.Response
    ) {

        try {
            return await this._movieRepository.find();
        } catch(e) {
            res.status(500);
            res.send(e.message);
```

```typescript
            }
        }

        @httpGet("/:year")
        public async getByYear(
            @response() res: express.Response,
            @requestParam("year") yearParam: string
        ) {

            try {
                const year = parseInt(yearParam);
                return await this._movieRepository.find({
                    year
                });
            } catch(e) {
                res.status(500);
                res.send(e.message);
            }
        }

        @httpPost("/")
        public async post(
            @response() res: express.Response,
            @requestBody() newMovie: Movie
        ) {

            if (
                typeof newMovie.title !== "string" |
                typeof newMovie.year !== "number"
            ) {
                res.status(400);
                res.send(`Invalid Movie!`);
            }

            try {
                return await this._movieRepository.save(newMovie);
            } catch(e) {
                res.status(500);
                res.send(e.message);
            }
        }
    }
```

InversifyJS configuration

We are going to declare some type bindings. We are going to declare the type bindings using `AsyncContainerModule` because we need to wait for the database connection to be ready. We are going to declare a binding for `MovieRepository`. We don't need to declare a binding for the `MovieController` because the `@controller(path)` annotation will create it for us. However, we need to import the controller to ensure that the decorator is executed and, as a result, the binding is declared:

```
import { AsyncContainerModule } from "inversify";

import { Repository, Connection } from "typeorm";

import { Movie } from "./entities/movie";

import { getDbConnection } from "./db";

import { getRepository } from "./repositories/movie_repository";

import { TYPE } from "./constants/types";

export const bindings = new AsyncContainerModule(async (bind) => {
    await getDbConnection();
    await require("./controllers/movie_controller");
    bind<Repository<Movie>>(TYPE.MovieRepository).toDynamicValue(() => {
        return getRepository();
    }).inRequestScope();
});
```

Index

The index file is also different. Instead of creating a new *Express* app, we need to create a new *InversifyExpressServer* app. The `InversifyExpressServer` constructor requires an instance of `Container`. The type bindings for the container are declared in the bindings object, which is an instance of the `AsyncContainerModule`:

```
import "reflect-metadata";

import { Container } from "inversify";

import { InversifyExpressServer } from "inversify-express-utils";

import { bindings } from "./inversify.config";

(async () => {
```

```
    const port = 3000;
    const container = new Container();
    await container.loadAsync(bindings);
    const app = new InversifyExpressServer(container);
    const server = app.build();
    server.listen(port, () => {
        console.log(`Server running at http://127.0.0.1:${port}/`)
    });
})();
```

> Please refer to Chapter 5, *Working with Dependencies*, to learn more dependency injection and dependency inversion with InversifyJS. Please refer to the official InversifyJS express utils at `https://github.com/inversify/inversify-express-utils` to learn more about it.

Other applications of Node.js

Developing command-line applications or REST APIs is not the only real-world application of Node.js. For example, we can develop desktop applications using Electron. Node.js is also commonly used as a reverse proxy and powers many web development tools.

Summary

In this chapter, we have learned the main characteristics of Node.js as a platform and its main components. We have also learned a little bit about the Node.js ecosystem and the kind of applications that we can create using it.

Toward the end of the chapter, we implemented a very small REST API. In the next two chapters, we are going to learn how we can use TypeScript to create web-based user interfaces that consume these APIs.

11
Frontend Development with React and TypeScript

In the preceding chapter, we learned how to implement web services with Node.js. In this chapter, we are going to learn how to implement a **single-page application** (**SPA**) that consumes the web services that we created in the preceding chapter. The web services might change slightly in this chapter, but the changes should be small enough not to require us to cover them in this chapter.

The companion source code includes an updated version of the backend application that we implemented in the preceding chapter. The new upgraded version contains new controllers and web services that allow us to manage a catalog of movies and actors, as opposed to just movies.

In this chapter, we are going to learn how to consume a web service from a React application and how we can use React components to display the data fetched from the backend in a web user interface. We are also going to learn how to implement client-side routing powered by the `react-router` and how to implement smart components powered by MobX.

Working with React

React is a library that allows us to implement web user interfaces. In this chapter, we are going to create a small frontend application using React and MobX. A frontend web application is quite different from a Node.js backend web application. It is true that both the web browser and Node.js can understand JavaScript natively, but the environments are quite different. For example, in the Node.js environment, we can access system resources like the filesystem, and we can use CommonJS modules natively. On the other hand, in a web browser, we cannot access resources like the filesystem and CommonJS modules are not supported natively. Also, the performance of a frontend web application is extremely influenced by its loading times. This means that in a frontend web application we must pay special attention to the number of HTTP requests and the size of the contents being loaded through the network.

The lack of native support for modules and the need for size optimization explains the need for a module bundler when we are working on a frontend web application. Throughout this book, we have been using Webpack as our module bundler, and we will do the same once more in this chapter.

We are going to use the following Webpack configuration:

```
const { CheckerPlugin } = require("awesome-typescript-loader");
const webpack = require("webpack");
const ExtractTextPlugin = require("extract-text-webpack-plugin");
const CopyWebpackPlugin = require("copy-webpack-plugin");

const corePlugins = [
    new CheckerPlugin(),
    new webpack.DefinePlugin({
        "process.env.NODE_ENV": JSON.stringify(process.env.NODE_ENV ||
"development")
    }),
    new ExtractTextPlugin({
        filename: "main.css",
        allChunks: true
    }),
    new CopyWebpackPlugin([
        { from: "./web/frontend/index.html", to: "index.html" }
    ])
];

const devPlugins = [];

const prodPlugins = [
    new webpack.optimize.UglifyJsPlugin({ output: { comments: false } })
```

```
];

const isProduction = process.env.NODE_ENV === "production";
const plugins = isProduction ? corePlugins.concat(prodPlugins) :
corePlugins.concat(devPlugins);

module.exports = {
    entry: "./web/frontend/index.tsx",
    devServer: {
        inline: true
    },
    output: {
        filename: "bundle.js",
        path: __dirname + "/public",
        publicPath: "/public"
    },
    devtool: isProduction ? "source-map" : "eval-source-map",
    resolve: {
        extensions: [".webpack.js", ".ts", ".tsx", ".js"]
    },
    module: {
        rules: [
            {
                enforce: "pre",
                test: /.js$/,
                loader: "source-map-loader",
                exclude: [/node_modules/]
            },
            {
                test: /.(ts|tsx)$/,
                loader: "awesome-typescript-loader",
                exclude: [/node_modules/]
            },
            {
                test: /.scss$/,
                use: ExtractTextPlugin.extract({
                    fallback: "style-loader",
                    use: ["css-loader", "resolve-url-loader", "sass-loader"]
                })
            }
        ]
    },
    plugins: plugins
};
```

Frontend Development with React and TypeScript

We have used some plugins to compile the SCSS files into one unique CSS file and to copy the HTML files into the build output directory (the `public` directory). If the build is successful, we should end up with three files under the `public` directory: `index.html`, `bundle.js`, and `main.css`.

> Please refer to `Chapter 9`, *Automating Your Development Workflow*, to learn more about Webpack.

About the sample application

The same application included in the companion source code is a very small web application that allows us to manage a database or movies and actors. The application is going to be divided into two main units: pages and components. In this section, we are going to learn about each of the pages and components used in the application.

The *home* page allows us to access the **Movies** and **Actors** pages. The **Home** page uses the Layout, Header, Container, Row, Column, Card, Card image, and Link components:

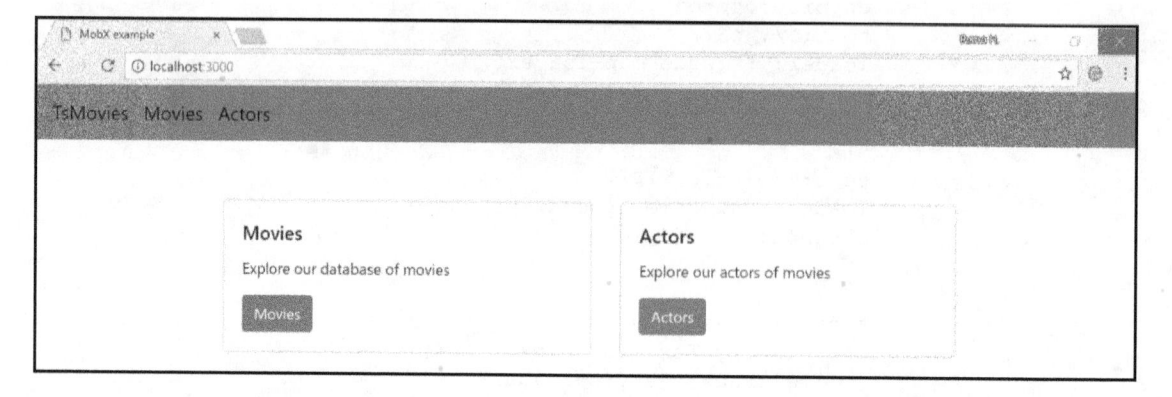

The **Movies** page allows us to see a list of existing movies in the database as well as to add and delete movies and uses the Layout, Header, Container, Row, Column, Modal, Button, Text field, and List Group components:

[344]

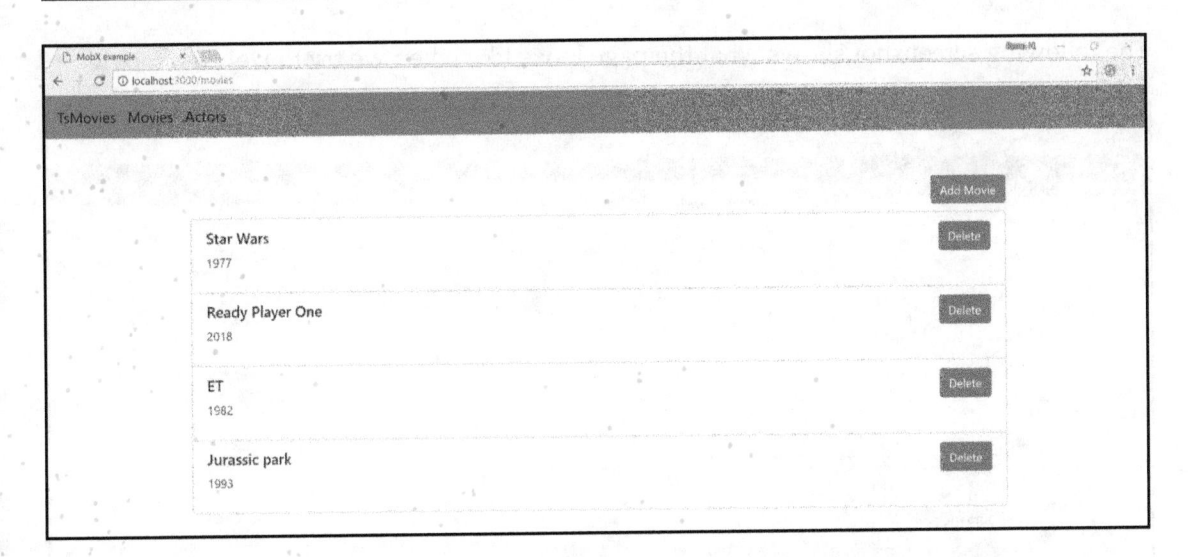

Chapter 11

The following screenshot shows what the page looks like when the **Movie Editor** is active:

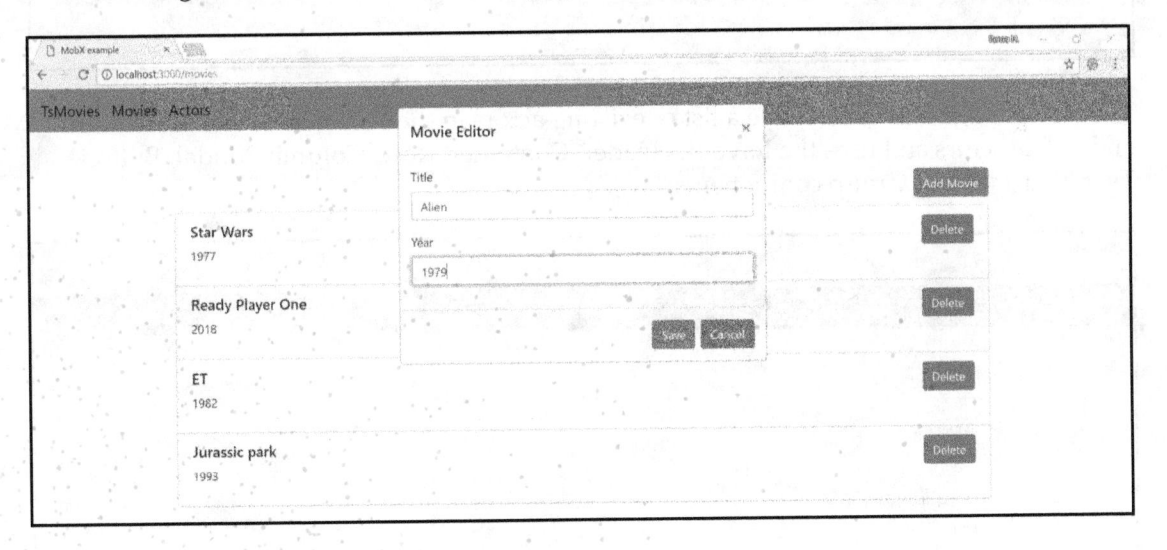

Frontend Development with React and TypeScript

The following screenshot shows what the page looks like when we try to **Delete** a movie:

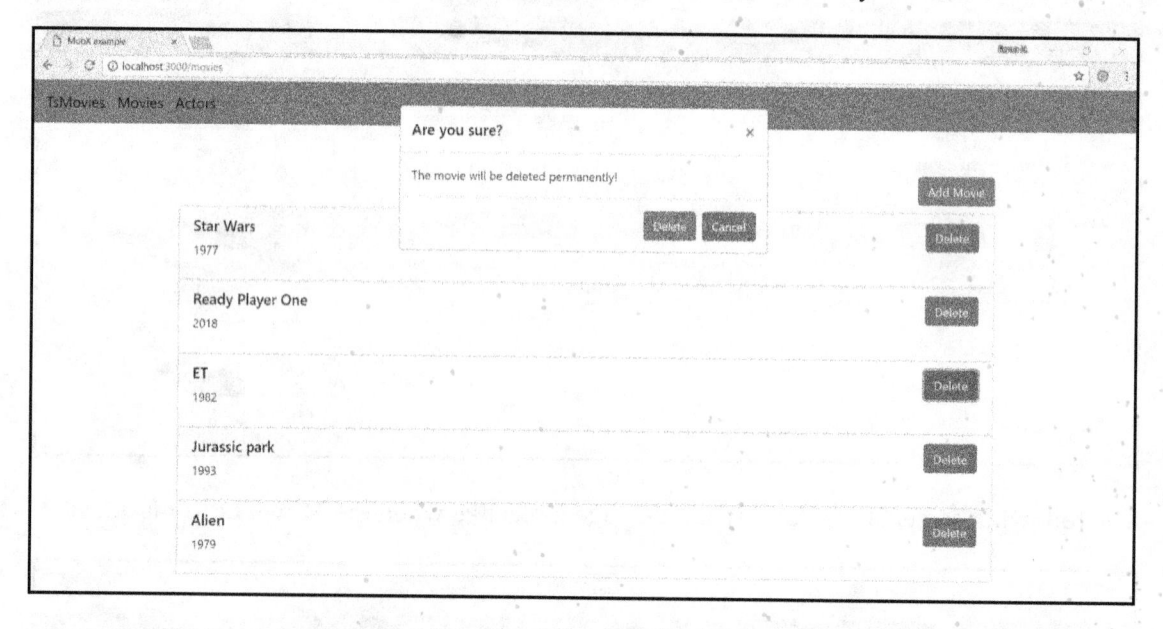

The **Actors** page allows us to see a list of existing actors in the database as well as to add and delete actors and uses the Layout, Header, Container, Row, Column, Modal, Button, Text field, and List Group components:

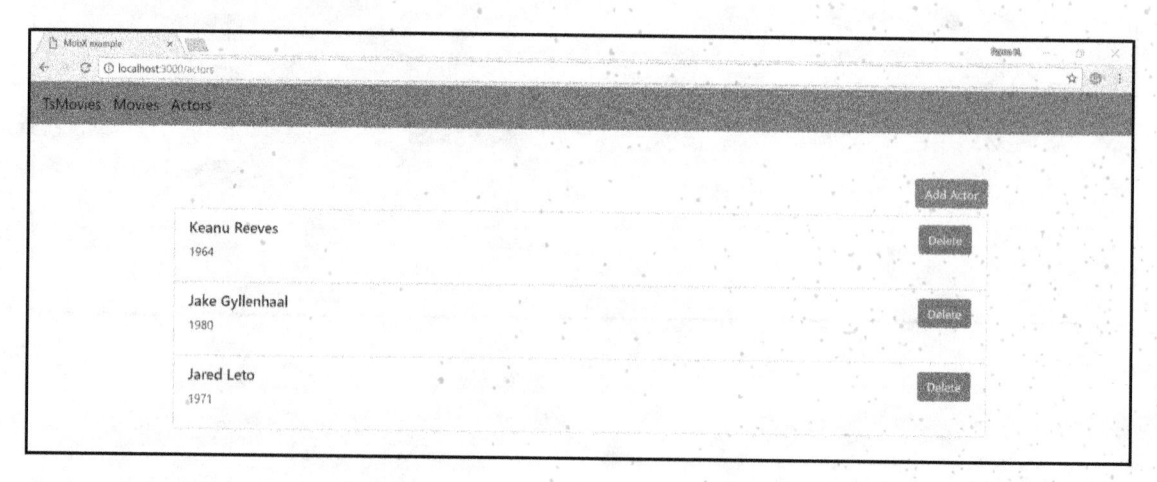

Creating or deleting an actor is almost identical to creating or deleting a movie. The following screenshot shows what the page looks like when the **Actor Editor** is active:

Chapter 11

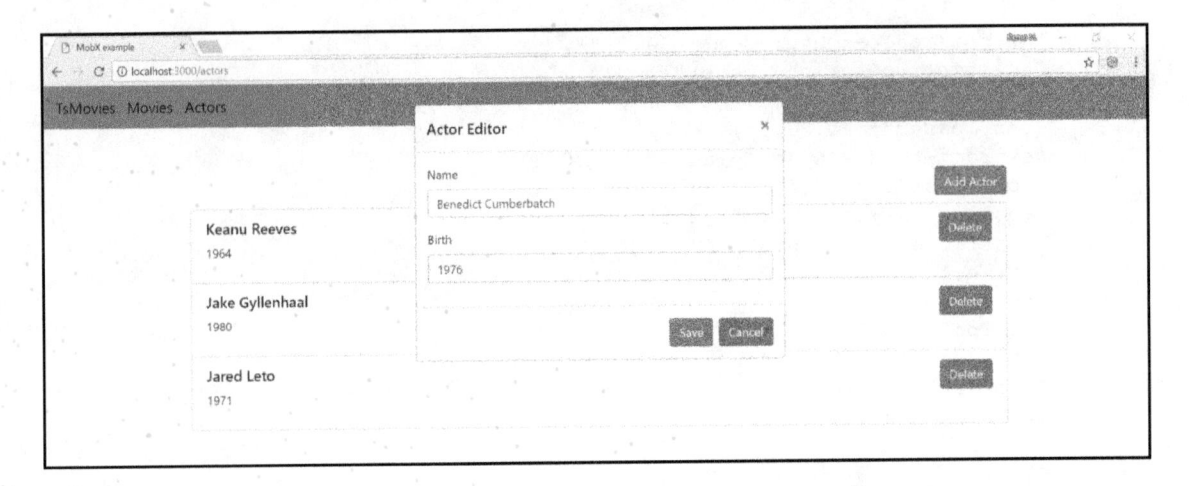

As you can see in the preceding screenshots, multiple pages can consume the same React components. The level of reusability of a component is one of the main strengths of React as a library for the development of user interfaces. React allows us to develop reusable *units of work* known as components that can later be reused across multiple applications.

The sample application included in the companion source code implements both a backend and a frontend web application and uses the following dependencies:

```
"dependencies": {
    "body-parser": "1.18.2",
    "bootstrap": "4.0.0",
    "express": "4.16.2",
    "inversify": "4.11.1",
    "inversify-binding-decorators": "3.2.0",
    "inversify-express-utils": "5.2.1",
    "inversify-inject-decorators": "3.1.0",
    "mobx": "4.1.0",
    "mobx-react": "5.0.0",
    "pg": "7.4.1",
    "react": "16.2.0",
    "react-dom": "16.2.0",
    "react-router-dom": "4.2.2",
    "reflect-metadata": "0.1.12",
    "typeorm": "0.1.14"
},
"devDependencies": {
    "@types/body-parser": "1.16.8",
    "@types/express": "4.11.1",
    "@types/node": "9.4.6",
    "@types/react": "16.0.40",
    "@types/react-dom": "16.0.4",
```

```
    "@types/react-router-dom": "4.2.5",
    "awesome-typescript-loader": "3.4.1",
    "copy-webpack-plugin": "4.5.1",
    "css-loader": "0.28.8",
    "extract-text-webpack-plugin": "3.0.2",
    "node-sass": "4.7.2",
    "resolve-url-loader": "2.2.1",
    "sass-loader": "6.0.6",
    "style-loader": "0.19.1",
    "ts-node": "5.0.1",
    "tslint": "5.9.1",
    "typescript": "2.8.1",
    "webpack": "3.10.0",
    "webpack-dev-server": "2.11.0"
}
```

We are also going to implement a very basic compilation pipeline using the following npm scripts commands:

```
"scripts": {
    "start": "ts-node ./web/backend/index.ts",
    "build": "webpack",
    "lint": "tslint --project tsconfig.json -c tslint.json ./web/**/*.ts ./web/**/*.tsx"
},
```

We can use the preceding command using the following npm commands:

```
npm run start
npm run build
npm run lint
```

To run the application, we must first run the build command, which will build our frontend application and transform it into bundled JavaScript and CSS files located under the directory named `public`. We can then run the application using the `npm run start` command. The Node.js server will then start listening to our API calls. The Node.js will also serve the files under the `public` directory as we will see in the following section.

Serving a React application with Node.js

In this chapter, we are going to try to avoid introducing changes to our existing Node.js backend. Some changes have been introduced to the web services declared by the controllers. We will not spend any time going through those changes in this chapter because they are trivial.

However, we are going to focus on some changes in the Express.js configuration required to serve the JavaScript and CSS files under the public directory. If we want our Express.js application to serve the static files of our frontend application, we are going to need to configure what is known as the **static middleware**.

The following code snippet contains the entire source code of the application's entry point:

```
import "reflect-metadata";
import * as express from "express";
import { Container } from "inversify";
import * as bodyParser from "body-parser";
import * as path from "path";
import { InversifyExpressServer } from "inversify-express-utils";
import { bindings } from "./inversify.config";

(async () => {

    try {

        const port = 3000;
        const container = new Container();
        await container.loadAsync(bindings);
        const app = new InversifyExpressServer(container);

        app.setConfig((a) => {
            a.use(bodyParser.json());
            a.use(bodyParser.urlencoded({ extended: true }));
            const appPath = path.join(__dirname, "../../public");
            a.use("/", express.static(appPath));
        });

        const server = app.build();

        server.listen(port, () => {
            console.log(`Server running at http://127.0.0.1:${port}/`); // tslint:disable-line
        });

    } catch (e) {
        console.log(e); // tslint:disable-line
    }

})();
```

Frontend Development with React and TypeScript

The preceding code snippet creates a new Express.js application. The key point to focus on here is the invocation to the `setConfig` method. We have configured the Express.js static middleware to serve all the files located under the `public` directory when the default path (`"/"`) is invoked. This means that if we run the application using `npm start` and we access `http://127.0.0.1:3000/`, the `index.html` file located under the `public` directory will be served. The `index.html` file will then request the JavaScript and CSS files; these files are also located under the `public` directory and can be accessed using `http://127.0.0.1:3000/main.css` and `http://127.0.0.1:3000/bundle.js` respectively.

> Please note that we have also configured our application to use the body-parser middleware. This is required to be able to parse JSON data contained in the body of an HTTP request. Please refer to *Chapter 10, Node.js Development with TypeScript*, if you need additional help with Node.js and Express.js.

Working with react-dom and JSX

Now that we know how we can use Webpack to build our frontend application and how we can use Express.js to serve its static files, we can focus on the code of the React application. We are going to start by examining the entry point of our frontend application. The application's entry point is located at `/web/frontend/index.tsx`.

As you can see, we have used the file extension .tsx instead of the .ts extension. This is the case because we are going to use a template system known as JSX. TypeScript supports JSX natively, but it requires us to use the .tsx file extension and to configure the JSX settings in our `tsconfig.json` file:

```
"jsx": "react"
```

The JSX setting determines if the JSX code should be compiled into JavaScript by TypeScript or by an external tool. In this case, we are working to set the JSX setting to `react`, which means that the JSX code will be compiled into JavaScript by TypeScript.

The application's entry point uses the `react-dom` module to render the application's root component. At this point, we don't know what a React component is yet. However, we don't need to go into detail just yet. All we need to understand here is that the `Layout` variable is a React component and that it is rendered into an HTML element using the `render` method from the `react-dom` library.

Chapter 11

We use the `querySelector` to find an existing DOM element in our `index.html` file and then we use the `render` function to render the output of the `Layout` component into the selected DOM element:

```
import "reflect-metadata";
import * as React from "react";
import * as ReacDOM from "react-dom";
import "../../node_modules/bootstrap/scss/bootstrap.scss";
import { Layout } from "./config/layout";

const selector = "#root";
const $element = document.querySelector(selector);

if (!$element) {
    throw new Error(`Node ${selector} not found!`);
} else {
    ReacDOM.render(
        <Layout/>,
        $element
    );
}
```

The first argument of the render function is a JSX element. As you can see, the JSX syntax is very similar to the HTML syntax, however it has some differences that we will explore throughout the rest of this chapter.

It is also worth mentioning that the preceding file is also importing some files required by the entire frontend application. For example, the file imports the `bootstrap.css` and the `reflect-metadata` modules. The first file contains the CSS required by the React components in this application, and the `reflect-metadata` module declares a polyfill required to implement dependency injection in some of our components.

Working with the react-router

In the preceding section, we learned how to use the `render` method from the `react-dom` module to render the `Layout` component. In this section, we are going to take a closer look at the `Layout` component.

Frontend Development with React and TypeScript

As we can see in the code snippet below, the `Layout` component is a function that returns a series of nested JSX elements; some of these JSX elements are other React components (such as `BrowserRouter`, `Header`, and `Switch` components). This is the first time that we have seen the actual implementation of a React component. In this case, a React component is a function that returns some JSX. However, it is important to mention that this is not always the case as a component can also be a class.

React is a component-based frontend development framework. This means that in React, everything is a component. Our application is a component, the pages within the application are components, and the elements in each of the pages are components.

The `Layout` component is the application's root component. The `Layout` component is always rendered on screen. However, the pages within the application are conditionally rendered as a child of the `Layout` component.

The `Layout` component uses the `react-router` module to implement routing in our React application. The `react-router` module includes the following React components:

- The `BrowserRouter` module is used to provide other components with access to some browser APIs required to implement client-side navigation (such as the History API).
- The `Switch` component allows us to define the routes available in our application.
- The `Route` component allows us to define a route in our application. The `Route` component takes a `path` and a `component` as properties. When the browser URL matches one of the routes, the respective component is rendered.
- The `Link` component is not used by the `Layout` component directly. However, it is the component used to declare a link to one of the existing routes.

The following code snippet showcases how the `Layout` component declares three different routes:

```
import { Route, Switch, BrowserRouter } from "react-router-dom";
import * as React from "react";
import { Header } from "../components/header_component";
import { HomePage } from "../pages/home_page";
import { MoviePage } from "../pages/movies_page";
import { ActorPage } from "../pages/actors_page";
import "../stores/movie_store";
import "../stores/actor_store";

export const Layout = () => (
    <BrowserRouter>
```

```
        <div>
            <Header
                bg="primary"
                title="TsMovies"
                rootPath="/"
                links={[
                    { path: "/movies", text: "Movies"},
                    { path: "/actors", text: "Actors"}
                ]}
            />
            <main style={{ paddingTop: "60px" }}>
                <Switch>
                    <Route exact path="/" component={HomePage}/>
                    <Route path="/movies" component={MoviePage}/>
                    <Route path="/actors" component={ActorPage}/>
                </Switch>
            </main>
        </div>
    </BrowserRouter>
);
```

As we have already mentioned, the `Link` component is not used by the `Layout` component, but it can be used as follows:

```
<Link className="btn btn-primary" to={props.linkPath} >
    {props.linkText}
</Link>
```

As we have already mentioned, the JSX syntax is almost identical to the HTML syntax. However, some attributes are not available or are named differently (for example, `className`). Another significant difference is that we must use a special syntax (`{ }`) to bind the value of a variable to one of the properties of a component.

Working with React components

In this section, we are going to take a close look at some of the components used by the application included in the companion source code. We will use multiple components to demonstrate multiple concepts.

Components as classes

The following code snippet declares three components named `Container`, `Row`, and `Column`. These components extend the `Component` class, which is imported from the `React` module. There are a few methods that we can implement in a class that extends the `Component` class, but at a bare minimum, we must implement the `render` method.

The `Container`, `Row`, and `Column` components are used to control the layout of a page. These components use the CSS classes from the Bootstrap (a library that allow us to style our application with ease) grid system. In Bootstrap, the layout has a maximum of 12 columns, and a different size can be declared for a given screen size:

```
import * as React from "react";

export class Container extends React.Component {
    public render() {
        return (
            <div className="container">
                {this.props.children}
            </div>
        );
    }
}

export class Row extends React.Component {
    public render() {
        return (
            <div className="row">
                {this.props.children}
            </div>
        );
    }
}

type ColumnWidth = 1 | 2 | 3 | 4 | 5 | 6 | 7 | 8 | 9 | 10 | 11 | 12;
type DeviceSize = "s" | "m" | "l" | "xl";

interface ColumnProps {
    width: ColumnWidth;
    size?: DeviceSize;
    style?: React.CSSProperties;
}

export class Column extends React.Component<ColumnProps> {
    public render() {
        return (
```

```
            <div className={this._getClass()} style={this.props.style ?
this.props.style : {}}>
                {this.props.children}
            </div>
        );
    }
    private _getClass() {
        if (this.props.size !== undefined) {
            return `col-${this.props.size}-${this.props.width}`;
        } else {
            return `col-${this.props.width}`;
        }
    }
}
```

Properties and state

As we can see in the preceding code snippet, the `Component` class is a generic class with two optional generic types: `Component<TProps, TState>`. These two generic types allow us to specify the type of the properties and state used in a React component.

As you can see, the `Container` and the `Row` components don't have any properties or state. However, the `Column` component defines the type of its properties because we need some additional data to be provided by its consumers. For example, when we declare the `Column` component, we don't know if the consumers will set its size to 1 or 12.

Properties are passed to a component via its constructor by the consumers of the component. For example, the following code snippet demonstrates how we can pass the property `width` to the `Column` component. The code snippet also demonstrates how we can pass other properties to the `Card` component:

```
import * as React from "react";
import { Card } from "../components/card_component";
import { Container, Row, Column } from "../components/grid_component";

export const HomePage = () => (
    <Container>
        <Row>
            <Column width={6}>
                <Card
                    title="Movies"
                    description="Explore our database of movies"
                    linkPath="/movies"
                    linkText="Movies"
                    img={null}
```

```
            />
        </Column>
        <Column width={6}>
            <Card
                title="Actors"
                description="Explore our actors of movies"
                linkPath="/actors"
                linkText="Actors"
                img={null}
            />
        </Column>
    </Row>
</Container>
);
```

A component can also have an internal state. The main difference between properties and states is that properties are immutable. In other words, the value of the properties of a component cannot change (be mutated) after the component instantiation. On the other hand, the state of a component mutates through the `setState` function. For example, the following code snippet declares a component that uses both properties and states. The component displays a basic numeric counter that increments when the users click on a button. The component properties are used to set the initial state of the component (the value of the counter). The state is then mutated by the `setState` function when the users click on the button:

```
import * as React from "react";
import { Button } from "./button_component";

interface CounterProps {
    initialValue: number;
}

interface CounterState {
    value: number;
}

export class Component extends React.Component<CounterProps, CounterState>
{
    public constructor(props: CounterProps) {
        super(props);
        this.state = { value: this.props.initialValue };
    }
    public render() {
        return (
            <div>
                The value is: {this.state.value}
```

```
                <Button onClick={() => this._increment()}>
                    Increment
                </Button>
            </div>
        );
    }
    private _increment() {
        this.setState({ value: this.state.value + 1 })
    }
}
```

The preceding component can be consumed as follows:

```
<Counter initialValue={1} />
```

The state of a component can only be changed by the component itself. In general, properties are preferred over internal states because it can lead to maintainability issues in very large projects. This is mainly because when we use an internal state, it is slightly more complicated to keep track of state mutations and the current state. We are going to learn more about this topic later in this chapter in the *Smart components and dumb components* section.

Functional stateless components

A **functional stateless component** (**FSC**) is a component that doesn't use an internal state, and it is a simple function, as opposed to a class that extends the Component class. For example, the Header component is an FSC:

```
import { Link } from "react-router-dom";
import * as React from "react";

type BgColor = "primary" | "secondary" | "success" |
               "danger" | "warning" | "info" | "light" |
               "dark" | "white";

interface HeaderProps {
    bg: BgColor;
    title: string;
    rootPath: string;
    links: { path: string; text: string }[];
}

export const Header = (props: HeaderProps) => (
    <nav className={`navbar navbar-expand-lg navbar-light bg-${props.bg}`}>
        <Link className="navbar-brand" to={props.rootPath}>
```

```
            {props.title}
        </Link>
        <ul className="navbar-nav">
            {
                props.links.map((link, linkIndex) => (
                    <Link
                        className="navbar-brand"
                        to={link.path}
                        key={linkIndex}
                    >
                        {link.text}
                    </Link>
                ))
            }
        </ul>
    </nav>
);
```

React component life cycle

When a component extends the `Component` class, it is possible to implement some component life cycle hooks. The companion source code includes a component named `MoviePage` that declares a component life cycle hook named `componentWillMount`:

```
class MoviePage extends React.Component {
    // ...
    public componentWillMount() {
        this.movieStore.getAll();
    }
    public render() {
        // ...
```

React allows us to declare multiple component life cycle hooks. Covering all the available React component life cycle hooks is out of the scope of this book. However, it is important to understand that the events are organized into three main phases:

- The mounting phase takes place before the component is rendered
- The updating phase included the rendering and the moment immediately before and after the component has been rendered
- The unmounting phase takes place when the component is about to stop being rendered

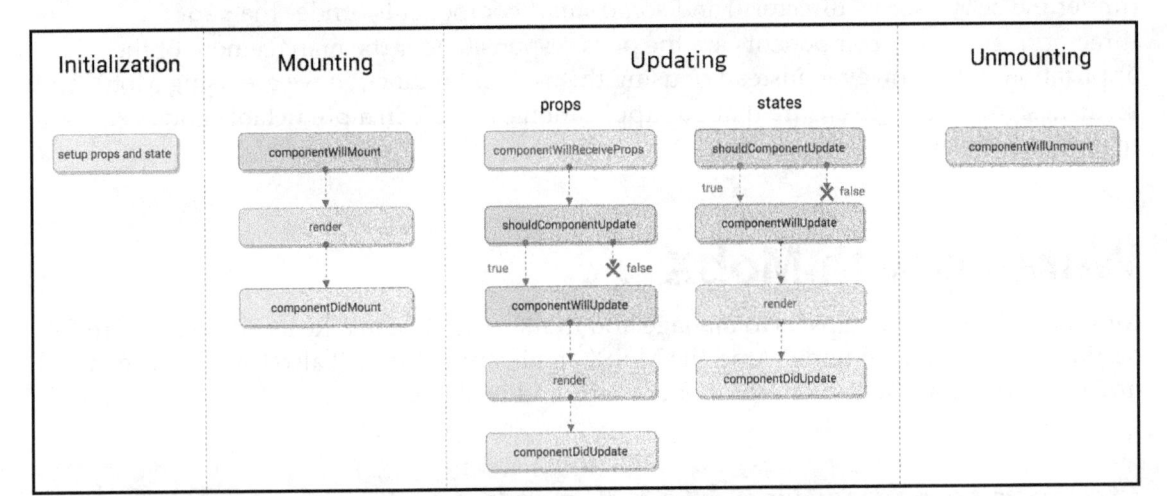

The following diagram showcases the order in which the main events are executed:

Initialization	Mounting	Updating		Unmounting
		props	states	
setup props and state	componentWillMount	componentWillReceiveProps	shouldComponentUpdate	componentWillUnmount
	↓	↓	true ↓ ✗ false	
	render	shouldComponentUpdate	componentWillUpdate	
	↓	true ↓ ✗ false	↓	
	componentDidMount	componentWillUpdate	render	
		↓	↓	
		render	componentDidUpdate	
		↓		
		componentDidUpdate		

> Please refer to the official React documentation at `https://reactjs.org/docs/react-component.html` to learn more about the component life cycle events.

Smart components and dumb components

In a real-world React application, we will have many stateless React components, but somewhere in our tree of components, a component must be responsible for the management of the application state. This means that we can group them into two main categories:

- **Dumb components** are also known as presentational components because their only responsibility is to present something to the DOM. Dumb components may be functional stateless components or not.
- **Smart components** are also known as container components because they are the ones that keep track of states and care about how the app works.

The separation between smart and dumb components can be achieved in many ways, and it is sometimes coupled to some implementation details. The most simplistic way to achieve this is to have a smart component that uses an internal state and the `setState` function and some dumb components that take their parent's internal state as their properties. However, it is also very common to use external state container libraries (such as Redux or MobX) to implement smart components.

The application included in the companion source code declares a lot of dumb components (under the `components` directory) and some smart components (under the `pages` directory). The smart components are the ones responsible for the management of the application state. However, instead of using the `setState` function we are using MobX and some design patterns to ensure that our application can scale in a predictable and maintainable way.

Working with MobX

MobX is a library that helps us to manage and mutate the state in a React application. In this section, we are going to understand the MobX architecture. We will also learn how to install and configure it, what its main components are, and its APIs.

Understanding the MobX architecture

The MobX architecture introduces an entity known as the `Store`. A `Store` is an object that contains some state and provides access to some actions that allow us to mutate its internal state:

- The state is observable; this means that when its value changes, an event is emitted and other parts of the application can subscribe to state changes
- The actions allow us to mutate the current state

Working with actions and observables

In this section, we are going to learn to use observables and actions. The following code snippet declares a `Store` named `ActorStore`:

```
import { ActorInterface } from "../../universal/entities/actor";
import * as mobx from "mobx";
import { provide } from "../config/ioc";
import { TYPE } from "../contants/types";
import * as interfaces from "../interfaces";

const { observable, action, runInAction, configure } = mobx;
configure({ enforceActions: true });

@provide(TYPE.ActorStore)
export class ActorStore implements interfaces.ActorStore {
```

Chapter 11

The `ActorStore` is a class that is decorated with the `@provide` decorators. This decorator is used to allow us to inject the `Store` into other elements in the application.

> Please note that we will learn more about the `@provide` decorator later in this chapter in the *Dependency injection in MobX* section.

The `Store` class also declares some properties that are decorated with the `@observable` decorator. This decorator allows other elements in our application to subscribe to the changes in the properties:

```
// Contains the actors that have been already loaded from the server
@observable public actors: ActorInterface[] = [];

// Used to represent the status of the HTTP GET calls
@observable public loadStatus: interfaces.Status = "pending";

// Used to represent the status of the HTTP DELETE call
@observable public deleteStatus: interfaces.Status = "idle";

// Used to represent the status of the HTTP POST and HTTP PUT calls
@observable public saveStatus: interfaces.Status = "idle";

// Used to display the confirmation dialog before deleting an actor
// null hides the modal and number display the modal
@observable public deleteActorId: null | number = null;

// Used to hold the values of the actor editor or null
// when nothing is being edited
@observable public editorValue: null | Partial<ActorInterface> = null;
```

After declaring the properties of the `Store`, we are going to declare its actions. As you can see in the following code snippet, an action is a method decorated with the `@action` decorator:

```
@action
public focusEditor() {
    runInAction(() => {
        this.editorValue = {};
    });
}

@action
public focusOutEditor() {
    runInAction(() => {
```

[361]

```
            this.editorValue = null;
        });
    }

    @action
    public focusDeleteDialog(id: number) {
        runInAction(() => {
            this.deleteActorId = id;
        });
    }

    @action
    public focusOutDeleteDialog() {
        runInAction(() => {
            this.deleteActorId = null;
        });
    }

    @action
    public edit<T extends ActorInterface, K extends keyof T>(
        key: K, val: T[K]
    ) {
        runInAction(() => {
            const actor = {...(this.editorValue || {}), ...{[key]: val}};
            this.editorValue = actor;
        });
    }
```

The `@action` decorator can be used to decorate methods that perform state mutations like the preceding methods, but we are not limited to only this kind of operation. The following methods perform state mutations, but they also send some HTTP requests to the server using the Fetch API. There is an action to fetch all actors from the actors REST API:

```
    @action
    public async getAll() {
        try {
            const response = await fetch(
                "/api/v1/actors/",
                { method: "GET" }
            );
            const actors: ActorInterface[] = await response.json();
            // We use setTimeout to simulate a slow request
            // this should allow us to see the loading component
            setTimeout(
                () => {
                    runInAction(() => {
                        this.loadStatus = "done";
```

```
                    this.actors = actors;
                });
            },
            1500
        );
    } catch (error) {
        runInAction(() => {
            this.loadStatus = "error";
        });
    }
}
```

There is also an action to create a new actor:

```
@action
public async create(actor: Partial<ActorInterface>) {
    try {
        const response = await fetch(
            "/api/v1/actors/",
            {
                body: JSON.stringify(actor),
                headers: {
                    "Accept": "application/json, text/plain, */*",
                    "Content-Type": "application/json"
                },
                method: "POST"
            }
        );
        const newActor: ActorInterface = await response.json();
        runInAction(() => {
            this.loadStatus = "done";
            this.actors.push(newActor);
            this.editorValue = null;
        });
    } catch (error) {
        runInAction(() => {
            this.loadStatus = "error";
        });
    }
}
```

There is also an action to delete an actor:

```
@action
public async delete(id: number) {
    try {
        const response = await fetch(
            `/api/v1/actors/${id}`,
```

```
                    { method: "DELETE" }
                );
                await response.json();
                runInAction(() => {
                    this.deleteStatus = "done";
                    this.actors = this.actors.filter((m) => m.id !== id);
                    this.deleteActorId = null;
                });
            } catch (error) {
                runInAction(() => {
                    this.deleteStatus = "error";
                });
            }
        }
    }
}
```

We use the `runInAction` function to wrap the state mutations. Using the `runInAction` function is required because we previously configured MobX to enforce that state mutations must only take place in actions:

```
configure({ enforceActions: true });
```

At this point, our `Store` is ready to be injected into one of our React smart components using the `@lazyInject` decorator.

> Please note that we will learn more about the `@lazyInject` decorator later in this chapter in the *Dependency injection in MobX* section.

The following code snippet declares a smart component named `MoviePages`. In our React application, the pages are smart components and the components are simply dumb components:

```
import * as React from "react";
import { observer } from "mobx-react";
import { MovieInterface } from "../../universal/entities/movie";
import { Container, Row, Column } from "../components/grid_component";
import { ListGroup } from "../components/list_group_component";
import { Modal } from "../components/modal_component";
import { TextField } from "../components/textfield_component";
import { Button } from "../components/button_component";
import { lazyInject } from "../config/ioc";
import { TYPE } from "../contants/types";
import * as interfaces from "../interfaces";
```

```
function isValidNewMovie(o: any) {
    if (
        o === null ||
        o === undefined ||
        // new movies don't have ID
        o.id !== undefined ||
        typeof o.title !== "string" ||
        isNaN(o.year)
    ) {
        return false;
    }
    return true;
}
```

This smart component is implemented using a class that extends the `Component` class and is decorated with the `@observer` decorator. The `@observer` decorator binds the React component to the state changes in the `Store`:

```
@observer
export class MoviePage extends React.Component {
```

The `MovieStore` is injected into the `Component` after an instance of it has been created by React. We can ignore the details about this for now because it will be explained in the following section:

```
@lazyInject(TYPE.MovieStore) public movieStore!: interfaces.MovieStore;
```

We use then the `componentWillMount` event hook to trigger the initial data-fetching action:

```
public componentWillMount() {
    this.movieStore.getAll();
}
```

Finally, we render the page. The `render` method accesses some of the properties (`@observables`) of the `Store`. Because our component is an observer (`@observer`), if an action (`@action`) is triggered, our component will be re-rendered. The component renders a list of movies:

```
public render() {
    const error = this.movieStore.loadStatus === "error" ? new Error("Movies could not be loaded!") : null;
    const movies = this.movieStore.loadStatus === "pending" ? null : this.movieStore.movies;
    return (
        <Container>
```

[365]

```
                <Row>
                    <Column width={12} style={{ textAlign: "right",
marginBottom: "10px" }}>
                        <Button
                            onClick={() => {
                                this.movieStore.focusEditor();
                            }}
                        >
                            Add Movie
                        </Button>
                    </Column>
                </Row>
                <Row>
                    <Column width={12}>
                        <ListGroup
                            error={error}
                            items={movies}
                            itemComponent={(movie: MovieInterface) => (
                                <Row>
                                    <Column width={8}>
                                        <h5>{movie.title}</h5>
                                        <p>{movie.year}</p>
                                    </Column>
                                    <Column width={4} style={{ textAlign:
"right" }}>
                                        <Button
                                            kind="danger"
                                            onClick={() => {
this.movieStore.focusDeleteDialog(movie.id);
                                            }}
                                        >
                                            Delete
                                        </Button>
                                    </Column>
                                </Row>
                            )}
                        />
                    </Column>
                </Row>
```

This component also renders a modal window that allows us to create a movie:

```
                <Modal
                    title="Movie Editor"
                    isVisible={this.movieStore.editorValue !== null}
                    onAcceptLabel="Save"
                    onAccept={() => {
                        if (isValidNewMovie(this.movieStore.editorValue)) {
```

```
                    const movie: any = this.movieStore.editorValue;
                    this.movieStore.create(movie);
                }
            }}
            onCancelLabel="Cancel"
            onCancel={() => {
                this.movieStore.focusOutEditor();
            }}
            error={this.movieStore.saveStatus === "error" ? new Error("Something went wrong") : undefined}
        >
            <form>
                <TextField
                    id="movie_title"
                    value={this.movieStore.editorValue ? this.movieStore.editorValue.title : ""}
                    title="Title"
                    placeholder="Title"
                    isValid={(val) => val !== undefined && val !== ""}
                    onChange={(val) => {
                        this.movieStore.edit("title", val);
                    }}
                />
                <TextField
                    id="movie_year"
                    value={this.movieStore.editorValue ? this.movieStore.editorValue.year : 2018}
                    title="Year"
                    placeholder="Year"
                    isValid={(val) => !isNaN(val as any)}
                    onChange={(val) => {
                        const n = parseInt(val);
                        if (!isNaN(n)) {
                            this.movieStore.edit("year", n);
                        }
                    }}
                />
            </form>
        </Modal>
```

This component also renders a modal window that allows us to confirm that we wish to delete a movie from the database:

```
<Modal
    title="Are you sure?"
    isVisible={this.movieStore.deleteMovieId !== null}
    onAcceptLabel="Delete"
    onAccept={() => {
        if (this.movieStore.deleteMovieId) {
            this.movieStore.delete(this.movieStore.deleteMovieId);
        }
    }}
    onCancelLabel="Cancel"
    onCancel={() => {
        this.movieStore.focusOutDeleteDialog();
    }}
    error={this.movieStore.deleteStatus === "error" ? new Error("Something went wrong") : undefined}
>
    The movie will be deleted permanently!
</Modal>
    </Container>
    );
  }
}
```

Dependency injection in MobX

In the preceding section, we decorated the `ActorStore` class with the `@provide` decorators:

```
@provide(TYPE.ActorStore)
export class ActorStore implements interfaces.ActorStore {
```

This decorator is an alternative to the InversifyJS biding syntax and is equivalent to the following:

```
container.bind<ActorStore>(TYPE.ActorStore).to(ActorStore);
```

The `@provide` decorator is not required but it is more convenient than the binding API. The `@provide` decorator can be created using the `inversify-binding-decorators` module as follows:

```
import { Container } from "inversify";
import { makeProvideDecorator } from "inversify-binding-decorators";
```

```
const container = new Container();
const provide = makeProvideDecorator(container);

export { provide };
```

> Note that the examples use the version 3.2.0 of the `inversify-binding-decorators` module and the upcoming version (4.0.0) will introduce some breaking changes. You can refer to the documentation at https://github.com/inversify/inversify-binding-decorators to learn more about the new API.

The `@provider` decorator declares a binding automatically for us when it is executed, and decorators are executed when a class is declared. This means that we need to import the files that use the `@provider` decorator at least once in our application to trigger the class declaration, or no bindings will be declared:

```
import "../stores/movie_store";
import "../stores/actor_store";
```

After declaring the bindings, the `Store` is injected into a React component. However, we cannot use the `@injectable` and `@inject` annotations as we did in some of the preceding chapters because React components are instantiated by React. This means that our IoC container will not be able to create instances of our React components and will therefore not be able to perform any constructor injection. We can overcome this limitation by using the `@lazyInject` decorator:

```
@lazyInject(TYPE.MovieStore) public movieStore!: interfaces.MovieStore;
```

The `@lazyInject` decorator injects a dependency immediately before it is used instead of injecting it when an instance of its dependent is created. The `@lazyInject` decorator can be created using the `inversify-inject-decorators` module as follows:

```
import { Container } from "inversify";
import getDecorators from "inversify-inject-decorators";

const container = new Container();
const { lazyInject } = getDecorators(container);

export { lazyInject };
```

> Please refer to `Chapter 5`, *Working with Dependencies*, to learn more about dependency injection and InversifyJS.

Using dependency injection in MobX is useful because we can inject a different store with hardcoded results during the execution of the unit tests. This allows us to test the components in complete isolation.

MobX alternatives

We have been using MobX to manage the state of our application and the required state mutations (actions). MobX is a great library and it has great support for TypeScript. However, it is not the only option.

One of the best features of React is that we have the freedom to select many different state management tools and architectures. Freedom of choice can lead to confusion and is a problem for junior engineers because they don't have the experience required to judge if a library is better than another. On the other hand, freedom can lead to more innovation and better solutions.

The two most popular alternatives to MobX are Redux and Flux. You can learn more about Redux at `https://redux.js.org`. Please refer to `https://facebook.github.io/flux` to learn more about Flux.

Development tools

We can install the React development tools extensions for Google Chrome to help us to debug our frontend React applications. The extension can be downloaded at `https://chrome.google.com/webstore/detail/react-developer-tools/fmkadmapgofadopljbjfkapdkoienihi`.

There is also a Google Chrome extension available that can help us to debug a MobX application. We can download the extension at the official installation page: `https://chrome.google.com/webstore/detail/mobx-developer-tools/pfgnfdagidkfgccljigdamigbcnndkod`.

These tools allow us to see components being rendered, their **properties** and **state**, and the MobX actions:

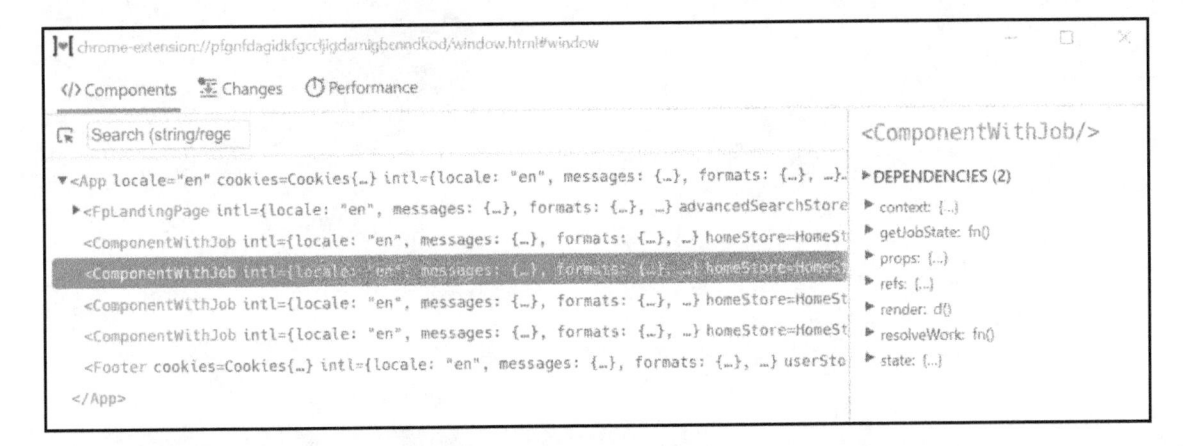

Summary

In this chapter, we have learned the basic principles of component-based web development and how to use React. We have also learned about concepts like stateless functional components and dumb components.

In the next chapter, we are going to implement the same application one more time. However, we will use Angular instead of React and MobX as our application development framework. We will try to implement a copy of the application as close as possible to enable us to compare both frameworks.

12
Frontend Development with Angular and TypeScript

In this chapter, we are going to learn how to develop a frontend web application with Angular and TypeScript. Just like in the previous chapter, we are going to try to use the backend Node.js application that we previously implemented. The application that we are going to develop is a clone of the frontend application that we developed in the previous chapter.

The features and styling of the application will be identical. However, the implementation will present some significant differences because we are going to use Angular instead of React as our frontend application development framework.

We are not going to go through the requirements of the application that we are going to implement in this chapter because we have covered them already in the preceding chapter.

Working with Angular

Angular is a library that allows us to implement web user interfaces. In this chapter, we are going to create a small frontend application using Angular.

As we learned in the preceding chapter, the JavaScript environment in Node.js and a web browser are quite different. The browser environment doesn't support modules natively and loading time is one of the major factors that influence the performance of a frontend application, which explains the need for a module bundler like webpack when we are working on a frontend web application.

In this chapter, we are going to use Webpack just as we have been doing throughout this book. We are going to use the following Webpack configuration. It is almost identical to the configuration used in the preceding chapter, but we have introduced a few modifications:

```
const { CheckerPlugin } = require("awesome-typescript-loader");
const webpack = require("webpack");
const ExtractTextPlugin = require("extract-text-webpack-plugin");
const CopyWebpackPlugin = require("copy-webpack-plugin");
const path = require ("path");

const corePlugins = [
    new CheckerPlugin(),
    new webpack.DefinePlugin({
        "process.env.NODE_ENV": JSON.stringify(process.env.NODE_ENV || "development")
    }),
    new ExtractTextPlugin({
        filename: "[name].css",
        allChunks: true
    }),
    new CopyWebpackPlugin([
        { from: "./web/frontend/index.html", to: "index.html" }
    ]),
```

We have introduced the `CommonChunkPlugin`. This plugin is used to identify pieces of code that repeat or that match a given rule. When a piece of code matches a condition, it is extracted from the main application bundle and is added to a second bundle named `vendor`. In this case, we are going to move all the pieces of code located under the `node_modules` folder to the vendor bundle, which means that we are going to end up with two bundles, one for the application and one for the third-party libraries:

```
    new webpack.optimize.CommonsChunkPlugin({
        name: "vendor",
        minChunks: (module) => {
            return module.context &&
                module.context.includes("node_modules");
        }
    })
];

const devPlugins = [];

const prodPlugins = [
    new webpack.optimize.UglifyJsPlugin({ output: { comments: false } })
];
```

```
const isProduction = process.env.NODE_ENV === "production";
const plugins = isProduction ? corePlugins.concat(prodPlugins) :
corePlugins.concat(devPlugins);
```

We have also introduced an additional application entry point. We import the `zone.js` module. This module is a polyfill for the Zones API, which is a mechanism for intercepting and keeping track of asynchronous work. Zones are defined as follows in the Zone.js documentation:

> *"A Zone is a global object which is configured with rules about how to intercept and keep track of the asynchronous callbacks. Zone has these responsibilities:*
>
> *Intercept asynchronous task scheduling*
> *Wrap callbacks for error-handling and zone tracking across async operations*
> *Provide a way to attach data to zones*
> *Provide a context-specific last frame error handling*
> *(Intercept blocking methods)*
>
> *In its simplest form, a Zone allows one to intercept the scheduling and calling of asynchronous operations, and execute additional code before as well as after the asynchronous task."*

We need Zone.js because it is one of the dependencies of Angular. The rest of the Webpack configuration doesn't present any other major differences:

```
module.exports = {
    entry: [
        "zone.js/dist/zone",
        "./web/frontend/main.ts"
    ],
    devServer: {
        inline: true
    },
    output: {
        filename: "[name].js",
        chunkFilename: "[name]-chunk.js",
        publicPath: "/public/",
        path: path.resolve(__dirname, "public")
    },
    devtool: isProduction ? "source-map" : "eval-source-map",
    resolve: {
        extensions: [".webpack.js", ".ts", ".tsx", ".js"]
    },
    module: {
        rules: [
```

```
            {
                enforce: "pre",
                test: /.js$/,
                loader: "source-map-loader",
                exclude: [/node_modules/]
            },
            {
                test: /.(ts|tsx)$/,
                loader: "awesome-typescript-loader",
                exclude: [/node_modules/]
            },
            {
                test: /.scss$/,
                use: ExtractTextPlugin.extract({
                    fallback: "style-loader",
                    use: ["css-loader", "resolve-url-loader", "sass-loader"]
                })
            }
        ]
    },
    plugins: plugins
};
```

> Please refer to Chapter 9, *Automating Your Development Workflow*, to learn more about webpack.

About the sample application

In this chapter, we are going to implement the same application that we implemented in the preceding chapter one more time. However, we will use Angular instead of React and MobX as our application development framework. We will try to implement a copy of the application as close as possible, to enable us to compare both frameworks.

The application is included in the companion source code and it is a very small web application that allows us to manage a database of movies and actors. We will not explain the features of the application in detail here because we already explained them in the preceding chapter.

> Please refer to Chapter 11, *Frontend Development with React and TypeScript*, to learn more about the application features and requirements. Please refer to the companion source code to have access to the entire source code of the application as well as its configuration, including things like the entire package.json file.

Serving an Angular application with Node.js

Just like we did in the preceding chapter, we need to configure Node.js to server the files of our frontend web application. We use the Express static middleware to implement this feature just like we did in the preceding chapter.

> Please refer to Chapter 11, *Frontend Development with React and TypeScript*, to learn more about the Express static middleware. In particular, please refer to the *Serving React applications with Node.js* section.

Bootstrapping an Angular application

The entry point of the frontend application is in the web/frontend/main.ts file:

```
import { platformBrowserDynamic } from "@angular/platform-browser-dynamic";
import { AppModule } from "./app.module";

platformBrowserDynamic().bootstrapModule(AppModule).catch((err) => {
  console.error(err); // tslint:disable-line
});
```

We use the `platformBrowserDynamic` module to bootstrap our application. We do this by invoking the `bootstrapModule` method and passing the main module in our application as an argument. We will learn more about modules in the following section.

In this section, we are going to focus on the `platformBrowserDynamic` module. The `platform-browser-dynamic` module can be installed using `npm` as follows:

```
npm install --save platform-browser-dynamic
```

[377]

We use `platformBrowserDynamic` because we expect our application to be executed in a browser environment. An Angular application can also be executed in a server-side environment like Node.js, but it requires a slightly different bootstrapping configuration. Executing an Angular application in Node.js can be used to improve the initial loading time of the application. We will not cover this topic in this chapter because it is an advanced feature and the purpose of this chapter is just to introduce Angular.

> Please refer to the documentation at `https://angular.io/guide/universal` if you wish to learn more about server-side rendering with Angular.

Working with NgModules

In the preceding section, we used a module named `AppModule` to bootstrap our Angular application. The `AppModule` is in the `web/frontend/app.module.ts` file and its content looks as follows:

```typescript
import { NgModule } from "@angular/core";
import { BrowserModule } from "@angular/platform-browser";
import { CommonModule } from "@angular/common";
import { AppRoutingModule } from "./app-routing.module";
import { AppComponent } from "./app.component";
import { LayoutModule } from "./config/layout.module";
import "../../node_modules/bootstrap/scss/bootstrap.scss";
import "./app.scss";

@NgModule({
    bootstrap: [AppComponent],
    declarations: [AppComponent],
    imports: [
        BrowserModule,
        CommonModule,
        AppRoutingModule,
        LayoutModule
    ]
})
export class AppModule {
}
```

The `AppModule` is the entry point of our application, and it provides access to every other element in the application. The Angular documentation defines a module as follows:

> *"An NgModule is a class marked by the @NgModule decorator. @NgModule takes a metadata object that describes how to compile a component's template and how to create an injector at runtime. It identifies the module's own components, directives, and pipes, making some of them public, through the exports property, so that external components can use them. @NgModule can also add service providers to the application dependency injectors.*
>
> *Modules are a great way to organize an application and extend it with capabilities from external libraries. Angular libraries are NgModules, such as FormsModule, HttpClientModule, and RouterModule. Many third-party libraries are available as NgModules. NgModules consolidate components, directives, and pipes into cohesive blocks of functionality, each focused on a feature area, application business domain, workflow, or common collection of utilities."*

A module allows us to group features; we can group all the elements (components, services, and so on) required for certain feature into a module.

The `@NgModule` decorator allows us to set up certain settings. The following list defines the purpose of some of the fields used by the application included in the companion source code:

- The `bootstrap` field is used to declare which component must be the root component during the bootstrapping process
- The `declarations` field is used to declare which components are going to be used within the Angular templates
- The `imports` field is used to make other components available within the module
- The `exports` field is used to make components available to other modules
- The `providers` field is used to configure the dependency injection bindings

It is important to clarify that Angular's `@NgModule` imports/exports and ES6 import/export modules are entirely different concepts.

> Please refer to the documentation at https://angular.io/guide/ngmodules to learn more about modules.

Working with Angular components

In this section, we are going to learn how to work with components. We are going to learn how to work to implement components and routing, as well as other concepts such as how to implement dependency injection in an Angular application.

Our first component

In this section, we are going to look at our first Angular component. Earlier in this chapter, we learned how to bootstrap an Angular application, and we used the `AppModule`. Later, we learned that the `AppModule` uses the `AppComponent` as the root component of our application. We will now look at the `AppComponent`:

```
import { Component } from "@angular/core";

@Component({
    selector: "app-root",
    template: `
    <app-layout></app-layout>`,
})
export class AppComponent {
}
```

As you can see, in Angular, a component is a class decorated with the `@Component` decorator. The `@Component` decorator takes some settings.

In this case, we use the `selector` setting to declare the name used to reference this component within a template. The `AppComponent` is the root component in our application; this means that it must be displayed as the root element in our `index.html` page. We can achieve this by adding a reference to the selector of our component in our `index.html` page:

```
<body>
    <app-root>Loading...</app-root>
    <script src="./vendor.js"></script>
    <script src="./main.js"></script>
</body>
```

When the page loads it will display **Loading...** within the `<app-root>` DOM element at first. As soon as the vendor and main bundle files are loaded, the Angular application will be executed, and the `bootstrap` function will render the template of the `AppComponent` within the `<app-root>` DOM element, which will cause the `Loading...` label to disappear.

We use the `template` setting to define the output that we wish to be generated when the component is rendered. In this case, the template is rendering another component that uses `app-layout` as its selector. We defined the template in-line, but it is also possible to define the template in a separate HTML file and reference it by using the `templateUrl` setting.

It is important to note that we can only use a component in a template if both components have been configured correctly within an `NgModule`, as explained in the preceding section.

Sometimes the components will use additional settings; we will not explain all the available settings in this chapter because our goal is only to provide a basic introduction to Angular.

It is also interesting to mention that, in Angular, a component is always a class. In React, it was possible to implement a component as a function or as a class, but in Angular components are always classes, which means that there are no functional stateless components in Angular.

> Please refer to the documentation at `https://angular.io/guide/architecture-components` to learn more about Angular components.

Components and directives

The existing Angular literature contains a lot of references to what are known as directives. Sometimes directives are mentioned as something that can be used together with components as if they were the same thing. The truth is that components are a kind of directive. The following has been extracted from the official Angular documentation:

> There are three kinds of directives in Angular:
> - Components-directives with a template.
> - Structural directives-change the DOM layout by adding and removing DOM elements.
> - Attribute directives-change the appearance or behavior of an element, component, or another directive.

We are not going to learn how to create custom attribute directives in this chapter. However, is it important to understand that components are a kind of directive.

> Please refer to the documentation at `https://angular.io/guide/attribute-directives` to learn more about directives.

Data binding

In Angular, we use data binding to coordinate the application's state with the content rendered on screen. Angular supports three kinds of binding, distinguished by the direction of data flow:

Data direction	Syntax	Type
One-way from data source to view target	`{{expression}}` `[target]="expression"`	• Interpolation • Property • Attribute • Class • Style
One-way from view target to data source	`(target)="statement"`	Event
Two-way	`[(target)]="expression"`	Two-way

Binding types other than interpolation have a target name to the left of the equals sign, surrounded by punctuation (`[]` and `()`).

> Please refer to the documentation at `https://angular.io/guide/template-syntax` to learn more about the data binding syntax.

Working with @Attribute and @Input

In the preceding section, we learned that the `AppComponent` renders the `AppLayout` component. In this section, we are going to look at the `AppLayout`:

```
import { Component, OnInit } from "@angular/core";
import { Route } from "../components/header.component";

@Component({
  selector: "app-layout",
  template: `
    <div>
        <app-header
            bg="primary"
            title="TsMovies"
            rootPath=""
            [links]="appRoutes"
        ></app-header>
        <main>
            <router-outlet></router-outlet>
        </main>
    </div>
  `
})
export class LayoutComponent {
    public appRoutes: Route[] = [
        { label: "Movies", path: "movies" },
        { label: "Actors", path: "actors" }
    ];
}
```

The `Layout` component uses the `app-layout` selector and declares an inline template. The template uses two other components with the `app-header` and `router-outlet` selectors. We will ignore the component with the `router-outlet` selector for now because we will learn more about it later, in the *Working with the Angular router* section.

Frontend Development with Angular and TypeScript

Let's focus on the component with the selector `app-header` for now. As we can see in the preceding code snippet, some arguments are passed to the `HeaderComponent`. However, not all the arguments are passed in the same manner.

We have some arguments passed as follows (one-way data binding from data source to view target):

```
bg="primary"
```

In this case, we are passing the string value primary as what is known as an attribute. We also have some arguments passed as follows:

```
[links]="appRoutes"
```

In this case, we are binding the value of the property `appRoutes` and passing it to the `AppHeader` component. This means that any changes to the `appRoutes` value will trigger the `AppHeader` component to be re-rendered.

We will now look at the `AppHeader` component to see how attributes and inputs are defined:

```
import { Component, Input, Attribute } from "@angular/core";

type BgColor = "primary" | "secondary" | "success" |
               "danger" | "warning" | "info" | "light" |
               "dark" | "white";

export interface Route {
    label: string;
    path: string;
}

@Component({
    selector: "app-header",
    template: `
        <nav [ngClass]="navClass">
        <a class="navbar-brand" [routerLink]="rootPath"
routerLinkActive="active">
            {{title}}
        </a>
        <ul class="navbar-nav">
            <li *ngFor="let link of links">
                <a class="navbar-brand" [routerLink]="link.path"
routerLinkActive="active">
                    {{link.label}}
                </a>
```

```
            </li>
        </ul>
    </nav>`
})
export class HeaderComponent {
    public navClass!: string;
    public title!: string;
    public rootPath!: string;
    @Input() public links!: Route[];

    public constructor(
        @Attribute("bg") bg: BgColor,
        @Attribute("title") title: string,
        @Attribute("rootPath") rootPath: string,
    ) {
        this.navClass = `navbar navbar-expand-lg navbar-light bg-${bg}`;
        this.title = title;
        this.rootPath = rootPath;
    }
}
```

The `HeaderComponent` takes some attributes, which are defined with the `@Attribute` decorator. The `HeaderComponent` also takes one input, which is defined with the `@Input` decorator:

- The `@Input` decorator is used to pass values into the component or to pass data from one component to another (typically parent to child)
- The `@Attribute` directory is used to retrieve the constant value of an attribute available in the host element of the component, and it must be used with a parameter of a component's constructor

Using structural directives

In the preceding section, we looked at the `HeaderComponent`. However, we skipped some details about its template. The `HeaderComponent` uses what is known as a structural directive:

```
<li *ngFor="let link of links">
    // ...
</li>
```

Structural directives are responsible for HTML layout. They shape or reshape the DOM's structure, typically by adding, removing, or manipulating elements.

> Please refer to the documentation at https://angular.io/guide/structural-directives to learn more about structural directives.

Using the <ng-content> directive

We can use the `ng-content` directive to <indexentry content="Angular components: directive, using">render the child of a component. For example, the following component can be used to define a row in <indexentry content=" directive:using">the application's layout. However, when we define the `RowComponent`, we don't know which content will be placed into the row. We use the `ng-content` directive to refer the yet to be known child component:

```
@Component({
    selector: "app-row",
    template: `
        <div class="row">
            <ng-content></ng-content>
        </div>
    `
})
export class RowComponent {}
```

The `RowComponent` can then be used within a template as follows:

```
<app-row>
    <h1>Title</h1>
</app-row>
<app-row>
    <h2>Subtitle</h2>
</app-row>
```

Working with @Output and EventEmitter

In Angular, we can handle user events using a property whose value is an event emitter. The property must be decorated with the `@Output` decorator as demonstrated by the following code snippet:

```
import { Component, EventEmitter, Input, Output } from "@angular/core";

@Component({
```

```
        selector: "app-text-field",
        template: `
            <input
                type="text"
                className="form-control"
                [id]="id"
                [placeholder]="placeholder"
                (input)="onEdit($event)"
            />
    })
    export class TextFieldComponent {

        @Input() public id!: string;
        @Input() public placeholder!: string;
        @Output() public onChange = new EventEmitter<{k: string; v: string}>();

        public onEdit(event: any) {
            const value = (event.target as any).value;
            const key = (event.target as any).id;
            this.onChange.emit({ v: value, k: key });
        }

    }
```

In our template, we have linked an event with one of the methods in the component as follows (one-way data binding from view target to data source):

```
(input)="onEdit($event)"
```

The `onEdit` method will receive an event object that allows access to the target (the DOM element that started the event). We can use the event target to access the attributes of the DOM element.

Finally, we invoke the `emit` method of our output to pass some data to the parent component as output:

```
public onEdit(event: any) {
    const value = (event.target as any).value;
    const key = (event.target as any).id;
    this.onChange.emit({ v: value, k: key });
}
```

Finally, the parent component can set one of its methods as the event handler for the `onChange` output as follows:

```
<app-text-field
    [id]="'title'"
    [placeholder]="'Title'"
    (onChange)="edit($event)"
></app-text-field>
```

> Please refer to the documentation at `https://angular.io/guide/component-interaction` to learn more about event handlers in Angular.

Working with the component's host

In this section, we are going to demonstrate how we can use the `host` setting in our components to control how the component host is rendered. When a component is rendered, Angular will always create a DOM element that matches the name of the component selector. This DOM element is known as the host. For example, take a look at the following component:

```
@Component({
    selector: "app-row",
    template: `
        <div class="row">
            <ng-content></ng-content>
        </div>
    `
})
export class RowComponent {}
```

It can be consumed by other components as:

```
<app-row>
    Hello!
</app-row>
```

However, it will be rendered as:

```
<app-row>
    <div class="row">
        Hello!
    </div>
</app-row>
```

As you can see, there is an additional DOM node. Sometimes, having an additional node can lead to some layout issues and it would be much better if we could control how the host is rendered to achieve the following output:

```
<app-row class="row">
    Hello!
</app-row>
```

We can achieve this by using the `host` setting when we declare a component:

```
@Component({
    host: {
        "[class]": "'row'"
    },
    selector: "app-row",
    template: `
        <ng-content></ng-content>
    `
})
export class RowComponent {}
```

Working with the Angular router

Earlier in this chapter, we mentioned a component known as the `router-outlet`. The component was used by the `Layout` component as follows:

```
<main>
    <router-outlet></router-outlet>
</main>
```

However, this component was not defined by us because it is defined by the `@angular/router` npm module. In order to use the module, we must import it and declare a `NgModule` that exports `RouteModule`. We must also declare the configuration for the router. The configuration is a map or a dictionary that links a given path with a given component:

```
import { NgModule } from "@angular/core";
import { Routes, RouterModule } from "@angular/router";
import { HomePageComponent } from "./pages/homepage.component";
import { MoviesPageComponent } from "./pages/moviespage.component";
import { ActorsPageComponent } from "./pages/actorspage.component";

export const appRoutes: Routes = [
    { path: "", component: HomePageComponent },
    { path: "movies", component: MoviesPageComponent },
    { path: "actors", component: ActorsPageComponent }
];

@NgModule({
    exports: [RouterModule],
    imports: [
        RouterModule.forRoot(
            appRoutes,
            { useHash: false }
        )
    ]
})

export class AppRoutingModule {}
```

When the browser URL matches one of the paths in the router configuration, the corresponding component is rendered into the `router-outlet` component:

```
<main>
    <router-outlet></router-outlet>
</main>
```

We can trigger a change in the URL using a `routerLink`:

```
<a class="navbar-brand" [routerLink]="link.path" routerLinkActive="active">
    {{link.label}}
</a>
```

We have provided the path that we wish to navigate to and the CSS class to be used when the link is active. When we click on a router link, the browser URL will change, and the router will render the matching component under the `router-outlet` component.

Angular component life cycle hooks

Angular allows us to declare multiple component life cycle hooks. For example, in the companion source code, the `Movie` component extends the `OnInit` interface, which declares the `ngOnInit` method. The `ngOnInit` method is one of the available component life cycle hooks in Angular:

- The `constructor` of the component class is called before any other component life cycle hook. The constructor is the best place to inject dependencies.
- The `ngOnInit` method is invoked immediately after the constructor and after the `ngOnChange` is triggered for the first time, which is the perfect time for initialization work.
- The `ngOnChanges` method is invoked first when the value of a bound property changes. It executes every time the value of an input property changes.
- The `ngDestroy` method is invoked just before the instance of the component is finally destroyed. It is the perfect place to clean a component (for example, canceling background tasks).

There are more life cycle hooks available, but they are out of the scope of this book.

> Please refer to the Angular documentation at `https://angular.io/guide/lifecycle-hooks` to learn more about all the available life cycle hooks.

Working with services

In Angular, it is a common practice to use a service to interact with a REST API or with other resources, such as the localStorage API. The class below defines a service named `MovieService`, which can be used to send HTTP requests to the backend Node.js application.

Frontend Development with Angular and TypeScript

A service is just a class, and it doesn't require any special decorators. However, the following code snippet uses the `@Injectable` decorator because it is going to be injected into the `MovieComponent`. We will learn more about dependency injection later, in the *Dependency injection in Angular* section.

The following methods perform some HTTP requests to the server using the Fetch API. There is a method to fetch all movies from the movies REST API:

```
import { Injectable } from "@angular/core";
import { MovieInterface } from "../../universal/entities/movie";
import * as interfaces from "../interfaces";

@Injectable()
export class MovieService implements interfaces.MovieService {

    public async getAll() {
        return new Promise<MovieInterface[]>(async (res, rej) => {
            try {
                const response = await fetch("/api/v1/movies/", { method: "GET" });
                const movs: MovieInterface[] = await response.json();
                // We use setTimeout to simulate a slow request
                // this should allow us to see the loading component
                setTimeout(
                    () => {
                        res(movs);
                    },
                    1500
                );
            } catch (error) {
                rej(error);
            }
        });
    }
```

There is also a method to create a new movie:

```
    public async create(movie: Partial<MovieInterface>) {
        const response = await fetch(
            "/api/v1/movies/",
            {
                body: JSON.stringify(movie),
                headers: {
                    "Accept": "application/json, text/plain, */*",
                    "Content-Type": "application/json"
                },
                method: "POST"
```

```
        }
    );
    const newMovie: MovieInterface = await response.json();
    return newMovie;
}
```

There is also a method to delete a movie:

```
    public async delete(id: number) {
        const response = await fetch(`/api/v1/movies/${id}`, { method: "DELETE" });
        await response.json();
    }

}
```

In the following section, we will learn how the movie service is consumed by the `Movie` component.

Smart components and dumb components

The Angular components don't draw a clear separation between properties and states like React does, but we can still use the same mental model. A component renders some data. If the data is mutated by the component, we are talking about a smart component. If the component only reads the data, we are talking about a dumb component.

Just like we did in the React example, we have organized our project using multiple directories in a way that allows us to have very clear differentiation between smart and dumb components. The `components` directory contains only dumb components while the `pages` directory contains smart components.

In Angular, the dumb components, most of the time, don't require life cycle hooks, and they also don't require services. On the other hand, the smart components will most likely require some services.

The following code snippet declares a smart component named `MoviePages`. In our Angular application, the pages are smart components and the components are simply dumb components:

```
import { Component, OnInit, Inject } from "@angular/core";
import { MovieInterface } from "../../universal/entities/movie";
import * as interfaces from "../interfaces";
import { MOVIE_SERVICE } from "../config/types";
```

Frontend Development with Angular and TypeScript

```
function isValidNewMovie(o: any) {
    if (
        o === null ||
        o === undefined ||
        // new movies don't have ID
        o.id !== undefined ||
        typeof o.title !== "string" ||
        isNaN(o.year)
    ) {
        return false;
    }
    return true;
}
```

The component renders a list of movies:

```
@Component({
    selector: "movies-page",
    template: `
        <app-container>
            <app-row>
                <app-column width="12">
                    <div style="text-align: right; margin-bottom: 10px">
                        <app-button (clicked)="focusEditor()">
                            Add Movie
                        </app-button>
                    </div>
                </app-column>
            </app-row>
            <app-row>
                <app-column width="12">
                    <app-list-group [isLoaded]="isLoaded" [errorMsg]="fetchErrorMsg">
                        <app-list-group-item *ngFor="let movie of movies">
                            <app-row>
                                <app-column width="8">
                                    <h5>{{movie.title}}</h5>
                                    <p>{{movie.year}}</p>
                                </app-column>
                                <app-column width="4" style="text-align: right">
                                    <app-button kind="danger" (clicked)="focusDeleteDialog(movie.id)">
                                        Delete
                                    </app-button>
                                </app-column>
                            </app-row>
                        </app-list-group-item>
```

```
            </app-list-group>
        </app-column>
    </app-row>
```

This component also renders a modal window that allows us to create a movie:

```
<div *ngIf="editorValue">
    <app-modal
        [title]="'Movie Editor'"
        [acceptLabel]="'Save'"
        [cancelLabel]="'Cancel'"
        [error]="saveStatus"
        (onCancel)="focusOutEditor()"
        (onAccept)="saveMovie()"
    >
        <form>
            <app-text-field
                [id]="'title'"
                [title]="'Title'"
                [placeholder]="'Title'"
                [errorMsg]="isValidTitle"
                (onChange)="edit($event)"
            ></app-text-field>
            <app-text-field
                [id]="'year'"
                [title]="'Year'"
                [placeholder]="'Year'"
                [errorMsg]="isValidYear"
                (onChange)="edit($event)"
            ></app-text-field>
        </form>
    </app-modal>
</div>
```

This component also renders a modal window that allows us to confirm that we wish to delete a movie from the database:

```
<div *ngIf="deleteMovieId !== null">
    <app-modal
        [title]="'Delete?'"
        [acceptLabel]="'Delete'"
        [cancelLabel]="'Cancel'"
        [error]="deleteStatus"
        (onCancel)="focusOutDeleteDialog()"
        (onAccept)="deleteMovie()"
    >
        Are you sure?
    </app-modal>
```

```
            </div>
        </app-container>

})
```

The `MoviesPageComponent` is a smart component. As we can see in the following code snippet, it holds and manages the entire state required for all the dumb components used in its template:

```
export class MoviesPageComponent implements OnInit {

    // Contains the movies that have been already loaded from the server
    public movies: MovieInterface[];

    // Used to represent the status of the HTTP GET calls
    public isLoaded!: boolean;

    // Display error if loading fails
    public fetchErrorMsg: null | string;

    // Used to represent the status of the HTTP DELETE call
    public deleteStatus: null | string;

    // Used to represent the status of the HTTP POST and HTTP PUT calls
    public saveStatus: null | string;

    // Used to display the confirmation dialog before deleting a movie
    // null hides the modal and number displays the modal
    public deleteMovieId: null | number;

    // Used to hold the values of the movie editor or null when nothing is being edited
    public editorValue: null | Partial<MovieInterface>;
    public isValidTitle!: null | string;
    public isValidYear!: null | string;

    public movieService!: interfaces.MovieService;
```

The `MovieService` is injected into the component. We can ignore the details about this for now because it will be explained in the following section:

```
        public constructor(
            @Inject(MOVIE_SERVICE) movieService: interfaces.MovieService
        ) {
            this.movieService = movieService;
            this.movies = [];
            this.fetchErrorMsg = null;
```

```
    this.isLoaded = false;
    this.deleteStatus = null;
    this.saveStatus = null;
    this.deleteMovieId = null;
    this.editorValue = null;
    this.isValidTitle = null;
    this.isValidYear = null;
}
```

We then use the `ngOnInit` event hook to trigger the initial data fetching:

```
public async ngOnInit() {
    this.isLoaded = false;
    try {
        this.movies = await this.movieService.getAll();
        this.isLoaded = true;
        this.fetchErrorMsg = null;
    } catch (err) {
        this.isLoaded = true;
        this.fetchErrorMsg = "Loading failed!";
    }
}
```

After declaring the properties, the constructor, and the `ngOnInit` event of the component, we are going to declare some methods. As you can see in the following code snippet, these methods are used to mutate the state of the application:

```
public focusEditor() {
    this.editorValue = {};
}

public focusOutEditor() {
    this.editorValue = null;
}

public focusDeleteDialog(id: number) {
    this.deleteMovieId = id;
}

public focusOutDeleteDialog() {
    this.deleteMovieId = null;
}
public edit(keyVal: any) {
    const movie = {
        ...(this.editorValue || {}),
        ...{[keyVal.k]: keyVal.v}
    };
```

```
            if (movie.title) {
                this.isValidTitle = (movie.title && movie.title.length) > 0 ?
    null : "Title cannot be empty!";
            }
            if (movie.year) {
                this.isValidYear = isNaN(movie.year) === false ? null : "Year
    must be a number!";
            }
            this.editorValue = movie;
        }
```

In the preceding chapter, we learned the basics about the MobX architecture. There are some significant differences between the MobX architecture and the Angular architecture:

- In MobX, the application state belongs to the Store. The smart component talks to the Store via actions. The Store is the entity that ultimately mutates the state, not the smart component.
- In Angular, the application state belongs to the smart component, which is the entity that ultimately mutates the state.

In Angular, we used a service to perform the Ajax calls; on the other hand, in MobX, we performed the Ajax calls inside the Store. This is a minor difference because we can create a service in MobX to perform the Ajax calls. The Store could then talk to the service. The key takeaway here is the difference in state management.

The following methods use the MovieService to perform some Ajax calls and to mutate the state of the MovieComponent:

```
        public async saveMovie() {
            if (isValidNewMovie(this.editorValue)) {
                const newMovie = await
    this.movieService.create(this.editorValue as any);
                this.movies.push(newMovie);
                this.saveStatus = null;
                this.editorValue = null;
            } else {
                this.saveStatus = "Invalid movie!";
            }
        }

        public async deleteMovie() {
            try {
                if (this.deleteMovieId) {
                    await this.movieService.delete(this.deleteMovieId);
                    this.movies = this.movies.filter((m) => m.id !==
    this.deleteMovieId);
```

```
                this.deleteStatus = null;
                this.deleteMovieId = null;
            }
        } catch (err) {
            this.deleteStatus = "Cannot delete movie!";
        }
    }
}
```

Dependency injection in Angular

Dependency injection in Angular requires us to define some unique identifiers using the `InjectionToken` class. Injection tokens are unique identifiers used to represent a type at runtime. The concept of `InjectionToken` in Angular is very similar to the concept of symbols in InversifyJS:

```
import { InjectionToken } from "@angular/core";
import { MovieService, ActorService } from "../interfaces";

export const ACTOR_SERVICE = new
InjectionToken<MovieService>("ActorService");
export const MOVIE_SERVICE = new
InjectionToken<MovieService>("MovieService");
```

After creating an `InjectionToken`, we must decorate the class that we wish to inject with the `@injectable` decorator, as demonstrated by the following code snippet:

```
import { InjectionToken } from "@angular/core";
// ...
@Injectable()
export class MovieService implements interfaces.MovieService {
    // ...
```

We also must declare a binding between the `InjectionToken` and an implementation of the type that it represents. This can be achieved using the `providers` setting when we declare an `NgModule` as follows:

```
import { NgModule } from "@angular/core";
import { CommonModule } from "@angular/common";
import { MoviesPageComponent } from "./moviespage.component";
import { ComponentsModule } from "../components/components.module";
import { MovieService } from "../services/movie_service";
import { MOVIE_SERVICE } from "../config/types";
```

```
@NgModule({
    declarations: [
        MoviesPageComponent
    ],
    exports: [
        MoviesPageComponent
    ],
    imports: [CommonModule, ComponentsModule],
    providers: [
        { provide: MOVIE_SERVICE, useClass: MovieService }
    ]
})
export class MoviesPageModule {
}
```

The preceding code snippet binds the `InjectionToken MOVIE_SERVICE` to the implementation `MovieService`. Finally, we can use the `@Inject` decorator to declare a dependency in one of our Angular components:

```
import { Component, Inject } from "@angular/core";
// ...
public constructor(
        @Inject(MOVIE_SERVICE) movieService: interfaces.MovieService
    ) {
        this.movieService = movieService;
        // ...
    }
```

> Please refer to the documentation at https://angular.io/guide/dependency-injection to learn more about dependency injection in Angular.

Summary

In this chapter, we have learned the basic principles of component-based web development and how to use Angular. We learned how to bootstrap an Angular application, how to implement routing, and how to create components.

We also learned how to implement dumb and smart components as well as how to work with services and implement dependency injection.

In the next chapter, we are going to learn about application performance.

13
Application Performance

In computer science, a system resource, or simply a resource, is any physical or virtual component of limited availability within a computer system. Every device connected to a computer system is a resource. Every internal system component is also a resource.

In this chapter, we are going to learn how we can manage the available resources of a system efficiently to achieve great application performance. We will learn about the different kinds of resources, performance factors, and performance profiling techniques.

The chapter starts by introducing some core performance concepts, such as latency or bandwidth, and continues showcasing how to measure and monitor performance as part of the continuous integration process.

As we have already learned in previous chapters, we can use TypeScript to generate JavaScript code that can be executed in many different environments. In this chapter, we are going to learn about performance profiling and optimization techniques, which are mainly applicable to the development of web applications. We are going to cover the following topics:

- Performance and resources
- Aspects of performance
- Memory profiling
- Network profiling
- CPU and GPU profiling
- Performance testing
- Performance recommendations
- Performance automation

Prerequisites

We are about to learn how to perform some performance analysis tasks; however, before that, we need to install a few tools in our development environment.

Google Chrome

Before we get started, we need to install Google Chrome. We can download it at `https://www.google.com/chrome/browser/desktop/index.html`. We are going to learn how to use the Google Chrome developer tools to perform some performance analysis tasks.

Node.js

If you didn't install Node.js in the previous chapters, you can visit `https://nodejs.org/en/download/` to download the installer for your operating system. There are two main versions of Node.js available: **Long Term Support** (**LTS**) and **Current**. We recommend using the LTS version.

Performance and resources

Before we get our hands dirty doing some performance analysis, we must first spend some time understanding some core concepts and aspects of performance.

A good application is one that has a set of desirable characteristics, which includes:

- Functionality
- Reliability
- Usability
- Reusability
- Efficiency
- Maintainability
- Portability

Over the course of this book so far, we have learned a lot about maintainability and reusability. In this chapter, we will focus on performance, which is closely related to reliability and maintainability.

The term performance refers to the amount of useful work accomplished compared with the time and resources used. A resource is a physical (such as CPU, RAM, GPU HDD, and so on) or virtual (such as CPU times, RAM regions, files, and so on) component with limited availability. Because the availability of a resource is limited, each resource is shared between processes. When a process finishes using a resource, it must release it before any other process can use it. Managing available resources in an efficient manner will help reduce the time other processes spend waiting for the resources to become available.

When we work on a web application, we need to keep in mind that the following resources will have limited availability:

- **Central Processing Unit (CPU)**: This carries out the instructions of a computer program by performing the basic arithmetic, logical, control, and input/output (I/O) operations specified by the instructions.
- **Graphics Processor Unit (GPU)**: This is a specialized processor used in the manipulation and alteration of memory to accelerate the creation of images in a frame buffer. A frame buffer is an area of the RAM used to hold the frame of data that is continuously being sent to the screen. The GPU is used when we create applications that use the WebGL API or when we use CSS animations.
- **Random Access Memory (RAM)**: This allows data items to be read and written in approximately the same amount of time, regardless of the order in which data items are accessed. When we declare a variable, it will be stored in RAM; when the variable is out of the scope, it will be removed from RAM by the garbage collector.
- **Hard Disk Drive (HDD)** and **Solid-State Drive (SSD)**: Both of these resources are data storage devices used to store and retrieve data. Frontend web applications don't usually use persistent data storage extensively. However, we should keep in mind that whenever we store an object in a persistent manner (such as cookies, local storage, IndexedDB and so on), the performance of our application will be affected by the availability of the HDD or SSD.
- **Network throughput**: This determines how much actual data can be sent per unit of time across a network. The network throughput is determined by factors such as the network latency or bandwidth (we will discover more about these factors later in this chapter).

Common performance metrics

Performance can be affected by the availability of multiple types of physical and virtual devices. This explains the existence of multiple performance metrics (factors to measure performance). Some popular performance metrics include availability, response time, processing speed, latency, bandwidth, and scalability. These measurement mechanisms are usually directly related to one of the general resources (such as CPU, network throughput and so on) that were listed in the preceding section. We will now look at each of these performance metrics in detail.

Availability

If a system is not available at some stage, even if it is only partially unavailable, we will perceive it as bad performance. The availability of a system can be improved by improving its reliability, maintainability, and testability. If the system is easy to test and maintain, it will also be easy to increase its reliability.

Response time

The response time is the amount of time that it takes to respond to a request for a service. A service here does not refer to a web service; a service can be any unit of work. The response time is influenced by the network throughput can be divided into three parts:

- **Wait time**: The amount of time that the requests will spend waiting for other requests that took place earlier to be completed.
- **Service time**: The amount of time that it takes for the service (unit of work) to be completed.
- **Transmission time**: Once the unit of work has been completed, the response will be sent back to the requester. The time that it takes for the response to be transmitted is known as the transmission time.

Processing speed

Processing speed (also known as clock rate) refers to the frequency at which a processing unit (CPU or GPU) runs. An application contains many units of work. Each unit of work is composed of instructions for the processor; usually, the processors can perform an instruction in each clock tick. Since a few clock ticks are required for an operation to be completed, the higher the clock rate (processing speed), the more instructions that will be completed.

Bandwidth

Whenever we mention bandwidth in this chapter, we will be referring to the network bandwidth. The bandwidth, or data transfer rate, is the amount of data that can be carried from one point to another in a given time. The network bandwidth is usually expressed in bits per second.

Latency

Latency is a term we can apply to many elements in a system; however, when working on web applications, we will use this term to refer to network latency. Network latency indicates any delay that occurs in data communication over the network.

High latency creates bottlenecks in the communication bandwidth. The impact of latency on network bandwidth can be temporary or persistent, based on the cause of the delays. High latency can be caused by problems in the medium (cables or wireless signals), problems with routers and gateways, and anti-virus, among others.

> Network performance can be affected by many factors. Some of these factors can degrade the network throughput. For example, a high packet loss, latency, and jitter will reduce the network throughput, while a high bandwidth will increase it.

Scalability

Scalability is the ability of a system to handle a growing amount of work. A system with good scalability will be able to pass some performance tests, such as spike or stress testing. We will learn more about performance tests (such as spike and stress) later in this chapter.

Performance analysis

Performance analysis (also known as performance profiling) is the observation and study of the usage of the available system resources by an application. We will perform profiling to identify performance issues in our applications. A different performance profiling process with specific tools will be carried out for each type of resource. For example, CPU profiling can be performed using the system monitor of our OS.

We will now learn how to use the Google Chrome's developer tools to perform some network profiling tasks.

Network performance analysis

We are going to start by analyzing network performance. Not so long ago, to be able to analyze the network performance of an application, we would have to write a small network logging application from scratch. Fortunately, today, things are much easier thanks to the arrival of the performance timing API.

> The performance timing API allows us to access detailed network timing data for each loaded resource. You can learn more about it at http://www.w3.org/TR/resource-timing/.

The following diagram illustrates the network timing data points that the API provides:

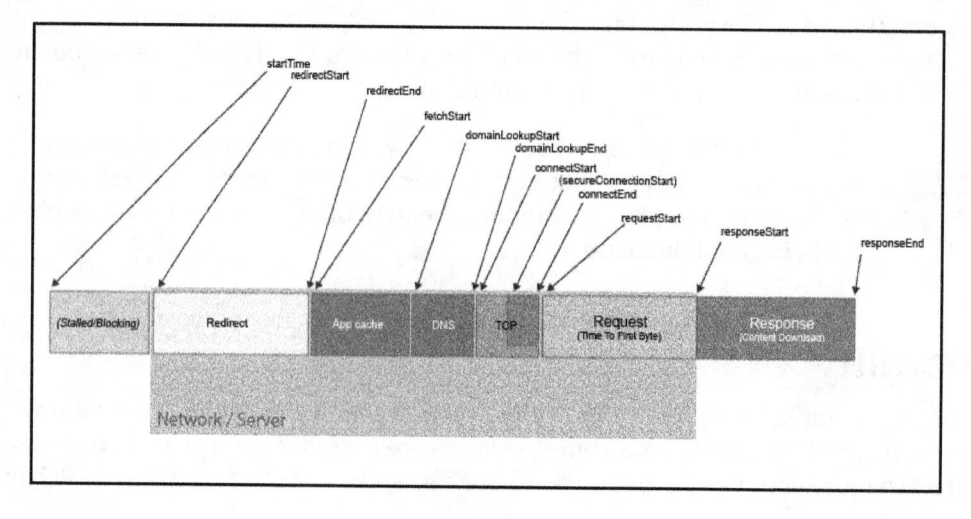

network timing data points

We can access the performance timing API via the `window` object:

```
window.performance
```

The performance attribute in the `window` object has some properties (`memory`, `navigation`, and `timing`) and methods (`clearMarks`, `clearMeasures`, and `getEntries`). We can use the `getEntries` function to access an array which contains the taming data points of each request:

```
window.performance.getEntries()
```

Each entity in the array is an instance of `PerformanceResourceTiming`, which contains the following information:

```
{
    connectEnd: 1354.525000002468
    connectStart: 1354.525000002468
    domainLookupEnd: 1354.525000002468
    domainLookupStart: 1354.525000002468
    duration: 179.89400000078604
    entryType: "resource"
    fetchStart: 1354.525000002468
    initiatorType: "link"
    name: "https://developer.chrome.com/static/css/out/site.css"
    redirectEnd: 0
    redirectStart: 0
    requestStart: 1380.8379999827594
    responseEnd: 1534.419000003254
    responseStart: 1533.6550000065472
    secureConnectionStart: 0
    startTime: 1354.525000002468
}
```

Unfortunately, the timing data points in the preceding format may not be useful if they are not presented in a visual way. Fortunately, there are some tools that can help us to analyze it with ease. We will now learn about some of these tools.

The first tool is a browser extension called **performance-bookmarklet**. This extension is open source and is available for Chrome and Firefox. The extension download links can be found at `https://github.com/micmro/performance-bookmarklet`.

Application Performance

In the following screenshot, we can see one of the graphs generated by the extension. The graphs display the performance typing API information visually, allowing us to spot performance issues with ease:

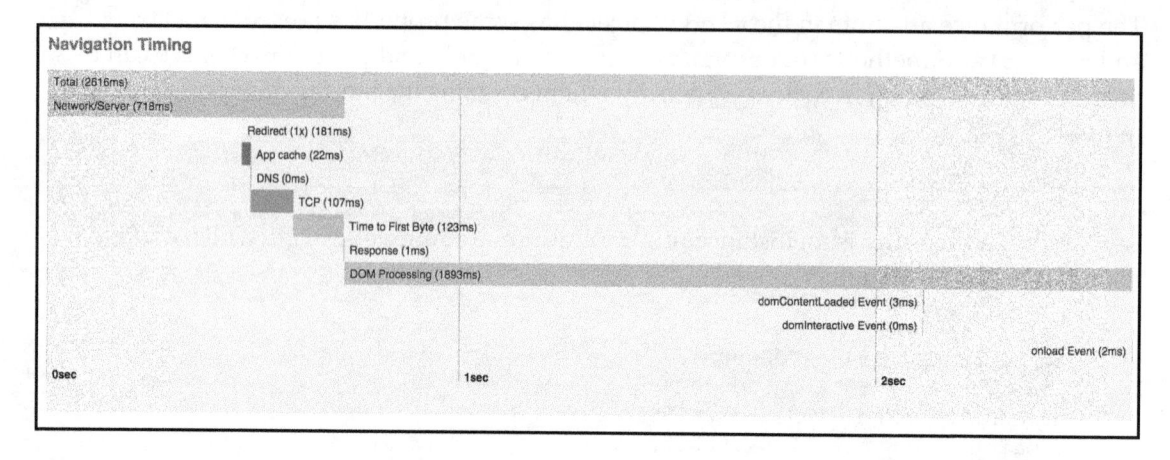

Alternatively, we can use the network panel in the Chrome developer tools to perform network performance profiling. To access the network panel, open Google Chrome, navigate to **View** | **Developer**, and then navigate to **Developer Tools**:

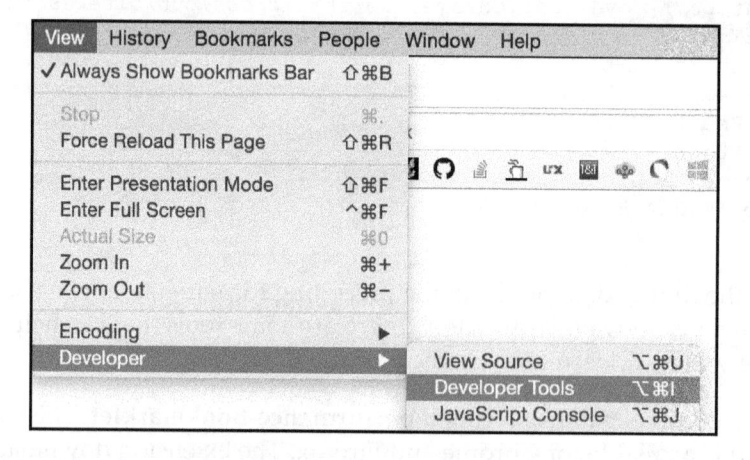

> Windows and Linux users can access the developer tools by pressing the *F12* key. OS X users can access it using the *Alt + Cmd + I* shortcut.

[408]

Chapter 13

Once the developer tools are visible, we can access the **Network** tab by clicking on it:

| Q | 🗔 | Elements | Network | Sources | Timeline | Profiles | Resources | Audits | Console | Ember | PageSpeed |

Network tab

Clicking on the **Network** tab will lead us to a screen like the one seen here:

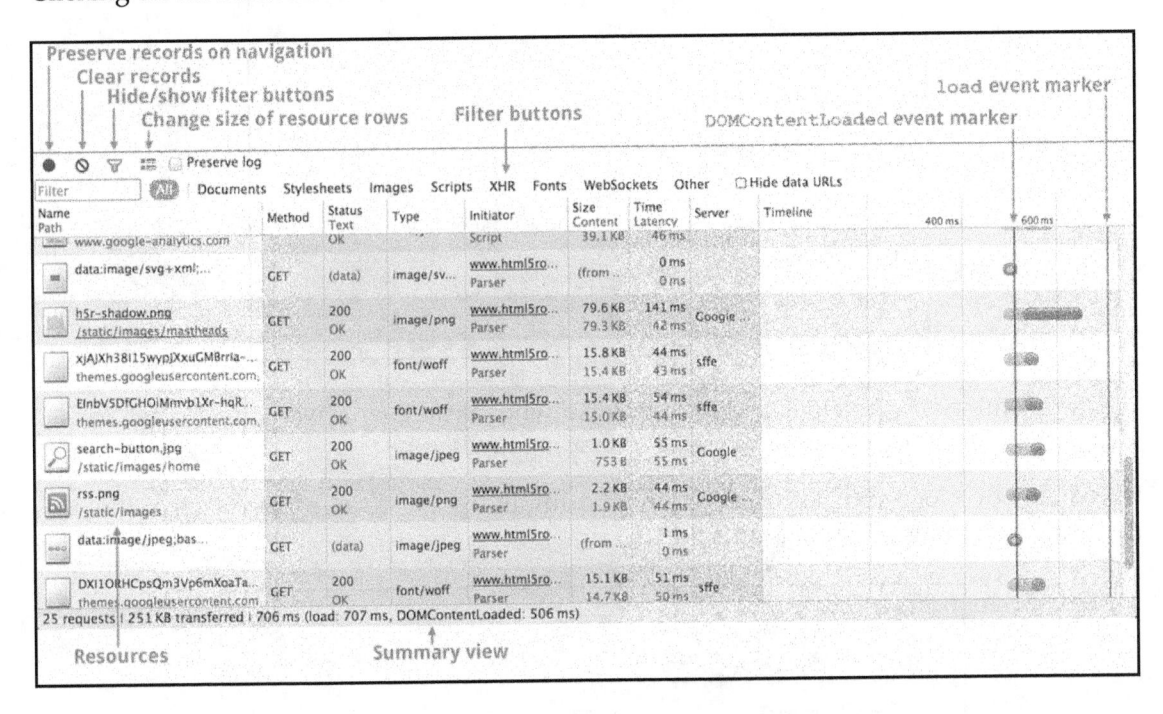

[Screenshot of browser developer tools Network tab with annotations: Preserve records on navigation, Clear records, Hide/show filter buttons, Change size of resource rows, Filter buttons, load event marker, DOMContentLoaded event marker, Resources, Summary view — showing a table of 25 requests, 251 KB transferred, 706 ms (load: 707 ms, DOMContentLoaded: 506 ms)]

As we can observe, the information is presented in a table in which each file loaded is displayed as a row. On the right-hand side, we can see the timeline column. The timeline displays the performance timing API in a visual way, just like the performance-bookmarklet extension.

Two very important elements in the timeline column are the red and blue vertical lines. These lines let us know when the `DOMContentLoaded` event is triggered (blue line), after which the `onLoad` event is triggered (red line):

- The blue line indicates when the `DOMContentLoaded` event was fired. The `DOMContentLoaded` event is fired when the engine has completed parsing of the main document.

[409]

Application Performance

- The red line indicates when the `onLoad` event was fired. The `onLoad` event is fired when all the page's resources have been loaded:

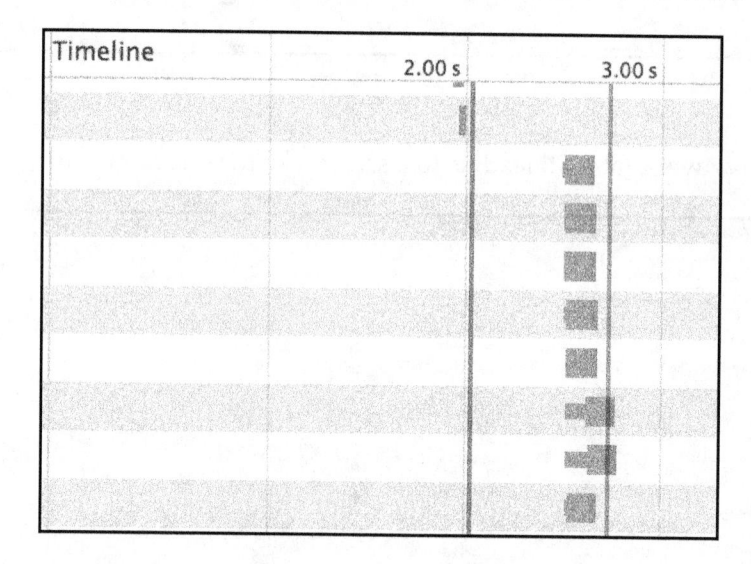

We can examine which requests were completed when these events were fired to get an idea of the overall page responsiveness and loading times.

If we hover over one of the cells of the timing column, we will be able to see each of the performance timing API data points:

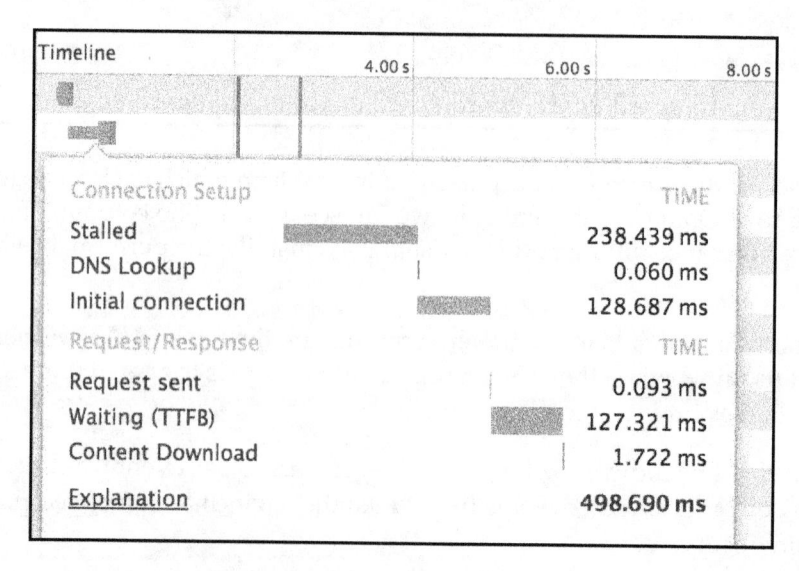

Connection Setup	TIME
Stalled	238.439 ms
DNS Lookup	0.060 ms
Initial connection	128.687 ms
Request/Response	TIME
Request sent	0.093 ms
Waiting (TTFB)	127.321 ms
Content Download	1.722 ms
Explanation	498.690 ms

It is interesting to know that this developer tool reads this information using the performance timing API. We will now learn more about the meaning of each of the data points:

Performance timing API data point	Description
Stalled/Blocking	The amount of time spent waiting by the request before it can be sent; there is a maximum number of open TCP connections for an origin. When the limit is reached, some requests will display blocking time, rather than stalled time. There is a maximum of 6 TCP connections to the same origin (domain address).
Proxy negotiation	The amount of time spent negotiating a connection with a proxy server.
DNS lookup	The amount of time spent resolving a DNS address; resolving a DNS requires a full round-trip to do the DNS server for each domain on the page.
Initial connection / connecting	The amount of time spent establishing a connection.
SSL	The amount of time spent establishing an SSL connection.
Request sent / sending	The amount of time spent issuing the network request; typically, a fraction of a millisecond.
Waiting (TTFB)	The amount of time spent waiting for the initial byte to be received—**time to first byte** (**TTFB**); the TTFB can be used to find out the latency of a round trip to the server in addition to the time spent waiting for the server to deliver the response.
Content download / downloading	The amount of time spent waiting for the response data to be received.

> Please refer to the official Google Chrome documentation at `https://developers.google.com/web/tools/chrome-devtools/network-performance/reference#timing-explanation` to learn more about the timing API.

Network performance and user experience

Now that we know how we can analyze network performance, it is time to identify the performance goals we should aim for. Numerous studies have proved that it is important to keep loading times as low as possible to achieve a great **user experience** (**UX**). The Akamai study, published in September 2009, interviewed 1,048 online shoppers and found that:

- 47 percent of people expect a web page to load in two seconds or less
- 40 percent of people will abandon a web page if it takes more than three seconds to load
- 52 percent of online shoppers claim that quick page loads are important for their loyalty to a site
- 14 percent of people will start shopping at a different site if page loads are slow
- 23 percent of people will stop shopping or even walk away from their computer if page loads are slow
- 64 percent of shoppers who are dissatisfied with their site visit will go somewhere else to shop next time

> You can read the full Akamai study at
> `https://www.akamai.com/us/en/about/news/press/2009-press/akamai-reveals-2-seconds-as-the-new-threshold-of-acceptability-for-ecommerce-web-page-response-times.jsp`.

From the preceding study conclusions, we should assume that network performance matters. Our priority should be to try to improve the loading speed of our applications.

If we try to improve the performance of a site to ensure that it loads in less than two seconds, we might make a common mistake: trying to get the `onLoad` event to be triggered in under two seconds.

While triggering the `onLoad` event as early as possible will probably improve the network performance of an application, it doesn't mean that the user experience will be equally improved. The `onLoad` event is insufficient in determining performance. We can demonstrate this by comparing the loading performance of the Twitter and Amazon websites. As we can see in the following screenshot, users can engage with Amazon much sooner than with Twitter. Even though the `onLoad` event is the same on both sites, the user experience is drastically different:

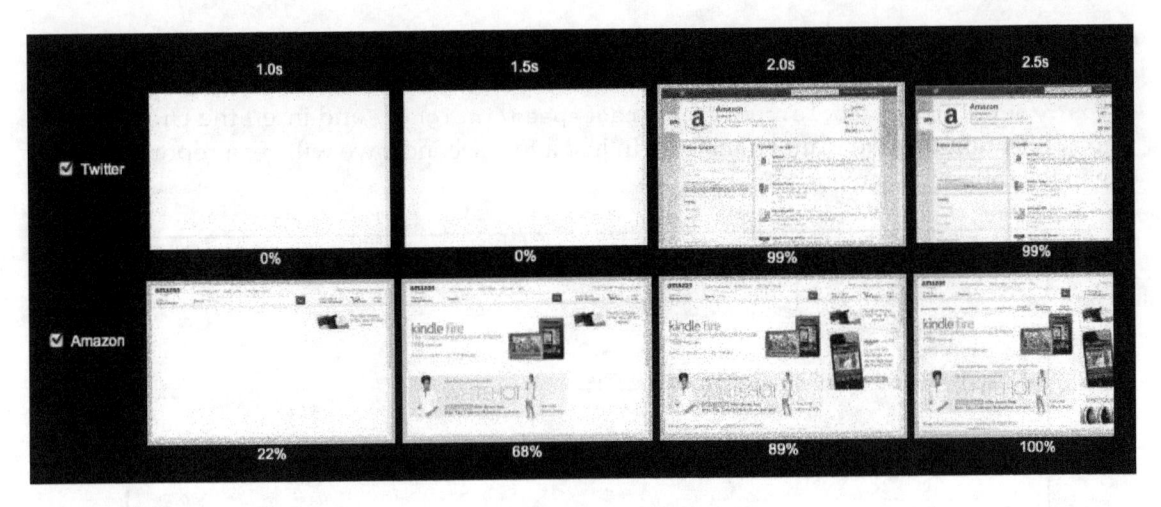

Twitter and Amazon websites

The preceding example demonstrates why it is important to try to load the web contents in such a way that the user engagement can begin as early as possible. One way to achieve this is by ensuring that we only load the minimum necessary assets on initial page load. We can then asynchronously load all the secondary assets.

> Refer to `Chapter 3`, *Working with Functions*, to learn more about asynchronous programming with TypeScript.

Network performance best practices and rules

Another way to analyze the performance of a web application is by using a best practices tool for network performance, such as the **Google PageSpeed Insights** application or the **Yahoo YSlow** application.

Application Performance

Google PageSpeed Insights can be used online or as a Google Chrome extension. To try this tool, we can visit the online version at `https://developers.google.com/speed/pagespeed/insights/` and insert the URL of the web application that we want to analyze. In just a few seconds, we will get a report like the one in the following screenshot:

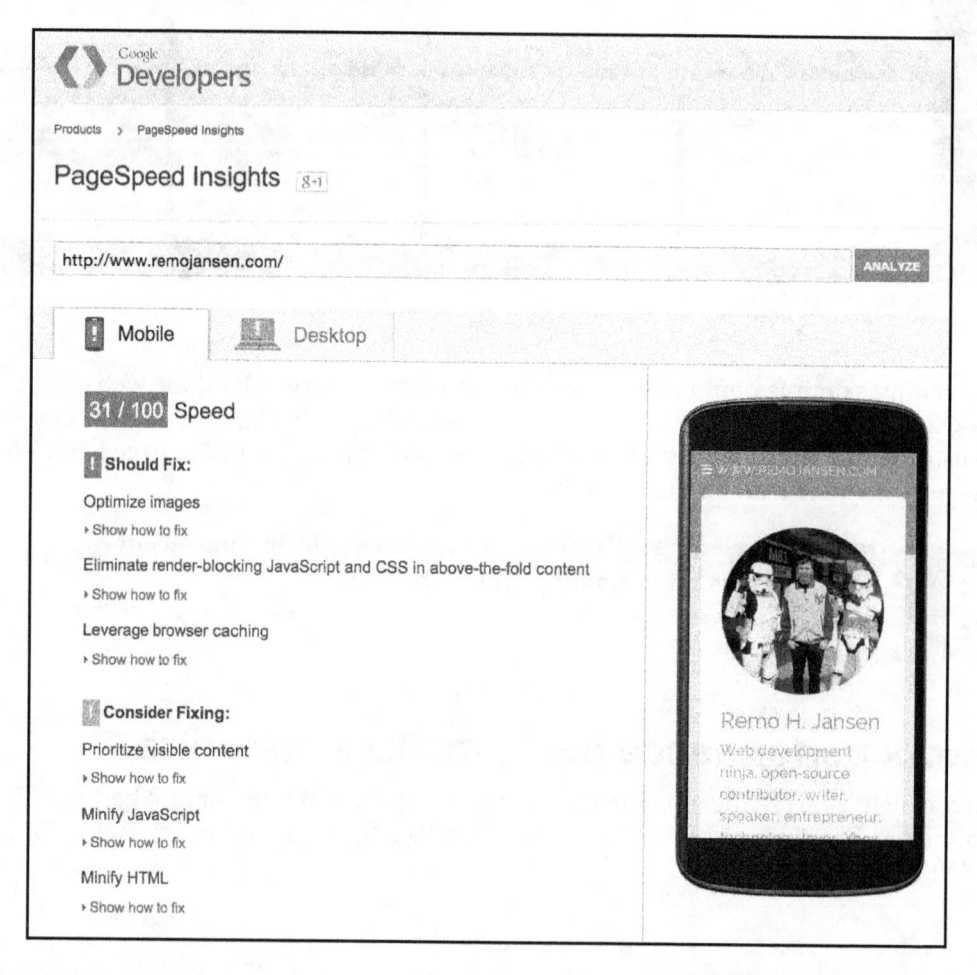

The report contains some effective recommendations that will help us to improve network performance and overall user experience of our web applications. Google PageSpeed Insights uses the following rules to rate the speed of a web application:

- Avoid landing page redirects
- Enable compression

- Improve server response time
- Leverage browser caching
- Minify resources
- Optimize images
- Optimize CSS delivery
- Prioritize visible content
- Remove render-blocking JavaScript
- Use asynchronous scripts

If we click on the score of one of the rules, we will be able to see recommendations and details that will help us to understand what is wrong and what we need to do to increase the score achieved.

On the other hand, Yahoo YSlow is available as a browser extension, a Node.js module, and a PhantomJS plugin, among other options. We can find the right version for our needs at `http://yslow.org/`. YSlow generates a report that will provide us with a general score and a detailed score of the website, like the one in the following screenshot:

Grade B Overall performance score 82 Ruleset applied: YSlow(V2) URL: http://www.remojansen.com/		
ALL (23) FILTER BY: CONTENT (6) | COOKIE (2) | CSS (6) | IMAGES (2) | JAVASCRIPT (4) | SERVER (6)		
C Make fewer HTTP requests	**Grade C on Make fewer HTTP requests**	
F Use a Content Delivery Network (CDN)	This page has 4 external Javascript scripts. Try combining them into one. This page has 8 external stylesheets. Try combining them into one.	
A Avoid empty src or href		
F Add Expires headers	Decreasing the number of components on a page reduces the number of HT Some ways to reduce the number of components include: combine files, com style sheet, and use CSS Sprites and image maps.	
A Compress components with gzip		
A Put CSS at top		
A Put JavaScript at bottom	»Read More	
A Avoid CSS expressions		
n/a Make JavaScript and CSS external	Copyright © 2015 Yahoo! Inc. All rights reserved.	
A Reduce DNS lookups		
A Minify JavaScript and CSS		
A Avoid URL redirects		
A Remove duplicate JavaScript and CSS		

YSlow uses the following set of rules to rate the speed of a web application:

- Minimize HTTP requests
- Use a content delivery network
- Avoid empty `src` or `href`
- Add an expires or a cache-control header
- GZIP components
- Put stylesheets at the top
- Put scripts at the bottom
- Avoid CSS expressions
- Make JavaScript and CSS external
- Reduce DNS lookups
- Minify JavaScript and CSS
- Avoid redirects
- Remove duplicate scripts
- Configure ETags
- Make Ajax cacheable
- Use GET for Ajax requests
- Reduce the number of DOM elements
- Prevent 404 errors
- Reduce cookie size
- Use cookie-free domains for components
- Avoid filters
- Do not scale images in HTML
- Make `favicon.ico` small and cacheable

If we click on the score of one of the rules, we will see some recommendations and details that will help us to understand what is wrong and what we need to do to increase the score achieved for one particular rule.

> If you want to learn more about network performance optimization, please look at the book *High Performance Browser Networking* by *Ilya Grigorik*.

GPU performance analysis

Rendering elements in a web application is sometimes accelerated by the GPU. The GPU is specialized in the processing of graphics-related instructions and can, therefore, deliver a much better performance than the CPU when it comes to graphics. For example, CSS3 animations in modern web browsers are accelerated by the GPU, while the CPU performs JavaScript animations. In the past, the only way to achieve some animations was via JavaScript. But today, we should avoid its usage when possible and use CSS3 instead.

In recent years, direct access to the GPU from a web browser has become possible thanks to the WebGL API. This API allows web developers to create 3D games and other highly visual 3D applications powered by the GPU.

Frames per second (FPS)

We will not go into much detail about the performance of 3D applications, because it is an extensive field and we could write an entire book about it. However, we will learn about an important concept that can be applied to any web application: **frames per second** (**FPS**), or frame rate. When the web application is displayed on the screen, it is done at several images (frames) per second. A low frame rate can be detrimental to the overall user experience when perceived by the users. A lot of research has been carried out on this topic, and 60 frames per second seem to be the optimum frame rate for great user experience. It is also worth mentioning that maintaining a constant frame rate, even if it is a low one like 30 FPS, is considered better than an inestable frame rate.

Whenever we develop a web application, we should look at the frame rate and try to prevent it from dropping below 40 FPS, which is especially important for animations and user actions.

Application Performance

We can use Google Chrome to monitor the FPS in our web applications. We need to open the development tools (*Ctrl + Shift + I*), click on the upper-right icon next to the *X* icon with the tooltip *Customize and control devtools*. We can then select **More tools | Rendering**:

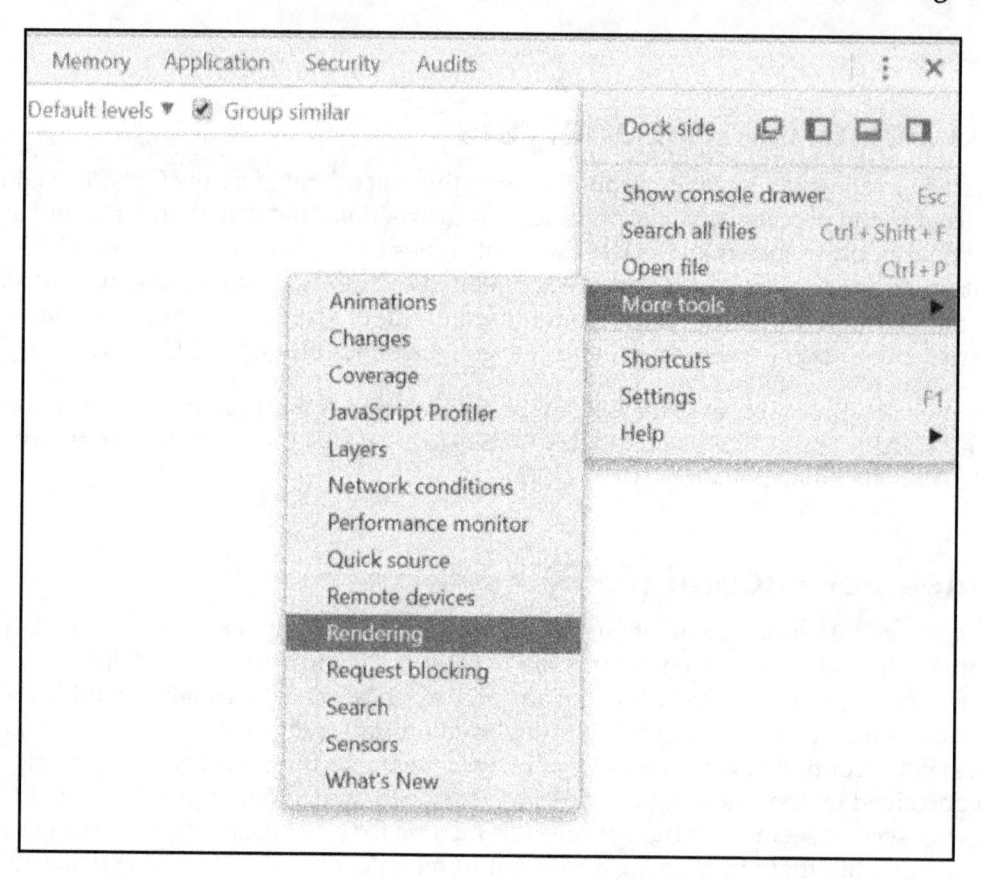

The preceding instructions will display a new panel with the title **Rendering**. We must then enable the FPS meter:

[418]

Chapter 13

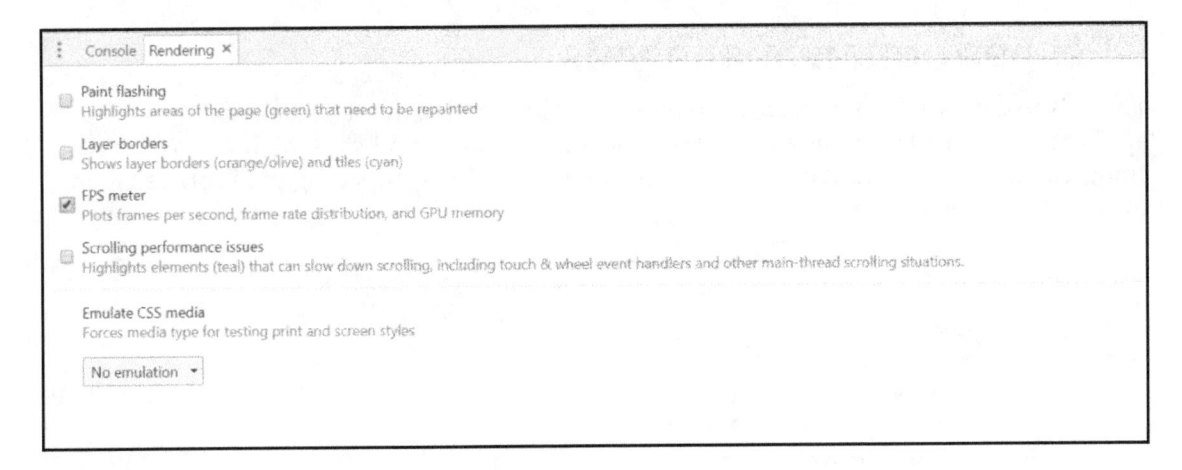

> Console | Rendering ×
>
> ☐ **Paint flashing**
> Highlights areas of the page (green) that need to be repainted
>
> ☐ **Layer borders**
> Shows layer borders (orange/olive) and tiles (cyan)
>
> ☑ **FPS meter**
> Plots frames per second, frame rate distribution, and GPU memory
>
> ☐ **Scrolling performance issues**
> Highlights elements (teal) that can slow down scrolling, including touch & wheel event handlers and other main-thread scrolling situations.
>
> **Emulate CSS media**
> Forces media type for testing print and screen styles
>
> [No emulation ▾]

The FPS meter should be displayed in the upper-right corner of the screen:

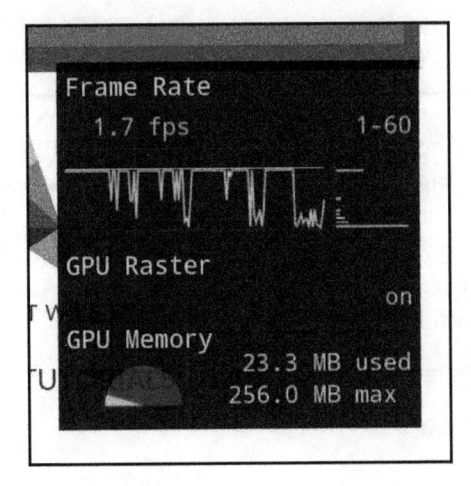

```
Frame Rate
  1.7 fps                    1-60
  ╱╲╱╲╱╲╱╲╱╲╱╲╱╲╱╲╱╲╱╲

GPU Raster
                               on
GPU Memory
                    23.3 MB used
                   256.0 MB max
```

The FPS counter allows us to see the number of frames per second and the GPU memory being consumed.

> ℹ Some advanced WebGL applications may require an in-depth performance analysis. For such cases, Chrome provides the Trace Event Profiling Tool. If you wish to learn more about this tool, visit the official page at
> `https://www.chromium.org/developers/how-tos/trace-event-profiling-tool`.

[419]

CPU performance analysis

To analyze the usage of the processing time, we will examine the call stack of our application. We will examine each of the functions invoked and how long it takes to complete their execution. We can access all this information by opening the **Profiles** tab in the Google Chrome developer tools:

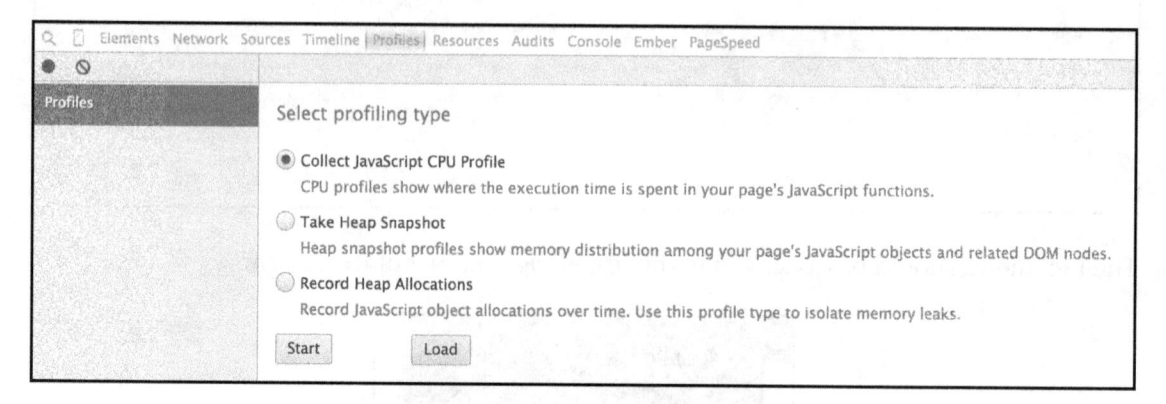

In this tab, we can select **Collect JavaScript CPU Profile** and then click on the **Start** button to start recording the CPU usage. Being able to select when we want to start and stop recording the CPU usage helps us select the specific functions that we want to analyze. If, for example, we want to analyze a function named `foo`, all we need to do is start recording the CPU usage, invoke the `foo` function, and stop recording. A timeline like the one in the following screenshot will then be displayed:

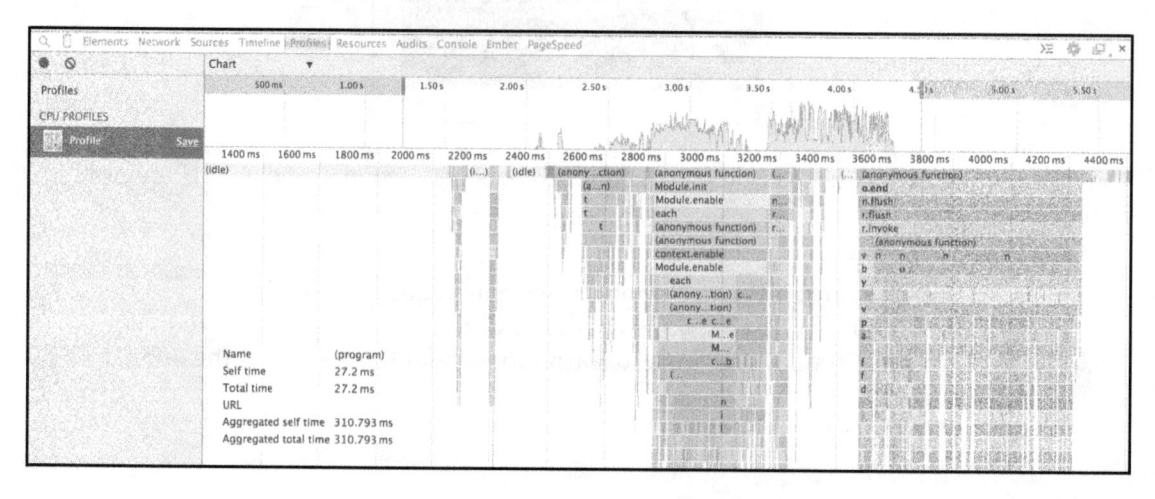

Timeline

The timeline displays the functions invoked in chronological order (horizontal axis). The timeline also displays the call stack of these functions (vertical axis). When we hover over one of these functions, we will be able to see its details in the lower-left corner of the timeline:

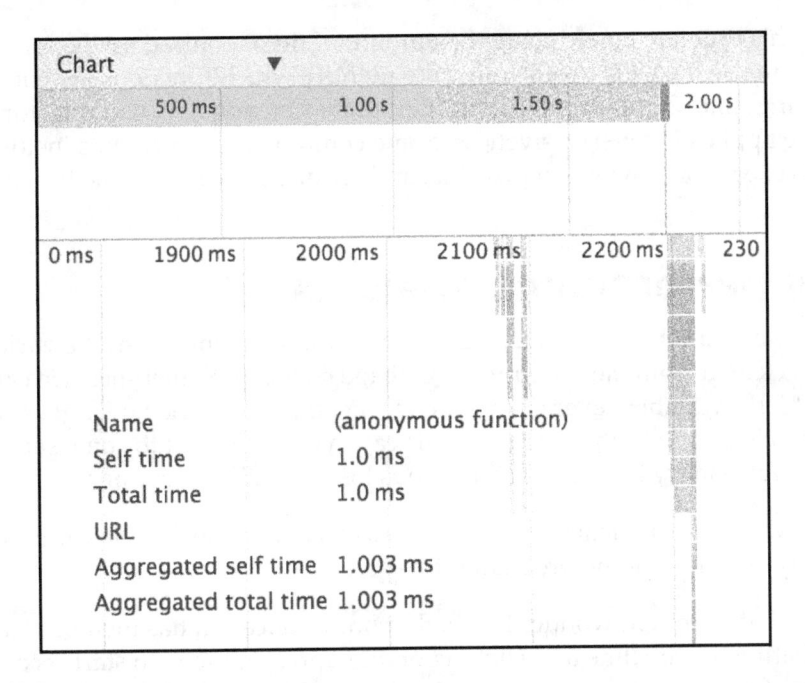

Chart ▼				
500 ms	1.00 s	1.50 s		2.00 s
0 ms 1900 ms	2000 ms	2100 ms	2200 ms	230

Name   (anonymous function)
Self time   1.0 ms
Total time   1.0 ms
URL
Aggregated self time   1.003 ms
Aggregated total time   1.003 ms

The details include the following information:

- **Name**: The name of the function
- **Self-time**: The time spent on the completion of the current invocation of the function; we will consider the time spent in the execution of the statements within the function, not including any functions that it called
- **Total time**: The total time spent on the completion of the current invocation of the function; we will consider the time spent in the execution of the statements within the function, including functions that it called
- **Aggregated self-time**: The time for all invocations of the function across the recording, not including functions called by this function
- **Aggregated total time**: The time for all invocations of the function across the recording, including functions called by this function

Application Performance

As we have learned in the previous chapters, all the JavaScript code is executed in one single thread at runtime; for this reason, when a function is executed, no other function can be executed. When the execution of a function takes too long to be completed, the application becomes unresponsive.

We can solve this problem by reducing the amount of time required by the long-running function. We can use the CPU profile report to identify which functions are consuming too much processing time. Once we have identified these functions, we can refactor them to try to improve the application responsiveness. Some common improvements include using an asynchronous execution flow when possible, and reducing the size of the functions.

Memory performance analysis

When we declare a variable, it is allocated in the RAM. Sometime after, the variable is out of the scope; it is cleared from memory by the garbage collector. Sometimes, we can generate a scenario in which a variable never goes out of scope. If the variable never goes out of scope, it will never be cleared from the memory. This can eventually lead to some serious memory leaking issues. A **memory leak** is the continuous loss of available memory.

When dealing with memory leaks, we can take advantage of the Google Chrome developer tools to identify the cause of the problem with ease.

The first thing that we might wonder is whether our application has memory leaks. We can find out by visiting the timeline and clicking on the upper-left icon to start recording the resource usage. Once we stop recording, a timeline graph like the one in the following screenshot will be displayed:

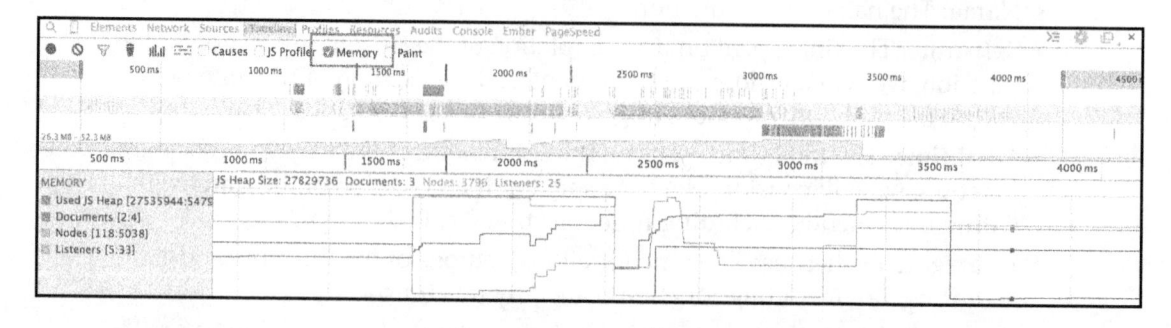

Chapter 13

In the timeline, we can select **Memory** to see the memory usage (**Used JS Heap**) over time (blue line in the screenshot). In the preceding example, we can see a notable drop towards the end of the line. That is a good sign because it indicates that most of the used memory has been cleared when the page has finished loading.

The memory leaks can also take place after loading; in that case, we can use the application for a while and observe how the memory usage varies in the graph to identify the cause of the leak.

An alternative way to detect memory leaks is by observing the memory allocations. We can access this information by recording the heap allocations in the **Memory** tab:

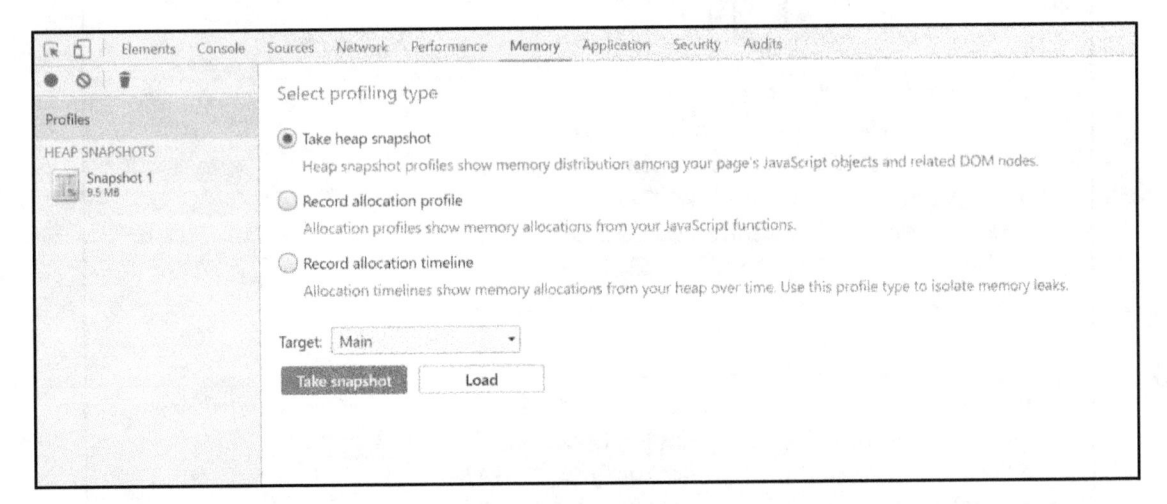

The report will be displayed after we have recorded some usage of the resources. We can do this by selecting **Record allocation timeline** and clicking on the **Stake snapshot** button. We then need to stop recording by clicking on the red dot displayed on the upper-left side of the development tools.

[423]

Application Performance

The memory allocation report will display a timeline like the one in the following screenshot. Each of the blue lines is a memory allocation that took place during the recorded period. The height of the line represents the amount of memory used. As we can see, the memory is almost cleared completely around the eighth second:

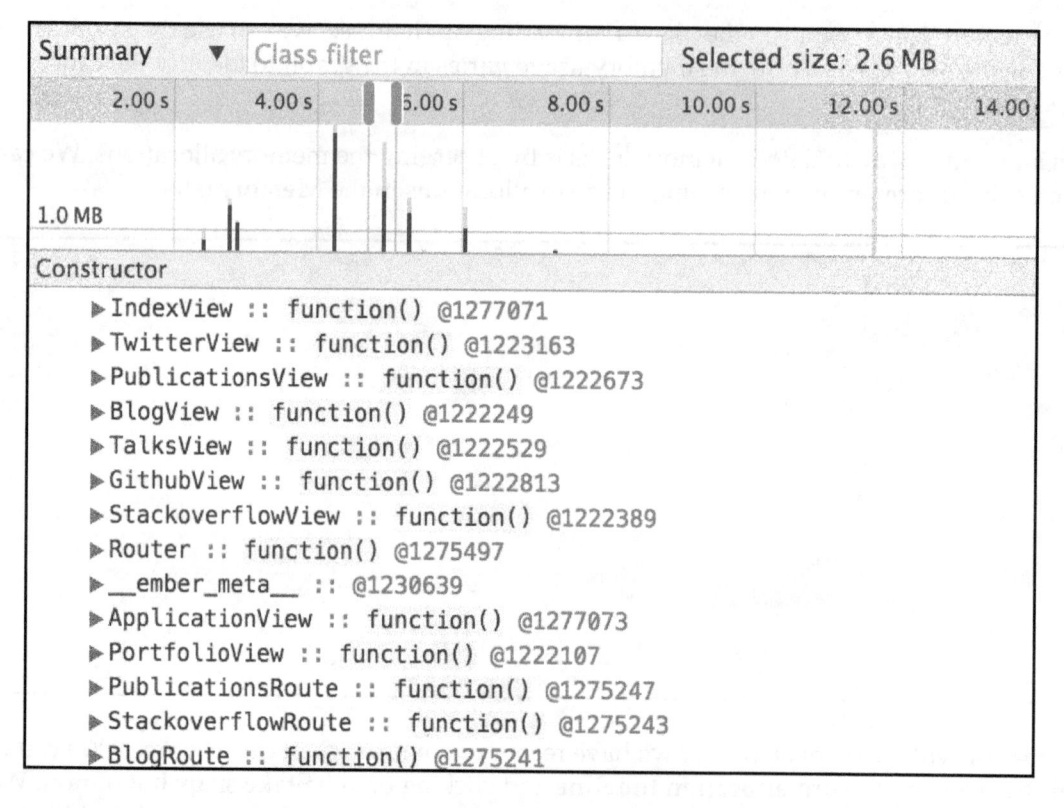

```
Summary    ▼   Class filter                          Selected size: 2.6 MB
      2.00 s      4.00 s    5.00 s     8.00 s    10.00 s    12.00 s    14.00


1.0 MB

Constructor
    ▶ IndexView :: function() @1277071
    ▶ TwitterView :: function() @1223163
    ▶ PublicationsView :: function() @1222673
    ▶ BlogView :: function() @1222249
    ▶ TalksView :: function() @1222529
    ▶ GithubView :: function() @1222813
    ▶ StackoverflowView :: function() @1222389
    ▶ Router :: function() @1275497
    ▶ __ember_meta__ :: @1230639
    ▶ ApplicationView :: function() @1277073
    ▶ PortfolioView :: function() @1222107
    ▶ PublicationsRoute :: function() @1275247
    ▶ StackoverflowRoute :: function() @1275243
    ▶ BlogRoute :: function() @1275241
```

If we click on one of the blue lines, we will be able to navigate through all the variables that were stored in memory when the allocation took place and examine their values. It is also possible to take a memory snapshot at any given point from the **Profiles** tab:

```
◉ Take Heap Snapshot
   Heap snapshot profiles show memory distribution among your page's JavaScript objects and related DOM nodes.
```

This feature is particularly useful when we are debugging and we want to see the memory usage at a breakpoint. The memory snapshot works like the details view in the previously explained allocations view:

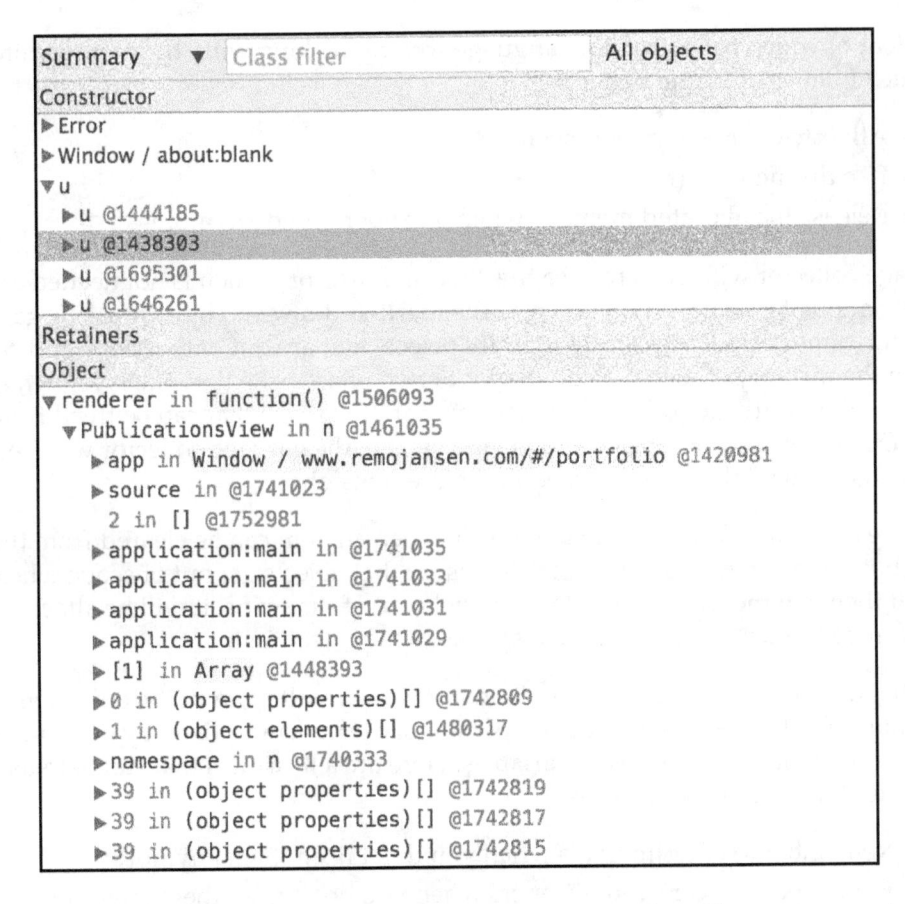

```
Summary        ▼  Class filter              All objects
Constructor
▶ Error
▶ Window / about:blank
▼ u
   ▶ u @1444185
   ▶ u @1438303
   ▶ u @1695301
   ▶ u @1646261
Retainers
Object
▼ renderer in function() @1506093
   ▼ PublicationsView in n @1461035
      ▶ app in Window / www.remojansen.com/#/portfolio @1420981
      ▶ source in @1741023
        2 in [] @1752981
      ▶ application:main in @1741035
      ▶ application:main in @1741033
      ▶ application:main in @1741031
      ▶ application:main in @1741029
      ▶ [1] in Array @1448393
      ▶ 0 in (object properties)[] @1742809
      ▶ 1 in (object elements)[] @1480317
      ▶ namespace in n @1740333
      ▶ 39 in (object properties)[] @1742819
      ▶ 39 in (object properties)[] @1742817
      ▶ 39 in (object properties)[] @1742815
```

As we can see in the preceding screenshot, the memory snapshot allows us to navigate through all the variables that were stored in memory when the snapshot was taken and examine their values.

The garbage collector

Programming languages with a low level of abstraction have low-level memory management mechanisms. On the other hand, in languages with a higher level of abstraction, such as C# or JavaScript, the memory is automatically allocated and freed by a process known as the garbage collector.

The JavaScript garbage collector does a great job when it comes to memory management, but it doesn't mean that we don't need to care about memory management.

Application Performance

Independent of which programming language we are working with, the memory life cycle pretty much follows the same pattern:

- Allocate the memory you need
- Use the memory (read/write)
- Release the allocated memory when it is not needed anymore

The garbage collector will try to release the allocated memory when is not needed anymore, using a variation of an algorithm known as the **mark-and-sweep algorithm**. The garbage collector performs periodical scans to identify objects that are out of the scope and can be freed from the memory. The scan is divided into two phases: the first one is known as a **mark**, because the garbage collector will flag or mark the items that can be freed from memory. During the second phase, known as a **sweep**, the garbage collector will free the memory consumed by the items marked in the previous phase.

The garbage collector is usually able to identify when an item can be cleared from the memory; but we, as developers, must try to ensure that objects get out of scope when we don't need them anymore. If a variable never gets out of the scope, it will be allocated in memory forever, potentially leading to a severe memory leak issue.

The number of references pointing to an item in memory will prevent it from being freed from memory. For this reason, most cases of memory leaks can be fixed by ensuring that there are no permanent references to variables. Here are a few rules that can help us to prevent potential memory leak issues:

- Remember to clear intervals when you don't need them anymore
- Remember to clear event listeners when you don't need them anymore
- Remember that when you create a closure, the inner function will remember the context in which it was declared, which means that there will be some extra items allocated in memory
- Remember that when using object composition, if circular references are created, you can end up having some variables that will never be cleared from memory

It is important to mention that Node.js processes assume that there will be at least 1.5 GB of RAM available, which can cause some problems when the system has less than 1.5 GB of RAM available because the garbage collector will not try to free any unused memory until the process has consumed almost 1.5 GB of RAM. If only 1 GB is available, the process will crash, because we will run out of memory before the garbage collector tries to clean the unused memory. We can solve this problem using the max_old_space_size flag:

```
node --max_old_space_size=1024 server.js --production
```

Performance analysis in Node.js applications

We have learned how to use the Google Chrome development tools to analyze frontend application. However, the same tools can also be used to analyze backend applications powered by Node.js.

To use the Google Chrome development tools to analyze a Node.js application, we need to start the Node.js application using the `--inspect` flag:

```
ts-node --inspect main.ts
```

Then we need to visit the `chrome://inspect` URL using Google Chrome.

If everything went well, we should be able to see the following screen:

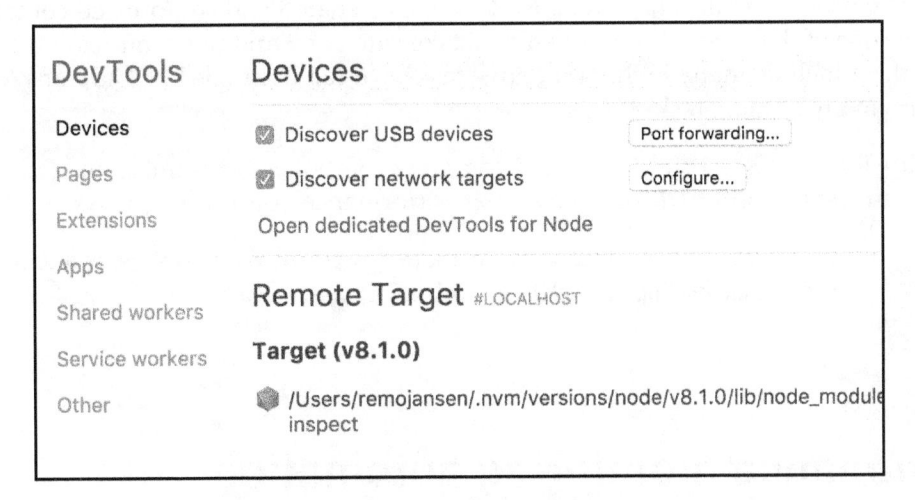

DevTools	Devices
Devices	☑ Discover USB devices Port forwarding...
Pages	☑ Discover network targets Configure...
Extensions	Open dedicated DevTools for Node
Apps	
Shared workers	**Remote Target** #LOCALHOST
Service workers	**Target (v8.1.0)**
Other	/Users/remojansen/.nvm/versions/node/v8.1.0/lib/node_module inspect

We then need to click on the **inspect** link, which should be available under the **Remote Target** section. A new window should be opened then. The window will display the Google Chrome developer tools, ready to analyze the Node.js application.

> Alternatively, we can use the **Node.js V8 --inspector Manager** (NiM) extension for Google Chrome, which allows us to access the Node.js inspector more easily. You can download the extension by visiting `https://chrome.google.com/webstore/detail/nodejs-v8-inspector-manag/gnhhdgbaldcilmgcpfddgdbkhjohddkj`.

Performance automation

In this section, we will understand how we can automate many of the performance optimization tasks, from concatenation and compression of contents to the automation of the performance monitoring and performance testing processes.

Performance optimization automation

After analyzing the performance of our application, we will start working on some performance optimizations. Many of these optimizations involve the concatenation and compression of some of the application's components.

We will also have to create a new version of the concatenated and compressed contents every time one of the original components (not concatenated and not compressed) changes. Because these include many highly repetitive tasks, we can use tools like Gulp or Webpack to perform many of these tasks for us.

We can use these tools to concatenate and compress components, optimize images, generate a cache manifest file, and perform many other performance optimization tasks.

> If you would like to learn more about Gulp and Webpack, refer to `Chapter 9`, *Automating Your Development Workflow*.

Performance monitoring automation

We have seen that we can automate many of the performance optimization tasks using the Gulp task runner. Similarly, we can also automate the performance monitoring process.

To monitor the performance of an existing application, we will need to collect some data that will allow us to compare the application performance over time. Depending on how we collect the data, we can identify three different types of performance monitoring:

- **Real user monitoring (RUM)**: This is a type of solution used to capture performance data from real user visits. The collection of data is performed by a small JavaScript code snippet loaded in the browser. This type of solution can help us to collect data and discover performance trends and patterns.

- **Simulated browsers**: This type of solution is used to capture performance data from simulated browsers, which is the cheaper option, but it is limited, because simulated browsers cannot offer as accurate a representation of the real user experience.
- **Real-browser monitoring**: This is used to capture performance data of real browsers. This information provides a more accurate representation of the real user experience, as the data is collected using exactly what a user would see if he or she visited the site with the given environment (browser, geographic location, and network throughput).

Web browsers can be configured to generate **HTTP Archive** (**HAR**) files. A HAR file uses a common format for recording HTTP tracing information. This file contains a variety of information, but, for our purposes, it has a record of each object being loaded by a browser.

There are multiple scripts available online that showcase how to collect the data. One of the examples, `netsniff.js`, exports the network traffic in HAR format. The `netsniff.js` file (and other examples) can be found at `https://github.com/ariya/phantomjs/blob/master/examples/netsniff.js`.

Once we have generated the HAR files, we can use another application to see the collected performance information in a visual timeline. This application is called HAR Viewer and can be found at `https://github.com/janodvarko/harviewer`.

Alternatively, we could write a custom script or Gulp task to read the HAR files and break the automated build if the application performance doesn't meet our needs.

It is also possible to run the YSlow performance analysis report and integrate it with the automated build.

> If you are considering using RUM, look at the New Relic solutions at `http://newrelic.com/` or Google Analytics at `http://www.google.com/analytics/`.

Performance testing automation

Another way to improve the performance of an application is to write automated performance tests. These tests can be used to guarantee that the system meets a set of performance goals. There are multiple types of performance testing, but some of the most common ones include the following:

- **Load testing**: This is the most basic form of performance testing. We can use a load test to understand the behavior of the system under a specific expected load (number of concurrent users, number of transactions, and duration).
- **Stress testing**: This is normally used to understand the maximum capacity limits of an application. This kind of test determines if an application can handle an extreme number of requests. Stress testing is not useful when working on a client-side application. However, it can be helpful when working on a Node.js application, since Node.js applications can have many simultaneous users.
- **Soak testing**: Also known as endurance testing. This kind of test is like the stress test, but instead of using an extreme load, it uses the expected load for a continued period. It is a common practice to collect memory usage data during this kind of test to detect potential memory leaks. This kind of test helps us to tell if the performance suffers degradation after a continued period.
- **Spike testing**: This is also like the stress test, but instead of using an extreme time load during a continued period, it uses sudden intervals of the extreme and expected load. This kind of test helps us to determine if an application can handle dramatic changes in load.
- **Configuration testing**: This is used to determine the effects of configuration changes to the performance and behavior of an application. A common example would be experimenting with different methods of load balancing.

Exception handling

Understanding how to use the available resources efficiently will help us to create better applications. Similarly, understanding how to handle runtime errors will help us to improve the overall quality of our applications. Exception handling in TypeScript involves three main language elements.

The Error class

When a runtime error takes place, an instance of the `Error` class is thrown:

```
throw new Error();
```

We can create custom errors in a couple of different ways. The easiest way to achieve it is by passing a string as an argument to the `Error` class constructor:

```
throw new Error("My basic custom error");
```

If we need more customizable and advanced control over custom exceptions, we can use inheritance to achieve it:

```
export class Exception extends Error {
    public constructor(public message: string) {
        super(message);
        // Set the prototype explicitly.
        Object.setPrototypeOf(this, Exception.prototype);
    }
    public sayHello() {
        return `hello ${this.message}`;
    }
}
```

In the preceding code snippet, we have declared a class named `Exception`, which inherits from the `Error` class. In the class constructor, we have set the prototype explicitly. This is a requirement since TypeScript 2.1, caused by some limitations. You can learn more details about this limitation at
`https://github.com/Microsoft/TypeScript-wiki/blob/master/Breaking-Changes.md#extending-built-ins-like-error-array-and-map-may-no-longer-work`.

The try...catch statements and throw statements

A `catch` clause contains statements that specify what to do if an exception is thrown in the `try` block. We should perform some operations in the `try` block and, if they fail, the program execution flow will move from the `try` block to the `catch` block. Additionally, there is an optional block known as `finally`, which is executed after both the `try` and `catch` (if there was an `exception` in the `catch`) blocks:

```
try {
    // code that we want to work
    throw new Error("Oops!");
}
catch (e) {
    // code executed if expected to work fails
    console.log(e);
}
finally {
    // code always executed after try or try and catch (when
     errors)
    console.log("finally!");
}
```

It is also important to mention that in the majority of programming languages, including TypeScript, throwing and catching exceptions is an expensive operation regarding resource consumption. We should use these statements if we need them, but sometimes it is necessary to avoid them because they can potentially negatively affect the performance of our applications.

Summary

In this chapter, we have learned what performance is and how the availability of resources can influence it.

We have also learned how to use some tools to analyze the way a TypeScript application uses available resources. These tools allow us to spot some possible issues, such as a low frame rate, memory leaks, and high loading times. We have also discovered that we can automate many kinds of the performance optimization tasks as well as the performance monitoring and testing processes.

In the following chapter, we are going to learn how we can automate the testing process of our TypeScript applications to achieve great application maintainability and reliability.

14
Application Testing

In Chapter 9, *Automating Your Development Workflow*, we learned how to write unit tests and generate a test coverage report. However, application testing is a very extensive subject, and we barely touched its surface.

In this chapter, we are going to learn how to write multiple kinds of automated tests for a TypeScript application. We are going to cover the following topics:

- Testing terminology
- Testing planning and methodologies
- Writing unit tests
- Isolating components during tests
- Writing integration tests
- Writing end-to-end (e2e) tests

We are going to get started by learning about the core terminology used in the field of software testing.

Testing terminology

Throughout this chapter, we are going to use some concepts that may not be familiar to readers without previous experience in the field of software testing. For this reason, we are going to take a quick look at some of the most popular concepts in software testing before we get started.

Assertions

An **assertion** is a condition that must be tested to confirm that a certain piece of code behaves as expected, or, in other words, to confirm conformance to a requirement.

Application Testing

Let's imagine that we are working as part of the Google Chrome development team, and we must implement the JavaScript `Math` API. If we are working on the `pow` method, the requirement could be something like, the `Math.pow` (base, exponent) function should return the base (the base number) to the exponent (the exponent used to raise the base) power-that is, base ^ exponent.

With this information, we could create the following implementation:

```
class MathAPI {
    public static pow(base: number, exponent: number) {
        let result = base;
        for (var i = 1; i < exponent; i++) {
            result = result * base;
        }
        return result;
    }
}
```

> Please note that we use the name `MathAPI` instead of `Math` in this example because the `Math` variable is already declared by the real JavaScript Math API.

To ensure that the method is correctly implemented, we must test its accordance with the requirement. If we analyze the requirements closely, we should identify at least two necessary assertions:

- The function should return the base to the exponent:

    ```
    const actual1 = MathApi.pow(3, 5);
    const expected1 = 243;
    const asertion1 = actual1 === expected1;

    if (asertion1 === false) {
        throw new Error(
            `Expected 'actual1' to be ${expected1} ` +
            `but got ${actual1}!`
        );
    }
    ```

- The exponent is not being used as the base (or the base is not used as the exponent):

    ```
    const actual2 = MathApi.pow(5, 3);
    const expected2 = 125;
    const asertion2 = actual2 === expected2;
    ```

[434]

```
    if (asertion2 === false) {
        throw new Error(
            `Expected 'actual2' to be ${expected2} ` +
            `but got ${actual2}!`
        );
    }
```

If both assertions are valid, then our code adheres to the requirements, and we know that it will work as expected.

Specs

Spec is a term used by software development engineers to refer to test specifications. A test specification (not to be confused with a test plan) is a detailed list of all the scenarios that should be tested and how they should be tested, as well as other details.

Test cases

A **test case** is a set of conditions used to determine whether one of the features of an application is working as it was originally intended to work. We might wonder what the difference between a test assertion and a test case is. While a test assertion is a single condition, a test case is a set of conditions.

Suites

A **suite** is a collection of test cases. While a test case should focus on only one test scenario, a test suite can contain test cases for many test scenarios.

> We will learn how to define assertions, test cases, and test suites later in this chapter, in the *Unit tests and integration tests with Mocha* section).

Spies

Spies are a feature provided by some testing frameworks. They allow us to wrap a method or function and record its usage. We can record things such as the method or function arguments, their return type, or the number of times that they have been invoked. When we wrap a method or function with a spy, the underlying method's functionality does not change.

Dummies

A **dummy** object is an object that is passed around during the execution of a test, but it is never actually used.

Stubs

A **stub** is a feature provided by some testing frameworks. Like spies, stubs also allow us to wrap a method or function to record its usage. Unlike in the case of spies, when we wrap a function with a stub, the underlying method's functionality is replaced with new behavior.

Mocks

Mocks are often confused with stubs. Martin Fowler once wrote the following in an article titled *Mocks Aren't Stubs*:

> "In particular, I see them (mocks) often confused with stubs - a common helper to testing environments. I understand this confusion - I saw them as similar for a while too, but conversations with the mock developers have steadily allowed a little mock understanding to penetrate my tortoiseshell cranium. This difference is actually two separate differences. On the one hand, there is a difference in how test results are verified: a distinction between state verification and behavior verification. On the other hand, is a whole different philosophy to the way testing and design play together, which I term here as the classical and mockist styles of Test Driven Development."

Both mocks and stubs provide some input to the test case, but despite their similarities, the flow of information from each is very different:

- Stubs provide input for the application under test so that the test can be performed on something else. Stubs are used to replace behavior.
- Mocks provide input to the test to decide whether the test should pass or fail. Mocks are used to declare an expectation.

The difference between mocks and stubs will become clearer as we move towards the end of this chapter.

Test coverage

The term **test coverage** refers to a unit of measurement, which is used to illustrate the number of portions of code in an application that have been tested via an automated test. Test coverage can be obtained by automatically generating test coverage reports.

> Refer to `Chapter 9`, *Automating Your Development Workflow*, to learn how to generate a test coverage report.

Prerequisites

Throughout this chapter, we will be using third-party tools. In this section, we are going to learn how to install these. Before we get started, however, we need to use npm to create a `package.json` file in the folder that we are going to use to implement the examples in this chapter.

Let's create a new folder and go inside it to generate a new `package.json` file using the `npm init` command:

```
npm init
```

> Please refer to `Chapter 5`, *Working with Dependencies*, for additional information about npm.

Mocha

Mocha is a popular JavaScript testing library that facilitates the creation of test suites, test cases, and test specs. Mocha can be used to test TypeScript in the frontend and backend, identify performance issues, and generate different types of test reports, among many other functions. We can install Mocha using the following command:

```
npm install --save-dev mocha @types/mocha
```

Chai

Chai is a test-assertion library that supports **test-driven development** (**TDD**) and **behavior-driven development** (**BDD**) test styles. The main goal of Chai is to reduce the amount of work necessary to create a test assertion and make the test more readable. We can install Chai using the following command:

```
npm install --save-dev chai @types/chai
```

> Please note that we are going to learn more about TDD and BDD later in this chapter in the section titled *Testing methodologies*.

Sinon.JS

Sinon.JS is a library that provides us with a set of APIs that can help us to test a component in isolation, thanks to its usage of spies, stubs, and mocks. Testing software components can be very difficult when there is a high level of coupling between them. However, a library such as Sinon.JS can help us isolate the components to test their features. We can install Sinon.JS using the following command:

```
npm install --save-dev sinon @types/sinon
```

nyc

As we already learned in `Chapter 9`, *Automating Your Development Workflow*, we can use nyc to generate test coverage reports for our applications. We can install nyc using the following command:

```
npm install --save-dev nyc
```

Webpack

As we already learned in `Chapter 9`, *Automating Your Development Workflow*, we can use nyc to generate test coverage reports for our applications. We can install Webpack and some additional plugins using the following command:

```
npm install --save-dev webpack css-loader extract-text-webpack-plugin node-sass sass-loader style-loader
```

Enzyme

Enzyme is an open source testing library developed by Airbnb that can help us to test React components. We can install enzyme using the following command:

```
npm install --save-dev enzyme enzyme-adapter-react-16 @types/enzyme @types/enzyme-adapter-react-16
```

SuperTest

SuperTest is a library that can help us to test HTTP web services developed with Node.js and Express.js. We can install SuperTest using the following command:

```
npm install supertest @types/supertest
```

PM2

PM2 is a production process manager for Node.js applications with a built-in load balancer. PM2 allows us to run a Node.js application as a background process, which is something that we are going to need to run our e2e tests. We can install PM2 using the following command:

```
npm install pm2
```

Nightwatch.js and ChromeDriver

Nightwatch.js is a library that helps us to implement **end-to-end** (**e2e**) tests. We also need a tool known as ChromeDriver. Nightwatch.js can run our test in multiple web browsers, but in our example, we are going use Google Chrome. The `chromedriver` library is an adapter that allows Nightwatch.js to communicate with Google Chrome during the test's execution. We can install Nightwatch.js and ChromeDriver using the following command:

```
npm install chromedriver nightwatch @types/nightwatch
```

> Refer to the companion source code to check the exact versions used in the `package.json` file. If you use `npm install`, the latest version will be installed by default. The version used in these examples might become outdated over time, which could lead to some configuration issues. If you want to use the latest version (which is recommended), you will have to check the documentation of each of the modules to learn about potential breaking changes.

Testing methodologies

Every time we develop a new application, we need to make a lot of decisions. For example, we need to choose the type of database, architecture, libraries, and frameworks that we will use. However, not all our choices are about technologies, and we can also choose a software development methodology, such as extreme programming or scrum. When it comes to testing, there are two major styles or methodologies: TDD and BDD.

Test-driven development (TDD)

Test-driven development is a testing methodology that focuses on encouraging developers to write tests before they write application code. Usually, the process of writing code in TDD consists of the following basic steps:

1. Write a test that fails. There is no application code at this point, so the test should fail.
2. Run the test and ensure that it fails.
3. Write the code to pass the test.
4. Run the test and ensure that it works.

5. Run all the other existing tests to ensure that no other parts of the application are broken because of the changes.
6. Repeat the process for every new feature or bug fix.

This process is often represented as the "red-green-refactor" diagram:

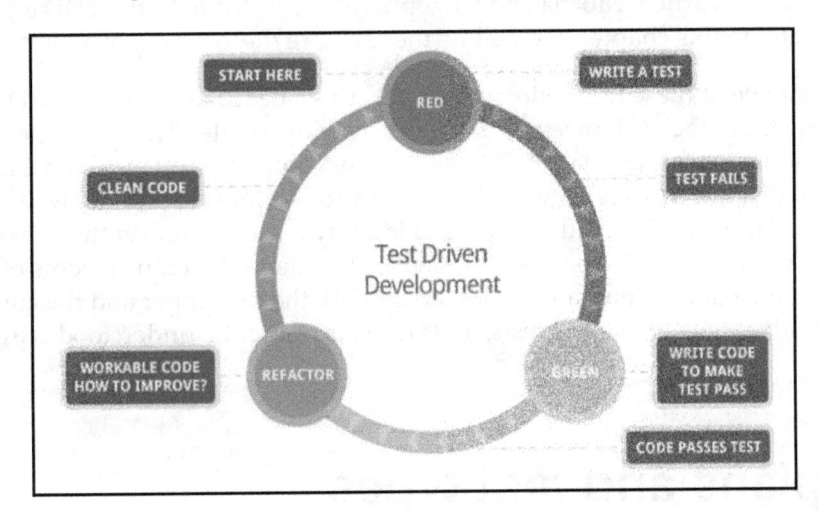

The choice between using TDD or not comes down to the mindset you wish to adopt. Many developers don't like writing tests, so the chances are that if we leave their implementation as the last task in the development process, the tests will never be implemented or the application will just be partially tested. It is also possible that the application could be implemented in a way that is harder to test. If we are planning to write a test, doing it upfront can lead to a reduction in the implementation cost.

TDD is recommended because it effectively helps you and your team to increase the test coverage of your applications and, therefore, significantly reduce the number of potential issues, which eventually ends up saving money.

Behavior-driven development (BDD)

Behavior-driven development appeared after TDD, with the mission of being a refined version of TDD. BDD focuses on the way tests are described (specs) and states that the tests should focus on the application requirements and not the test requirements. Ideally, this will encourage developers to think less about the tests themselves and think more about the entire application.

Application Testing

> The original article in which the BDD principles were introduced by *Dan North* is available at `http://dannorth.net/introducing-bdd/`.

As we have already learned, Mocha and Chai provide APIs for both the TDD and BDD approaches. Later in this chapter, we will further explore these two approaches.

Recommending one of these methodologies is not trivial because TDD and BDD are both good testing methodologies. However, BDD was developed after TDD with the objective of improving it, so we can argue that BDD has some additional advantages over TDD. In BDD, the description of a test focuses on what the application should do and not what the test code is testing. This can help the developers to identify tests that reflect the behavior desired by the customer. BDD tests can be used to document the requirements of a system in a way that can be understood and validated by both the developer and the customer. This is a clear advantage over TDD tests, as TDD tests cannot be understood with ease by the customer.

Tests plans and test types

The term "test plan" is sometimes incorrectly used to refer to a test specification. While test specifications define the scenarios that will be tested and how they will be tested, a test plan is a collection of all the test specs for a given area.

It is recommended that you create an actual planning document, because a test plan can involve many processes, documents, and practices. One of the main goals of a test plan is to identify and define what kind of test is adequate for a component or set of components in an application. The following are the most commonly used test types.

Unit tests

These are used to test an isolated component. If the component is not isolated—that is, if the component has some dependencies—we will have to use some tools and practices, such as stubs or dependency injections, to try to isolate it as much as we can during the test. If it is not possible to manipulate the component's dependencies, we will use spies to facilitate the creation of the unit tests. Our main goal should be to achieve the total isolation of a component when it is tested. A unit test should also be fast, and we should try to avoid input/output, network usage, and any other operations that could potentially affect the speed of the test.

Integration tests

Integration tests are used to test a set of components (partial-integration test) or the entire application (full-integration test). In integration, we will normally use known test data to feed the backend with information that will be displayed on the frontend. We will then assert that the displayed information is correct.

Regression tests

Regression tests are used to verify that an issue has been fixed. If we are using TDD or BDD, whenever we encounter an issue, we should create a unit test that reproduces the issue before we fix the issue. By doing this, we will be able to reproduce past issues and ensure that we don't have to deal with the same issue ever again.

Performance and load tests

Performance and load tests verify whether the application meets our performance expectations. We can use performance tests to verify that our application will be able to handle many concurrent users or activity spikes. To learn more about this type of test, look at `Chapter 13`, *Application Performance*.

End-to-end (e2e) tests

End-to-end tests are not that different from full-integration tests. The main difference is that in an e2e testing session, we will try to emulate an environment that is almost identical to the real user environment. We will use Nightwatch.js and ChromeDriver for this purpose.

User-acceptance tests (UAT)

User-acceptance tests help us to ensure that the system meets all the requirements of the end users.

The example application

In this chapter, we are going to develop an entire web application. The application itself is not a very realistic example, but should be realistic enough to demonstrate many kinds of testing practices and technologies. We are going to develop a calculator that can perform the `pow` operation. The calculator application is composed of the following components:

- A graphic user interface that is implemented using React, and fetches the result of the `pow` operation from a web service using an HTTP client
- A web service that is implemented using Node.js and Express.js, and finds the result of the `pow` operation using a small math library

The application's graphic user interface looks as follows:

Base	Exponent	Result	
2	3	8	Submit

We are going to define many different automated tasks using npm scripts. Each task uses different tools, and some tasks must take place before others. We could use a more complex setup to run some tasks in parallel and reduce the execution time of the whole process, or use a more realistic application, but we want to keep things as simple as possible to focus on the test techniques and tools.

We are going to define the following tasks in our `package.json` file:

```
"scripts": {
  "all": "npm run clean && npm install && npm run lint && npm run build && npm test",
  "clean": "rimraf ./dist ./public",
  "start": "./node_modules/.bin/pm2 start ./dist/src/backend/main.js",
  "kill": "./node_modules/.bin/pm2 kill",
  "lint": "tslint --project tsconfig.json -c tslint.json ./src/**/*.ts ./test/**/*.ts",
  "build": "npm run build-frontend && npm run build-e2e",
  "build-frontend": "webpack",
  "build-e2e": "tsc -p tsconfig.e2e.json",
  "test": "npm run nyc && npm run e2e",
  "nyc": "nyc --clean --all -x webpack.config.js -x test/*.e2e.ts -x public -x dist -x globals.js --require ./jsdom.js --require isomorphic-fetch --require ts-node/register --extension .ts -- mocha --timeout 5000 **/*.test.ts **/*.test.tsx",
  "e2e": "npm run start && npm run nw && npm run kill",
```

Chapter 14

```
"nw": "nightwatch --config nightwatch.json",
"coverage": "nyc report --reporter=text --reporter=lcov"
},
```

> If you are using Windows, the commands defined in the preceding code will fail because the relative paths use the Unix notation. You can solve this problem by installing Git and then installing Git Bash on Windows from `https://git-scm.com/downloads`, and then setting up npm to use Git Bash using the following command:
> `npm config set script-shell "C:Program FilesGitbinbash.exe"`
> You might also need to install Python and the C++ build tools because both are required by the `node-sass` module.
> Remember that the entire source code is included in the companion source code.

The process has been designed in a way that allows us to run it entirely by using the `npm run all` command. This command will execute all the other tasks in order, as described in the following diagram:

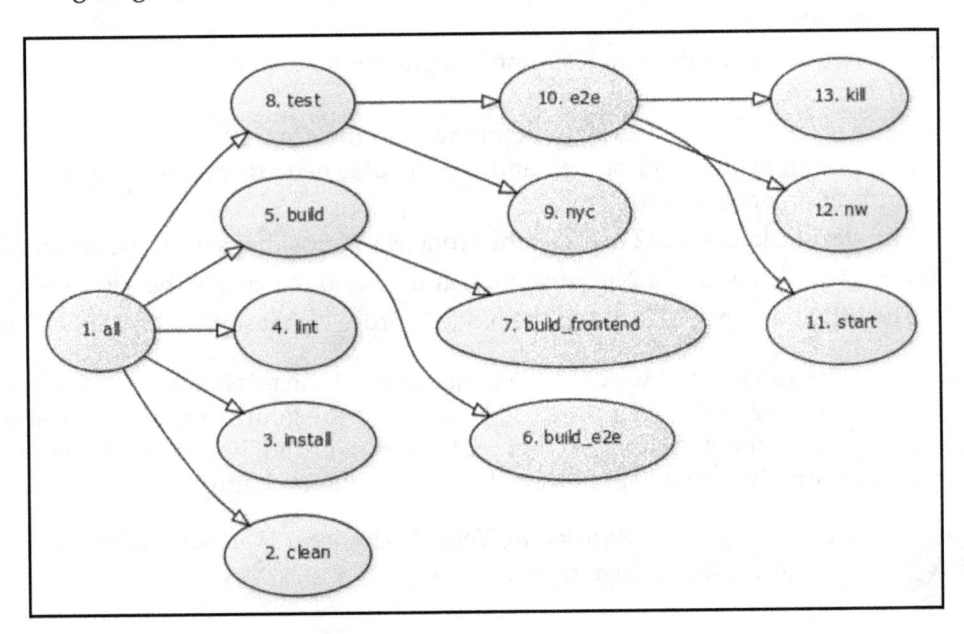

[445]

Application Testing

The preceding diagram allows us to visualize which tasks are initialized by a parent task. For example, the clean, install, lint, build, and test tasks are all started by the **all** task. The diagram also helps us to visualize the order in which the tasks are executed. For example, we can see that the first task is the **all** task and the last task is the **kill** task.

We will now examine the purpose of each of these tasks:

- The **all** task is the root task, and it is used to start other tasks.
- The **clean** task removes some of the previous outputs to ensure that results are not influenced by any cache issues.
- The **install** task downloads all the required dependencies.
- The **lint** task enforces some code-styling rules.
- The **build** task starts the compilation tasks for both frontend and end-to-end tests. Compilation for the backend and the unit tests is not required because the tools used (nyc and ts-node) don't require it.
- The **build_e2e** task compiles the e2e tests using tsc.
- The **build_frontend** task compiles the frontend application using Webpack.
- The **test** task runs both the unit tests with nyc and the e2e tests with Nightwatch.js.
- The **nyc** task runs the unit tests and integration tests, and generates a test-coverage report.
- The **e2e** task runs the e2e tests. Before we run the e2e tests, we need to serve the application using a web server, and we will also need to stop serving the application once we are done.
- The **start** task uses PM2 to starts the Node.js process that serves the application.
- The **nw** task stands for Nightwatch.js, and is used to execute the e2e tests.
- The **kill** task uses PM2 to stop the Node.js process that serves the application.

We shouldn't worry too much if we don't understand what the mission is of each of the tasks or tools mentioned in the preceding list, because we are going to spend the rest of this chapter learning about them in detail, except for the clean, install, lint and build tasks, because we have already learned about these tasks in previous chapters.

> Refer to `Chapter 9`, *Automating Your Development Workflow*, to learn how to generate a test-coverage report.

Unit tests and integration tests with Mocha

In `Chapter 9`, *Automating Your Development Workflow*, we learned the basic details of the unit tests and test-coverage reports with nyc, ts-node, Mocha, and Chai. In this chapter, we are going to learn how to test asynchronous APIs using Mocha and how to combine Mocha with other powerful tools, such as Sinon.JS, SuperTest, and Enzyme:

- We are going to learn how to write tests for every layer of an application.
- We are going to start by testing a math library used in the backend.
- We will then test a web service, which consumes the math library, and a client, which consumes the web service.
- We will finish the section by writing tests for the graphic user interface and creating some e2e tests.

Back to basics

The companion source code includes a class named `MathDemo`. This class allows us to perform the pow calculation in a few different ways. One of them is the synchronous pow function:

```
public pow(base: number, exponent: number) {
  let result = base;
  for (let i = 1; i < exponent; i++) {
    result = result * base;
  }
  return result;
}
```

As we learned in `Chapter 9`, *Automating Your Development Workflow*, we can test the method declared in the preceding function using the following test case:

```
it("Should return the correct numeric value for pow", () => {
  const math = new MathDemo();
  const result = math.pow(2, 3);
  const expected = 8;
  expect(result).to.be.a("number");
  expect(result).to.equal(expected);
});
```

Application Testing

We can then use the `nyc` command with ts-node and Mocha to run our tests and generate a test-coverage report. In the companion source code, this is wrapped with npm scripts as the following command to facilitate the usage:

```
npm run nyc
```

If everything goes according to plan, we should see a list of all the tests that have been executed. The result generated by the tests that were included in the companion source code should look as follows:

```
  MathDemo
    ✓ Should return result of pow calculation

  MathDemo
before() invoked!
beforeEach() invoked!
    ✓ Should return the correct numeric value for PI
afterEach() invoked!
beforeEach() invoked!
    ✓ Should return the correct numeric value for pow
afterEach() invoked!
beforeEach() invoked!
    ✓ Should return the correct numeric value for pow (async)
afterEach() invoked!
beforeEach() invoked!
    ✓ Should return the correct numeric value for pow (async)
afterEach() invoked!
beforeEach() invoked!
    ✓ Should throw an exception when no parameters passed
afterEach() invoked!
after() invoked!

  Math Service
    ✓ Should be able to HTTP GET /api/math/pow/:base/:exponent

  Calculator Component
    ✓ Should invoke client and set #result value when #submit.click is triggered (90ms)


  8 passing (182ms)
```

The command should also generate a test coverage report as shown in the following screenshot:

```
File                                    | % Stmts | % Branch | % Funcs | % Lines | Uncovered Lines
All files                               |  82.86  |    50    |  73.17  |  84.25  |
 02_frontend_testing                    |  90.91  |   100    |  66.67  |  90.91  |
  jsdom.js                              |  90.91  |   100    |  66.67  |  90.91  |      8
 02_frontend_testing/src/backend        |  60.34  |    50    |  47.37  |  63.46  |
  interfaces.ts                         |    0    |   100    |   100   |    0    |      2
  main.ts                               |    0    |   100    |   100   |    0    | 2,3,4,5,6
  math_demo.ts                          |  56.76  |    50    |  43.75  |  59.38  | ... 62,64,65,75
  server.ts                             |  93.33  |   100    |  66.67  |   100   |
 02_frontend_testing/src/frontend       |   100   |   100    |   100   |   100   |
  math_client.ts                        |   100   |   100    |   100   |   100   |
 02_frontend_testing/test               |   100   |   100    |   100   |   100   |
  match_client.test.ts                  |   100   |   100    |   100   |   100   |
  math_demo.test.ts                     |   100   |   100    |   100   |   100   |
  pow_service.test.ts                   |   100   |   100    |   100   |   100   |
```

Once we have executed our tests with the `nyc` command, we can generate a test coverage report by running the following command:

```
nyc report --reporter=text --reporter=lcov
```

This will generate a folder named `coverage` in the current directory. The coverage folder contains some HTML files that we can open using a web browser:

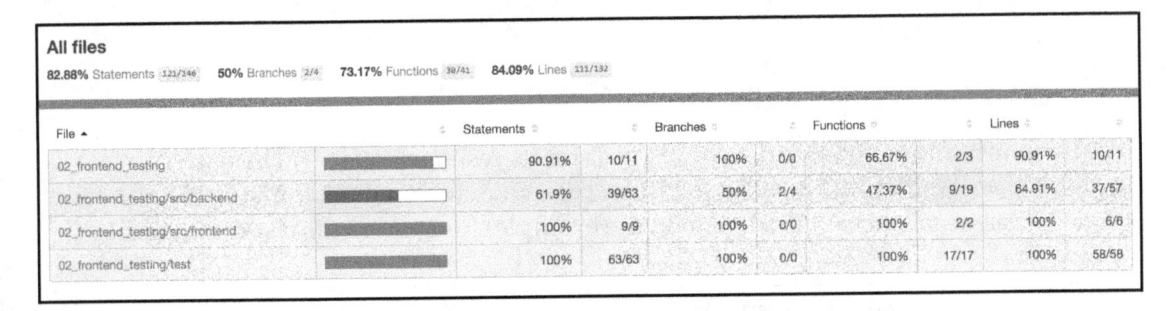

File ▲	Statements		Branches		Functions		Lines	
All files 82.88% Statements 121/146 50% Branches 2/4 73.17% Functions 30/41 84.09% Lines 111/132							
02_frontend_testing	90.91%	10/11	100%	0/0	66.67%	2/3	90.91%	10/11
02_frontend_testing/src/backend	61.9%	39/63	50%	2/4	47.37%	9/19	64.91%	37/57
02_frontend_testing/src/frontend	100%	9/9	100%	0/0	100%	2/2	100%	6/6
02_frontend_testing/test	100%	63/63	100%	0/0	100%	17/17	100%	58/58

Application Testing

If we click on one of the files, we will be able to see a line-by-line test coverage report for the selected file:

```
All files / 02_frontend_testing/src/frontend  math_client.ts
100% Statements 9/9    100% Branches 0/0    100% Functions 2/2    100% Lines 6/6

1  1x   export class MathClient {
2  1x       public async pow(base: number, exponent: number): Promise<string> {
3  1x           const res = await fetch(`/api/math/pow/${base}/${exponent}`);
4  1x           const json = await res.json();
5  1x           return json.result.toString();
6           }
7  1x   }
8
```

Testing asynchronous code

The `MathDemo` class also includes an asynchronous version of the same method:

```
public powAsync(base: number, exponent: number) {
  return new Promise<number>((resolve) => {
    setTimeout(
      () => {
        const result = this.pow(base, exponent);
        resolve(result);
      },
      0
    );
  });
}
```

If we try to test this method, and we don't wait for its result, our test will be useless. However, if we wait for the result, using the `Promise.then` method, our test will also fail, unless we pass a callback (named `done` in the example) function to the test-case handler:

```
it("Should return the correct numeric value for pow", (done) => {
  const math = new MathDemo();
  math.powAsync(2, 3).then((result: number) => {
    const expected = 8;
    expect(result).to.be.a("number");
    expect(result).to.equal(expected);
    done();
  });
});
```

Chapter 14

Alternatively, we can use async and await, as demonstrated in the following code snippet:

```
it("Should return the correct numeric value for pow", async () => {
    const math = new MathDemo();
    const result = await math.powAsync(2, 3);
    const expected = 8;
    expect(result).to.be.a("number");
    expect(result).to.equal(expected);
});
```

When testing asynchronous code, Mocha will consider the test as failed (timeout) if it takes more than 2,000 milliseconds to invoke the `done` function. The time limit before a timeout can be configured, as can warnings for slow functions. By default, when a test takes more than 40 milliseconds, a warning will be displayed. The warning suggests that our test is somehow slow. If the test execution takes over 100 milliseconds, the warning will suggest that our test is quite slow. We can change this configuration using the `--timeout` command-line argument of the `mocha` command.

> The companion source code includes examples of each kind of warning and failure.

Asserting exceptions

In the previous examples, we have learned how to assert the type and value of a variable:

```
const expected = 8;
expect(result).to.be.a("number");
expect(result).to.equal(expected);
```

However, there is one scenario that is perhaps not as intuitive as the previous one—testing for an exception.

Application Testing

The `MathDemo` class also contains a method named `bad`, which was added with the sole purpose of illustrating how to test for an exception. The `bad` method throws an exception when it is invoked with a `null` argument:

```
public bad(foo: any) {
  if (foo === null) {
    throw new Error("Error!");
  } else {
    return this.pow(5, 5);
  }
}
```

In the following test, we can see how we can use the `expect` API to assert that an exception is thrown:

```
it("Should throw an exception when no parameters passed", () => {
  const math = new MathDemo();
  expect(math.bad).to.throw(Error);
});
```

> If you wish to learn more about assertions, visit the Chai official documentation available at `http://chaijs.com/api/bdd/`.

Testing a web service with SuperTest

The demo application included in the companion source code declares a web service that allows us to get the result of the `pow` calculation:

```
import * as express from "express";
import * as path from "path";
import { MathDemo } from "./math_demo";

export function getApp() {

    const app = express();

    // ...

    app.get("/api/math/pow/:base/:exponent", (req, res) => {
        const mathDemo = new MathDemo();
        const base = parseInt(req.params.base, 10);
        const exponent = parseInt(req.params.exponent, 10);
        const result = mathDemo.pow(base, exponent);
```

```
        res.json({ result });
    });

    return app;
}
```

The initialization of the application is separated into two files: `main.ts` and `server.ts`. The `server.ts` file defines the `getApp` function that we have examined in the preceding code snippet. The `main.ts` file uses the `getApp` function to start the server:

```
import { getApp } from "./server";

const app = getApp();
const port = 3000;

app.listen(port, () => {
    console.log(`App listening at http://localhost:${port}`); // tslint:disable-line
});
```

Sometimes, it is a good idea to test a web service as a whole in what is known as integration tests. As we learned earlier in this chapter, integration tests are used to test a set of components. In this case, we are going to test the server-side route handlers and their usage of the `MathDemo` class. We can define a test for the `pow` service as follows:

```
import { expect } from "chai";
import * as request from "supertest";
import { getApp } from "../src/backend/server";

describe("Math Service", function() {
    it("HTTP GET /api/math/pow/:base/:exponent", async () => {
        const app = getApp();
        return request(app).get("/api/math/pow/2/3")
                    .set("Accept", "application/json")
                    .expect("Content-Type", /json/)
                    .expect(200)
                    .then((response) =>
                        expect(response.body.result).eql(8)
                    );
    });
});
```

Application Testing

As we can see in the preceding code snippet, we have used a function named `getApp` to get the instance of the Express.js app. Once we have the app instance, we can use the request method from the `supertest` module to send a request to the service. We can use SuperTest together with Chai to assert that the response of the request matches an expected result. It is important to mention that the `getApp` function creates an app, but it doesn't launch the app. Or, in other words, the `getApp` function avoids invoking the `app.listen` method.

Working with tests suites

A test suite is a group of test cases. We have already learned that we can use the `describe` function from Mocha to define a test suite and the `it` function to define a test case. However, we have not learned that we can define event handlers that can be invoked before and after all the tests in a test suite. The following code snippet demonstrates how we can define these event handlers:

```
describe("My test suite", () => {
    before(() => {
       // Invoked once before ALL tests
    });

    after(() => {
       // Invoked once after ALL tests
    });

    beforeEach(() => {
       // Invoked once before EACH test
    });

    afterEach(() => {
       // Invoked once before EACH test
    });

    it(() => {
       // Test case
    });
});
```

This can be useful if we want to reuse some of the initialization logic across multiple test cases. For example, we can rewrite the example that we used to test a web service earlier in the preceding section, in a way that will allow us to share the Express.js application instance across multiple test cases:

```
import { expect } from "chai";
import * as express from "express";
import * as request from "supertest";
import { getApp } from "../src/backend/server";

describe("Math Service", function() {

    let app: express.Application | null;

    before(() => {
        app = getApp();
    });

    after(() => {
        app = null;
    });

    it("HTTP GET /api/math/pow/:base/:exponent", async () =>
        request(app).get("/api/math/pow/2/3")
            .set("Accept", "application/json")
            .expect("Content-Type", /json/)
            .expect(200)
            .then((response) =>
                expect(response.body.result).eql(8)
            )
    );

});
```

> Usually, testing frameworks (regardless of the language we are working with) won't allow us to control the order in which the unit tests and test suites are executed. The tests can even be executed in parallel by using multiple threads. For this reason, it is important to ensure that the unit tests in our test suites are independent of each other.

Application Testing

Isolating components with Sinon.JS

We have learned that unit tests are used to test individual components, and integration tests are used to test a set of components and their interactions. When we write a unit test, and a component has a dependency on another, we will need to provide stubs, mocks, or dummies instead of real dependencies to ensure that the component is being tested in isolation. However, sometimes this can be more complicated than it sounds. Luckily, Sinon.JS can help us to ensure that our components are tested in isolation.

The following code snippet is used to test the web client of the `pow` web service that we described earlier in this chapter. We use Sinon.JS to define a stub for a global object named `fetch`. The `fetch` global object is a function that allows us to send an AJAX request to the backend from the frontend. Replacing the `fetch` object with a stub is a good idea because it will help us to ensure that the client class is not interacting with the backend, and, thus, that it is tested in complete isolation:

```
import { expect } from "chai";
import { stub } from "sinon";
import { MathClient } from "../src/frontend/math_client";

describe("MathDemo", () => {
    it("Should return result of pow calculation", async () => {

        const expectedResult = "8";

        const response = {
            json: () => Promise.resolve({
                result: expectedResult
            })
        };

        const stubedFetch = stub(global, "fetch" as any);
        stubedFetch.returns(Promise.resolve(response));

        const mathClient = new MathClient();
        const actualResult = await mathClient.pow(2, 3);
        expect(expectedResult).to.eq(actualResult);
        expect(stubedFetch.callCount).to.eq(1);

    });
});
```

Using a global is a bad idea because it goes against the dependency inversion principle and makes our applications harder to test. Fortunately, Sinon.JS can help us to overcome this kind of difficulty.

> Refer to `Chapter 5`, *Working with Dependencies*, to learn more about dependency inversion and its underlying principles.

It is also worth mentioning that the stubs provide us with an API that can help us to check things, such as the number of times that the stub was used or which arguments were passed to it. This was demonstrated by the last assertion in the preceding code snippet.

jsdom

Some testing tools, such as Enzyme (we will learn about this in the following section), expect to be used in a web browser. In our example, the application uses nyc and ts-node to execute all our unit tests, which means that we are not using a web browser. Sometimes, it is possible to overcome this problem by using jsdom, which is described by its creators as follows:

> *"jsdom is a pure-JavaScript implementation of many web standards, notably the WHATWG DOM and HTML Standards, for use with Node.js. In general, the goal of the project is to emulate enough of a subset of a web browser to be useful for testing and scraping real-world web applications."*

If we examine the `nyc` command in the `package.json` file included in the companion source code, we will see that one of the arguments provided to the nyc binary is `--require ./jsdom.js`. This will force Mocha to need the `jsdom.js` file before any tests are executed. The `jsdom.js` file is used to initialize jsdom, and looks as follows:

```
const { JSDOM } = require("jsdom" );
const jsdom = new JSDOM(" <!doctype html><html><body></body></html>" );
const { window } = jsdom;

function copyProps(src, target) {
  const props = Object.getOwnPropertyNames(src)
    .filter(prop => typeof target[prop] === " undefined" )
    .reduce((result, prop) => ({
      ...result,
      [prop]: Object.getOwnPropertyDescriptor(src, prop),
    }), {});
  Object.defineProperties(target, props);
```

Application Testing

```
}

global.window = window;
global.document = window.document;
global.navigator = {
  userAgent: " node.js",
};

copyProps(window, global);
```

The preceding file creates a few global variables that allow us to run the backend code that was originally designed to be executed in a web browser. In the Node.js execution environment, we don't have certain variables, such as the window variable. The preceding code snippet initializes all the required variables to enable the execution of frontend code in our backend execution environment (Node.js). This is useful, for example, when we want to write a test for a frontend component because we can execute our tests without the need for a web browser.

> Refer to the Enzyme documentation at `https://github.com/airbnb/enzyme/blob/master/docs/guides/jsdom.md` to learn more about the jsdom configuration.

Testing React web components with Enzyme

At this point, we have tested the backend of our application using both unit tests and integration tests (with SuperTest). We have also tested our client in complete isolation, thanks to the usage of Sinon.JS. However, our application can still fail if something is wrong in the presentation layer (the graphic user interface). In this section, we are going to learn how we can use some libraries to help us to test each of the components of our graphic user interface.

> Refer to `Chapter 11`, *Frontend Development with React and TypeScript*, to learn more about React.

The companion source code includes the following React component:

```
import * as React from "react";
import { MathClient } from "./math_client";
import { NumericInput } from "./numeric_input_component";

const ids = {
  base: "#base",
  exponent: "#exponent",
  result: "#result",
  submit: "#submit"
};

interface CalculatorProps {
  client: MathClient;
}

interface CalculatorState {
  base: string;
  exponent: string;
  result: string;
}

export class Calculator extends React.Component<CalculatorProps,
CalculatorState> {

  public constructor(props: CalculatorProps) {
    super(props);
    this.state = {
      base: "1",
      exponent: "1",
      result: "1"
    };
  }

  public render() {
    return (
      <div className="well">
        <div className="row">
          <div className="col">
            <NumericInput
              id="base"
              name="Base"
              value={this.state.base}
              onChangeHandler={(v) => this.setState({ base: v })}
            />
          </div>
          <div className="col">
```

Application Testing

```jsx
            <NumericInput
              id="exponent"
              name="Exponent"
              value={this.state.exponent}
              onChangeHandler={(v) => this.setState({
                  exponent: v
              })}
            />
        </div>
        <div className="col">
          <div className="form-group">
              <label>Result</label>
              <div id="result">{this.state.result}</div>
          </div>
        </div>
        <div className="col">
          <button
            id="submit_btn"
            type="Submit"
            className="btn btn-primary"
            onClick={() => this._onSubmit()}
          >
            Submit
          </button>
        </div>
      </div>
    </div>
  );
}

private _onSubmit() {
  (async () => {
    const result = await this.props.client.pow(
      parseFloat(this.state.base),
      parseFloat(this.state.exponent)
    );
    this.setState({ result });
  })();
}

}
```

Chapter 14

As we learned earlier in this chapter, the preceding component will display a web form on the screen. The users of the application need to provide two numbers (base and exponent) as inputs. The input is then sent to a web service in the backend, and the response is displayed as a result. The following code snippet demonstrates how we can isolate the preceding component from the HTTP client using a stub. The code snippet also demonstrates how we can configure Enzyme to work with version 16 of React and then use it to simulate user events, such as clicking on an element or typing in an input:

```
import { expect } from "chai";
import * as Enzyme from "enzyme";
import * as Adapter from "enzyme-adapter-react-16";
import * as React from "react";
import { stub } from "sinon";
import { Calculator } from "../src/frontend/calculator_component";
import { MathClient } from "../src/frontend/math_client";

Enzyme.configure({ adapter: new Adapter() });

describe("Calculator Component", () => {

  it("Should invoke client #submit is clicked", (done) => {

    const mathClient = new MathClient();

    const mathClientStub = stub(mathClient, "pow");
    mathClientStub.returns(Promise.resolve(8));

    mathClientStub.callsFake((base: number, exponent: number) => {
      expect(base).to.equal(2);
      expect(exponent).to.equal(3);
      done();
    });

    const wrapper = Enzyme.mount(<Calculator client={mathClient} />);

    expect(wrapper.find("input#base")).to.have.length(1);
    expect(wrapper.find("input#exponent")).to.have.length(1);
    expect(wrapper.find("button#submit_btn")).to.have.length(1);

    wrapper.find("input#base").simulate("change", { target: { value: "2" } });
    wrapper.find("input#exponent").simulate("change", { target: { value: "3" } });
    wrapper.find("button#submit_btn").simulate("click");

  });

});
```

[461]

Application Testing

```
});
```

The preceding tests insert a value for the base and exponent inputs and then click on the **Submit** button. This will invoke the web client, which has been replaced by a stub.

Enzyme has been designed to work with React. However, each major version of React requires a specific adapter. Other frameworks might require other libraries. For example, in Angular, we can use the utilities provided by the `@angular/core/testing` module to do something like the following:

```
import {TestBed, ComponentFixture, inject, async} from
"@angular/core/testing";
import {LoginComponent, User} from "./login.component";
import {Component, DebugElement} from "@angular/core";
import {By} from "@angular/platform-browser";

// Refine the test module by declaring the test component
TestBed.configureTestingModule({
    declarations: [LoginComponent]
});

// Access the component
let fixture: ComponentFixture<LoginComponent> =
TestBed.createComponent(LoginComponent);
let component: LoginComponent = fixture.componentInstance;

// Access an element
let submitEl: DebugElement = fixture.debugElement.query(By.css("button"));
submitEl.triggerEventHandler("click", null);
```

> Please refer to the documentation at `https://angular.io/api/core/testing` to learn more about testing in Angular.

TDD versus BDD with Mocha and Chai

As we have already seen, TDD and BDD follow many of the same principles, but have some differences in their style. While these two styles provide the same functionality, BDD is considered to be easier to read by many developers.

The following table compares the naming and style of the suites, tests, and assertions used by the TDD and BBD styles:

TDD	BDD
suite	describe
setup	before
teardown	after
suiteSetup	beforeEach
suiteTeardown	afterEach
test	it
assert.equal(math.PI, 3.14159265359);	expect(math.PI).to.equals(3.14159265359);

End-to-end tests with Nightwatch.js

Writing an e2e test with Nightwatch.js is very simple because its API is very readable. We should be able to read an e2e test and be able to understand it, even if it is the first time that we see one. For example, the following is an example of an e2e test that is used to test the application included in the companion source code:

```
import { NightwatchBrowser } from "nightwatch";

const test = {
  "Calculator pow e2e test example": (browser: NightwatchBrowser) => {
    browser
      .url("http://localhost:3000/")
      .waitForElementVisible("body", 1000)
      .assert.title("Calculator")
      .assert.visible("#base")
      .assert.visible("#exponent")
      .clearValue("#base")
      .setValue("#base", "2")
      .clearValue("#exponent")
      .setValue("#exponent", "3")
      .click("#submit_btn")
      .pause(500)
      .assert.containsText("#result", "8")
      .end();
  }
```

Application Testing

```
    };

    export = test;
```

We use the `NightwatchBrowser` instance to navigate to a URL, wait for a few elements to be visible, set the value of a few inputs, and then click on the **Submit** button.

While the e2e tests API is very simple, the process behind it is not so simple. If we examine the `npm script` commands in the `package.json` file included in the companion source code, we will be able to observe that the command triggers four other commands:

- Compile the e2e tests
- Run the application
- Run the e2e tests
- Kill the application

The first command uses PM2 and ts-node to run the application. PM2 is a very powerful process management tool that allows us to run a Node.js app as a cluster and to monitor it. However, this is not why we are using it here. We use PM2 because it is a very easy way to run the application as a background process. We need to run the entire application before our e2e tests are executed. The problem is that when the app starts waiting for HTTP requests, it blocks all the subsequent commands. PM2 solves this problem by allowing us to run the app in a background process.

Another thing worth mentioning is that our e2e tests are browser-independent. This explains why Nightwatch.js requires us to configure a driver. The driver provides native access to the web browser that will execute the e2e tests.

In the demo application, we are using ChromeDriver. We have created a file named `globals.js` that is used to define some global events that will be executed before and after our e2e tests. The event handlers are very similar to the ones that we learned about while defining a test suite with Mocha earlier in this chapter.

We use the event handlers declared in the `globals.js` file to create and destroy instances of `chromedriver`:

```
    const chromedriver = require("chromedriver");

    module.exports = {
        before: (done) => {
            chromedriver.start();
            done();
        },
        after: (done) => {
```

```
            chromedriver.stop();
            done();
        },
        reporter: function(results) {
            if (
                (typeof(results.failed) === "undefined" || results.failed === 0) &&
                (typeof(results.error) === "undefined" || results.error === 0)
            ) {
                process.exit(0);
            } else {
                process.exit(1);
            }
        }
    }
};
```

> The version of the `chromedriver` npm module used in this example is 2.36.0. This version has been tested with Google Chrome 65.0. If you are using a later version of Google Chrome, please ensure that you also upgrade the `chromedriver` module.

We then create a file named Nightwatch.js that contains the following configuration:

```
{
    "src_folders": [
        "dist/test"
    ],
    "output_folder": "reports",
    "custom_commands_path": "",
    "custom_assertions_path": "",
    "page_objects_path": "",
    "globals_path": "./globals.js",
    "selenium": {
        "start_process": false
    },
    "test_settings": {
        "default": {
            "selenium_port": 9515,
            "selenium_host": "localhost",
            "default_path_prefix": "",
            "desiredCapabilities": {
                "browserName": "chrome",
                "chromeOptions": {
                    "args": [
                        "--no-sandbox"
                    ]
                },
```

```
                "acceptSslCerts": true
            }
        },
        "chrome": {
            "desiredCapabilities": {
                "browserName": "chrome"
            }
        }
    }
}
```

As we can see in the preceding code snippet, we are configuring ChromeDriver to use the `globals.js` events and Google Chrome as the web browser to be used to run our tests. We have also configured Nightwatch.js to look for our test under the `dist` folder. Nightwatch.js cannot understand TypeScript natively, which explains why we need to compile the tests into the `dist` folder before we can run them.

We need to define a second `tsconfig.json` file named `tsconfig.e2e.json` with some additional options to ensure that we only compile the required files:

```
{
    "compilerOptions": {
        "outDir": "./dist/"
    },
    "extends": "./tsconfig",
    "include": [
        "test/*.e2e.ts",
        "src/backend/*.ts"
    ],
    "exclude": [
        "node_modules"
    ]
}
```

Please note that the `extends` filed in the `tsconfig.json` file allows us to inherit all the settings from a previously declared `tsconfig.json` file.

If everything goes well, we should be able to see results like the following on the console:

```
> nightwatch --config nightwatch.json

[Src / Backend / Interfaces] Test Suite
=======================================
/Users/remojansen/CODE/LearningTypeScript/chapters/chapter_11/02_frontend_testing
App listening at http://localhost:3000

[Src / Backend / Main] Test Suite
=================================

[Src / Backend / Math Demo] Test Suite
======================================

Running: MathDemo
No assertions ran.

[Src / Backend / Server] Test Suite
===================================

Running: getApp
/Users/remojansen/CODE/LearningTypeScript/chapters/chapter_11/02_frontend_testing
No assertions ran.

[Test / Pow E2e] Test Suite
===========================

Running: Calculator pow e2e test example
 ✓ Element <body> was visible after 84 milliseconds.
 ✓ Testing if the page title equals "Calculator".
 ✓ Testing if element <#base> is visible.
 ✓ Testing if element <#exponent> is visible.
 ✓ Testing if element <#result> contains text: "8".

OK. 5 assertions passed. (2.54s)

OK. 5 total assertions passed. (4.552s)
```

Summary

In this chapter, we discussed some core testing concepts, such as stubs, suites, and more. We also looked at the test-driven development and behavior-driven development approaches, and how to work with some of the leading JavaScript testing frameworks, such as Mocha, Chai, Sinon.JS, Enzyme, SuperTest, and Nightwatch.js.

In the next chapter, we will learn how to use the TypeScript language services to create our development tools.

15
Working with the TypeScript Compiler and the Language Services

In this chapter, we are going to learn about the internals of the TypeScript compiler and the TypeScript language services.

These topics may seem very advanced and not something that everybody will find useful. While it is true that it is a topic for advanced users, the truth is that everybody can benefit from understanding the TypeScript language services. Understanding the compiler API of the TypeScript compiler can help us to develop many kinds of development tools and to automate certain aspects of our development workflow.

The goal of this chapter is not to make you an expert in the compiler's internals or the development of TypeScript tools, but to gently introduce you to this very extensive topic. In this chapter, we will cover the following topics:

- The internal architecture of the TypeScript compiler
- Using the compiler API programmatically
- Working with `ts-simple-ast`
- Implementing custom code-analysis tools

The TypeScript compiler's internal architecture

In this section, we are going to learn what the main components in the TypeScript compiler are. We are going to learn the main responsibility of each of the components, as well as what their expected inputs and outputs are.

The following diagram describes the main components of the TypeScript architecture:

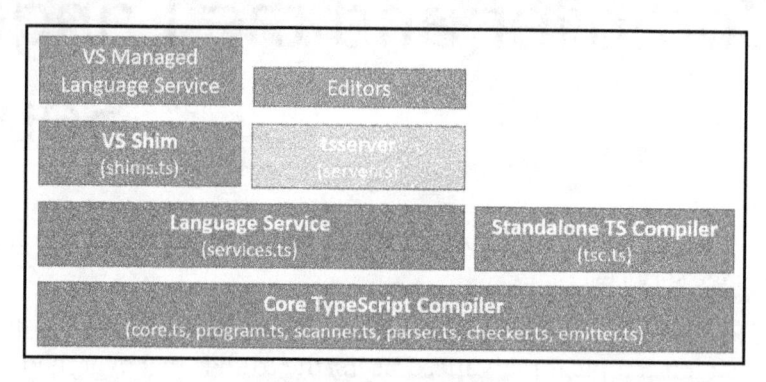

Components of the TypeScript architecture

The core TypeScript API is the foundation of everything, and is composed of elements such as the scanner, parser, binder, type checker, and emitter.

The language services and the standalone compiler (the `tsc` command-line tool) sit on top of the core compiler APIs. Finally, the Visual Studio shim and the TypeScript standalone server (`tsserver`) are designed to facilitate the integration of TypeScript with Visual Studio and other source code editors.

The official TypeScript documentation defines the TypeScript standalone server as follows:

> *"The TypeScript standalone server (aka tsserver) is a node executable that encapsulates the TypeScript compiler and language services and exposes them through a JSON protocol. tsserver is well suited for editors and IDE support."*

Scanner

The scanner transforms the source code files into streams of tokens. The scanner is also known as the **lexer** in other resources about compilers. The scanner is used by the parser.

Lexemes and tokens

A lexeme is a sequence of characters in the source program that matches the pattern for a token. We can say that a token has a pattern and a pattern can be matched by many lexemes, in some cases. As a result, in a programming language, there are an infinite number of potential lexemes and a limited number of tokens.

The easiest way to understand the difference between a lexeme and a token is to take a look at an example, such as the following code snippet:

```
while (y >= t) y = y - 3;
```

The preceding code snippet will be parsed into the following lexemes and tokens:

Lexeme	Token
while	WhileKeyword
(	OpenParenToken
y	Identifier
>=	GreaterThanEqualsToken
t	Identifier
)	CloseParenToken
y	Identifier
=	EqualsToken
y	Identifier
-	MinusToken
3	NumericLiteral
;	SemicolonToken
	EndOfFileToken

In TypeScript, the tokens are defined in the `SyntaxKind` enumeration:

```
export const enum SyntaxKind {
    Unknown,
    EndOfFileToken,
    SingleLineCommentTrivia,
    MultiLineCommentTrivia,
```

```
        NewLineTrivia,
        WhitespaceTrivia,
        ShebangTrivia,
        ConflictMarkerTrivia,
        NumericLiteral,
        StringLiteral,
        JsxText,
        //...
```

The `SyntaxKind` enumeration is defined in the `/src/compiler/types.ts` file in the TypeScript source code.

> Refer to the official TypeScript repository on GitHub at `https://github.com/Microsoft/TypeScript` if you wish to explore the entire source code of the TypeScript project.

Parser

The TypeScript parser uses the scanner to traverse our source code files and transform them into a stream of tokens.

The TypeScript parser then transforms the stream of tokens into a tree-like data structure known as an abstract syntax tree (AST). Each of the elements in this tree-like data structure is known as a node. A node is the basic building block of the AST.

AST

The **abstract syntax tree** (**AST**) is a tree-like data structure created by the parser. This data structure allows the TypeScript compiler to traverse our source code to perform many core tasks, such as emitting the output JavaScript code. We are going to learn more about the AST later in this chapter.

Symbols

The TypeScript textbook by Basarat Ali Syed describes symbols as follows:

> "Symbols connect declaration nodes in the AST to other declarations contributing to the same entity. Symbols are the basic building block of the Semantic system."

The symbol class is defined in the TypeScript source code as follows:

```
function Symbol(this: Symbol, flags: SymbolFlags, name: __String) {
    this.flags = flags;
    this.escapedName = name;
    this.declarations = undefined;
    this.valueDeclaration = undefined;
    this.id = undefined;
    this.mergeId = undefined;
    this.parent = undefined;
}
```

A symbol contains a reference to the declarations of a type and some flags that help us to identify some of its characteristics.

Binder

The TypeScript textbook by Basarat Ali Syed describes the binder as follows:

> "The binder is used to connect the various parts of the source code into a coherent type system that can then be used by the checker. The main responsibility of the binder is to create the Symbols."

TypeScript supports a feature known as *declaration merging*, which allows us to merge two separate declarations declared with the same name into a single definition. For example, the following code snippet declares two interfaces named `Person` and a variable named `person`:

```
interface Person {
    name: string;
}

interface Person {
    surname: string;
}

const person: Person = { name: "Remo", surname: "Jansen" };
```

The type of the variable is Person, and as we can see, the type contains the properties declared in both previously declared interfaces. This is the case because the declaration merging mechanism merges both declarations into one unique type. This is directly related to the behavior of the binder.

Type checker

The type checker is probably the most important component in the TypeScript compiler. The type checker uses the abstract syntax trees (one per file) and the symbols as inputs, and it oversees the identification of type errors in our source code.

Emitter

The emitter is the component responsible for the generation of the output code. The output is usually JavaScript that adheres to one of the supported specifications (ES3, ES5, or ES6), but it can also be type definitions or source map files.

Language service

The TypeScript compiler includes an additional component that has been specifically designed to provide developers with a great developer experience. The following paragraph has been extracted from the official TypeScript documentation:

> *"The "Language Service" exposes an additional layer around the core compiler pipeline that is best suiting editor-like applications. The language service supports the common set of a typical editor operations like statement completions, signature help, code formatting and outlining, colorization, etc... Basic re-factoring like rename, Debugging interface helpers like validating breakpoints as well as TypeScript-specific features like support of incremental compilation (--watch equivalent on the command-line). The language service is designed to efficiently handle scenarios with files changing over time within a long-lived compilation context; in that sense, the language service provides a slightly different perspective about working with programs and source files from that of the other compiler interfaces."*

Understanding the abstract syntax tree (AST)

As we have already learned, an **abstract syntax tree**, or **AST**, is a tree-like data structure used to represent the abstract syntactic structure of source code written in a programming language. Each node of the AST represents a construct that occurs in the source code.

We are now going to look at a small TypeScript code snippet to understand the AST in detail. There is nothing very special about the following code snippet—it simply declares an interface named `Weapon` and a couple of classes, named `Katana` and `Ninja`. It then creates an instance of the `Ninja` class and invokes one of its methods:

```
interface Weapon {
    tryHit(fromDistance: number): boolean;
}

class Katana implements Weapon {
    public tryHit(fromDistance: number) {
        return fromDistance <= 2;
    }
}

class Ninja {
    private _weapon: Weapon;
    public constructor(weapon: Weapon) {
        this._weapon = weapon;
    }
    public fight(fromDistance: number) {
        return this._weapon.tryHit(fromDistance);
    }
}

const ninja = new Ninja(new Katana());
ninja.fight("5");
```

The AST for the preceding code snippet generated by the TypeScript compiler looks as follows:

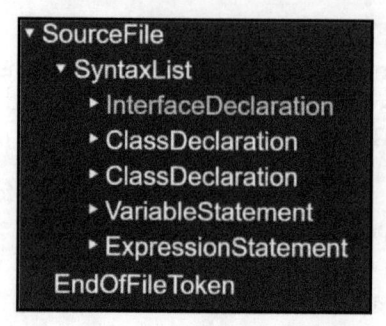

```
▼ SourceFile
    ▼ SyntaxList
        ▶ InterfaceDeclaration
        ▶ ClassDeclaration
        ▶ ClassDeclaration
        ▶ VariableStatement
        ▶ ExpressionStatement
  EndOfFileToken
```

Some of the nodes of the preceding AST have been removed for ease of understanding. We can see how the AST starts with a `SourceFile` node and ends with an `EndOfFileToken` node. Between these two nodes, we have a node for the interface declaration (`InterfaceDeclaration`), two nodes for the class declarations (`ClassDeclaration`), one node for the variable declaration (`VariableStatement`), and, finally, a node for the method invocation (`ExpressionStatement`).

We are now going to focus on one of these nodes: the node that represents the interface declaration (`InterfaceDeclaration`). As we saw earlier, the interface declaration looks as follows:

```
interface Weapon {
    tryHit(fromDistance: number): boolean;
}
```

The `InterfaceDeclaration` node in the AST for the preceding code snippet looks as follows:

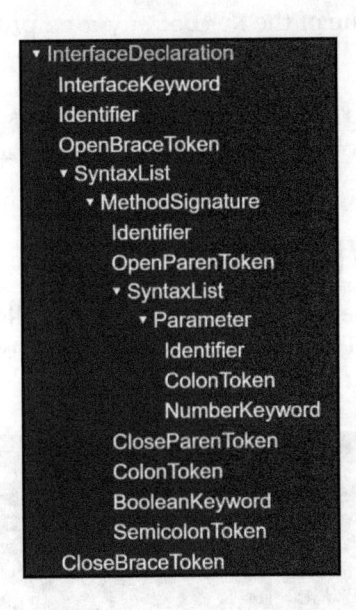

```
▼ InterfaceDeclaration
    InterfaceKeyword
    Identifier
    OpenBraceToken
    ▼ SyntaxList
        ▼ MethodSignature
            Identifier
            OpenParenToken
            ▼ SyntaxList
                ▼ Parameter
                    Identifier
                    ColonToken
                    NumberKeyword
            CloseParenToken
            ColonToken
            BooleanKeyword
            SemicolonToken
    CloseBraceToken
```

In the preceding representation of the AST, we can see the names of each of the nodes that compose the AST of an interface declaration with a unique method signature. For example, we can see that the declaration starts with a node that represents the interface keyword (`InterfaceKeyword`), and that it is followed by the name of the interface (`Identifier`). We can also see that the `tryHit` method takes a number (`NumberKeyword`) as an argument and returns a boolean (`BooleanKeyword`).

The AST nodes have certain properties. For example, the `NumberKeyword` in the preceding example has the following properties:

```
NumberKeyword
pos:43
start:44
end:50
flags:0
kind:133
```

These properties allow us to identify the kind of the node (the `kind` property) and its position within the source code (the `pos` and `end` properties). The `kind` is a reference to a `Token`. The value `133` is the value of the `NumberKeyword` property in the `SyntaxKind` enum.

Now we know what the TypeScript AST is and what it looks like. In the following section, we are going to learn about a tool that can help us to visualize the AST.

TypeScript AST Viewer

TypeScript AST Viewer is an open source application that allows us to explore the AST for a given TypeScript code snippet. This application is available online at `http://ts-ast-viewer.com`:

```
TypeScript AST Viewer
 1  interface Weapon {
 2      tryHit(fromDistance: number): boolean;
 3  }
 4
 5  class Katana implements Weapon {
 6      public tryHit(fromDistance: number) {
 7          return fromDistance <= 2;
 8      }
 9  }
10
11  class Ninja {
12      private _weapon: Weapon;
13      public constructor(weapon: Weapon) {
14          this._weapon = weapon;
15      }
16      public fight(fromDistance: number) {
17          return this._weapon.tryHit(fromDistance);
18      }
19  }
20
21  const ninja = new Ninja(new Katana());
22  ninja.fight("5");
23
```

- ▼ SourceFile
  - ▼ SyntaxList
    - ▶ InterfaceDeclaration
    - ▶ ClassDeclaration
    - ▶ ClassDeclaration
    - ▶ VariableStatement
    - ▶ ExpressionStatement
  - EndOfFileToken

Sample application

The companion source code includes a very small application that we are going to use throughout the rest of this chapter. The following subsections describe each of the components in the sample application.

interfaces.ts

The `interfaces.ts` file declares and exports a couple of interfaces:

```
export interface Weapon {
    tryHit(fromDistance: number): boolean;
}

export interface Named {
    name: string;
}
```

katana.ts

The `katana.ts` file declares a base class named `BaseWeapon` and a derived class named `Katana`:

```
import { Weapon, Named } from "./interfaces";

export class BaseWeapon {
    damage = 25;
}

export class Katana extends BaseWeapon implements Weapon, Named {
    name = "Katana";
    public tryHit(fromDistance: number) {
        return fromDistance <= 2;
    }
}
```

ninja.ts

The `ninja.ts` file declares a class named `Ninja`:

```
import { Weapon } from "./interfaces";

export class Ninja {
    private _weapon: Weapon;
    public constructor(weapon: Weapon) {
        this._weapon = weapon;
    }
    public fight(fromDistance: number) {
        return this._weapon.tryHit(fromDistance);
    }
}
```

main.ts

The `main.ts` file is the application's entry point. It creates an instance of `Katana` and an instance of `Ninja` and then invokes one of the methods of the `Ninja` instance:

```
import { Ninja } from "./ninja";
import { Katana } from "./katana";

const ninja = new Ninja(new Katana());

ninja.fight(5);
```

broken.ts

The companion source code also includes a file named `broken.ts`. This file contains some compilation errors on purpose because it is used to demonstrate how to perform error diagnostics:

```
import { Ninja } from "./ninja";
import { Katana } from "./katana";

const ninja = new Ninja(new Katana());

ninja.fight("5");
```

Traversing the TypeScript AST

We have learned how to visualize the TypeScript AST using the TypeScript AST viewer online. At this point, it is normal to ask ourselves where all this information is coming from. In this section, we are going to demonstrate how to use the TypeScript compiler APIs to access the AST.

After creating a `package.json` file and installing TypeScript using `npm`, the first thing that we need to do is to create a new TypeScript file and import TypeScript as a module:

```
import * as ts from "typescript";
```

Then we need to declare the configuration of the TypeScript compiler using an object literal:

```
const options = {
    module: ts.ModuleKind.CommonJS,
    target: ts.ScriptTarget.ES5,
};
```

Next, we need to create a new program:

```
const program = ts.createProgram(
    [
        "./app/interfaces.ts",
        "./app/ninja.ts",
        "./app/katana.ts",
        "./app/main.ts"
    ],
    options
);
```

A program is a collection of source files and a set of compilation options that represent a compilation unit. The program is the main entry point to the type system and code generation system.

Then we need to create an instance of the TypeScript type checker:

```
const checker = program.getTypeChecker();
```

At this point, we can write some code to iterate through the source files in the program. The following code snippet traverses the AST of the given source files and returns a list of the classes and interfaces declared in each file.

Working with the TypeScript Compiler and the Language Services

It uses the `getSourceFiles` method of the program instance to access the source files in the program. The `lib.d.ts` file and the files under the `node_modules` directory are ignored.

The code snippet uses a recursive function named `visit` to traverse the nodes in the AST. The recursive function compares each of the nodes with the tokens that we are looking for (`ClassDeclaration` and `InterfaceDeclaration`) to identify the classes and interfaces:

```
interface Result {
    fileName: string;
    classes: string[];
    interfaces: string[];
}
const entities = program.getSourceFiles().map(file => {

    if (
        file.fileName.indexOf("lib.d.ts") !== -1 ||
        file.fileName.indexOf("node_modules") !== -1
    ) {
        return null;
    }

    const result = {
        fileName: file.fileName,
        classes: [] as string[],
        interfaces: [] as string[]
    };

    const visit = (node: ts.Node) => {
        if (node.kind === ts.SyntaxKind.ClassDeclaration) {
            // Find class identifier
            node.getChildren().forEach(n => {
                if (n.kind === ts.SyntaxKind.Identifier) {
                    const name = (n as ts.Identifier).getFullText();
                    result.classes.push(name);
                }
            });
        } else if (node.kind === ts.SyntaxKind.InterfaceDeclaration) {
            // Find interface identifier
            node.getChildren().forEach(n => {
                if (n.kind === ts.SyntaxKind.Identifier) {
                    const name = (n as ts.Identifier).getFullText();
                    result.interfaces.push(name);
                }
            });
        } else if (node.kind === ts.SyntaxKind.ModuleDeclaration) {
            // Iterate module nodes
```

```
            ts.forEachChild(node, visit);
        }
    };

    ts.forEachChild(file, visit);
    return result;

}).filter(e => e !== null) as Result[];
```

If the token found is a module declaration, we will invoke the recursive function `visit` once more. Once we have managed to find all the classes and interfaces in our source code, we can display them in the console using a simple `forEach` loop:

```
entities.forEach(e => {
    console.log(chalk.cyan(`
        FILE: ${e.fileName}n
        CLASSES: ${e.classes.length > 0 ? e.classes : "N/A"}n
        INTERFACES: ${e.interfaces.length > 0 ? e.interfaces : "N/A"}n
    `));
});
```

> Note that the `chalk` module can be installed via `npm`, and is used to display colored text in the console output.

Now we know how we can access and traverse the TypeScript AST. As we can see, the process required to create this kind of task is quite tedious. However, there is an open source tool that can help us to traverse the TypeScript AST with ease: `ts-simple-ast`.

Working with ts-simple-ast

As we learned in the preceding section, when it comes to working with the TypeScript, AST is not very complicated. However, there is an open source npm module named `ts-simple-ast` that makes working with the TypeScript AST even easier! In this section, we are going to take a look at multiple examples to learn how to use `ts-simple-ast`.

Traversing the AST with ts-simple-ast

The following code snippet implements an application that is almost identical to the application that we implemented in the preceding section. The most notable difference is that, instead of using the core TypeScript compiler APIs, we are going to use the `ts-simple-ast` helpers:

```
import chalk from "chalk";
import Ast, { DiagnosticMessageChain } from "ts-simple-ast";
```

The following function is used in many of the examples in this chapter, and it is used to get an instance of the TypeScript AST, given certain files and the desired compiler settings:

```
function getAst(tsConfigPath: string, sourceFilesPath: string) {
  const ast = new Ast({
    tsConfigFilePath: tsConfigPath,
    addFilesFromTsConfig: false
  });
  ast.addExistingSourceFiles(sourceFilesPath);
  return ast;
}
```

We can use the `getAst` function to access the `ts-simple-ast` AST and then the `getSourceFiles` method to access the source files in the program:

```
const myAst = getAst("./tsconfig.json", "./app/*.ts");
const files = myAst.getSourceFiles();
```

At this point, we can use `getFilePath` to get the path of a source file and the `getClasses` and `getInterfaces` methods to access the class and interface declarations in a source file:

```
const entities = files.map(f => {
  return {
    fileName: f.getFilePath(),
    classes: f.getClasses().map(c => c.getName()),
    interfaces: f.getInterfaces().map(i => i.getName())
  };
});
```

As we can see, the `ts-simple-ast` helpers can greatly simplify traversing the TypeScript AST or searching for a certain kind of entity.

Finally, we can display the name of the classes on the command-line interface:

```
entities.forEach(e => {
  console.log(
    chalk.cyan(`
        FILE: ${e.fileName}n
        CLASSES: ${e.classes.length > 0 ? e.classes : "N/A"}n
        INTERFACES: ${e.interfaces.length > 0 ? e.interfaces : "N/A"}n
    `)
  );
});
```

Diagnostics with ts-simple-ast

The following code snippet implements a very small application that uses `ts-simple-ast` to find errors in a TypeScript file using the error diagnostic APIs. The application uses the `chalk` npm module to display errors using a red font in the command-line interface:

```
import chalk from "chalk";
import Ast, { DiagnosticMessageChain } from "ts-simple-ast";
```

The following function is the same `getAst` function that we used in the preceding section:

```
function getAst(tsConfigPath: string, sourceFilesPath: string) {
  const ast = new Ast({
    tsConfigFilePath: tsConfigPath,
    addFilesFromTsConfig: false
  });
  ast.addExistingSourceFiles(sourceFilesPath);
  return ast;
}
```

The AST provided by `ts-simple-ast` includes a method named `getDiagnostics`, which allows us to access the detected compilation errors. The `getErrors` function showcases how to traverse each of the diagnostics and how to access the underlying `DiagnosticMessageChain`.

The method `diagnostic.getMessageText` returns a string or a `DiagnosticMessageChain`. The `DiagnosticMessageChain` implements the iterator pattern, which explains why we use the `DiagnosticMessageChain.getNext` method:

```
function getErrors(ast: Ast) {

  const diagnostics = ast.getDiagnostics();

  function dmcToString(dmc: DiagnosticMessageChain, msg: string = ""): string {
    const messageText = dmc.getMessageText();
    const code = dmc.getCode();
    msg += `${code} ${messageText}n`;
    const next = dmc.getNext();
    return next ? dmcToString(next, msg) : msg;
  }

  const errors = diagnostics.map(diagnostic => {
    const code = diagnostic.getCode();
    const sourceOrUndefined = diagnostic.getSourceFile();
    const source = sourceOrUndefined ? sourceOrUndefined.getFilePath() : "";
    const line = sourceOrUndefined
      ? sourceOrUndefined.getLineNumberFromPos(diagnostic.getStart() || 0)
      : "";
    const stringOrDMC = diagnostic.getMessageText();
    const messageText =
      typeof stringOrDMC === "string" ? stringOrDMC : dmcToString(stringOrDMC);
    return `
            ERROR CODE: ${code}
            DESCRIPTION: ${messageText}
            FILE: ${source}
            LINE: ${line}
        `;
  });

  return errors;
}

const myAst = getAst("./tsconfig.json", "./app/broken.ts");

getErrors(myAst).forEach(err => console.log(chalk.red(err)));
```

Accessing class details with ts-simple-ast

The following code snippet demonstrates how we can use the `ts-simple-ast` APIs to access and manipulate class declarations.

> Note that the preceding example is not meant to be executed. It is a showcase of the available methods in the `ts-simple-ast` API, but it is not an executable demo.

Just like in the preceding examples, we are going to use the `getAst`, `getSourceFiles`, and `getClasses` methods to find all the class declarations in our source code.

We will then use some tools to access the details of the class declaration, including methods, derived classes, and properties, among others. We will also demonstrate how we can modify the class declaration by performing operations such as adding a base class or a new method:

```
import chalk from "chalk";
import Ast, { DiagnosticMessageChain } from "ts-simple-ast";

function getAst(tsConfigPath: string, sourceFilesPath: string) {
    const ast = new Ast({
        tsConfigFilePath: tsConfigPath,
        addFilesFromTsConfig: false
    });
    ast.addExistingSourceFiles(sourceFilesPath);
    return ast;
}

const myAst = getAst("./tsconfig.json", "./app/*.ts");
const files = myAst.getSourceFiles();

files.forEach(file => {

    // Find all classes
    const classes = file.getClasses();

    // Find class by name
    const class1 = file.getClass("Katana");

    // Find class with no constructors
    const firstClassWithConstructor = file.getClass(
        c => c.getConstructors().length > 0
    );
```

[487]

```typescript
// Add a class
const classDeclaration = file.addClass({
    name: "ClassName"
});

// Get extends
const extendsExpression = classDeclaration.getExtends();

// Set extends
classDeclaration.setExtends("BaseClass");

// Remove extends
classDeclaration.removeExtends();

// Get derived classes
const derivedClasses = classDeclaration.getDerivedClasses();

// Remove one class
if (classDeclaration) {
    classDeclaration.remove();
}

// Get instance methods
const instanceMethods = classDeclaration.getInstanceMethods();

// Get static methods
const staticMethods = classDeclaration.getStaticMethods();

// Add method
const method = classDeclaration.addMethod(
    { isStatic: true, name: "myMethod", returnType: "string" }
);

// Remove method
method.remove();

// Get instance properties
const instanceProperties = classDeclaration.getInstanceProperties();

// Get static properties
const staticProperties = classDeclaration.getStaticProperties();

// Add a property
const property = classDeclaration.addProperty({ isStatic: true, name: "prop", type: "string" });

// Remove property
property.remove();
```

    });

Accessing module details with ts-simple-ast

The following code snippet demonstrates how we can use the `ts-simple-ast` APIs to access and manipulate module `import` and `export` declarations.

> Note that the preceding example is not meant to be executed. It is a showcase of the available methods in the `ts-simple-ast` API, but it is not an executable demo.

Just like in the preceding examples, we are going to use the `getAst` and `getSourceFiles` methods to access the source code's objects:

```
import chalk from "chalk";
import Ast, { DiagnosticMessageChain } from "ts-simple-ast";

function getAst(tsConfigPath: string, sourceFilesPath: string) {
    const ast = new Ast({
      tsConfigFilePath: tsConfigPath,
      addFilesFromTsConfig: false
    });
    ast.addExistingSourceFiles(sourceFilesPath);
    return ast;
}

const myAst = getAst("./tsconfig.json", "./app/*.ts");
const files = myAst.getSourceFiles();
```

We will then use some methods to access the details of the module `import` and `export` declarations. We also demonstrate how we can add and remove module `import` and `export` declarations by performing operations such as adding a default `export`:

```
files.forEach(file => {

  const functionDeclaration = file.getFunction("someFunction");

  if (functionDeclaration) {

    // Is exported
    functionDeclaration.isExported();
    functionDeclaration.isNamedExport();
    functionDeclaration.isDefaultExport();
```

Working with the TypeScript Compiler and the Language Services

```
    // Has export keyword
    functionDeclaration.hasExportKeyword();
    functionDeclaration.hasDefaultKeyword();

    // Access export keywords
    functionDeclaration.getExportKeyword();
    functionDeclaration.getDefaultKeyword();

    // Set is export
    functionDeclaration.setIsDefaultExport(true);
    functionDeclaration.setIsDefaultExport(false);

    // Set is exported
    functionDeclaration.setIsExported(true);
    functionDeclaration.setIsExported(false);

}

// Get all imports
const imports = file.getImportDeclarations();

// Add import
const importDeclaration = file.addImportDeclaration({
    defaultImport: "MyClass",
    moduleSpecifier: "./file"
});

// Remove import
importDeclaration.remove();

// Get default import
const defaultImport = importDeclaration.getDefaultImport();

// Get named imports
const namedImports = importDeclaration.getNamedImports();

// Add named import
const namedImport = importDeclaration.addNamedImport({
    name: "MyClass",
    alias: "MyAliasName" // alias is optional
});

// Remove named import
namedImport.remove();

});
```

Accessing the language services API

The language services API is built on top of the core compiler APIs, and it was designed to provide software engineers with a great developer experience independent of their IDE or code editor of choice.

We are going to use `ts-simple-ast` to access the language services API. We can access the language services API using the `getLanguageService` method in an AST instance:

```
myAst.getLanguageService();
```

The language services API implements methods that allow us to perform a common editing task, such as renaming a variable or automatically implementing an interface. The following screenshot shows some of the available methods in the language services API:

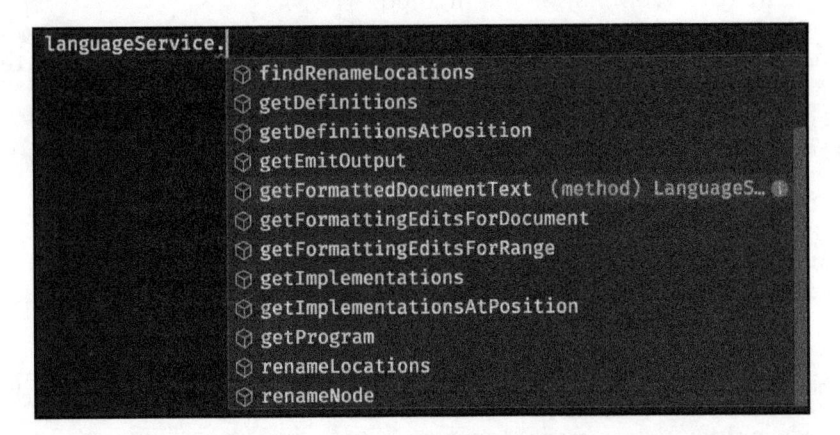

```
languageService.
            findRenameLocations
            getDefinitions
            getDefinitionsAtPosition
            getEmitOutput
            getFormattedDocumentText   (method) LanguageS...
            getFormattingEditsForDocument
            getFormattingEditsForRange
            getImplementations
            getImplementationsAtPosition
            getProgram
            renameLocations
            renameNode
```

We are now going to create a very small application that uses the language services API to find interfaces in the sample application included in the companion source code. The application will display the name of each of the interfaces and the name of each of their implementations:

```
import chalk from "chalk";
import { flatten, join } from "lodash";
import Ast, { DiagnosticMessageChain } from "ts-simple-ast";
import * as ts from "typescript";

function getAst(tsConfigPath: string, sourceFilesPath: string) {
    const ast = new Ast({
      tsConfigFilePath: tsConfigPath,
      addFilesFromTsConfig: false
    });
    ast.addExistingSourceFiles(sourceFilesPath);
```

```
        return ast;
}

const myAst = getAst("./tsconfig.json", "./app/*.ts");
const languageService = myAst.getLanguageService();
const files = myAst.getSourceFiles();
const interfaceDeclarations = flatten(files.map(f => f.getInterfaces()));
```

We then need to find the name of each of the interface declarations using the `getName` method.

We are also going to try to find each of their implementations using the `getImplementations` method, which is part of the language services API. The method expects us to pass the node that declares the interface. The node can be accessed using the `interfaceDeclaration.getNameNode` method.

Once we have found the implementations, we need to find their names. We do this by searching for the name of the nodes of the kind called `Identifier`:

```
const result = interfaceDeclarations.map(interfaceDeclaration => {

    const interfaceName = interfaceDeclaration.getName();

    const implementations = languageService.getImplementations(
        interfaceDeclaration.getNameNode()
    );

    const implementationNames = implementations.map(implementation => {
        const children = implementation.getNode().getChildren();
        const identifier = children.filter(
            child => child.getKind() === ts.SyntaxKind.Identifier
        )[0];
        const implementationName = identifier.getText();
        return implementationName;
    });

    return {
        interface: interfaceName,
        implementations: implementationNames
    };

});
```

Finally, we display the results in the console:

```
console.log(
    result.forEach(
        o => console.log(
            `- ${o.interface} is implemented by ${join(o.implementations,
",")}`
        )
    )
);
```

If we execute the application, we should be able to see the following displayed in our console:

```
- Weapon is implemented by Katana
- Named is implemented by Katana
```

> Since TypeScript 2.2, it is possible to write language services plugins to extend the language services API. Custom language services can help to provide developers with a better developing experience. For example, there is a language service that provides developers with autocomplete and error diagnostic features while working with GraphQL queries. Before this, GraphQL queries were just text, and as a result, they were somewhat tedious to implement. Implementing our language services plugins is out of the scope of this book, but if you wish to learn more, you will be able to do so at `https://github.com/Microsoft/TypeScript/wiki/Writing-a-Language-Service-Plugin`.

Implementing a yUML compiler

In this section, we are going to put together everything that we have learned so far during this chapter to create a custom developer tool. We are going to write a tool that takes TypeScript source code as input and generates a **unified modeling language** (UML) class diagram. A class diagram describes the structure of a system by showing the system's classes, their attributes, methods, and the relationships among the objects.

Working with the TypeScript Compiler and the Language Services

A class diagram looks as follows:

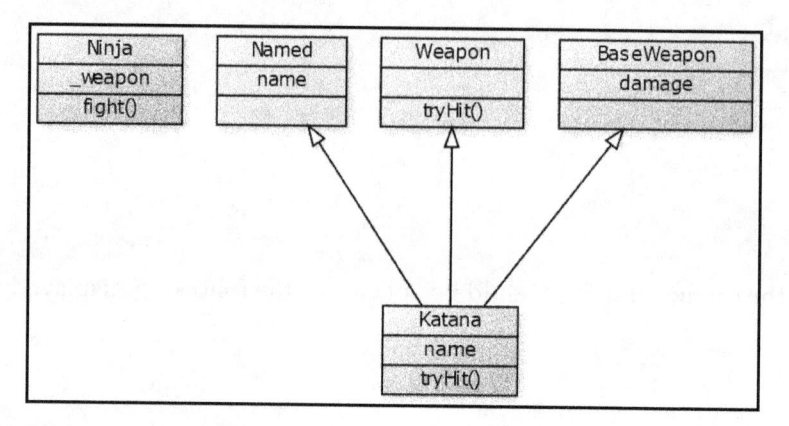

```
┌─────────────────────────────────────────────────────────────────┐
│   ┌──────────┐      ┌────────┐      ┌────────┐     ┌────────────┐│
│   │  Ninja   │      │ Named  │      │ Weapon │     │ BaseWeapon ││
│   ├──────────┤      ├────────┤      ├────────┤     ├────────────┤│
│   │ _weapon  │      │  name  │      │        │     │  damage    ││
│   ├──────────┤      ├────────┤      ├────────┤     ├────────────┤│
│   │ fight()  │      │        │      │ tryHit()│    │            ││
│   └──────────┘      └────────┘      └────────┘     └────────────┘│
│         △               △               △                       │
│          \              │              /                         │
│           \             │             /                          │
│            \        ┌────────┐       /                           │
│             \       │ Katana │      /                            │
│              \      ├────────┤     /                             │
│               \     │  name  │    /                              │
│                     ├────────┤                                   │
│                     │tryHit()│                                   │
│                     └────────┘                                   │
└─────────────────────────────────────────────────────────────────┘
```

We are going to use the TypeScript compiler API and `ts-simple-ast` to traverse the AST generated by the sample application included in the companion source code. We will then emit some code in a **domain-specific language** (**DSL**) known as yUML. Finally, we will post the yUML DSL to an online service to generate the diagram as an image. We are going to translate from TypeScript to yUML, which means that we can think about this as creating a yUML compiler.

We are going to start by importing some required modules:

```typescript
import * as fs from "fs";
import { flatten, join } from "lodash";
import * as path from "path";
import * as request from "request";
import Ast, * as SimpleAST from "ts-simple-ast";
import * as ts from "typescript";
```

The `fs` and `path` modules are native core Node.js modules and don't need to be installed. However, we are going to need the type definitions for Node.js (`@types/node`).

> Note that the `flatten` function is part of the `lodash` npm module. This function allows us to transform a multidimensional array (for example, an array of arrays) into an array with only one dimension.

We are then going to declare two interfaces that are used to represent the relevant details about a class, method, or property. In this example, we are going to only use the name of the method or property:

```
interface MethodDetails {
  name: string;
}

interface PropertyDetails {
  name: string;
}
```

The following code snippet declares a constant variable named `templates`. Templates are functions that take names and return strings that contain yUML DSL snippets:

```
const templates = {
  url: (dsl: string) => `http://yuml.me/diagram/scruffy/class/${dsl}`,
  composition: "+->",
  implementsOrExtends: (abstraction: string, implementation: string) => {
    return (
      `${templates.plainClassOrInterface(abstraction)}` +
      `^-${templates.plainClassOrInterface(implementation)}`
    );
  },
  plainClassOrInterface: (name: string) => `[${name}]`,
  colorClass: (name: string) => `[${name}{bg:skyblue}]`,
  colorInterface: (name: string) => `[${name}{bg:palegreen}]`,
  class: (name: string, props: PropertyDetails[], methods: MethodDetails[])
  => {
    const pTemplate = (property: PropertyDetails) => `${property.name};`;
    const mTemplate = (method: MethodDetails) => `${method.name}();`;
    return (
      `${templates.colorClass(name)}` +
      `[${name}|${props.map(pTemplate)}|${methods.map(mTemplate)}]`
    );
  },
  interface: (
    name: string,
    props: PropertyDetails[],
    methods: MethodDetails[]
  ) => {
    const pTemplate = (property: PropertyDetails) => `${property.name};`;
    const mTemplate = (method: MethodDetails) => `${method.name}();`;
    return (
      `${templates.colorInterface(name)}` +
      `[${name}|${props.map(pTemplate)}|${methods.map(mTemplate)}]`
    );
```

Working with the TypeScript Compiler and the Language Services

```
    }
  };
```

The following function is used to get the AST for the given source files:

```
function getAst(tsConfigPath: string, sourceFilesPaths?: string[]) {
  const ast = new Ast({
    tsConfigFilePath: tsConfigPath,
    addFilesFromTsConfig: !Array.isArray(sourceFilesPaths)
  });
  if (sourceFilesPaths) {
    ast.addExistingSourceFiles(sourceFilesPaths);
  }
  return ast;
}
```

The following function emits the yUML DSL for the class declarations. We traverse the AST, searching for properties and methods:

```
function emitClass(classDeclaration: SimpleAST.ClassDeclaration) {

  const className = classDeclaration.getSymbol()!.getName();
  const propertyDeclarations = classDeclaration.getProperties();
  const methodDeclarations = classDeclaration.getMethods();

  const properties = propertyDeclarations.map(property => {
      const sym = property.getSymbol();
      if (sym) {
          return {
              name: sym.getName()
          };
      }
  }).filter((p) => p !== undefined) as PropertyDetails[];

  const methods = methodDeclarations.map(method => {
    const sym = method.getSymbol();
    if (sym) {
        return {
            name: sym.getName()
        }
    }
  }).filter((p) => p !== undefined) as MethodDetails[];

  return templates.class(className, properties, methods);
}
```

The following function emits the yUML DSL for interface declarations. We traverse through the AST, searching for properties and methods:

```
function emitInterface(interfaceDeclaration:
SimpleAST.InterfaceDeclaration) {

    const interfaceName = interfaceDeclaration.getSymbol()!.getName();
    const propertyDeclarations = interfaceDeclaration.getProperties();
    const methodDeclarations = interfaceDeclaration.getMethods();

    const properties = propertyDeclarations.map(property => {
        const sym = property.getSymbol();
        if (sym) {
            return {
                name: sym.getName()
            }
        }
    }).filter((p) => p !== undefined) as PropertyDetails[];

    const methods = methodDeclarations.map(method => {
        const sym = method.getSymbol();
        if (sym) {
            return {
                name: sym.getName()
            }
        }
    }).filter((p) => p !== undefined) as MethodDetails[];

    return templates.interface(interfaceName, properties, methods);
}
```

The following function emits the yUML DSL for heritage clauses. This includes relationships defined in our source code by the use of the `extends` and `implements` keywords:

```
function emitInheritanceRelationships(
    classDeclaration: SimpleAST.ClassDeclaration
) {

    const className = classDeclaration.getSymbol()!.getName();
    const extended = classDeclaration.getExtends();
    const implemented = classDeclaration.getImplements();
    let heritageClauses: HeritageClause[] = [];

    if (extended) {
        const identifier =
extended.getChildrenOfKind(ts.SyntaxKind.Identifier)[0];
```

[497]

Working with the TypeScript Compiler and the Language Services

```
            if (identifier) {
                const sym = identifier.getSymbol();
                if (sym) {
                    heritageClauses.push(
                        {
                            clause: sym.getName(),
                            className
                        }
                    );
                }
            }
        }

        if (implemented) {
            implemented.forEach(i => {
                const identifier =
    i.getChildrenOfKind(ts.SyntaxKind.Identifier)[0];
                if (identifier) {
                    const sym = identifier.getSymbol();
                    if (sym) {
                        heritageClauses.push(
                            {
                                clause: sym.getName(),
                                className
                            }
                        );
                    }
                }
            });
        }

        return flatten(heritageClauses).map((c: HeritageClause) =>
          templates.implementsOrExtends(c.clause, c.className)
        );

}
```

The following function renders the UML diagram into a .png file using the yUML web service. We invoke the web service using the `request` npm module.

The `request` module is used to download the rendered image. The image is then saved into the current directory using the code's Node.js FileSystem API:

```
function render(dsl: string) {
    const download = (uri: string, filename: string, callback: () => void) =>
    {
        request.head(uri, (err, res, body) => {
```

```
      request(uri)
        .pipe(fs.createWriteStream(filename))
        .on("close", callback);
    });
  };

  const url = templates.url(dsl);
  const file = `uml_diagram_${new Date().getTime()}.png`;
  const absolutePath = path.join(__dirname, file);

  download(url, file, () =>
    console.log(`Saved UML diagram available at ${absolutePath}`)
  );
}
```

The following function generates the yUML DSL for the given TypeScript files. This function delegates work to the previously defined `getAst`, `emitClass`, `emitInterface`, and `emitInheritanceRelationships` functions:

```
function yUML(tsConfigPath: string, sourceFilesPaths: string[]) {
  const ast = getAst(tsConfigPath, sourceFilesPaths);
  const files = ast.getSourceFiles();

  const declarations = files.map(f => {
    return {
      fileName: f.getFilePath(),
      classes: f.getClasses(),
      interfaces: f.getInterfaces()
    };
  });

  const entities = declarations.map(d => {
    const classes = d.classes.map(emitClass);
    const interfaces = d.interfaces.map(emitInterface);
    const inheritanceRelationships = d.classes.map(
      emitInheritanceRelationships
    );
    return [...classes, ...interfaces, ...inheritanceRelationships];
  });

  return join(flatten(entities), ",");
}
```

At this point, we have implemented the entire application and we can invoke the yUML function to generate the yUML DSL for the given files:

```
const yuml = yUML("./tsconfig.json", [
  "./app/interfaces.ts",
  "./app/ninja.ts",
  "./app/katana.ts",
  "./app/main.ts"
]);
```

Finally, we can invoke the `render` function:

```
render(yuml);
```

> Refer to the official `ts-simple-ast` documentation at https://dsherret.github.io/ts-simple-ast/ to learn more about the available APIs.

VS Code extensions

Developing Visual Studio extensions is out of the scope of this book. However, it is worth mentioning that VS Code extensions can be developed using TypeScript. This means that it is possible to transform our custom command-line TypeScript tools, such as the UML diagram generator, into VS Code extensions without too many complications.

> Refer to the official VS Code documentation about the development of extensions at https://code.visualstudio.com/docs/extensions/overview to learn more.

Summary

In this chapter, we have learned about the internal components of the TypeScript compiler. We have also learned how to use the compiler APIs and how we can take advantage of these features to develop our TypeScript development tools.

I hope that this chapter will foster your curiosity of the TypeScript compiler internals and the development of software development tools powered by TypeScript. Their potential and growing popularity will take the JavaScript ecosystem to the next level.

Other Books You May Enjoy

If you enjoyed this book, you may be interested in these other books by Packt:

TypeScript 2.x By Example
Sachin Ohri

ISBN: 978-1-78728-003-8

- Design your first project in Visual Studio
- Learn about the different data types in TypeScript
- Create web applications in an object-oriented fashion using TypeScript
- Build a Trello application using TypeScript's complex features.
- Explore the tools available in a web application ecosystem to write unit test cases
- Deploy web applications to cloud and assign resources to the application

Other Books You May Enjoy

TypeScript High Performance
Ajinkya Kher

ISBN: 978-1-78528-864-7

- Learn about the critical rendering path, and the performance metrics involved along the same
- Explore the detailed inner intricacies of a web browser
- Build a large scale front end applications and learn the thought process behind architecting such an effort
- Understand the challenges of scalability and how TypeScript renders itself to the cause
- Learn efficient usage of TypeScript constructs to deliver high performance and avoid common mistakes and pitfalls that can hamper performance
- Monitor performance, resolve and detect performance bottlenecks in production, and learn the tools involved

Leave a review - let other readers know what you think

Please share your thoughts on this book with others by leaving a review on the site that you bought it from. If you purchased the book from Amazon, please leave us an honest review on this book's Amazon page. This is vital so that other potential readers can see and use your unbiased opinion to make purchasing decisions, we can understand what our customers think about our products, and our authors can see your feedback on the title that they have worked with Packt to create. It will only take a few minutes of your time, but is valuable to other potential customers, our authors, and Packt. Thank you!

Index

-

--strict mode 47

@

@Attribute
  working with 383
@Input
  working with 383
@Output
  working with 386

A

abstract classes 146
abstract syntax tree (AST)
  about 472, 475, 477, 478
  broken.ts 480
  interfaces.ts 479
  katana.ts 479
  main.ts 480
  ninja.ts 480
  sample application 479
  traversing, with ts-simple-ast 484
  ts-simple-ast, working with 483
  TypeScript AST Viewer 478
  TypeScript AST, traversing 481, 483
access modifiers
  about 116
  private access modifier 117
  protected access modifier 119
  public access modifiers 116
aggregation 136
Akamai study
  URL 412
algebraic data types 235
AMD modules 179

Angular application
  bootstrapping 377
  serving, with Node.js 377
Angular components life cycle hooks
  URL 391
Angular components
  @Attribute, working with 383
  @Input, working with 383
  @Output, working with 386
  about 380
  data binding 382
  dependency injection 399
  directives 382
  dumb components 393, 398
  EventEmitter, working with 386
  host, working with 388
  life cycle hooks 391
  router, working with 389
  services, working with 391
  smart components 393, 398
  structural directives, using 385
  working with 380
Angular router
  working with 389
Angular
  working with 373, 375
annotations
  versus decorators 250
any type 15
application programming interface (API) 157
Applicative 237
arithmetic operators 18
arrow functions 93
assertion 433
assignment operators 21
association 136
async and await 106

asynchronous generators 108
asynchronous programming
  about 92
  arrow functions 93
  async and await 106
  asynchronous generators 108
  asynchronous iteration 109
  callback hell 95
  callbacks 92
  covariant, checking in callback parameters 102
  generator, delegating 109
  generators 104
  promises 98, 101
asynchronous scripts
  URL 290
attributes 112

B

behavior-driven development (BDD)
  about 438, 441
  versus test-driven development (TDD) 462
binary function 222
binder 473
bindings 313
bitwise operators 20
blocking model 309
Browser Object Model (BOM) 69, 190, 314
built-in conditional types 66

C

callback 92
callback hell 95, 97
callback parameters
  covariant, checking 102
category theory
  about 235
  functor 237
Central Processing Unit (CPU) 403
Chai
  about 438
  TDD, versus BDD 462
ChromeDriver 440
circular dependency 188
class 112

class decorators 251, 253
class expressions 121
classes
  about 29, 111
  access modifiers 116
  aggregation 136
  association 136
  class expressions 121
  composition 136
  generic classes 127
  inheritance 114
  iterables 144
  method overriding 126
  multiple inheritance 138
  optional members 123
  parameter properties 120
  read-only properties 124
  static members 121
  strict property initialization 112
closures
  about 210, 211
  private members 214
  static variables 212
command-line interface (CLI)
  about 279
  using 307
CommonJS modules 180
companion source code
  about 274
  URL 274
comparison operators 18
complex type serialization 267
composition 137, 225
conditional types 65
constructor 112
continuous integration tools 305, 306
control flow analysis 51
CPU performance analysis 420, 421, 422
cross-file internal modules 172
Current 402
currying 230
custom type guards 48

[506]

D

data binding
  about 382
  URL 383
data type
  any 15
  array 15
  boolean 14
  empty object type {} 16
  enum 15
  never 16
  null 16
  number 14
  object (lowercase) 16
  object (uppercase) 16
  string 15
  tuple 15
  undefined 16
  void 16
declaration files 69
decorator factory 267
decorators
  class decorators 251, 253
  decorator factory 267
  factory decorators 270
  method decorators 253, 256
  parameter decorators 259
  property decorators 257
  reflect metadata API 262, 266
  versus annotations 250
  with arguments 262
default parameters 78
DefinitelyTyped 71
dependencies, OOP
  about 183
  circular dependency 188
  dependency injection, versus dependency inversion 183
  inversion of control (IoC) containers 185
dependency injection 399
dependency inversion principle (DIP) 150, 159
depth of the inheritance tree (DIT) 115
diamond problem 139
directives

URL 382
discriminated unions 52
Document Object Model (DOM) 69, 170, 190, 314
Domain Name Servers (DNS) 315
domain-specific language (DSL) 494
dummy object 436
dynamic scoping 84

E

Either data type 240
emitter 474
end-to-end (e2e) tests 440, 443
enumerations 55
enzyme 439
Enzyme
  React web components, isolating 462
  React web components, testing 458
Error class 431
ES6 modules 176
event loop
  about 191, 193
  frames 192
  heap 193
  queue 193
  stack 193
EventEmitter
  working with 386
example application 444, 446
exception handling
  about 431
  Error class 431
  throw statements 432
  try...catch statements 432
Express middleware 329
Express.js 328
Express
  routing with 328
external modules
  about 173
  AMD modules 179
  at design time 175
  at runtime 175
  CommonJS modules 180
  definition syntaxes 174
  ES6 modules 176

legacy external modules 178
module loaders 174
summary 182
SystemJS modules 182
UMD modules 181

F

factory decorators 270
first-in-first-out (FIFO) 128
flow control statements
  about 22
  counter-controlled repetition (for) 27
  do-while expression, testing 25
  double-selection structure (if...else) 22
  for-in statement, iterating 25
  for...of statement 26
  inline ternary operator (?) 23
  multiple-selection structure (switch) 23
  single-selection structure (if) 22
  while expression 25
fluent interfaces
  URL 67
for await...of expression 109
frame 192
frames per second (FPS) 417
function arity 222
function declaration 74
function expression 74
function overloading 82
functional programming (FP)
  about 217
  benefits 224
  concepts 218
  function arity 222
  functions, as first-class citizens 221
  higher-order function 223
  immutability 221
  lambda expressions 221
  limitations 220
  pure functions 219
  referential transparency 221
  techniques 225
  TypeScript, testing 225
functional stateless component (FSC) 357
functions
  about 27
  declaration 74
  expressions 74
  function overloading 82
  immediately invoked function expression (IIFE) 87, 90
  scope 84, 87
  specialized overloading signature 83
  tag functions 91
  tagged templates 91
  trailing commas, using in function arguments 76
  types 75
  using, as first-class citizens 221
  with default parameters 78
  with optional parameters 77
  with REST parameters 80
  working with 74
Functor
  about 237
  applicative 237
  Either data type 240
  Maybe data type 238
  monad 243

G

garbage collection 84
garbage collector 425, 426
generators 104
generic classes
  about 127
  generic constraints 130, 134
  operator 135
  types 134
generic constraints 60
generic types 59
Git
  URL 273
GitHub
  URL 273
Google Chrome
  URL 402
Google PageSpeed Insights
  about 413
  URL 414
GPU performance analysis

about 417
  frames per second (FPS) 417
Graphics Processor Unit (GPU) 403
Grunt
  URL 285
Gulp
  about 285, 287
  task execution order, controlling 287
  URL 289

H

HAR Viewer
  URL 429
Hard Disk Drive (HDD) 403
heap 193
higher-order functions 92
hoisting 85
HTTP Archive (HAR) files 429
http module 327

I

immediately invoked function expression (IIFE) 87, 90, 201
immutability 221
Immutable.js 245
implementation signature 82
index signature 57
infer keyword 66
inheritance
  about 114
  depth of the inheritance tree (DIT) 115
input/output (IO) operations 97
instance properties
  about 202
  versus class properties 201
instances 112
integrated development environments (IDEs) 10
integration tests 443, 447
interface segregation principle (ISP) 150, 157
interfaces 30, 147
internal architecture, TypeScript compiler
  about 470
  AST 472
  binder 473

emitter 474
language service 474
lexemes 471
parser 472
scanner 470
symbols 473
tokens 471
type checker 474
internal modules
  about 31, 171
  compiling 173
  cross-file internal modules 172
  internal module aliases 173
  nested internal modules 171
intersection types 43
inversify-express-utils
  database 336
  index file 339
  InversifyJS configuration 339
  model 336
  repository 336
  types 336
  used, for routing 335
  using, with controllers 335, 336
  view 336
inversion of control (IoC) container
  about 185
  InversifyJS 186
iterables 144
iterator 104

J

jsdom 457
JSX
  working with 350, 351

K

keyof operator 57

L

language service 474
last-in-first-out (LIFO) 193
legacy external modules 178
lexeme 471

lexical scoping 84
Libuv
　URL 313
linting tool 282
liskov substitution principle (LSP) 149, 156
literal types
　about 52
　advance features 59
　ambient declarations 69
　built-in conditional types 66
　conditional types 65
　discriminated unions 52
　enumerations 55
　generic constraints 60
　generic types 59
　index signature 57
　infer keyword 66
　keyof operator 57
　local types 58
　lookup types 63
　mapped type modifiers 64
　mapped types 61
　never type 53
　object literals 56
　polymorphic this type 67
　type casting 59
　type declarations 70
　weak types 56
load test 443
local types 58
logical operators 19
Long Term Support (LTS) 402
lookup types 63

M

mapped type modifiers 64
mapped types 61
mark-and-sweep algorithm 426
Maybe data type 238
members 112
memory leak 422
memory performance analysis 422, 425
method decorators 253, 256
method overriding 126, 127
methods 112

mixins 140
MobX application
　URL 370
MobX
　about 248
　actions, working with 360, 361, 364, 368
　alternatives 370
　architecture 360
　dependency injection 368, 370
　observables, working with 360, 361, 364, 368
　working with 360
Mocha
　about 438
　asynchronous code, testing 450
　components, isolating with Sinon.JS 456
　exceptions, asserting 451
　integration tests 447
　jsdom 457
　React web components, isolating with Enzyme 462
　React web components, testing with Enzyme 458
　synchronous pow function, using 447
　TDD, versus BDD 462
　test suites, working with 454
　unit tests 447
　web service, testing with SuperTEst 452
Model-View-Controller (MVC) design pattern
　about 331
　controller 332
　database 334
　index 335
　model 332
　repository 332
　view 335
modern development workflow
　about 271
　companion source code 274
　Git 273
　GitHub 273
　Node.js 272
　prerequisites 272
　Visual Studio Code 272
Modernizr
　URL 190

[510]

monad 243
multiple inheritance
  about 138
  diamond problem 139
  implementing 140, 143

N

namespaces 31
nested internal modules 172
netsniff.js file
  URL 429
network performance analysis 406, 408, 410, 411
network performance
  about 412
  best practices 413
  rules 413
network throughput 403
never type 53
new operator 210
NgModules
  working with 378, 380
Nightwatch.js
  about 440
  end-to-end tests 463, 466
node package manager (npm)
  about 12
  URL 318
node version manager (nvm) 319
Node.js applications
  performance analysis 427
Node.js core API
  about 314
  style 318
  styles 316
Node.js ecosystem
  about 314
  Node.js core API 314
  Node.js core API, style 316
  npm ecosystem 318
Node.js environment
  versus browser environment 314
Node.js V8 --inspector Manager (NiM)
  URL 427
Node.js
  about 272, 309

Angular application, serving 377
applications 340
bindings 313
components 312
databases, working with 323, 325, 326
development 320
environment, versus browser environment 314
filesystem, working with 320, 322, 323
inversify-express-utils, used for routing 335
inversify-express-utils, using with controllers 335
Libuv 313
Node.js core API 313
non-blocking I/O 309, 312
React application, serving 348
REST APIs, working with 327
setting up 319
URL 272, 402
V8 313
non-blocking I/O 309, 312
non-nullable types 44
nonspecialized signature 83
npm documentation
  URL 285
npm scripts
  working with 284
nyc 438

O

object literals 56
object-oriented programming (OOP) 111, 149
object-relational mapping (ORM) 323
objects 112
open/close principle (OCP)
  about 149, 153
  polymorphism 155
optional members 123
optional parameters 77
optional static type annotations 13, 37
overload signatures 82

P

package management tools
  about 162, 281
  npm 162, 166

[511]

rise and fall 162
  type definitions 166
parameter decorators 259
parser 472
partial application 227
pattern matching 49
performance 402
performance analysis
  about 406
  CPU performance analysis 420, 421, 422
  garbage collector 425, 426
  GPU performance analysis 417
  in Node.js applications 427
  memory performance analysis 422, 425
  network performance 412
  network performance analysis 406, 408, 410, 411
  user experience 412
performance automation
  about 428
  performance monitoring automation 428
  performance optimization automation 428
  performance testing automation 430
performance metrics
  about 404
  availability 404
  bandwidth 405
  latency 405
  processing speed 405
  response time 404
  scalability 405
performance monitoring
  about 428
  Real user monitoring (RUM) 428
  real-browser monitoring 429
  simulated browsers 429
performance test 443
performance testing
  about 430
  configuration testing 430
  load testing 430
  soak testing 430
  spike testing 430
  stress testing 430
performance-bookmarklet 407

pipeline operator proposal
  URL 232
pipes 231
PM2 439
pointfree style 232
polymorphic this type 67
private access modifier 117
promises 98, 101
properties 112
property decorators 257
property shadowing 209
protected access modifier 119
prototypal inheritance 204
prototype chain 207
prototypes
  about 199, 201
  accessing, of an object 209
  instance properties, versus class properties 201
public access modifier 116
pure functions 219

Q

queue 193
quick fixes 299

R

Ramda 247
Random Access Memory (RAM) 403
React applications
  URL 370
React development tools 370
react-dom
  working with 350, 351
react-router
  working with 351, 352
React
  about 248
  application, serving with Node.js 348
  component life cycle 358, 359
  components, as classes 354
  components, working with 353
  dumb components 359
  functional stateless component (FSC) 357
  JSX, working with 350, 351

[512]

properties 355
react-dom, working with 350, 351
react-router, working with 351, 352
sample application 344, 346, 348
smart components 359
state 355
working with 342
read-only properties 124
real-world FP application
  about 245
  Immutable.js 245
  MobX 247
  Ramda 247
  React 247
recursive function 235
Redux
  URL 370
referential transparency 221
reflect metadata API 262, 266
regression tests 443
resources 403
REST APIs
  Express middleware 329
  Express.js 328
  http module 327
  MVC design pattern 331
  routing, with Express 328
  working with 327
REST parameters 80
runtime environment 190

S

sample application 376, 479
Scaffolding tools 306
server-side rendering
  URL 378
single responsibility principle (SRP)
  about 149, 150
  encapsulation 152
single-page application (SPA) 341
Sinon.JS 438
  components, isolating 456
SOLID principles
  Dependency inversion principle (DIP) 150
  Interface segregation principle (ISP) 150, 157

Liskov substitution principle (LSP) 149, 155
open/close principle (OCP) 153
Open/closed principle (OCP) 149
single responsibility principle 150
Single responsibility principle (SRP) 149
Solid-State Drive (SSD) 403
source control tools 276, 278, 280
specialized overloading signature 83
specs 435
spies 436
spread operator 21
static members 121
static middleware 349
static variables 212, 214
structural directives
  URL 385
  using 385
structural type system 39
stub 436
suites 435
SuperTest 439
symbols 473
SystemJS modules 182

T

tag function 91
tagged templates 91
task execution order
  callback, passing 288
  controlling 287
  promise, returning 288
  stream, returning 288
techniques, functional programming (FP)
  composition 225
  currying 230
  partial application 227
  pipe 231
  pointfree style 232
  recursion 235
ternary function 223
test cases 435
test coverage 296, 437
test fixture 297
test plan 442
test types

about 442
end-to-end (e2e) tests 443
integration tests 443
load test 443
performance test 443
regression tests 443
unit tests 442
user-acceptance tests (UAT) 443
test-driven development (TDD)
about 438
versus behavior-driven development (BDD) 462
testing methodologies
about 440
behavior-driven development (BDD) 441
test-driven development (TDD) 440
testing terminology
about 433
assertions 433
dummies 436
mocks 436
specs 435
spies 436
stub 436
suites 435
test cases 435
test coverage 437
third-party dependencies
about 161
package management tools 162
this operator
about 194
apply method 197
bind method 197
call method 196
property shadowing 207
prototypal inheritance 204
prototype chain 207
prototype, accessing of object 209
using, in function context 195
using, in global context 195
throw statements 432
time to first byte (TTFB) 411
tokens 471
trailing commas
using, in function arguments 76

transpiler 10
Travis CI
URL 305
try...catch statements 432
ts-node 304
ts-simple-ast
AST, traversing 484
class details, accessing 487
diagnostics with 485, 486
language services API, accessing 491, 493
module details, accessing 489
working with 483
tslint 282
type aliases 42
type binding 187
type casting 59
type checker 474
type definitions
about 166
ECMAScript specification type definitions (lib.d.ts) 169
external TypeScript helpers (tslib) 170
modules, with external support 166
modules, with native support 166
modules, with no support 167
type guards 48
type inference 14, 36
type system
--strict mode 47
characteristics 35
control flow analysis 51
core features 41
custom type guards 48
intersection types 43
non-nullable types 44
optional static type annotations 37
structural type system 39
type aliases 42
type guards 48
type inference 36
typeof operator 48
TypeScript, versus JavaScript 36
union types 41
typeof operator 48
TypeScript architecture

[514]

about 7
  components 9
  design goals 8
TypeScript AST Viewer
  URL 478
TypeScript AST
  traversing 481, 483
TypeScript compiler 281
TypeScript
  arithmetic operators 18
  assignment operatos 21
  bitwise operators 20
  classes 29
  comparison operators 18
  flow control statements 22
  functions 27
  implementing 32
  interfaces 30
  language features 10
  logical operators 19
  namespaces 31
  operators 14
  optional static type annotations 13
  references 11
  spread oeprator 21
  type 13
  type inference 13
  types 14
  URL 10
  variable scope 17
  variables 14

U

UMD modules 181
unary functions 222
unified modeling language (UML) 493

union types 41
unit testing 296
unit tests 442, 447
user experience (UX) 412
user interface (UI) 331
user-acceptance tests (UAT) 443

V

V8
  URL 313
variable hoisting 74
variable scope 17
variadic functions 223
Visual Studio Code
  about 272, 299
  quick fixes 299
  source control utilities 303
  URL 272, 299
  utilities, debugging 300, 302
VS Code extensions
  about 500
  URL 500

W

weak types 56
webpack
  about 290, 292, 294, 439
  development server 295

Y

Yahoo YSlow 413
yield* expression 109
YSlow
  URL 415
yUML compiler
  implementing 493, 495, 497, 500

CPSIA information can be obtained
at www.ICGtesting.com
Printed in the USA
FSHW02n1302240918
52488FS